the fragile alliance

fifth edition

the fragile alliance

an orientation to psychotherapy
of the adolescent

JOHN E. MEEKS, M.D.
Medical Director
The Foundation Schools
Rockville, Maryland

WILLIAM BERNET, M.D.
Professor in the Department of Psychiatry
Vanderbilt University School of Medicine
Nashville, Tennessee

KRIEGER PUBLISHING COMPANY
MALABAR, FLORIDA

Original Edition 1971
Second Edition 1980
Third Edition 1986
Fourth Edition 1990
Fifth Edition 2001, 2005 with updates

Printed and Published by
KRIEGER PUBLISHING COMPANY
KRIEGER DRIVE
MALABAR, FLORIDA 32950

Library of Congress Cataloging-in-Publication Data

Meeks, John E.
    The fragile alliance : an orientation to psychotherapy of the
adolescent / John E. Meeks, William Bernet.—5th ed.
      p. ; cm.
    Includes bibliographical references and index.
    ISBN 1-57524-125-0 (alk. paper)—ISBN 1-57524-126-9
(pbk. : alk. paper)
    1. Adolescent psychotherapy. I. Bernet, William. II. Title.
[DNLM: 1. Psychotherapy—Adolescence. WS 463 M494f 2001]
RJ503.M44 2001
616.89′14′0835—dc21   00-061708

10 9 8 7 6 5 4 3 2

contents

preface to the fifth edition

The Fragile Alliance was first published almost 30 years ago. During this time there have been remarkable and even drastic changes in the way adolescent culture influences our society; the way medical care and mental health care are delivered in this country; and the way practitioners conceptualize psychotherapeutic work with adolescents. For example, the expressed concerns of high school teachers about their students is one way to track our society's view of adolescents. In the 1950s high school teachers said that one of their main concerns was students who chew gum in class; in the 1970s it was kids with long hair who smoked marijuana; by the 1990s high school teachers were most concerned about students who might come to school armed and ready to kill.

A generation ago there was a strong psychoanalytic bent to the psychotherapy of adolescents. Whether in private practice or in community mental health centers, therapists treated teenagers and their families for long periods of time with little oversight. Now there are many more services and treatments available—such as a multitude of diagnosis-specific groups, manualized treatment, wrap-around programs in which a counselor goes to the client's home, cognitive-behavioral treatment, new medications, and several models of residential treatment—and also much more oversight in the form of case management and tight budgets.

In some respects *The Fragile Alliance* has changed with the times. But the fundamental principles in creating and managing the fragile therapeutic alliance in working with adolescent clients remain the same. The central message remains the same, although it has been packaged and repackaged through five editions.

The first edition of *The Fragile Alliance* was published in 1971 by Williams & Wilkins. It was 282 pages long. Dr. John Meeks observed in the introduction that there wree increasing numbers of adolescents being referred for psychotherapy, but not enough therapists. He commented that many therapists who were skillful at treating adult clients became discouraged and frustrated when they tried to treat adolescents. He thought that this book would help therapists understand the special issues involved in dealing with teenagers and also provide practical suggestions regarding therapeutic technique. Part One of the book covered general principles for the diagnostic evaluation, the therapeutic alliance, and ongoing psychotherapy; Part Two addressed specific clinical situations, including "Illegitimate Pregnancy" and "The Adolescent on the Drug Scene."

Since the second edition, which was in 1980, *The Fragile Alliance* has been published by Robert E. Krieger Publishing Co. The second edition was 400 pages long. The book was enlarged to include Part Three, which addressed the design and the process of inpatient treatment programs. The second edition contained chapters that were not in the first edition, such as "Atypical Alliances in the Psychotherapy of Adolescents" and "Group Therapy of the Adolescent."

When the third edition was published in 1986, *The Fragile Alliance* had grown to 475 pages. By that time there was greater awareness of and interest in treating youngsters with narcissistic and borderline features, so Dr. Meeks enlarged the chapter on atypical alliances to become the new chapter, "Malignant Defenses, Malignant Resistances, and Atypical Alliances." He rewrote the chapter on adolescent drug use and made other changes to make the book more contemporary.

When the fourth edition was published in 1990, Dr. William Bernet joined Dr. Meeks as coauthor. The book was updated, expanded, and lengthened to 602 pages. Several chapters were added, including "The Adolescent at School," "The Adolescent Victim," "Adolescents in Divorced and Remarried Families," and "Medical and Neurological Considerations."

The fifth edition of *The Fragile Alliance* will be published in

2001. We have decided that new methods of mental health care delivery over the past decade require further changes in *The Fragile Alliance*. Like much of present treatment, our book is briefer, less expensive, but in some ways more comprehensive than previous editions. We have not included the chapters on inpatient treatment in this edition. Other material has been shortened or eliminated. Additional material has been presented in tabular form and highlighted in boxes. References and terminology have been updated. The references are now all in one chapter at the end of the book and are annotated, to help the student locate additional reading.

Although we have introduced many changes and improvements, which keep this book contemporary, the fundamental principles in *The Fragile Alliance* are the same as they were 30 years ago:

- Effective therapy with the adolescent client requires a solid alliance based on an understanding of the development and psychological realities of adolescent functioning. For instance, the therapist needs to be aware of and respect the youngster's ambivalence about independence.
- Adolescents are driven by both conscious and unconscious motives. Sometimes, although not always, it is therapeutic to help the adolescent client get in touch with unconscious issues.
- Generally the role of the therapist is to help the adolescent make decisions for himself or herself regarding current activities and future plans, but there are times when the therapist should intervene in a very active manner.
- Although the primary client is the adolescent, it is important to consider the concerns and needs of the parents.
- Flexibility and therapeutic creativity is important. Although this book emphasizes individual psychotherapy, there are times when the therapist should consider other approaches: family meetings, group therapy, medication, meditation, cognitive-behavioral therapy, and referral to intensive residential programs.

The clinical material in *The Fragile Alliance* has been disguised. The names and other identifying data have been changed. Many of the clinical vignettes are composites of several actual cases. To avoid the awkward repetition of "he" or "she," the pronoun "he" is understood to refer to either gender in some chapters and "she" is used in other chapters.

Annotated references are found at the end of the book. The reader is also referred to Internet web sites for additional information on many topics. *DSM-IV-TR* in the text refers to *Diagnostic and Statistical Manual of Mental Disorders,* Fourth Edition, Text Revision (American Psychiatric Association, 2000).

We thank our colleagues for their counsel and constructive criticism. Dr. Michael Meagher and Dr. Catherine Fuchs read the manuscript and helped us clarify sections that were ambiguous or unclear. We appreciate very much the support and suggestions of our wives, Anita Meeks and Susan Bernet. Our secretaries, Cathy Maloney in Rockville and Nikki Kirby in Nashville, have tirelessly helped in organizing the various drafts of this book. Also, Peggy Westlake, M.L.S., Eskind Biomedical Library, helped enormously by checking the references.

acknowledgments

Grateful acknowledgement is made to the following for permission to reprint their material:

1. *Adolescent Psychiatry,* excerpt from Katz P., "The Psychotherapeutic Treatment of Suicidal Adolescents." 20: 325–341, 1995.
   Excerpt from Sugar M., "Diagnostic Aspects of Underachievement in Adolescents. 14: 427–440, 1987.
2. American Psychiatric Association, excerpts from *Diagnostic and Statistical Manual of Mental Disorders,* Fourth Edition, Text Revision, 2000.
3. Taylor & Francis, New York, excerpt from Sager C. J., *Treating the Remarried Family,* 1983.
4. *Journal of the American Academy of Child and Adolescent Psychiatry,* excerpt from Aug R. G., Bright T. P, "A Study of Wed and Unwed Motherhood in Adolescents and Young Adults." 9: 577–594, 1970.
   Excerpt from Bernet W., "The Therapist's Role in Child Custody Disputes." 22: 180–183, 1983.
5. *Journal of the American Psychoanalytic Association,* excerpt from Adatto C. P., "On the Metamorphosis from Adolescence into Adulthood." 14: 485–509, 1966.

Part

One

introduction

At the core of all psychotherapy is the relationship with the patient. The process of developing an understanding of the adolescent, forming a working relationship or therapeutic alliance, managing the ongoing therapy, and then constructively dissolving the therapeutic contract is the subject of Part One. Specific diagnoses and special technical problems will be largely deferred to Part Two.

The emphasis in Part One is on general principles of therapy and the primary focus is on individual therapy. The discussion of the individual therapist and the individual patient is vital to the structure of the book. Part One also includes a chapter discussing the role of the adolescent's family in treatment. The focus of that chapter is on the therapist's relationship with the parents of those adolescents the therapist is seeing in individual therapy.

The remainder of Part One includes brief chapters presenting the basics of group and family psychotherapy. These therapeutic modalities are discussed primarily to show their relationship to the more traditional individual approach and to suggest some of their special applications in planning treatment for adolescent patients.

Our hope is that Part One will provide the reader with a general grasp of the aims and methods of psychotherapy with the adolescent in any setting. This basic understanding should never be forgotten whenever a therapist approaches an adolescent patient. This sense of the therapeutic alliance is the core of the book and the solid grounding of all successful adolescent therapy.

CHAPTER 1
adolescents are different

Adolescence as a developmental stage has not always been as obvious as it is today. In Western Europe and America, adolescence was confused with childhood at least until the eighteenth century. When most society was rural and there was little formal education, the population was divided into the younger people (children, who were dependent and a financial drain) and the older people (individuals who could work and were an economic asset). In most families there was no time or place for young people to engage in a "psychosocial moratorium." All this changed in the nineteenth century because of broad social transitions to increasing urbanization, industrialization, and universal education. The growth of schools with multiple grades—rather than the one-room school house—and the creation of high schools made it official that adolescents were different from children. The word "adolescence" was mentioned as far back as the Middle Ages, but came into general use in the mid-nineteenth century. The term "teenager" originated in the 1940s (Hine, 1999).

It has gotten to the point, of course, that adolescents are hardly an invisible or silent minority, but are almost always in the face of the rest of us. The distinct aspects of youth culture (whether it be black-clad youth of both sexes, outrageous hairdos, overly macho jocks, overly loud music, overly violent schools, whatever) are the most blatant feature of our social landscape (Esman, 1995). The twentieth century was a time for the definition and study of adolescents and adolescence, starting with the landmark book by G. Stanley Hall in 1904 and the creation of the first juvenile court clinic by William Healy in

5

1909. The full title of Hall's book (*Adolescence: Its Psychology and Its Relations to Physiology, Anthropology, Sociology, Sex, Crime, Religion, and Education*) still defines the scope of our interest in this important developmental stage.

As we enter the twenty-first century there continues to be a remarkable interest in studying adolescence as a discrete phase in the development of the human personality. The information converging from many sources has shown that adolescence cannot be understood as merely a recapitulation of previous development. Increasing awareness of the specific role of cultural opportunities and restrictions, the characteristics of adolescent thought processes, the importance of childhood experiences, and the synthetic role of the ego during adolescence—to mention only a partial list of pertinent topics—has expanded our picture of the adolescent toward a three-dimensional view.

Two of the pioneers in the psychological study of adolescence were Erik H. Erikson and Peter Blos. Erikson (1963, 1968) developed a useful framework for thinking about human development—the eight stages from infancy through old age—and offered an overview of the adolescent process as a regression in the service of progression. It is as though the adolescent must at times drag himself and the adults who care for him through the mud of old conflicts, enmities, and attachments to inoculate himself against both the seductive memories and the frightening dangers of the past. If all goes well, he emerges into adulthood with immunity to some of the more virulent pathogens from his past and the ability to host others without apparent damage to his psychological integrity.

Blos (1962) described several phases of adolescence—that latency is followed by preadolescence, early adolescence, adolescence proper, late adolescence, and postadolescence. See the outline on page 7. The overall goal of adolescence is to achieve what Erikson (1968) called "identity" and what Blos (1967) called the "second individuation." Both terms refer to the achievement of a workable self-awareness that accepts inner complexity and is able to relate this multifaceted sense of selfhood to others in an interpersonal and larger social context.

STAGES WITHIN ADOLESCENCE

Adolescence can be divided into several substages of development, which have their own physical, psychological, and social characteristics.

Early adolescence starts with the onset of puberty. For girls, the average age of the first menstrual period (menarche) is 12.5 years; for boys, the average age of the first ejaculation is 13. Secondary sexual characteristics make their appearance a year or so prior to those events and continue to develop for several years after. Early adolescents are typically 12 to 14 years old and are in junior high school, the 7th and 8th grades. Peers are important and the early adolescent's best friend is usually a child of the same gender.

Middle adolescence typically extends from age 14 to 16, when teenagers are in the 9th, 10th, and 11th grades. During this time, girls are maturing earlier than boys in sexual development and in achieving their adult height. Social relationships usually revolve around a specific group of friends, with many teenagers pairing off in heterosexual dating. This is a time for much experimentation and many firsts: first sexual relationship; first driver's license; first real job; first checking account; first substance use; first serious rebellion against parents or other adults.

Late adolescence typically extends from age 17 to 20, from the latter part of high school until one or two years following graduation. The developmental emphasis during this time is on autonomy from parents; emotional investment in a significant relationship with another person; and commitment to a general career area.

This sense of self is still tentative and is largely a recognition of potentials, not a static and finalized state. As Erikson pointed out, the adolescent who is involved in the quest for identity does not actually ask himself, "Who am I?" as we often loosely say. Instead, he asks, "What do I want to make of myself and what do I have to work with?" Recognition of this distinction has implications for defining the goals of psychotherapy with adolescents and setting appropriate end points for therapy, which we will consider later.

Perhaps a metaphor based on the world of theater will help convey a sense of the adolescent experience. For the adolescent, the external world is sometimes a distant stage on which skillful players are easily producing a successful performance. The young spectator can hardly imagine that he will ever have sufficient skill to handle anything more than a walk-on part. At other times, the world is seen as a cast of faltering and untutored players, totally available to be molded to the adolescent's personal sense of drama. In short, the adolescent shifts from seeing reality as a malleable medium in which he can implant an image of his inner struggles to viewing it as a relatively fixed situation to which he must mold himself. Generally speaking, the younger adolescent tends toward the view of himself as the undiscovered director, whereas the older adolescent gradually comes to accept a less inflated role in the grand production of life. The theatrical metaphor was deliberately chosen to emphasize the experimental and tentative quality of the adolescent's feelings, attitudes, and relationships. One often has the impression that the adolescent is assuming a role and "playing at" life.

We do not mean to imply that the adolescent is necessarily playful or frivolous in his approach to living. The fact that he is often very serious indeed is revealed by the intense emotions that are typical of adolescence. What is lacking is a readiness to make permanent commitments or form irreversible loyalties. The adolescent cannot take positions or roles that imply finality because these may prove later to be poorly suited to what he wants to make of himself or what he has to work with. Still, he can only answer these questions by involving himself with life.

We cannot expect him to learn to swim without getting into the water. The adolescent's compromise solution involves trial dips that are always undertaken with the option of jumping out if the currents are too swift, if the eddies are too deep, or even if he decides he is a landlubber after all.

The average adolescent quietly conducts his experiments in living. His surface behavior remains for the most part well within the confines of acceptability. The inner struggle is hardly apparent even to the adolescent himself and is accomplished with only a few dramatic displays. The relative peacefulness of the ordinary adolescent experience was described by Offer (1969) and Offer and Offer (1975) who spent much of their professional lives studying the habits of normal American adolescents. Their data did not support the classic explanation of adolescence, especially the description of adolescence as an angry, difficult time. Offer (1987) stated that 80% of nonpatient adolescents are happy with themselves most of the time. It should be recognized that there is a range of development patterns even within normal adolescence. Some adolescents have a rather turbulent path to adulthood; others show periodic external distress; while others move through the developmental stage with minimal observable evidence of upset.

For the most part, those adolescents who present (or are presented) for psychotherapy are a very different group. Their struggle is desperate and highly visible. For them, adolescence is quite literally a question of life or death. If they cannot find a part in the drama that fits both their sense of personal integrity and their notion of a good show, they refuse to play. The applause of an audience—that they would feel they were both exploiting and being exploited by—seems to them insufficient reward. They will not be roped into a command performance.

There are three general groups who might be caught in this quandary. One group is composed of those youngsters whose experiences and emotional development have been atypical to a degree that forces them to demand a role that is simply not realistically available.

An 18-year-old adolescent told his therapist that he was

sure his work paralysis would disappear if only he could be entrusted with some worthwhile task. When he was asked to give an example of a worthwhile task, he told at length of his plans for restructuring the executive branch of the United States government.

Other adolescents, even more impaired by their early experience or constitution, are faced with needs and wishes that may be internally inconsistent and even explicitly psychotic. They cannot imagine any role in the real world of adulthood that would even approach a satisfactory level of gratification.

Paul, a 13-year-old, was seen for psychological evaluation during his hospitalization for a crash weight-loss program. His internist insisted on this approach after Paul's weight rose above 300 pounds despite outpatient dietary management. Paul told the evaluating therapist that he saw no reason to lose weight, since it was his plan to establish an absolute monarchy on an uninhabited island. He anticipated that he would be totally cared for by his subjects, emphasizing the gastronomic delights that they would prepare for him. His affect was inappropriate and associations were loose. He appeared to be convinced of the reality of his delusional empire.

When he was released from the hospital, his mother attempted to carry out the dietary restrictions imposed by the internist. She relented, however, when Paul threatened her with a kitchen knife if she did not give him the food he wanted. The mother called the therapist in panic, but explained that she and Paul could not enter therapy since Paul's father "did not believe in psychiatry."

Five years later, the therapist was again contacted by Paul's mother. She wondered if the therapist would testify that Paul was emotionally ill. He was facing trial on charges of air piracy after hijacking an airplane to another country. Paul's psychotic mission in life eventually led him to an extremely dangerous impulsive venture in the real world. He was found to be legally insane and committed to receive the treatment that he should have had five years sooner.

A third group of troubled adolescents consists of those who are largely whole within, but who are dismayed by the possibilities that society presents them. Many of the adolescents who come for psychotherapy present a convincing argument for this view of their difficulty. If only society (their parents, their school, their community, their country, their world) were different, everything would be simple for them. They have studied the play and find it to be of inferior quality, lacking any suitable vehicle for their talents. Since social institutions are far from perfect, their argument has surface merit. On closer examination, however, one usually comes to feel that the particular social imperfections that trouble them most are remarkably similar to those features within themselves that they regard as unacceptable. The devil without is easier to abide than the devil within, especially for the conflicted adolescent.

Most adolescents today seem almost too eager to accept society's status quo, in that there is little sustained and consensual social criticism extant among today's adolescents. This does not mean that the adolescent no longer battles the adult world. At this time, however, the battle tends to be closer to home, perhaps more interpersonal than political, and less strident. Of course, more seriously disturbed adolescents may be very opposed to society but their rejection tends to be indiscriminate, obviously impassioned, and clearly self-destructive.

However, it does seem that many adolescents come to therapy somewhat more willingly today or at least are prepared to view themselves as unhappy and in need of some kind of assistance. Even when this is true, the adolescent must test the therapist and this test casts the therapist in a variety of roles—mostly adversarial at first. He will often be cast in roles far removed from his actual attitudes, capabilities, or intentions. Early in therapy, the adolescent tends to utilize the new adult in his life as a screen on which he can externalize the negative aspects of his self-image and his more distressing introjects. The therapist also may be a convenient embodiment of all the social, cultural, and family evils that the adolescent deplores. Later, we will consider more fully both the problems that this tendency poses for the therapist in the establishment of a therapeutic alliance and some of the technical approaches that may be useful in managing this hazard.

Later in therapy, the therapist frequently finds himself unrealistically elevated and venerated to the point of idealization. Although this reaction of the adolescent is not nearly so distressful to the therapist, it can also interfere with the adolescent's emotional growth if it is not properly utilized and eventually dissolved. The countertransference problems that occur when one is faced with adulation are especially marked when this attitude follows upon a previous disdain for the therapist.

These extremes of relating often take different paths that depend on the basic pathology of the adolescent. If the client lacks capacity to imagine help from others or even to emotionally recognize the separateness of another person, the passage through this "testing" phase may be very difficult. With some youngsters it is almost impossible to respond therapeutically to this peculiar style of adolescent relating. The observing ego, with which the therapist has allied himself in working with adults, seems rudimentary or absent in many adolescents. The seasoned psychotherapist expects his clients to distort his intentions and his personality, as long as the client is able to localize the origins of the distortions within himself and to reflect on their possible meanings. In early therapy with adolescents, one commonly encounters an intensity of feeling and a lack of introspection that produce a degree of uncooperativeness and explosiveness usually seen only in very disturbed individuals in adult psychotherapeutic work. If the adolescent's capacity to relate is seriously impaired or undeveloped before the vicissitudes of this developmental phase, the task can become overwhelming for patient and therapist alike.

THE ADOLESCENT'S STYLE OF RELATING

When adolescence begins, a youngster is subjected to a multipronged attack on his sense of self-esteem. The invading forces include the impact of unpredictable, uneven, sudden changes in body configuration and size; an unacceptable upsurge of forbidden impulses; and the adolescent's own need to devalue his parents, thereby losing a valued part of himself. The subjective response to this onslaught is a vague, anxious sense of inner loss and injury. The adolescent, as a result, is eager for new human relationships but is equally driven to use these relationships primarily to bind his psychic wounds. Although he desperately needs human identification patterns to restore a sense of direction, he is unable for several reasons to involve himself in any relationship that requires him to take a consistent interest in the other person. His attachment to other people—other adolescents as well as adults—is primarily narcissistic.

This does not mean that the adolescent will necessarily exploit the people to whom he relates, although he may. It merely means that the tie to others is strongly colored and mainly determined by the adolescent's inner needs. The actual characteristics of the other person are not totally ignored, but they are important primarily as orientation points around which the adolescent weaves complex fantasies and suppositions that are emotionally important to him. Other equally obvious characteristics are simply ignored if they do not fit the adolescent's view.

An inhibited 14-year-old boy in therapy for six months expressed amazement on learning that his therapist was married.

"You seem more like the swinger type," he exclaimed.

The therapist had worn a clearly visible wedding band throughout his contact with the adolescent. The same therapist had been accused of being hopelessly old-fashioned and an obvious nerd by other adolescents with different needs.

The adolescent's hunger to merge with an individual who seems to have a workable identity structure must live in uneasy coexistence with the fear that merger may actually occur. The adolescent's opposition to therapy, his therapist, and the therapist's ideas is often a reaction to a fear that the fragile identity he is nurturing may simply be overwhelmed by the strength of the therapist's personality. Perhaps this is the core of the dread of dependency that the adolescent frequently demonstrates.

DEVELOPMENTAL TASKS OF ADOLESCENCE

Adolescence is a time of great change—physically, psychologically, and socially. The major tasks of adolescence are listed here, with authors who emphasized particular issues. Gemelli (1996) has integrated these factors into a broad biopsychosocial model of mental development.

Survive puberty, which means accepting one's primary and secondary sexual characteristics and having a satisfying, realistic body image.

Develop a sense of identity, which means defining one's own values, ideals, and preferences and accepting one's race, sexual orientation, intellectual strengths and weaknesses, and personal foibles (Erikson, 1968).

Accomplish secondary separation-individuation, which means having a sense of oneself as a psychologically independent person who has his or her own thoughts, feelings, and opinions (Blos, 1962).

Expansion of relationships outside the home, so that self-esteem is derived from peers and adults in the community, not from parents (Harris, 1998).

Contemplation of a realistic plan to achieve social and economic independence, which involves giving up the idealized view of oneself, one's parents, and societal institutions.

Achieve abstract conceptualization. Most adolescents progress from concrete operations to formal operations, i.e., making theoretical statements about objects and situations that have not been experienced first-hand (Piaget, 1972).

Integration of a mature value system. Most adolescents achieve a sense of morality based on personal ethical principles, not just self-interest (Kohlberg, 1981).

Certainly one often notices that youngsters who are most fearful of the dependent role in the psychotherapeutic relationship have parents who frequently intrude into the adolescent's psychological privacy in an attempt to dictate his style of life.

The observable adolescent style of relating to others is the outer manifestation of inward distress. The adolescent often shows an intense but still fleeting and superficial attachment to other people. There is a searching quality, frequently described as fickle, as the adolescent reacts to real or fantasized qualities in new objects that promise an external solution to his inner turmoil. It is also characteristic that he hopes for total solutions and therefore is regularly disillusioned by those to whom he attaches himself. Of course, with the progression of adolescence, the attachments take on an increasingly adult form, although an ebb and flow of mature and immature attitudes toward the loved or admired person will continue until young adulthood. The impact of these characteristic adolescent styles of relating on the problem of establishing a therapeutic alliance will be immediately apparent to the reader. Not only will the styles of relating affect the early phases of therapy, but they must also be considered in attempting to understand transference phenomena in this age group.

THE THOUGHT OF THE ADOLESCENT

For many years, the peculiar thought processes of the adolescent have been noted by both the clinician and the creative artist. Prior to the monumental contribution of Jean Piaget, however, the unusual nature of these cognitive processes was explained on the basis of the emotional changes characteristic of the developmental phase. Piaget pointed out that we must also consider the way in which the intellectual functioning of the adolescent influences his behavior and emotions.

According to Piaget (1972), the capacity for formal operations appears in early adolescence. This style of thought allows the youngster for the first time to manipulate logically thought itself. In the preceding phase of concrete operations, the child

developed a capacity for logical manipulation of isolated problems and an understanding of the interrelationships of material
objects. The advent of formal operations allows the construction of general theories of the interrelationship between various
facts, problems, and ideas. As the adolescent develops the capacity to think about thought itself, he is able to manipulate mere
possibilities. Piaget states further that the emergence of a new
stage in conceptual development is invariably marked by an
increase in the egocentric use of the new cognitive ability and by
a preoccupation with testing and utilizing the recently acquired
skill. The adolescent is therefore fascinated with his shining toy
of truly abstract thought, and he plays with it endlessly.

The adolescent applies this ability for abstract thinking to his
world and overemphasizes its strengths and capacities as a tool
for reshaping the reality around him. Clinically, this tendency
appears as a belief in the omnipotence of thought and a grandiose overestimation of the adolescent's capacity to alter his world
by merely thinking about it. There is often a sense of impatience
with adults, who seem to be dawdling and needlessly complicating problems that could easily be solved by a logical approach.
In many youngsters, this development is accompanied by a
quickness and acuity of logical thinking that is truly outstanding. In this regard, it is of interest to note that many mathemati-
cians and theoretical scientists, who deal almost entirely in symbolic logic, make their most important theoretical contributions
during late adolescence and early adulthood.

This development in the cognitive area reinforces the emotional predisposition to narcissism during adolescence. The omnipotent, messianic preoccupations in the thought of the adolescent may be determined not only by his narcissistic withdrawal
from the real world and internal objects, but also by the parallel
developments in the unfolding of the cognitive apparatus. It
seems that the adolescent needs and deserves the opportunity to
play with his thoughts and to develop elaborate if unrealistic
and fanciful plans to revolutionize social, political, and scientific
practice just as the infant needs to shake his rattle and the

latency child to build his collections as they master and consolidate earlier cognitive development.

A related area in which the adolescent makes use of his newly developed skill in manipulating thought is in the discussion of ideologies. The adolescent is struggling toward a sense of commitment to some life view and therefore spends a great deal of time thinking about and talking about lifestyles and the meaning of existence. This interest in ideology is readily observed in the articulate, studious, middle-class adolescent with his endless dialogue about life goals and values. The therapist who wishes to treat adolescents must be prepared to listen to extended discussions that he would dismiss as intellectual defensiveness and resistance in adult patients. In fact, he should not only listen, but at appropriate times join the ideological discussion. Some guidelines for dealing with intellectualizing in adolescents are offered later.

THE ADOLESCENT AND SOCIETY

The adolescent's view of adult, organized society contains inherent elements of ambivalence. If the adolescent intends to find a place for himself in society, he naturally will have a strong curiosity about the nature and structure of this organization he plans to join. As noted, however, the adolescent is above all things a deductive thinker. His curiosity about society does not necessarily lead to an active study of its institutions, methods of operation, and reward systems. In addition, he is sadly deficient in knowledge of the behavior of human beings. Since he is utopian in outlook, he can develop only a limited interest in a historical perspective. He is more likely to devote himself to extensive fantasy, speculation, and theorization based on the most superficial and cursory examination of the data.

The adolescent who "drops out" and cannot accept the possibility of amalgamation into the adult world may be more interested in a depth study of society, but the value of his efforts may be decreased by the strong bias that accompanies his work. He is interested only in verifying his opinion, already self-validated, that society is corrupt, unchangeable, and inimical to basic human needs.

Even the adolescent who is more favorably inclined toward the adult world will have some mixed feelings about accepting an apprentice's or student's role despite the value of this intermediate step on the path to adulthood. The adult world is, after all, his parents' world. The adolescent is still engaged in the struggle to escape dependent ties to his parents. He is reluctant to place himself in a comparable position with other adults. It is very difficult, especially for the younger adolescent, to accept his limitations comfortably, even those that are simply human. Internal conflicts, as well as shortcomings, tend to be externalized and dealt with as though they were environmental enemy forces. The adolescent cannot be entirely at peace with the world because he is not at peace within.

The capacity to tolerate inner strife is developed only gradually. Often, the adolescent cannot afford to learn the truth about society when that information would interfere with some of his self-protective fictions. This is often most clearly apparent in his dealings with the aspect of adult society closest to him, namely, his parents.

This state of affairs is complicated by adult society's views of the adolescent, which is often as irrational and unconsciously determined as are the adolescent's attitudes. Parents may unconsciously harbor competitive, fearful, erotic, and envious attitudes toward their adolescent children. Adults may view adolescents as a minority group and respond to them, as a group, with stereotyped attitudes and expectations that could only be described as prejudiced.

Adolescents struggle along an unstable interface between their peer culture and adulthood. In even the smoothest adolescence, there is some mutual shaping and accommodation between the adolescent and his parents. The game is one of negotiation and compromise, no matter how much some adults may wish that a stricter approach would simplify life. Our society eventually guides the adolescent into an acceptable adult role in most instances, but, after all the arguments, threats, cajolery, coercion, and capitulations, we find that the process of molding our youth also has altered our notion of adulthood. Maturity and youth constantly shape one another.

Viewed objectively, the battle of the generations would seem to end in victory for both sides in the yield of a wider and more flexible set of adaptive skills. Subjectively, however, both sides often feel defeated. Too often, the young person feels that he has compromised his ideals whereas the adult suffers a nostalgic longing for a simpler and somehow nobler past, now lost forever.

Unfortunately, as we will discuss in detail later, some adolescents are committed to extending their energy to construct a purely fanciful view of themselves, the world around them, and the intentions of other people. These young people, whose sense of "potential competence" has been severely restricted due to early trauma or constitutional deficiencies, are often trapped by the upsurge of omnipotence and omnipotentiality in adolescence. They are no longer influenced by most life events and, without therapy, may simply continue to be preoccupied with adolescent dreams. Often they live these out with tragic, even fatal results. These are the youngsters who suffer "malignant" emotional disorders.

THE ADOLESCENT AS UNCLE TOM

Erikson (1968) has argued well that autonomy and a clear sense of identity are always found in some workable and personally meaningful alliance with dominant cultural themes and available role patterns. Although one may yearn personally for the more individualistic, self-directed, and ethically oriented American character of past generations, such an identity may be poorly adapted to current American culture. A workable personality for the new millennium may need to emphasize easy amiability and compromise rather than strict adherence to principle in all matters. Current social conditions may favor a generalized, although possibly superficial, friendliness rather than a pattern of mannered formality counterpointed with passionate involvement with a few intimates. The social conditions of urbanization, easy geographic mobility, corporate business structure, and massive population growth that have fostered these styles of relating are factors to which the adolescent must adapt, not conditions that he has created.

Adolescents, despite their affinity for ideological discussion, are not effective agents of real social change. They are more frequently noisy and highly visible riders on a bandwagon they cannot afford to miss. It seems unfair to expect the adolescent, struggling with internal turmoil and possessing only a superficial understanding of the cultural landscape, to do the adult world's dirty work of social criticism and reconstruction. It is enough that he stand ready to follow intelligent and passionate leadership, carrying the banners of the cause and shouting its slogans. Adolescents, as a group, are well informed and thoughtful consumers of new or at least historically relevant ideologies. They are in no position to assume the responsibility of devising and manufacturing them. It has been suggested that the hope for a solution of our social problems lies with our youth. This may be true, if sensible and knowledgeable adults will provide reasonable blueprints for reconstruction. Our youth will labor untiringly if they are provided a job description that makes sense to them and then are left to their own techniques of implementation.

The adolescent who comes to psychotherapy needs assistance in gaining enough freedom from his internal strictures so that he can voluntarily commit himself to the lifestyle of his own choice. His therapist has no right to select the leaders the adolescent will follow, only the responsibility for assuring a reasonably free election.

IMPORTANCE OF PEERS

The friendless adolescent and the adolescent who prefers adult companionship are good examples of patterns that should alert the therapist to probable areas of emotional conflict. The turn toward peers is an almost universal adaptive technique for the adolescent. This hunger to have friends is related to at least four pressures on the adolescent.

1. *His internal need for narcissistic support.* Friends of the same age group can provide support not only by offering the sense of acceptability inherent in belonging to a group, but also by sharing guilt and thus reducing the shattering impact on self-esteem of a superego outraged by the increase in libidinal and aggressive drives at puberty.

2. *The strongly felt need to loosen both dependent and unconscious erotic ties to the parents* in preparation for eventual independence and mature love. The companionship of peers offers some substitution for the loss of support entailed in this process of leave-taking.

3. *The absence of a comfortable, or even bearable, sense of individual identity.* That is, a teenager might not be ready to take a stand on his own, but would be very comfortable being part of a group that is asserting some opinion or demand.

4. *To a large extent, group formation is forced on the adolescent by social realities.* The process of secondary education and the college experience in a specialized and technological society requires us to place large numbers of adolescents together apart from their families. This spatial contiguity, coupled with the "minority group" status of the adolescent, strongly encourages the formation of intense ties between young people.

Adolescents use their peers to back their demands for greater freedom and to validate their grievances toward their parents and the remainder of the adult world. In unity, there is some strengthening in their vulnerable position. The use of the group to avoid awareness of anxiety is especially evident in the preoccupation of adolescent groups with "fun" and "action." The complaint "there is nothing to do" is not so much the jaded grumbling of a pleasure-mad sophisticate as the anxious lament of a trembling soul desperate to stay one jump ahead of a pursuing host of internal demons.

The importance of adolescent peer relationships has been studied from almost every perspective. In his classic book, Hall (1904) said, "Every adolescent boy ought to belong to some club or society marked by as much secrecy as is compatible with safety," since "something esoteric, mysterious, a symbolic badge . . . and perhaps other things owned in common give a real basis for comradeship." As a psychotherapist in the early twentieth century, Harry Stack Sullivan emphasized the importance of having a same-gender pal during early adolescence. A psychoanalyst, Deutsch (1967), explained that the adolescent often prefers the safety of belonging to a "we" to the terror of becoming an "I," when faced with the struggle to define an acceptable sense of self. A developmental psychologist, Harris (1998) recently criticized researchers who overemphasize the impact of parental nurture on children and adolescents. According to Harris's "group socialization theory," parents have little lasting influence on children and adolescents, but children and adolescents are greatly influenced by each other and by their culture.

THE POWER OF WORDS

At times, the adolescent pauses in his flight to turn and face up to the enemy within. He rarely makes this stand alone. His choice of weapons against the demons requires the company of at least one other person who will be asked to serve as a listener. A listener is essential to the plan of action, since the adolescent seems intent on subduing his inner problems with words. He plans to talk them to death, and the adult listener sometimes wonders who will succumb first, the demons or the listener.

This adolescent chatter often has an incessant, driven quality because it is used in the service of intellectual defense. The content of the verbalizations may be frankly introspective at times. These monologues may contain rather accurate insights into some of the adolescent's conflicts that he is able to face by maintaining some distance from their associated affects. Still, as Blos (1962) pointed out, the defense of intellectualizing permits

NOTEWORTHY AUTHORS ON ADOLESCENCE

G. Stanley Hall (1844–1924) was the first president of the American Psychological Association. His comprehensive, two-volume work, *Adolescence,* was published in 1904.

William Healy (1869–1963), a pioneer in the study of juvenile delinquency, directed the first juvenile court clinic in Chicago in 1909. He was the first president of the American Orthopsychiatric Association.

August Aichorn (1878–1949) wrote *Wayward Youth* (1925), an account of psychoanalytically oriented treatment of teenagers in Vienna, Austria.

Anna Freud (1895–1982) was the first psychoanalyst of children and the author of *The Ego and the Mechanisms of Defence* (1958, 1966).

Jean Piaget (1896–1980), a Swiss psychologist, studied the cognitive and moral development of children and adolescents (1972).

Erik H. Erikson (1902–1994) introduced the concept of identity formation and psychosexual stages throughout the life cycle. He wrote *Childhood and Society* (1950, revised in 1963) and *Young Man Luther* (1958).

Peter Blos (1903–1997) was a psychoanalyst whose work has become part of the foundation of our understanding of the development and psychopathology of children and adolescents. His classic book was *On Adolescence* (1962).

Joseph D. Noshpitz (1922–1997) was a leader in child and adolescent psychiatry. He edited the encyclopedic *Handbook of Child and Adolescent Psychiatry* (1997, 1998).

Daniel Offer (1930–), a psychiatrist, did important research on normal adolescents (1987).

David Elkind (1931–), a contemporary psychologist, wrote *All Grown Up and No Place to Go: Teenagers in Crisis* (1997) and many other books about children and adolescents.

greater tolerance of instincts and is therefore largely a positive emergency measure during adolescence.

More often, the voluble ruminations are not so clearly related to the adolescent's personal feelings, but take the form of philosophic discussion. A very personal concern can usually be discovered underlying the philosophic issue when these weighty pronouncements are carefully attended.

A very unhappy 13-year-old spent her first few therapy hours bitterly accusing the adult world, including her therapist, of hypocrisy. No adult, she proclaimed, was what he pretended to be. This led to long and bitter tirades against religion and against her parents for forcing her to attend a church whose articles of faith she could not in conscience accept.

Shortly thereafter, when a therapeutic relationship was established, she wished to discuss her dangerous sexual provocation of older boys whom she told that she was 16. She noted in a letter to the therapist, "I've been yelling about all those hypocrites. I guess I'm the biggest one of all."

At a deeper level, she seemed to be referring to the incongruity between her rigid infantile superego and the emerging sexual feelings that seemed foreign to her. She had some awareness that her precocious leap into heterosexual behavior was "hypocritical" in the sense that it was defensive and by no means an expression of an actual readiness for heterosexual encounter. In her conflicts over denied dependency on her mother and her overwhelming guilt, she tried to maintain equilibrium by a spurious sexual aggressiveness.

If the adolescent can be garrulous at times, he can also be unbelievably taciturn. Total retreat into a glum and irritable silence is more disturbing to most adults than intellectual prattling. The intuitive feeling, often voiced by parents, that withdrawal is more serious than open conflict is correct. Usually, these silences cover a sense of being overwhelmed. During such times, the adolescent frequently adopts ascetic attitudes that cause him to experience almost unbearable feelings of guilt and shame. No progress in integrating the new instinctual striving is made in this atmosphere of self-suppression. At best, the adolescent can use these self-imposed exiles to lower the amount of external stimulation and to lick his wounds. At worst, he can paint himself into a misanthropic corner that he has too much pride to leave, even when he would like to do so.

MISDIRECTION

Magicians discovered long ago that it was not necessary for the hand to be faster than the eye if the observer could be led to look in the wrong place. To accomplish this, the magician uses large and obvious movements to divert attention from more subtle movements that are essential to the trick. Blackstone used to open his act by producing a live goat on stage. The great fuss he raised with his cape diverted attention from the fact that behind the cape he was carrying the goat under his arm! The technique is known as misdirection.

Adolescents seem to use these diversionary tactics frequently, especially in hiding attitudes and affects that they do not care to face or to have others notice. The method is especially effective when the affect to be hidden is a quieter, more gentle feeling. It is not always easy to detect the sadness and dependent longings a young person is experiencing when one's anxious and irritated attention is commanded by his belligerent and angry rantings.

The defensive technique that we are calling misdirection, then, could be defined as the exaggerated expression of one felt affect in order to hide from the self and others the presence of a concurrent, less acceptable affect. The utilization of this defensive operation explains why the adolescent often seems to go to extremes in the expression of a single feeling, especially of anger. Misdirection gives the adolescent a one-dimensional affective tone when it is employed. He appears at these times to be a real "Johnny-One-Note" on the emotional scale. The stereotyped and unchanging nature of the affective expression can be a clue that other shadowy feelings may be lurking behind the fireworks in the foreground.

Of course, a similar pattern has a wider defensive value in simplifying and resolving identity conflicts. Erikson (1968) has discussed this as a demand for "totality" when a richer sense of "wholeness" cannot be achieved. The adolescent who grasps at totality amputates not just single affects, but larger portions of his personality in order to achieve a constricted, but comfortable, sense of identity.

Special mention should be made of the adolescent's varied attempts to adapt to his superego conflicts. These behaviors are a frequent source of confusion to the adult observer. Very often, when it comes to the adolescent and his conscience, things are simply not as they seem to be.

Pattie was a 15-year-old whose rebellious behavior and apparent sexual promiscuity became so outrageous that her distraught family in desperation placed her in a psychiatric hospital. On the ward, she paraded her precocious pulchritude in a seductive display that made Madonna look like an inhibited old-maid schoolteacher. Since the adolescent boys on the ward were all racing about, tongues awag, approaching something that might have been called heterosexual panic, Pattie was seen in emergency daily therapy sessions.

In the first two sessions, she contented herself with systematically dismembering her parents with a cool, detached sophistication. By the third session, however, she was ready to give her therapist the full treatment. She somehow eluded the censoring eye of the nurses and arrived for therapy (barely) clad in a brief miniskirt, topped by a low-cut, skin-molded peasant blouse. She spun around in the office modeling her outfit. Then, hands on hips, she leaned seductively forward and innocently asked her therapist, "Now do you see anything wrong with these clothes?" Her therapist retained his composure and looked at her steadily for a long moment. "I think you secretly feel like a dirty slut," he said. "And I think that must be a lousy way to live. Why don't we talk about why you're doing this to yourself?" Pattie broke into tears. "You stupid ass," she shouted and fled the office.

Her flamboyant exhibitionism lessened over the next few days. During the weekend, she remarked to a ward nurse, "Dr. X (her therapist) is not such a bad shrink. At least you can't fool him."

As her therapy proceeded, it became clear that Pattie's extravagant delinquency was simultaneously an effort to disclaim and escape a rigid superego and an unconsciously calculated effort to force others to control her behavior.

The variety of similar patterns is virtually endless. Many adolescents who appear to exhibit poor ego structure and deficiencies in impulse control are actually thrashing helplessly in the grip of an infantile superego that will not permit the comfortable and orderly expression of impulses. These adolescents can permit gratification only by linking pleasure with self-destructive and self-punitive extremes.

Not all of them are so flamboyantly "going down in flames" as was Pattie. The self-destructive behavior may be quieter and more subtle. The adolescent may merely fail his school work, "rebelliously" refuse to accept honors, or demonstrate a sullen refusal to enjoy anything. The built-in self-punishment evens the tally and therefore allows some expression of pleasure-seeking behavior. The combination often appears to the puzzled, angry (and sometimes envious) adult as a self-indulgent and willful flaunting of social expectations. The typical adult response makes it easy for the adolescent to externalize his superego conflict. The adult who tries to set reasonable limits is invested with the viciousness, rigidity, and anhedonia that actually reside in the adolescent's own superego.

ASTROLOGY, SATANISM

Many adolescents show an intense interest in the supernatural. Some of their morbid preoccupations and beliefs would be quite pathological if expressed by an adult. Usually, these interests do not seem unpleasant or frightening to the adolescent. In fact, they are usually presented in a playful manner and may be the basis of entertainments such as visiting "haunted houses" in groups. Astrology and other occult sciences also hold great fascination for many adolescents.

Frankie, an intelligent, nonpsychotic 16-year-old girl, bounced cheerfully into a therapy session. Bubbling with enthusiasm she announced, "Now I know how to make myself invisible!"

Frankie had frequently discussed a fantasy wish to be invisible which seemed to have multiple dynamic origins. She now explained, "You get a human head and three black beads. You put one bead in each eye and one in the mouth. Then you draw this design on the head and bury it. You water it with the finest brandy for three days and then. . . ."

"Wait, wait," said the therapist. "I'm still back at the beginning. Where do you get the human head?"

Even risking the pun, the gleam in her eye could only be described as devilish.

It is striking that much of the interest in the supernatural seems related to the question of death and immortality. One gains the impression that not only is the fear of death very real to the adolescent but death often seems imminent. In typical adolescent fashion, however, this fear is usually handled in a counterphobic manner.

There seem to be two primary sources of this inclination toward the occult within the adolescent. The first we have already encountered as the adolescent's belief in the omnipotence of thought. Reality ties are loosened and magical thinking is easily accepted. It is a logical short step from a personal alteration of reality to a world peopled by witches, ghosts, and seers.

The second factor is the adolescent's effort to relinquish his parents and many aspects of his childhood self. In a psychological sense, death and mourning are an immediate part of the adolescent experience. Since the adolescent's greatest fear is fear itself, he sometimes happily embraces his demons and, gulping back his fears, takes them out for a romp.

Some youngsters become preoccupied with supernatural and occult topics to a degree that goes beyond curiosity about death and immortality and also goes beyond a rebellious interest in beliefs that most adults do not value. These disturbed young-sters make use of satanism, either individually or with a few like-minded friends, as an embodiment of evil power. The purpose of the preoccupation with and belief in evil power—whether it be satanism or the neo-Nazi philosophy of skinheads—is to orga-nize and represent the intense, chaotic sexual and aggressive feelings that these adolescents are experiencing. According to King (1988), self-styled satanism is a way for disturbed teen-agers to organize a value system that endorses violent and anti-social behavior. King also thought that this preoccupation with evil power is synergistic with serious drug use in teenagers, since each one seems to promote the other. In general, the adolescent interest in the supernatural is reinforced by a gener-alized awakened interest in the irrational and mystical. When these activities are linked with the use of psychedelic drugs and other substances, the potential for destructive interactions is frightening.

IMPLICATIONS FOR PSYCHOTHERAPY

These developmental characteristics of adolescence pose many problems in psychotherapy. Because of the adolescent's style of relating and his preference for peers, it is often difficult to establish a therapeutic relationship. This is true not only because of the adolescent's distrust of the therapist, but because of the countertransference attitudes that this negative approach arouses. In later chapters, we will be concerned with the tech-niques of establishing the therapeutic alliance and with the problems that are encountered by the therapist and the patient even after therapy is well under way and through the time of termination.

CHAPTER 2

the diagnostic evaluation of the adolescent patient

THE PERTINENT QUESTIONS

The evaluation process has the goal of understanding the adolescent's problem, accessing the youngster's strengths, and choosing a course of therapy that can utilize the strengths to move the adolescent toward maturity and emotional harmony with self and environment. This does not assume that harmony is necessarily compliance. The adolescent may develop into an effective, constructive critic of his or her world. In conducting an evaluation we should ask seven questions.

1. *Does the adolescent have constitutional, genetic, or other organic limitations that have significantly affected development and that may now limit the potential for ego growth? Are there indications of a severe learning disability or brain dysfunction? Does the adolescent have a major psychiatric disorder, such as bipolar disorder or schizophrenia, that is subtle or atypical in its presentation? If these problems were diagnosed earlier, has the youngster received understanding at home, remediation, and treatment?*

The presence of mental retardation, brain damage, attention-deficit/hyperactivity disorder, specific learning disability, and the like is an important consideration in the comprehensive understanding of any adolescent. These problems color early development and also impact adolescence in a direct way, often interfering with the efforts of the young person to individuate and gain an independent sense of self.

Severe physical illnesses, particularly if they are chronic and limit activity, may produce an enforced dependency that disrupts adolescent development. The illness may also set the adolescent apart from peers either in a factual way or in the adolescent's view of himself or herself as "different."

A serious mental disorder may be present, but not yet recognized because the symptoms have not fully developed or seem atypical. Examples include bipolar disorder, schizophrenia, and pervasive developmental disorder, such as Asperger's disorder. Feinstein (1982) described how adolescents with manic-depressive disorder (now called bipolar disorder) may have dramatic behavioral symptoms in addition to pathological mood swings. For instance, bipolar disorder can be manifested by severe adolescent rebellion; exaggerated self-esteem with grandiose conceptions of physical and mental powers; and sexual acting-out. Some youngsters with Asperger's disorder—which can be conceptualized as a mild form of autism—have puzzling behavioral and emotional symptoms. Children and adolescents with Asperger's disorder may have multiple assessments and diagnoses before their condition is identified and understood.

A strong family history of mental illness or addiction, major disorganization on mental status, and evidence of delusions or hallucinations in the absence of drug ingestion all suggest the possibility of major affective illness or psychosis. Even when the patient's primary symptoms are behavioral, these findings suggest the need for psychological and biological testing to search further for evidence of specific disease entities.

If the youngster's problems have been previously undetected, the years of failure and frustration have often scarred not only the adolescent's self-image but also relationships with other people. Severe narcissistic disorders, delinquency, drug use, and other "malignant" patterns of disability are often the end point by the time adolescence arrives. Treatment must address these defensive positions adequately before remediation is possible but the long-range need to help the youngster achieve success must be kept in mind even while struggling with unpleasant defenses.

2. *What is the best level of psychosocial development that the adolescent has achieved?*

This question is complex and difficult to answer for any psychiatric patient. In adolescents, who frequently deal with developmental stress by either regression or an equally confusing premature leap forward, the problem may be bewildering. The distinction between regression and fixation, so important to prognostication, is often very uncertain during the fluidity of the adolescent phase. Only meticulous attention to a complete developmental history and the capacity to decipher the latent content of the adolescent's behavior and verbalizations can yield the data for even a tentative conclusion on this point.

Although the adolescent may be obviously preoccupied with pregenital concerns and behavior at the time of referral, other diagnostic data may lead the therapist to suspect that this represents a regression. A documented history of performance at a better level is one observation that would encourage a better prognosis. In addition, the patient may present dreams, fantasies, or a style of relating during the diagnostic interviews which will belie the primitive psychological picture suggested by the presenting symptoms.

A 16-year-old boy was seen for evaluation because of stealing, destruction of property, and periods of staring vacantly into space. His parents stated that he was uncontrollable and they were concerned that he might become homicidal.

In his interview, he varied between angry silences, anal obscenities, and tight-lipped avowal to "get" his parents for arranging the consultation. Whenever the therapist asked a question or made a comment, the boy would lean forward menacingly and snarl, "What?"

The therapist repeated himself a few times, and then realized what was happening. He commented amiably to the boy, "I get the feeling that you're trying to scare me out of saying anything. You must be pretty worried about what I might say."

"I don't give a shit what you think of me," the boy snapped.

"How about what you think of you?" the therapist asked.

For a moment, the boy lowered his guard and grinned.

"Well, now that might be worth talking about some," he said.

Actually, he was not able to talk about his crippled self-esteem and foundered through the remainder of the interview, angry and suspicious. However, his brief comment did reveal that he was potentially capable of engaging in a human relationship at something other than a level of anal control.

3. *What kind of object relationships has the adolescent established, especially with his parents?*

Correct assessment of this side of the adolescent's development is obscured by the phase-specific peculiarities of relating that were described earlier. It is particularly hard to derive a realistic view of the adolescent's previous style of relating to the parents in the face of reversal of affect, disparagement, and other defenses calculated to help the adolescent divest himself of dependent ties to the parent. Again, the history plays a crucial role in arriving at the answer to this question. The adolescent's less guarded description of her relationships with peers may also be of assistance. Particular attention should be given to the covert expectations, hopes, and fears that the adolescent holds in regard to her friends. These frequently reveal a great deal about the strengths and conflicts present in the previous relationships with parents.

Although historical data will be of central importance in answering this question, much can be learned from observing what the adolescent emphasizes in rejecting her relationship to her parents. Generally speaking, those adolescents who have been most dependent on their parents are the most adamant in their demands for independence. Very often, their shrill and uncompromising insistence on total freedom and their denial of any attachment to their parents are accompanied by behavior that is unconsciously calculated to pull their parents into their affairs. The louder the adolescent screams that her parents treat her like a baby, the more likely it is that she is struggling with intense dependency yearnings toward them.

A similar situation exists in some adolescents who are extremely angry with their parents for not being omnipotent. These children have, for a variety of reasons, invested their parents with a fantasized capacity to protect them from all harm and to ensure their success in all endeavors. When this illusion collapses with the onset of adolescence, the youngster feels cheated. Often, the parents are denounced as phonies, hypocrites, or idiots. The tone of disappointment is conveyed by a joke that a teenage girl told her psychotherapist.

A teenage boy approached his father with questions about conflict in the Mid-East, abortion, government's role in social programs, and the like. He wanted his father to give him clear-cut judgments and answers, but instead the father, after each question, equivocated, noting that the situation was very complex and that there was no simple answer. He ended his comments each time by saying, "You're just going to have to make up your own mind on that, son."

After this happened five times, the son finally said, "Dad, would you rather I wouldn't bother you with all these questions?"

"Gosh, no!" said the father. "You have to ask questions. How else are you going to learn?"

In the joke, it is the father who fails to recognize that there are some things that he cannot teach, but in fact the disillusioned adolescent himself is begging, "Say it ain't so, Pop!"

We have already mentioned the adolescent who utilizes disdain to protect against incestuous feelings. One may also suspect Oedipal conflicts when the adolescent reports and demonstrates a pattern of constant bickering with and withdrawal from the parent of the opposite sex, especially when this is accompanied by accusations of sexual repression and unattractive personal qualities. This follows a general rule of thumb with the adolescent. When she stresses and emphasizes one particular vector of affect, you may get a glimpse of significant problems if you sight backward along the arrow in a reverse direction. Often, the adolescent unknowingly betrays her real feelings when she "doth protest too much."

4. *Why is the patient ill now?*

In many youngsters brought for therapy during adolescence, the answer is simply that they are ill now because they have always been ill. This is true of youngsters with very severe behavior disorders that result from a basic failure in the process of socialization. The parents may be antisocial themselves, overtly or covertly, or simply so rejecting of the child that they have never provided the affection and direction necessary for identification with society's rules and goals. These youngsters are brought to psychotherapy in adolescence, not necessarily for the first time, primarily because their increased strength, cleverness, and mobility have widened and deepened the impact of their antisocial behavior on their environment.

Other individuals, struggling with adolescence reasonably well, become ill in response to external traumatic events. Although their symptomatology is colored by their developmental phase, the focus of therapy should be on the mastery of the precipitating event. It should be noted that adolescents and their families are no more skilled than other psychiatric patients at recognizing the events that precipitate emotional illnesses. Often, the examiner must take the responsibility for noting temporal connections between life occurrences and the onset of symptoms of illness. The examiner can then search for the dynamic connections between the meaning of the particular event, the developmental history of the adolescent, the adolescent's verbal and nonverbal behavior during the diagnostic study, and the course of the illness. Only in this way can the true significance of the traumatic event be fully understood.

Most adolescent patients are victimized by specific developmental stresses. Their illness is precipitated by the onset of adolescence and the tasks inherent in that period. This is not to say that their conflicts are purely adolescent. Very often, perhaps usually, adolescence merely activates and highlights points of relative weakness in the personality structure. These unsolved growth problems may not have been troublesome in earlier stages, but careful review of the developmental history usually reveals their presence underground prior to their eruption into open view during the volcanic upheaval of adolescence. For most adolescents, this reactivation of latent conflicts has positive value that outweighs its negative implications. During the "trial run" at adulthood that adolescence permits, the young person has another opportunity to discover, demonstrate, and correct personality flaws without the severe and possibly irreversible consequences that might attend their emergence after commitment to adult goals and responsibilities.

Generally speaking, adolescent illnesses that are precipitated by clear-cut external events, such as the death of a family member, or that result primarily from the stress of the developmental crisis of adolescence respond well to outpatient psychotherapy. This is true even when the regressive features of illness are quite marked. On the other hand, even deviations that appear relatively minor on the surface may be very difficult to resolve if they reflect long-standing personality patterns. Generally, a chronic situation of this kind suggests a strong family involvement in the behavior pattern. Typically in these instances, the impetus for consultation comes from outside the family group. In these cases, the final three questions will usually be answered in the negative. The adolescent is not conflicted, the family has no real wish to permit or aid in change, and the adolescent will be unable to observe her own feelings objectively as a result of her comfortable immersion in a neurotic family pattern. Some alternate treatment approaches for these youngsters and their families will be discussed later.

5. *Is the adolescent conflicted?*

This question could be restated in two other ways. Is the adolescent concerned about her behavior? Is the adolescent motivated to change?

The problem in answering these questions is the adolescent's reluctance to admit directly to a sense of conflict. She is much more likely to try to bluff it out and make the best of a bad thing, although there are some exceptions to this rule, especially in older adolescents. Her indications that she is unhappy with herself and would welcome assistance are likely to be subtle and carefully hedged.

Many therapists, especially those who are relatively inexperienced, place too great an emphasis on verbalized motivation. All patients who approach therapy honestly are ambivalent about it. Conscious motivation is a straw in the whirlwind of primitive emotions unleashed by exploratory psychotherapy. Most patients weather these storms only because their attachment to the therapist strongly reinforces their rational wishes to improve. Often, it is possible to assess the true nature of the adolescent's motivation only after a trusting involvement with the therapist has developed. Actually, before this stage has arrived, the adolescent herself does not know whether she is "motivated" or not.

Except for some older adolescents, one rarely encounters an adolescent patient who views her symptoms as totally ego-alien, completely originating within herself, and subject to solution by self-understanding. The adolescent is largely self-justifying and resistant to any therapy that would require her to face up to herself. The examiner must content herself with minor clues that the adolescent is dissatisfied with herself. These brief self-disparaging comments, veiled hints of guilt, and half-admitted anxieties are viewed as surface evidence of workable discontents below ground that can be tapped later, when the adolescent is comfortable enough to permit exploration.

The examiner should also ask the parents if the adolescent has expressed discontent with herself or with her symptoms. Naturally, their answers must be studied in the full light of their motivations. Angry, rejecting parents may see the most anxious youngster as blissfully unregenerate. On the other hand, indulgent, overinvolved parents may misread deep self-concern in the faint scribblings of manipulative mock remorse.

Only when there is some real evidence of inner conflict, even if faint, should the adolescent be considered for individual outpatient treatment. If the conflicts are only between the adolescent and the outside world, the adolescent will not be motivated to form a therapeutic alliance. These youngsters will require other treatment approaches, at least initially, to produce any hope of success. Often, this question cannot be answered definitely without a trial period of treatment.

6. *Does the adolescent have the capacity to view herself with reasonable objectivity and the willingness to describe her view to the therapist?*

This is, of course, a central question, since in outpatient therapy the therapist will have to rely heavily on the adolescent to report honestly both her behavior and her feelings as a basis for the therapeutic work. One cannot expect too much, however, especially in younger patients. Some defensiveness, distortion, and self-protection are anticipated and do not contraindicate outpatient work. All adolescents can be expected to "play games." One only expects that they will gradually develop a capacity to discuss the rules of the game and the prizes they are trying to win.

In the case of some youngsters with narcissistic and borderline disorders, the initial goal of therapy is to draw their unrealistic game playing into the therapy relationship. This "make believe" relationship is tolerated until the patient is gradually able to see the world and himself or herself more clearly.

Many aspects of the diagnostic information must be considered in seeking the answer to this question. The presence of at least low average intellectual ability is probably a necessary basis for a therapeutic approach that relies on a verbal readjustment of attitudes and experiences. Youngsters with serious impairments in brain functioning may be unable to face themselves honestly without benefit of a specially constructed living situation that could be adjusted to their special needs. Outpatient psychotherapy, with its emphasis on personal responsibility, may place undue demands on the coping mechanisms of these youngsters.

Some adolescents adapt neurotically but successfully to a neurotic family situation. If the parents can offer such a youngster sufficient gratification within the pathological family configurations, there may be little impetus for growth and honest evaluation of the skewed contract that the adolescent has accepted. One can often suspect such a state of affairs when the adolescent accepts the absence of satisfactory peer relationships without complaint and without any apparent drive to achieve them.

These youngsters are best treated either in conjoint family therapy or in a residential setting if their symptoms are severe.

Other youngsters may reveal chronic impairment in the capacity to put feelings into words or to share their feelings with others. Rather than showing the disguised and distorted feelings that one expects in adolescent patients, these youngsters are either totally cut off from knowledge of their inner experience or else have never developed the trust in another person that would encourage them to make the effort of trying to explain themselves to someone. The examiner should accept this view of an adolescent patient with great reluctance and only in the face of overwhelming evidence. Many adolescents have temporary problems in recognizing and describing their emotions that would not interfere with the eventual utilization of outpatient psychotherapy. With only a diagnostic evaluation to guide him, the examiner can erroneously assume that these defects are chronic and irremediable, especially if he is angered or frightened by the adolescent's initial inability to cooperate.

Frankly psychotic adolescents are unable to assess their feelings and behavior realistically. These youngsters usually require inpatient treatment until their reality testing becomes more reliable. Many of those with transient psychotic symptoms may then be candidates for outpatient psychotherapy.

A final group of youngsters who cannot objectively observe their own behavior are those who are intoxicated with their control of the environment and are virtually convinced of their own omnipotence. Usually, their conflicts can be studied only when they are prevented from discharging their every anxiety in action. As a rule, this can be accomplished only with the control and leverage offered by a residential setting.

7. *Will the adolescent's family permit and help the adolescent to change?*

In adolescent patients, this is usually not a serious problem. Most of the youngsters come to therapy after at least having begun to fight for autonomy. The therapist usually will find that, although the parents may be distressed by this turn of events, the family has recognized that the previous homeostatic balance must be altered.

In the older adolescent, this alteration can often be effected without the parents' active assistance. In fact, in the course of successful psychotherapy, the adolescent can learn to recognize and to accept a reasonable degree of parental ambivalence toward her effort to wrench herself away from the family.

In the younger adolescent, however, the parents may need to involve themselves in the therapy. Most parents are sufficiently troubled by the overt family strife to be somewhat more cooperative than many parents of latency-age children are.

Occasionally, one encounters parents who are desperately committed to maintaining a pathological tie to their child, even in the face of the adolescent's efforts to force a separation. These parents typically seek the therapist's aid in forcing the youngster to remain under their infantilizing control. In such a situation, it is probably not therapeutic to offer psychotherapy for the adolescent until the parents can be brought to a healthier point of view.

A 17-year-old female high school senior was brought for psychiatric evaluation because of her refusal to accept her father's selection of the college she was to attend. The girl's objections to the college seemed fairly reasonable, since all of her friends were planning to attend a coeducational school in the area, whereas her father insisted that she attend an exclusive girls' college located some distance from her home. The girl was an outstanding student and correctly pointed out that the girls' school was noted more for its social prestige than its academic excellence. It was also obvious that she was attempting to assert her right to make this important decision in her life for herself.

The father, an extremely successful businessman, was an autocrat of the old school who had little interest in friends or intellectual achievement. He was self-made and put great store in his daughter's associating with "the right people." He asserted that his daughter's choice of school was very suspect and might be based on a wish to "run wild."

When the therapist asked about his evidence for this assertion and otherwise demonstrated a wish to explore the disagreement rather than accepting his view without question, he became quite angry. He stated that he certainly knew what was best for his own girl and had only hoped that "a doctor" could help bring his daughter to her senses. When the therapist asked whether the girl should have any decision-making power in regard to her college education, the father replied sarcastically, "Certainly! To the exact same degree that she intends to pay for it!"

In other cases the pathological tie is not limited to the parent, but also resides in the adolescent. There may be elements of protectiveness toward the adolescent that are understandable though ill-advised.

A 16-year-old male was referred for evaluation. There was a long history of erratic functioning and the patient was actively delusional—although one had to ask the right questions to bypass the boy's paranoid caution and elicit the delusions. There was reason for concern about possible homicidal violence. The psychiatrist recommended hospitalization. The mother wept and begged the therapist to treat the boy at home, "even if you have to see him twice a day." When she calmed down and began to accept the recommendation, the mother admitted the boy was concurrently being evaluated by a second psychiatrist. Interestingly, the adolescent had not mentioned the other doctor. Mother sighed, "I'm afraid he's going to say the same thing. We're going to meet with him next week."

He did and the family accepted hospital treatment.

Fortunately very few parents view their adolescent children as chattel as the father in the first example or as part of themselves like the mother in the second case. Most parents of adolescents are anxious or diffident and require support to function with the kind of helpful firmness that their children need.

Sometimes, however, it is best to permit ambivalent parents and adolescents to continue to resist treatment until greater discomfort leads to readiness for change. The techniques and problems of involving parents in the therapy of the adolescent are discussed more fully in chapter 8.

These seven questions are interrelated. One might even say that they are largely different ways of looking at the same basic question: how sound is the basic personality structure in this particular youngster?

The adolescent who has previously functioned in large measure at age-appropriate levels and has achieved fairly gratifying and stable object relationships probably has the capacity, if given proper assistance and if her family can allow it, to utilize the therapist as an ally in productive self-scrutiny. This remains true even if the presenting behavior is chaotic and bizarre. Trying to decide the true nature of the premorbid adjustment in the face of the distortions of the adolescent and her parents is truly a perplexing enigma. A tremendously important therapeutic step will have been accomplished if this problem can be resolved with substantial accuracy.

THE EVALUATION PROCESS

There are no set rules stipulating the form that the evaluation of the adolescent patient and her family should take. Procedures must be dictated by the circumstances of the individual case and by the particular preferences and skills of the examiner. Any approach that permits a contact with the adolescent and her family comfortable and extensive enough to allow the collection of sufficient data to answer the diagnostic questions posed above is acceptable. However, experience can offer some guidelines that will apply to most adolescents.

It is often preferable to set up the initial contact directly with the adolescent, especially the older adolescent. Many adolescents are very concerned that the therapist will form an alliance with their parents. Other adolescents may not resent the coalition between parents and therapist, but may be encouraged to take a passive role, hoping that the adults will straighten things out for them. Scheduling the initial interview with the adolescent clarifies the therapist's intention to appeal to that part of the adolescent that is striving for autonomy, self-direction, and responsibility. It also offers the therapist an opportunity to observe how the adolescent responds to this invitation to maturity.

When the adolescent patient is opposed to the consultation, she gives us the opportunity to observe how effective her parents can be in dealing with her. Many parents will ask how they should present and explain the necessity for the evaluation. This permits the therapist to demonstrate his willingness to help the parents, as well as his expectation that the parents take a significant portion of the responsibility for helping their youngster.

The parents should be advised to be honest with the adolescent not only about the nature of the interview, but also about the parents' reasons for requesting it. The therapist may freely offer advice about appropriate wording, since this is basically an attempt to educate the parents to a psychological view of their youngster's problem.

> The father of a 15-year-old boy who was tyrannizing his family and involving himself in minor delinquencies called to discuss therapy for his son. When the therapist suggested an interview with the boy, his father said, "I don't think he'll come. He is already mad at us, especially my wife. He'll think we're trying to say that he's crazy."
>
> "Do you think that he is?" the therapist asked.
>
> "No, but he is acting very strangely. Sometimes he sits and stares at nothing for hours."
>
> "I wonder if he's afraid that he may be going crazy," the therapist said. "Maybe you should discuss your concern with him. Tell him that you are worried about him and that you think he is probably worried about himself."
>
> After further discussion of the appropriate approach to the boy, the father finally asked, "What if he still doesn't want to come, even after all that?"

"From what you tell me, that's very likely the way it will be," the therapist said. "What do you feel you should do as his father if it turns out that way?"

There was a long pause. Then the father emitted a long sigh that seemed a mixture of resignation and resolution.

"He'll be there," the father said.

The therapist simply cannot be a party to any parental plan to skirt the issue by pretending the youngster is coming for a physical checkup, to discuss school planning, or to take some tests for an ill-defined purpose. Such dishonesty would defeat the whole effort to establish an atmosphere of honesty, trust, and open communication. In situations where there is a high level of family conflict, however, it is appropriate for the parent to present the evaluation as a family undertaking. The adolescent may be told, "We have arranged for a series of interviews with Dr. X since we all seem to be having trouble living successfully as a family." Since this is quite true, there can be no disadvantage in emphasizing it to the adolescent. Suggesting this approach also has the advantage of making this point quite clear to the parents.

Some parents will not be able to accomplish the task of bringing their adolescent to her initial interview in a reasonably acceptable frame of mind unless the therapist departs from this usual pattern and provides them with some direct assistance. In these instances, the therapist should honestly admit to the parents that his contact with them may pose some problems later with their youngster.

The parental interviews should focus tactfully on the parents' already demonstrated problem in discharging their appropriate function in family leadership. If their problem cannot be resolved in a few contacts with the therapist, this supplies an early negative answer regarding the parents' capacity to assist the therapy. The therapist must then consider whether therapy for the adolescent would be more appropriately conducted on an inpatient or residential basis or whether an extensive period of therapy for the parents should precede any effort to work directly with the youngster. It is impossible to treat the adolescent if she is in omnipotent control of her environment or if her parents are determined to destroy her if she remains in their company.

Many therapists do not follow the procedure outlined above. They feel that they can evaluate the adolescent more effectively if they follow a more traditional approach and obtain a full developmental history from the parents prior to the interview with the adolescent.

Both approaches probably have their advantages and pitfalls. It is probably wise to choose the approach that feels most comfortable and then to utilize it consistently. The therapist gradually becomes acquainted with the particular "side effects" of his favored style and develops skill in managing them. As stated earlier, the end result is more important than any rule of procedures.

At some time during the evaluation, however, the therapist has the right and the responsibility to insist on seeing the parents, no matter who is seen first. The occasional adolescent who objects to this reasonable request is actually revealing an aspect of her problem that needs to be carefully explored and acceded to only under the most unusual circumstances. The therapist who agrees to this arrangement usually finds that he is the next victim of his patient's secretive control and that his therapeutic usefulness is nil.

When the adolescent is interviewed, the therapist must decide how many sessions are needed to gain the necessary information for treatment planning. This may vary from one or two interviews with an articulate adolescent who is "ripe" for therapy to four or five or even more if the adolescent is silent or otherwise highly defensive.

Many therapists find that one or more family sessions are useful in the course of a diagnostic evaluation. These may even include other siblings or relatives, such as grandparents, who live in the home. These family sessions not only may reveal patterns of family interaction that might be missed in individual interviews, but may assist the family in defining their problems and understanding what must be accomplished later during therapy. These arrangements may need to be pre-approved by insurance companies or others, but the examiner must insist on adequate coverage.

Negativism

The initial task in the diagnostic interview with the adolescent patient is to define the purpose of the interview and to help the adolescent to recognize and deal with her reactions to the procedure. Unless some measure of cooperation can be obtained, the diagnostic process cannot proceed. The most common problem with the adolescent patient is an open reluctance or refusal to participate in the interview. Even in dealing with this initial negativism, however, the therapist can gain important diagnostic information. Although the manifest emphasis is on conscious feelings about the present situation, the adolescent will display her usual defensive techniques and reveal some of her conflicts when confronted with the request that she talk openly about herself. The therapist should make note of these responses, but should comment on them only as they relate to the evaluation procedure. This is especially true in the younger adolescent, who may be more frightened by the implications of a psychiatric or psychological evaluation than patients of any other age group. These children are old enough to realize some of the implications of the referral, but are not old enough to have the objectivity of the adult or older youngster. The strong upsurge of instinctual impulses with which they are struggling, as well as their tendency to confuse fantasy with action, makes the discussion of their inner feelings very threatening. In short, they are already secretly convinced that they are crazy—a confirmation they certainly do not need!

Adolescents of any age who are straining to maintain a shaky adjustment based on omnipotent defenses fight off self-disclosure for the same reason. They see honesty and exposure of limitations and vulnerability as threats to any sense of self-worth. Since they recognize only the extremes of triumphant, all powerful superiority or helpless worthlessness they do not welcome investigation that threatens their public façade.

Early Negotiations

In all adolescents, the decision to consult a therapist, even when self-initiated, gives rise to intense feelings. If the examiner does not attend carefully to these reactions and help the patient to deal with them, he will have great difficulty in obtaining the information he requires. The reactions that one anticipates are closely bound to the age of the patient. The early adolescent is likely to respond to the stress by denying that she has problems of any kind. The 14- to 16-year-old patient is likely to admit that there are problems, but then to blame them on her parents. The older adolescent is better able to appreciate that at least some of her difficulties are related to her own attitudes and feelings.

Adolescents of all ages, however, are skilled negotiators. Those who are resistant to the exploration of their problems begin testing the therapist even during the diagnostic process. They are interested to know whether the therapist will take an authoritarian, parental role with them. The testing may take the form of direct invitation. After having revealed something of herself in spontaneous conversation, the adolescent may suddenly ask, "Wouldn't you like to ask me some questions?" The unwary examiner may accept the invitation and confirm the adolescent's ambivalent hope and fear that she is faced with still another adult who wishes to arrange his life. A better response might be to comment, "I think you are doing very well in telling me about yourself. Please go on." With the younger adolescent, one might go even further in encouraging responsibility by commenting, "I sometimes ask a lot of questions with younger children, but with guys your age I have found this usually isn't necessary."

The patient may also try directly or indirectly to force the therapist to promise that he will reward the youngster for discussing certain topics or for simply participating in the diagnostic evaluation. This may be presented negatively, "I don't see how talking about all this is going to help me." At other times, the appeal may be more openly dependent. "Mother says if I tell you all about my problems, you can straighten me out."

"Can You Help Me?"

Of course, the therapist cannot permit himself to be pulled into such an unprofitable contract. The focus must be returned to the obvious fact that diagnostic understanding must precede any reasonable decision about what can be done to help matters. The youngster can be told that he and the therapist can discuss this question when the diagnostic work is completed. Some openly rebellious adolescents would challenge this comment by declaring that they already understand themselves and know that they do not need psychotherapy or help of any kind. The therapist must either ignore or challenge this opinion, since obviously it would dictate an untimely end to the diagnostic process. The manner in which the therapist chooses to respond to this ultimatum will depend on his tentative understanding of the particular adolescent. If anxiety appears to be the predominant obstacle to discussion, the approach would be sympathetic and supportive. The therapist might agree that the youngster has demonstrated ability to solve many of her own problems. The therapist can explain that he has no wish to interfere with that process, but can also comment that perhaps there are some problems that the youngster has not entirely solved as yet and that may be difficult to discuss. It may be wise at that point to add, "At any rate, I'd like to get to know you a bit better." The therapist can then ask a neutral question regarding the youngster's school, hobbies, or plans for the future. This may permit a more natural flow of talk with more subtle introduction of important topics. The youngster may comment, for example, that he is interested in motorcycles, but that his parents will not buy him one. The therapist can then open the discussion of the parent-child relationship in a natural manner by asking, "They're not too interested in Harleys, eh?"

Youngsters who appear more angry and rebellious may require a more direct approach. The therapist may need to state openly that he feels the patient is simply stating his opposition to the consultation when he says that he does not need any help. Since most rebellious youngsters have not originated the idea of psychiatric or psychological referral, this fact may be recalled to her. The therapist can then inquire directly about feelings and wonder whether the attitude toward the diagnostic evaluation is mainly derived from anger. This may allow a discussion of the youngster's feelings about doing things that her parents recommend or demand of her, including her feelings about the evaluation. If she is able to reveal her rebellious attitude toward her parents, he may go on to a more extended discussion of her feelings about rules and authority figures.

Other youngsters are merely being provocative and teasing when they say that they do not need help. They do not expect an answer to their dare, but are testing to see whether the therapist is an anxious and defensive adult who must rise to every bait thrown his way. They are best managed by ignoring the gauntlet and pressing forward with the real business at hand. Others deserve a light, "Frankly, I hope you're right. My schedule is pretty full right now. However, someone thought you needed help and it's my job now to form my opinion. I can't just accept yours. Let's go ahead and see whether you and I agree or disagree."

"You Better Not Help Me!"

Not infrequently, however, one encounters an adolescent who has successfully erected a defensive façade that depends upon an apparent omnipotent control of the environment. Often, these youngsters are quite successful in manipulating their families. Since they do manage to externalize their illness, they feel quite strongly that they "have it made" and feel absolutely no wish to have their arrangement interfered with. As a rule, such youngsters would not be candidates for outpatient psychotherapy and would have to be either placed in a controlled environment that they could not manipulate or managed quite differently by their parents before they would be amenable to psychotherapy.

If outpatient therapy is undertaken in these cases it is often necessary to utilize special approaches with the adolescent as well as the family. We will consider these youngsters in chapter 4, discussing the reasons for their "malignant" resistances in more detail and exploring techniques that may permit them to utilize therapy.

On Keeping Your Cool

Commonly, the early interviews with an adolescent resemble a verbal fencing match more than a typical psychotherapy interview. It is impossible to anticipate the myriad forms that the adolescent's testing behavior may assume during the diagnostic evaluation. The therapist must rely on his basic commitment to an open-minded, objective evaluation to guide his interaction with the adolescent. Since it is difficult, if not impossible, to work a confidence game on a person who is disinterested in larceny, the therapist can usually avoid being drawn into fruitless arguments with the adolescent.

Since therapists are human, however, they probably will lose some of their rounds with adolescents. The therapist who wishes to work with adolescents must be able to shrug these off and return to the work at hand. A relaxed humorous comment to the effect that the adolescent won that round can sometimes actually improve the relationship between the patient and the therapist. Adolescents often have great difficulty in laughing at themselves and are therefore very critical of adults who are too stiff and self-important. Perhaps the adolescent, with her own narcissistic problems, intuitively recognizes that she cannot work with an adult who is similarly afflicted. At any rate, a sense of humor and a casual attitude are valuable attributes in interviewing adolescents. They are rivaled in importance only by the trait of honesty.

Tell It Like It Is

Adolescent patients frequently test the therapist's willingness to call a spade a spade. The adolescent who is engaging in behavior that is either extremely antisocial or very bizarre may ask the therapist's opinion about the seriousness of the problem. It is important that this question not be dismissed lightly. The therapist can reply that he can see that these are things that would worry anyone and must be a source of great concern to the adolescent. When this concern appears to be lacking, the therapist may well comment on this and wonder why the child is so disinterested in her own welfare. This may include an objective recounting of the personal risk involved in the behavior in question, including its effect on the youngster's opinion of herself.

An intelligent 18-year-old dropped out of college, although his work was at an acceptable level. He readily accepted psychiatric referral, since his parents were extremely distraught and he saw the evaluation as an opportunity to prove to them that his decision was entirely rational.

He was extremely cooperative during the initial interview, but demonstrated a breezy nonchalance about his decision to leave school. He spoke at length about how "up tight" his parents were, laughing at their distress over his withdrawal from school. His own philosophy of life emphasized the pleasures of the moment, and he was good-naturedly critical of the competitive attitude at the college he had been attending. Toward the end of the first interview, the therapist commented that the patient described his situation as though he were recounting a story about a friend. He was told that the incongruity between the importance of his decision to leave school and the absence of any strong feelings in the matter puzzled the therapist.

The young man became grave, but did not reply. On the following day, he called for an appointment, stating that the therapist's words had caused him to do some thinking. He had slept poorly and wanted to discuss some of his thoughts and feelings.

In the next interview, he began to explore his long-standing competitive relationship with his father, although it was much later in therapy before he began to appreciate the origins and extent of his inability to succeed and his true motives for leaving college.

Youngsters who have given up on themselves more completely, such as the seriously delinquent adolescent who has wholeheartedly adopted a negative identity, cannot so readily utilize the invitation to treat themselves more kindly. Still, the invitation must be clearly conveyed and continually repeated. Even the delinquent who actually does harm others pays a great personal price in the bargain. He must be asked why he always seems to express his aggression by drowning others in his own blood.

ONCE THE INTERVIEW GETS GOING

If these gross resistances to the diagnostic process can be managed, the interview with the adolescent can be conducted more or less in the same way as the diagnostic interview with an adult. Although it would be beyond the scope of this book to deal exhaustively with the techniques of interviewing, some points of special interest in the initial interview of the adolescent should be mentioned.

The Adolescent and Silence

Silence is an important technique in psychotherapy, but most clinicians feel that it should be avoided in initial interviews. There is always the danger that the patient, who as yet has no relationship with the therapist, will interpret silence as disinterest and unresponsiveness. It is even less advisable to permit the adolescent to stew alone in mute discomfort. Silence is likely to accentuate the adolescent's anxiety, her fearful fantasies regarding the therapist, and her difficulty in perceiving the sympathetic and helpful attitude of the therapist. Any discussion, no matter how apparently or actually trivial or unrelated to the purpose of the evaluation, is preferable to an anxious silence. If necessary, the therapist should carry the conversation, periodically inviting the youngster's participation, and gradually assuming a more passive role as the child begins to talk more. As we have noted earlier, careful attention should be given to the youngster's feelings regarding the evaluation itself. Silence often results from anxiety or anger directly related to the evaluation.

The Adolescent and Confidentiality

Confidentiality is a point of great concern to many, perhaps most, adolescents. At times, the fear that the therapist will report their conversation to the parents becomes virtually a paranoid preoccupation. Often, this worry is not verbalized openly, but can be detected through its influence on the course of the interview. The adolescent may suddenly appear anxious after revealing something about herself and even retract the statement. The alert therapist will usually be able to guess when the question of confidentiality is troubling her patient. The problem should be openly discussed, not because this will always settle the issue, but to demonstrate an openness and honesty that may gradually convince the adolescent that she can trust the therapist.

It is usually possible to raise the subject of confidentiality as a natural part of the evaluation process. The youngster usually understands what you are driving at if you bring it up as a concrete issue rather than as an abstract concept. For instance, after interviewing the adolescent and before meeting with the parents, the therapist can ask, "Of all the things we have talked about, what is okay to discuss with your parents and what things do you not want them to know about?" The patient's answer may tell a lot about her relationship with his parents and it also protects the therapist from making some blunder with the parents early in the game. Of course, once the adolescent has given her view of confidentiality, the therapist should explain his own understanding of how it works.

Regarding confidentiality, the therapist is confronted with

the need for negotiation and discussion with the adolescent. The promise of complete confidentiality may pose serious problems. If the adolescent later confides plans for serious antisocial behavior, preparations for a suicide attempt, or other dangerous actions that require intervention, the therapist will have to break his promise in order to enlist the aid of parents or others. The admission by the adolescent patient that she is using illegal drugs without her parents' knowledge poses a delicate dilemma in this area, which today's adolescent therapist faces with painful regularity. Therapists generally do not promise to withhold knowledge of criminal activity from a minor's parents. In the case of the drugs, the activities are not only felonious, but are potentially quite dangerous to the adolescent. Still, many therapists who would be quite concerned and anxious in the knowledge that a female adolescent patient was engaging in active sexual behavior accept drug usage without blinking an eye! The problem of psychoactive drug usage is complex and is considered in detail later, but it is clear that it is another subject in which the adolescent should not be assured of blanket confidentiality.

What then can the therapist promise? First of all, and probably most reassuring to the adolescent, the promise can be given that the therapist will not convey any information to the parents without informing the adolescent of his intention to do so in advance. The adolescent's greatest fear is of a secret coalition between her parents and her therapist.

Second, the therapist should state clearly that the adolescent's feelings are confidential. Only the adolescent's actions will ever be considered for possible discussion with her parents, and then only if in the therapist's judgment the particular actions represent a danger to the therapeutic process, other people, or the adolescent herself.

ENTER THE PARENTS

Although some therapists suggest that the adolescent should be asked whether she is willing to permit the therapist to talk with her parents, this probably only confuses the youngster and creates an atmosphere of unreality. Parental involvement in their affairs is a fact of life for most adolescents, unless they have already left home. To play along with the adolescent's fantasy that she can solve her conflicts with her parents by wishing the adults out of existence can only block any rational therapy. The adolescent's parents have a right to know, in general terms, what their youngster's problem is, how serious it seems to be, the reasons behind the therapeutic recommendations, and what they can do to assist their youngster. These assertions remain true even when the adolescent's complaints against her parents are well grounded in objective evidence of parental inadequacy. To ask the adolescent's permission to talk with her parents implies that troubling family interactions can be safely ignored.

It does seem appropriate to offer the adolescent the option of attending the postdiagnostic conference with the parents. Youngsters of this age do have a right to be fully informed of plans that involve them. Conducting the treatment-planning session as a family interview may also be helpful in promoting an atmosphere of objective exploration toward family problems that have previously been the occasion for disruptive anger and mutual recrimination. This is also a good time to spell out the ground rules of psychotherapy (if this is the recommendation), including the rules regarding confidentiality mentioned above. This subject is explored more fully in chapter 8, "The Parents of the Adolescent Patient." Many adolescents, even when offered the opportunity of attending the postdiagnostic conference with their parents, will prefer to have an individual interview at the end of the diagnostic period to discuss the findings and recommendations.

OTHER DIAGNOSTIC PROCEDURES

At times, one needs information about the adolescent that requires referring her for psychological testing, physical examination, or other procedures. These recommendations tend to be resisted by adolescent patients. If the interview situation, which at least resembles typical social interaction, is frightening, the prospect of being tested with instruments that the patient does not understand poses an even greater threat. Adolescents are aware that psychological tests are designed to extract information that the patient may not have intended to reveal. Because of her many secrets, the adolescent certainly does not want her mind read.

It is important to explain honestly to the adolescent why the additional studies are necessary and what information they may reveal. When the adolescent is not given this information and allowed to discuss it fully, she often reacts to the diagnostic studies as though they were devious attempts to "get the goods on her." An electroencephalogram (EEG) may be interpreted as an underhanded effort to find out if she has damaged her brain by masturbating or by taking drugs or, in more disturbed youngsters, as a way of finding out her dirty thoughts.

In the postdiagnostic conference, it is important to report fully the findings of the special procedures and to correlate them with the youngster's life experiences. If, for example, an EEG has been ordered to rule out complex partial seizures in a youngster with episodic rage reactions, the negative findings should be correlated with the absence of postictal phenomena, amnesia, and other clinical data that have already been discussed with the patient. It should be noted briefly that projective tests may give a very misleading picture of the adolescent unless they are administered and interpreted by a psychologist with extensive experience with adolescents. Youngsters in this age group frequently appear much more ill than they actually are if their test productions are judged by adult norms.

Tests that screen for drugs have been much improved in recent years. Most necessary tests can be done with urine samples. When drug use is suspected the tests should be used even if the youngster denies usage. Many of the tests are quantitative and aid in understanding how extensive drug use has been. Adolescent refusal to submit to urine testing frequently has the same meaning as a positive test.

Although it hardly needs to be stated, no evaluation of an adolescent is complete without a current thorough physical examination. Most therapists arrange this through the family physician. Child and adolescent psychiatrists usually defer to the family physician or pediatrician because they are concerned that adolescents may find it confusing to have both psychological and physical testing and evaluation by the same person. Practitioners of adolescent medicine and behavioral pediatrics may feel comfortable handling both the physical and mental aspects of their patients.

DIAGNOSTIC INTERVIEWS WITH PARENTS

Several goals must be kept in mind simultaneously during the diagnostic sessions with the parents of an adolescent patient. The parents' feelings about their child's problems may range from a deep concern, verging on panic, through rage and wishes to reject the child, to subtle enjoyment of the youngster's behavior. Most often, the parents are puzzled and frightened, especially if the adolescent appeared to be adjusting adequately during earlier childhood. Their intense feelings result in a loss of perspective, which causes difficulty in gaining information about past family relationships and events in the youngster's earlier life. The parents must be offered the opportunity to ventilate these feelings, not only to clear the way for consideration of historical data, but because of the importance of such feelings to an understanding of the adolescent's current life situation.

Usually, it is possible to learn a great deal about the parents' conscious and unconscious attitudes toward the adolescent by carefully noting which aspects of the current situation they choose to emphasize in their discussion with the therapist. However, some caution should be exercised in drawing conclusions from observations made during the emotional turmoil that often characterizes initial diagnostic contacts. Defensive reactions both to the family crisis and the prospect of revealing their family problems to an outsider may produce confusing distortions.

The mother of a 14-year-old delinquent girl was referred for therapy by her daughter's therapist. The referring psychiatrist, who had performed the diagnostic evaluation on the family, apologized for the referral, stating, "I don't think there is much you can do. This mother would really just like to pretend that this girl is not her daughter. She's the coldest fish I ever saw."

Actually, the mother wept throughout most of her first therapy hour. She expressed her conviction that her daughter's problems were completely her fault and recognized that she was still struggling with antisocial impulses, especially in the sexual area, herself. When asked why she had not told the referring physician of these concerns, she could only say that she was in a state of shock after the daughter's delinquencies came to light.

"I guess I thought someone was going to come and arrest me," she said.

DEVELOPMENTAL HISTORY

The importance of detailed information about psychological development in children has been challenged in recent years. A number of studies have demonstrated that the accuracy of parental recall is rather poor. It is still worthwhile to spend some time in asking about the adolescent's earlier development even if one cannot accept the parents' statements as literal truth. One can often detect evidence of gross difficulties in psychosocial progression, such as serious maternal depression during infancy, separations from one or both parents, family deaths, and periods of poor adjustment such as difficulty in toilet training. It is also possible to draw some tentative conclusions about the extent of parental investment in the child and the quality of the parent-child relationship in the past. Parental statements in this area must be explored and taken as tentative, since the current family conflict may influence memory selectively and impart a retrospective overemphasis or denial of negative aspects in the parent-child relationships. Often, persistent attention to the his-

tory is rewarded with valuable data, such as the parental recollec-
tion that their belligerently independent adolescent has shown
considerable evidence of excessive dependency on one or both
parents in the past.

Even if the information gathered in a developmental history
only approximates the actual occurrences, the process of inquiring about longitudinal development helps the parents to refocus their efforts toward understanding their youngster's problems. The very act of exploring the past suggests to the parents
that their youngster's problems are comprehensible and possibly soluble. The investigation of the family history may also
bring to light any feelings of guilt that the parents harbor about
their role in the adolescent's difficulties. When these are openly
discussed, the therapist can compliment the parents for their
frankness, suggest that emotional problems are rarely so simply
understood, and state his intention to discuss frankly with them
all factors that may have had importance in creating the family
difficulties.

It is also important to do a careful search of the family history
for evidence of mental illness or substance abuse that might
have hereditary elements. This is valuable not only when it
turns up actual evidence of familial diseases but when it merely
gives the family the opportunity to ventilate concerns in that
area.

"Well, she's just like your wacky Aunt Ruth!"

"Don't be ridiculous, woman. Aunt Ruth's not blood kin
to us. She just married Uncle Sam."

"Oh, yeah. I forgot."

And so forth.

In the case of adopted youngsters this data is very important
although sometimes difficult to obtain since the adoptive parents may have limited information about the youngster's biological relatives. Certainly the adoptive parents' fantasies and projections in this area may prove very important.

Some therapists prefer to have the parents interviewed by a
colleague. This has some disadvantages in that the parents are
better able to support the therapy fully if they have had a

meaningful personal experience with the therapist. For this reason, it seems wise for the adolescent's therapist to spend some time with the parents, even if he is unwilling or unable to conduct the parental diagnostic interviews. The trust that can result will be invaluable during difficult periods in the adolescent's therapy. Even if there are few difficult periods, adolescents who undergo successful psychotherapy will move toward independence from the parents. Many parents find this transition emotionally painful, even if they intellectually recognize that it is necessary. A positive relationship with the therapist may permit the parents to tolerate essential growth without consciously or unconsciously sabotaging the therapy.

DIAGNOSIS IN ADOLESCENCE

There is a danger in assigning a clinical diagnosis to the adolescent. Erikson (1968) pointed out that the adolescent is very susceptible to the expectations of her society. The adolescent's present and future role is partially defined by the reaction of her culture to her. It is clear that some clinical psychiatric diagnoses, such as schizophrenia and antisocial personality, carry powerful implications for future functioning, and are in effect statements that the adolescent's problems are chronic and his prognosis relatively poor. The effect is to decree an identity as a sick individual for the adolescent. Since the troubled adolescent is especially unsure of what and who she is, she may be very sensitive to such definitions. For this reason, it is important to exercise caution in assigning clinical diagnoses during the fluidity of the adolescent period. Even if the patient and her family are not directly apprised of the diagnosis, it will certainly affect the therapist's attitude toward his patient and will be perceived indirectly by the youngster. Given the impressive gains in therapy for even the most serious psychiatric illnesses, optimism is warranted for all youth who receive treatment.

In general, it would seem preferable for the clinician to make every effort to arrive at the best possible clinical diagnostic category for every adolescent whom he evaluates. This clinical diagnosis may then be viewed as highly tentative, since it is recognized to represent a cross-sectional statement regarding personality structure during a period of life in which longitudinal changes may be quite rapid and very extensive. Despite the need to establish a tentative clinical diagnosis, prognostication and treatment planning depend more on an overall assessment of the strengths and weaknesses of the adolescent's personality functioning than on any diagnostic term. The diagnostic data should be reviewed with an eye to the seven questions posed earlier.

THE POSTDIAGNOSTIC FAMILY CONFERENCE

When the diagnostic information appears reasonably complete, it is necessary to arrange for one or more conferences with the parents and the adolescent to discuss the findings and recommendations. Many therapists like to invite the adolescent to sit in with the parents during this conference, whereas others prefer to have separate meetings with the parents and with the adolescent.

This conference is difficult to manage due to the intensity of feelings present both in the family members and in the examiner. However, the necessity for such a conference and its crucial role in setting the stage for the entire therapeutic undertaking cannot be ignored. A tremendous hurdle to successful treatment will have been passed if the family can leave this conference with some sense of direction and with the feeling that the therapist respects their individual feelings.

No matter how skillful the therapist becomes in conducting the postdiagnostic conference, he will not be able to use the skill without a clear formulation of the case in his own mind. The family dynamics, clinical diagnosis of the child, and the genetic and dynamic understanding of the adolescent must be carefully thought out prior to the postdiagnostic interview. Without this preparatory work, the therapist cannot hope for the kind of conciseness and clarity that will be necessary for effective communication with the family.

Full consideration of the diagnostic data will often suggest that individual psychotherapy for the adolescent is not the immediate treatment of choice. It is difficult to specify these situations with exactitude, but some general suggestions can be offered. These may be organized around the specific recommendations that might be made.

Hospitalization

The decision to hospitalize the adolescent is not to be taken lightly. The fact that the adolescent frequently views psychiatric hospitalization as a verification of her worst fears about herself is only one of several reasons that inpatient treatment is fraught with danger. The inevitable presence of restrictive structuring in even the most liberal group situation, the loss of contact with normal peer experiences and opportunities, and the invitation to regression and an accentuation of dependency conflicts all militate against a positive result in hospital treatment of the adolescent.

Still, some adolescents require hospitalization to ensure their safety. For these youngsters, hospitalization is aimed at dealing with the emergency situation, utilizing psychotropic medication, and support to avert disaster. Usually, the evaluating therapist will wish to be involved in the youngster's hospital care, hoping to establish a therapeutic relationship during the hospital stay. Outpatient therapy can then be utilized to deal with the chronic personality problems that predispose the youngster to emotional breakdown.

A 16-year-old boy, home from prep school during the Christmas holidays, developed marked suicidal ideation as the time for returning to school approached. A suicide attempt led to an emergency diagnostic study. Evaluation revealed marked confusion and a strong tendency toward impulsivity. The preoccupation with suicide as a solution to a chronic sense of failure suggested that hospital care was the only reasonable plan.

During the ten-day hospitalization, the boy formed an intense tie to the therapist and revealed a good capacity for self-observation and verbalization of feeling. Arrangements were made for the boy to return to school locally and attend outpatient psychotherapy sessions three times a week. Soon, it was possible to reduce the sessions to twice weekly and to explore the youngster's long-standing neurotic conflicts. The therapy continued for two years with no further need for inpatient care.

In order to succeed, the hospital program needs to accomplish several goals:

1. *Contain acting out and provide strong pressure to make pathological defenses ego-alien.* This is done through strong family intervention and utilization of nursing staff as supportive limit-setters. Medication may be important if symptoms result from psychosis or other organic factors.

2. *Discover important areas of weakness in adaptive functioning and plan intense remediation to strengthen them.* This includes learning problems, deficiencies in social skills, and difficulties in identifying and expressing feelings. Although a brief hospital stay may not allow sufficient time for correction of these deficiencies, hope can be established and the young person can anticipate some success in areas where she has become demoralized. This experience of success can lead to higher motivation for treatment and a decrease in the resistance and defensiveness based on hopelessness and lack of a realistic treatment plan.

3. *Active family therapy is an essential element in these hospital programs.* In many of the cases described above, the family has become dysfunctional and is not only not a help to the adolescent patient but may serve to permit or encourage continued maladaptive behavior. It is necessary to gain the family's support and to strengthen their capacity to assist the adoles-

cent. Successful family intervention usually includes combined education and psychotherapy.

Partial Hospitalization

The partial hospitalization or day hospitalization is a level of care that is less intensive than inpatient treatment. Adolescents who are treated in a partial hospitalization program continue to live and sleep at home, but come to the program during the day. For example, from 8:00 a.m. to 5:00 or 6:00 p.m. During the day they participate in a specialized educational program, but also have group therapy, individual therapy, medication management, and much work with the families. There should be frequent or even daily contact between the treatment staff and the client's parents, to ensure an active collaboration among the adults in the teenager's life.

In some instances, partial hospitalization is a step-down from inpatient treatment. For example, a client was initially admitted to an inpatient program and was treated there for one week to get the situation under control; then the youngster was in the partial hospitalization program for three weeks, until she was ready to return to his regular school. In other instances, partial hospitalization is an alternative to inpatient treatment. That is, the youngster skips the inpatient phase of treatment altogether and is admitted directly to the partial hospital program.

Several criteria should be met for a client to be appropriate for partial hospitalization. The youngster's clinical condition should be serious enough that outpatient appointments will not be helpful—such as instances of intractable school refusal, severe anorexia nervosa, and severe depression. On the other hand, the teenager should not be so disturbed that she is actively dangerous to herself or to others. For partial hospitalization to be safe and effective, it is important for the youngster's parents to be supportive and available to participate in the program. There is also the practical issue of living close enough to the partial hospitalization program to make it possible to travel back and forth every day.

Extended Residential Treatment

Those adolescents who require long-term residential treatment comprise a different group. This recommendation should be reserved for those with marked defects in early ego development usually associated with families that are unable or unwilling to correct these deficiencies in the present. These youngsters therefore require a prolonged corrective living experience. For these youngsters, there is no disadvantage in the structured nature of the residential setting. Structure is essential for them to learn adaptive techniques, adequate impulse control, and skills in interpersonal relations. The potential of the residential setting to induce regression is not a hindrance to their care, but can rather be turned to the advantage of the adolescent.

When this type of therapy is to be recommended, it is often wise to extend the diagnostic period, especially that portion spent with the parents. This precaution allows the development of the closest possible relationship with the parents, which may be utilized to aid them in dealing with their resistance to separation from the patient. In many adolescents who require residential care this will be a very difficult job, since the parents have often crippled the adolescent in order to bolster their own defensive structure. The parents will often resist placement in order to protect their personal equilibrium. In their resistance to the separation, grossly irrational fantasies tend to be projected onto the therapist who recommends the placement, the institution, and the staff of the residential center. Often, these can be dealt with if the therapist has had sufficient contact with the parents to establish open communication and a sense of trust. At times, a period of unsuccessful outpatient treatment is necessary, both to demonstrate that residential care is essential and to gain enough therapeutic ground to permit the parents to accept the recommendation. In the youngsters who truly need this intensive approach, problems are chronic and proper preparation is more important than speed of disposition.

Perhaps the most crucial element in successful referral for residential care is the diagnostician's conviction that long-term care is essential. This clarity of conviction must not be allowed to falter in response to patient or parental pleas, promises, or threats. Parents can be reassured to some extent in regard to their fears about social stigma, their child's anger at them for taking the step, the dangers of the youngster mingling "with all those crazy people," and the like, but there are problems in that. There is a social stigma associated with residential care. The child will likely be angry . . . and so on. The point is that the crucial need for treatment outweighs these concerns and that conviction must be clearly conveyed. In a very real sense, when one is recommended for residential care, there should be no viable alternative. If there were, the evaluator would be suggesting it!

Family Therapy and Group Psychotherapy

The indications for recommending group psychotherapy or family therapy as primary treatment approaches are covered in the chapters dealing with these modalities (chapter 6, "Group Psychotherapy of the Adolescent," and chapter 7, "Family Therapy").

Cognitive-Behavioral Treatment

Some mental conditions respond better to cognitive-behavioral treatment (CBT) than to traditional talk therapy, including psychodynamic insight-oriented therapy. A good example is obsessive-compulsive disorder. Some of these youngsters may talk about their feelings and fantasies and unconscious issues for years, but still have obsessions and compulsions. What they need is an approach that helps them understand, master, and defeat the anxiety that drives the obsessions and compulsions. March et al. (1998) developed a treatment manual for this purpose. In many cases, the CBT of obsessive-compulsive disorder is combined with appropriate medication with good results. CBT may also be useful in other conditions, such as depressive disorders that are not very severe (Reinecke et al., 1998) and posttraumatic stress disorder. One hopes that cognitive-behavioral therapists will know how to relate to and communicate with their adolescent clients, in addition to following the manualized treatment.

Evaluation as Brief Therapy

In many mild adolescent disturbances, the therapist may attempt to help the parents and the adolescent to define their problems more productively during the diagnostic contact and during the postdiagnostic family conference. The therapist may identify certain clear issues that allow immediate intervention and are also amenable to continuing family "homework." In other cases psychopharmacology with minimal follow-up may be the treatment of choice. Brief therapy is especially effective when it is undertaken with a cooperative family.

CHAPTER 3

the therapeutic alliance with the adolescent

Almost every form of serious psychotherapy requires that there be a therapeutic alliance or a working alliance between the therapist and the client. This is true of psychoanalysis and psychoanalytic psychotherapy (where the concept of the therapeutic alliance originated), as well as interpersonal psychotherapy, cognitive therapy, behavior therapy, hypnosis, client-centered therapy, transactional analysis, paradoxical therapy, family therapy, and group therapy. Furthermore, a therapeutic alliance is present in most uses of psychopharmacology. The therapeutic alliance refers to the collaboration between the therapist and the client, in which the therapist and the conscious, observing ego of the client work together on his or her problems. There is a pact between the therapist and the observing portion of the client's ego aimed at an honest and uncritical examination of the client's inner experience. The psychotherapist allies himself with the healthier, more reality-oriented aspect of the patient's ego for the purpose of observing the maladaptive, neurotically defended, and conflicted portions of the personality.

There are some forms of treatment—which most practitioners would not consider psychotherapy—for which a therapeutic alliance is not necessary. For instance: a therapist might devise a behavior modification program for a teenager who has no interest in having his behavior modified; a practitioner might arrange involuntary hospitalization for a youngster who currently has no observing ego to work with; a psychiatrist might administer psychotropic medication to a patient who is out of touch with reality. The talking therapies, however, require that there is a part of the client that wants to change. Of course,

68

many teenagers may desperately want to change some aspect of themselves, but are not the least bit interested in revealing that desire to parents, friends, therapists, or anybody else.

Early psychoanalysts identified the need to develop and utilize a conscious, cooperative portion of the patient's personality as an observing ally during the storms of transference feelings that appear during analysis. In Freud's 1912 paper, "The Dynamics of Transference," he pointed out that, paradoxically, transference is both the force that binds the patient to therapy and encourages cooperation, as well as the major resistance to analysis. In his book on analytic technique, Greenson (1967) emphasized the importance of this relationship with the therapist, which he preferred to call the "working alliance." Friedman (1969) reviewed the concept of the therapeutic alliance.

In working with adolescent clients, the first and most important step is the creation and strengthening of the therapeutic alliance. One of the major obstacles in developing a therapeutic alliance with an adolescent is the youngster's fear of dependency, which is most marked in the early adolescent. In fact, a major reason that the therapeutic alliance with the adolescent is fragile is that the therapist is trying to help the youngster see that he needs help despite the teenager's natural reluctance to collaborate with adults.

There are several specific techniques that the therapist may use during the early stage of therapy to encourage the formation of a therapeutic alliance (Meeks, 1997).

1. *The key element in developing an alliance is the therapist's ability to respond empathically to the adolescent's resistance to the very process of therapy and to respond to manifestations of negative transference as they appear in the therapy meetings.* The adolescent may not come right out and tell the therapist what he thinks about these lousy appointments, but may present his concerns in a disguised or displaced manner. For example, a 13-year-old boy gave his new therapist advice on how a person should approach an unfamiliar dog. The boy said that the person should not try to pet the dog on the head initially, since the dog may perceive that as a threatening gesture; but the person should put out his hand so

the dog can sniff it. The therapist agreed that the boy had a good plan for how to get acquainted with unfamiliar animals.

2. *It is important to accept without question the positive feelings that the youngster may have toward the therapeutic process.* This positive transference—although unrealistic—may help the adolescent get through the initial meetings and until he develops a more solid alliance with the therapist.

3. *The therapist should recognize and respond empathically to the adolescent's pain.* It is usually best to do this in an understated manner ("Gee, that was a rough time for you."), since teenagers are turned off by therapists who are "mushy" or infantilizing.

4. *The therapist can teach the youngster how to start the work of therapy.* There will be opportunities for the therapist to praise behaviors that indicate that the adolescent client is catching on to how the therapeutic alliance works. For instance, the youngster will open up a little about his concerns regarding family issues, friends, or some other significant topic. This is a chance for the therapist to comment in a positive manner ("It helps me understand your situation at home, when you told me what happened between you and your Dad.") and reinforce the youngster's tentative use of therapy.

WILL THE REAL OBSERVING EGO PLEASE STAND UP?

In adolescents, the capacity for self-scrutiny is something of a paradox. At times, the adolescent seems completely immersed in self-observation. Ruminative preoccupation with inner feelings, interminable musings over real or imagined inadequacies, and detached experimentation with new feelings states and altered states of consciousness all appear to signal the emergence of a capacity to stand aside and observe one's own psychological structure and functioning. This capacity is demonstrably unstable, however, and the adolescent also expends great effort in denying his impulses, affects, and needs. Often, this tendency to disavow his inner life is reinforced by an explosive tendency to act, rather than to think or feel.

A primary reason for this unstable state of affairs is the adolescent's conflict with his conscience. The emerging capacity for self-observation can flower only as the harsh and unrelenting superego of early adolescence is gradually modified toward a more flexible and humane code of conduct. When the capacity for noncritical self-observation appears, many adolescent patients seem virtually to "cure themselves" with relative rapidity.

It should be emphasized that the primary function of the therapeutic alliance with the adolescent is to assist the youngster in understanding the link between his feelings and his behavior in the present. The adolescent's anxiety about the future and his fear of regression contraindicate extensive focusing on the genetic determinants of his behavior. Early developmental defects and severe fixations cannot be worked through during early adolescence because the necessary degree of regression would threaten the progressive thrust of the developmental period. Brief regressive episodes appear spontaneously and account for the fluctuating transference of adolescent patients. However, only the older adolescent can tolerate the careful study of these ego states. The therapist must usually focus his efforts on helping the adolescent to recover from regressions. As a rule, adolescents respond to a correct and appropriate interpretation by a progressive developmental leap forward rather than by further regression and exploration of genetics. If the therapist tries to interfere with this tendency by encouraging the development of a regressive transference, many adolescents will bolt from therapy. The conscious, rational alliance must be emphasized, not the irrational, infantile bonds to the therapist.

STRENGTHENING THE EGO IDEAL

Blos (1962) described the adolescent's use of a special friendship to accelerate the development of the ego ideal. The special attachment is made to a friend of the same sex, usually somewhat older. An important aspect of this attachment is that the older person displays some essential traits that are lacking or that the young adolescent feels are lacking in himself. These traits are then idealized to provide the missing perfection of the self so that narcissistic balance is partially restored. This relationship is later internalized as a stabilizing but also liberalizing introject. The friend's values are gradually abstracted and detached from their origin and come to exist completely in their own right in the adolescent's mind. In the process of developing a therapeutic alliance with the adolescent patient, the therapist may find that he has become the youngster's "special friend" in the sense described above. Even when this does not happen, the therapist's permission to discover and relate to an older friend of this kind may be one of the most important gains in therapy

FOSTERING THE THERAPEUTIC ALLIANCE

Since the alliance is of central importance yet is often difficult to achieve even with the neurotic adolescent, the techniques and problems associated with this phase of therapy are discussed in some detail. This becomes even more crucial in brief psychotherapy.

The basic technique of establishing the therapeutic alliance is the timely interpretation of affect and defense. This process can be restated as helping the adolescent to recognize that his behavior is motivated by inner feeling states. Early in the therapeutic situation, these feeling states are commonly impatience, frustration, feelings of helplessness, and a sense of narcissistic impairment over the need to consult a psychotherapist. Some of the typical early defenses against these painful affects include rebelliousness; passive compliance; timidity; disdainful, condescending attitudes toward the therapist; and cool, aloof intellectualizing. Recognizing these defenses and the feeling states that they disguise is the first order of business in psychotherapy. This may be overlooked when the adolescent's primary defense is passive compliance. These adolescents appear to be "good" patients, eager to get right to work on their problems. The therapist should not be deceived into confusing this frightened obsequiousness with a true therapeutic alliance.

More often, the adolescent therapist must proceed to the clarification of the connection between feeling and action by means of a difficult way station, namely, through interrupting the adolescent's propensity to act in order to avoid feeling. When the therapist challenges this pattern, he is quickly cast in the role of a critical parent, a superego figure. It is a difficult but crucial undertaking to convince the adolescent that "Why did you do that?" is a neutral question, rather than a statement of moral disapproval.

SAYING NO THE EGO WAY

Adolescent acting up and acting out must be limited by the therapist. The only rational basis for the authority to direct behavior proceeds from the therapist's knowledge of the conditions required for effective therapy. In short, the adolescent is told that his behavior is none of the therapist's business except that some actions interfere with the therapeutic process and these must be controlled or therapy will not proceed properly. Often, it is also possible to demonstrate that acting out disrupts the youngster's psychological harmony or threatens to harm him. The therapist tries to convey his wish that the adolescent win the developmental war while keeping it clear that it is the youngster's battle and that the therapist cannot fight it for him. This position is more convincing to the adolescent when it becomes apparent that the therapist has the same benevolent, inquiring attitude toward all symptomatic behavior, whether it is "wrong" or not.

Sarah, a 15-year-old in psychotherapy because of promiscuity and poor academic performance, was openly skeptical of the therapist's assertion that his disapproval of this promiscuous behavior was not based on moral indignation. She jeered at the assertion that there were reasons behind her behavior that she did not understand and which could not be explained by her statement that she was "hypersexed." She continued to believe that the therapist was "another square" with "hang-ups about sex" who was trying in typical bluenose fashion to interfere with her fun. After some positive transference had developed, the girl began to study secretly. Eventually, she brought an excellent report card to a psychotherapy session as a seductive gift to the therapist and as proof of her value. She was at first offended, and then amazed that the therapist did not praise her "good" behavior. Instead, the therapist noted that she did not seem to be enjoying the grades and that this suggested she had worked hard because she felt for some reason that it was expected of her. She talked for a few moments about her motives for improving her academic performance, then said, "You know, I've been telling you what a sex expert I am. Actually, the only reason I was willing to come see you in the first place is that I have never enjoyed sex. Not once. I love the idea of sex, but in practice it's lousy for me. Yet I practice and practice and practice. I know that sounds crazy."

The therapist agreed that this must be a puzzling state of affairs and suggested that he and the patient try to understand it together.

The adolescent is exquisitely sensitive to any manipulative control that threatens his tenuous sense of autonomy. Unless the therapist maintains his neutral, sympathetic but inquiring attitude toward all the adolescent's behavior, he cannot convince the adolescent that his goal is to foster understanding, not to dominate the patient through psychological warfare.

"DON'T KNOCK YOURSELF"

The therapist should be quick to point out tendencies toward judgmental and self-critical attitudes in the adolescent. The adolescent should be encouraged to look for the sources of his behavior, attitudes, and affective states, rather than call himself names. The goal of therapy is to increase self-understanding and inner psychological strength and flexibility, not to suppress annoying behavior. Often, the demonstration of therapeutic neutrality and of the motivational origins of behavior can be made effectively through the office interaction with the patient.

A 16-year-old boy started his first three therapy sessions

by slouching in his chair and lighting a cigarette. The therapist's inquiry about the meaning of the behavior made him angry. "You mean I can't even smoke in this crummy office?"

"I didn't say there was a rule against it. I just have noticed that you never talk about smoking, yet you light up the moment you hit that chair."

"So what?"

"So we're here to understand why you do the things you do."

"Because I want to, okay?"

"Well, if you want to go through a session standing on your head and playing a harmonica, I guess that's okay, but I'd probably ask you why you wanted to."

The boy grinned, and then asked carefully, "Are you going to tell my parents I smoke here?"

"We can talk about that in a minute, but I wonder why you're doing something here that you know your parents disapprove of."

The boy hung his head. "Yeah. I know I shouldn't smoke. It would kill my parents if they knew. I don't know why I'm always bad."

"I don't think it's going to help to criticize yourself. Let's try to understand what's really going on here."

"Well, I kinda wanted to see what you'd say about the smoking."

The smoking represented an attempt to corrupt the therapist by implicating him as an accessory in a forbidden behavior. Without a persistent effort to expose the reasons behind the smoking, the therapist would have been either maneuvered into a compromised position or forced into an arbitrary prohibition. In either case, no therapeutic alliance could develop. Later, when the therapist was calmly able to confront the boy with his tendency to manipulate people, the boy said, "Yeah, I like to have my way with them, I guess."

The therapist did not pick up on the sexual implications in the wording, but commented, "I'm sure there are reasons why you can't trust people enough to be honest with them. That's one of the things we might try to understand."

Eventually, the boy was able to talk easily about what he called his "crook tendencies," both in terms of their disadvantage to him and the situations in which they appeared. The capacity to observe himself in action and in feelings was finally achieved.

TOWARD TRUE FREEDOM

The youngster discussed above was finally able to realize that "just wanting" to perform certain actions was actually the end result of many forces within himself. This recognition is extremely important in the treatment of the adolescent. The startling realization that his freedom of choice is being sabotaged by unknown inner forces greatly strengthens the adolescent's motivation for therapy. The young person's wish for freedom and autonomy will then be a support to the therapeutic effort to change rebellion into true freedom and self-direction rather than merely to substitute slavish submission to instinctual drives for earlier submission to the parents.

Several psychological forces within the adolescent interfere with his acceptance of this liberating insight. The typical narcissistic, omnipotent defensive conformation of adolescence, reinforced by the preoccupation with formal operations and the omnipotence of thought, is severely threatened by the idea of unconscious motivation. The adolescent feels a desperate need to see himself as absolute master of his fate. The idea that he is not infinitely malleable but must adapt himself to his own instinctual drives, his own conscience, and external social demands is offensive and frightening. The flip side of total control is total helplessness. When the bubble of his omnipotence is punctured, the adolescent tends to feel completely vulnerable and pitifully weak. The therapist must be extremely supportive and sometimes quite forceful to convince the adolescent that ignoring a fire in the basement or merely trying to "think it away" is an excellent way to get burned. The therapeutic support consists of helping the adolescent to see that his real abilities to devise methods of putting out the fire or confining it to safe areas are much greater than he thought. In short, the therapist supports the adolescent's ego skills to discourage his reliance on magic omnipotence.

'TIS AN ILL WIND—

It is important not to drift into a pattern of only observing and studying pathological and maladaptive behaviors within the therapeutic alliance. A fair and objective evaluation of the adolescent will always reveal areas of strength and competence, often unrecognized by the patient. These must be included in any total observation of psychological functioning. This is also true of the adaptive value of ego defenses. For example, a distrust of appearances may result in interpersonal touchiness in the adolescent, but it also characterizes the personality of many successful social and scientific innovators. If the adolescent is to learn to trust the objectivity and honesty of the therapist, he must have the opportunity to see the therapist patiently look at all sides of every question. This strengthens the client's faith in the therapist's position of friendly neutrality. It is a demonstration of the therapist's wish to avoid intruding and his determination to provide the adolescent with as much information as possible so that the youngster is better prepared to reach his own decisions.

ADOLESCENT ATTITUDES TOWARD A THERAPEUTIC ALLIANCE

The wishes and fears with which adolescents face the beginning of therapy have very little congruence with the goals of the therapist. Consciously, the adolescent is fearful of becoming embroiled in another dependency relationship, whereas unconsciously he hopes and fears to find in the therapist the gratification of various irrational and childish wishes. Because of these emotional currents, the adolescent typically utilizes various techniques to avoid the establishment of a therapeutic alliance. He may project negative attributes onto the therapist or externalize his difficulties and invite the therapist to criticize or reject him. Other adolescents attempt to convert the therapeutic situation into a friendly parent-child relationship in which they will be advised and assisted. Others are overwhelmed by massive super-ego pressure and can only condemn themselves and beg for mercy.

UNHOLY ALLIANCES

The distortions of the therapeutic relationship just described can usually be managed by the patient application of the princi-ples previously enumerated. However, Keith (1968) described in a timeless paper another group of resistances that he appro-priately designated as "unholy alliances." These must be recog-nized and avoided in order to achieve a usable therapeutic alli-ance. Keith classified these structurally as unholy alliances (1) with the id, (2) with pathological ego defenses, and (3) with the superego.

Id Alliances and the Swinging Therapist

All of the unholy alliances are dangers with the adolescent patient. Id alliances are especially seductive, since the therapist is often eager to appear more understanding, tolerant, and "hip" than the other adults whom the adolescent criticizes. The therapist who finds himself discussing specifics of sexual behav-ior, techniques of outwitting parents, or the absurdity of official authority early in therapy may well suspect that he has been drawn into an unholy alliance with the id or with id derivatives. The result of such an alliance is the weakening of the adoles-cent's controls and an upsurge in impulsive acting-out behavior. The lack of a true alliance may be demonstrated through overt hostility that the adolescent soon directs toward the therapist, probably with the unconscious goal of inviting external control. It is of crucial importance to avoid this alliance with the adoles-cent because of his tenuous controls and his resultant fear of his strong feelings and impulses. Because of these fears of loss of control, many adolescents will react to an id alliance with intense anxiety that leads to defensiveness, silence, and attempts to avoid the entire therapy process. The therapist is viewed as an actual threat, a tempter who is encouraging them to lose control of themselves and give rein to the worst aspects of their nature.

This pitfall can be avoided by remembering that it is unwise to interpret or discuss aggressive or sexual material until the distinction between thought and action is clearly established and the adolescent understands that the therapist's encouragement of free expression includes only thoughts and feelings. Only a comfortable recognition that the therapist is opposed to impulsive and unwise action can create a proper atmosphere for the open expression of strong feelings and lead to a true therapeutic alliance. To fantasize that one is omnipotent is a dangerous luxury. It is a game of pretense that the therapist must not play even temporarily. Stated differently, the adolescent can never be seduced into a therapeutic alliance, and the therapist who attempts to deal with his uncomfortable patient in this way is likely to end up with an unworkable and unholy alliance with the id.

A 15-year-old girl was referred for psychotherapy after her parents learned that she and her boyfriend were having sexual intercourse regularly. In early sessions, she admitted that she was promiscuous and eagerly volunteered specific information on her sexual fantasies and adventures in seduction. The therapist ignored her racy stories and merely commented repeatedly on the absence of affect in her friendships as well as her cool and distant way of relating to him. Her titillation gradually ceased and she began to describe her feelings of contempt for all her sexual partners and eventually her wish to outsmart the therapist and show him up as "another dumb, horny male."

Over a period of time, it was possible to create a friendly and honest therapeutic alliance that allowed a moderately successful exploration of the girl's serious character problems that had prevented her from forming close emotional ties. Therapeutic results were first apparent when she began to develop satisfying friendships with girls for the first time since early childhood.

Alliances with Pathological Ego Defenses

The primary pathological ego defense that may be utilized in an unholy alliance by the adolescent is intellectualization. The intelligent, psychologically minded adolescent, often well read in popular psychology (or even Freud, Erikson, Fromm, etc.) can discuss fascinating insights for hours on end while remaining totally untouched by therapy. The defense may even be actively used to act out competitive and demeaning attitudes toward the therapist under the guise of enthusiastic cooperation. If the therapist, relieved that he does not have to struggle with one of those belligerent, uncooperative adolescents, joins in an alliance with this defense, a therapeutic alliance will not appear. Instead, therapy will deteriorate into sterile, philosophical discussions gradually producing feelings of boredom and despair in both therapist and patient.

There is a place in the therapy of the adolescent for ideological discussion and even for the defense of intellectualization. However, it is important first to establish a therapeutic alliance strong enough to allow the experiencing and reporting of affect. This can only be accomplished by refraining from extensive discussion of conceptual content early in therapy when affective contact has not been established with the adolescent. The intellectualizing patient should be asked to define all jargon such as "hostility," "ambivalent," "erotic," "incestuous," "really meaningful," "I-Thou relationship," and the like. He is asked what he means by those words and asked to tie them to concrete experiences and his feelings during his involvement in those real-life interactions. The therapist, of course, avoids any technical terms, using instead emotionally laden, everyday words such as "mad," "angry," "burned up," "sexual," and even slang sexual phrases if these do not seem unduly seductive with the specific patient.

Generalities are discouraged and specifics are sought. The goal, of course, is to bring real emotion into the session. When affect does appear, either in the description of events outside the psychotherapy session or in direct relationship to the therapist, this is encouraged by a demonstration of interest and acceptance.

An 18-year-old college freshman was seen for psychiatric evaluation when he became psychotic following the ingestion of LSD. Even after the brief overt psychosis cleared, he remained rather grandiose, preoccupied with cosmic issues of good and evil. Psychotherapy with limited goals appeared feasible despite the fragility of the personality structure.

Initially, the general philosophic structure and preoccupation were accepted, although not encouraged. The therapist occasionally interjected the observation that personal feelings were important and seemed absent from the patient's thinking. The patient's objection that he intended to rise above his feelings was received with friendly skepticism. The extremely intelligent young man was reminded of historical examples in which philosophical systems were distorted by the personality quirks of their innovators. At the same time, the patient's infrequent references to "human weaknesses" in himself were applauded as evidence of his desire to know himself and thereby avoid the blind errors of other ideologists. Gradually, a capacity for self-observation was developed, although the therapist had to continually disavow the patient's attempt to cast him in role of maharisha.

The conviction that people did not rise above their feelings was constantly reiterated and was demonstrated to the patient in his own behavior whenever possible. The therapist himself continually insisted that his only area of competence was in understanding emotions and that this skill was the result of special training, rather than any supernatural power or mysterious talent. Gradually, the patient was able to admit that much of his aloof, mystical superiority covered anxiety and feelings of inferiority and that philosophical detachment was often his way of dealing with feelings of frustration and helplessness.

Greater caution was necessary in approaching the intense anger that he covered with a fervent pacifism and masochistic turnings of the other cheek. Only after repeatedly showing him evidence of his capacity to have strong feelings without acting on them was it possible to comment directly on his anger. The intensity of his fear of losing control of his aggressive impulses was illustrated by his delusional projection of a "conspiracy of evil" that he felt was trying to make him "homicidally insane" during his initial psychotic episode.

Since adolescents place such importance on logical thought and ideological speculation, it would be a gross technical error to dismiss their intellectual efforts in therapy as useless and unacceptable resistances. Instead, one accepts intellectualization but does not support it. The therapist continues to point out that feelings are also important. A patient and persistent effort is made to bring affect into the therapy hours without making a direct critical attack on the defense of intellectualization. The therapist does not ally himself with the pathological ego defense, but neither does he try to force the adolescent to abandon it before he is ready. In behavioral terms, the therapist positively reinforces affective expressions and attempts to extinguish intellectualization by failure to reinforce that behavior.

To a lesser extent, adolescents may attempt to draw the therapist into alliances with other pathological ego defenses, especially denial and reaction formation. In these instances, the therapist maintains his neutrality and encourages greater objectivity without directly assaulting essential defenses. In the emergency states that appear during adolescence, many pathological defenses will be utilized by adolescent patients. The wise therapist approaches them with respect and caution, but it is rarely necessary for the therapist to give his stamp of approval to distortions of inner or outer reality.

The Unholy Alliance with the Superego

It is almost impossible to avoid completely an unholy alliance with the superego in adolescent psychotherapy. It is natural for the adolescent to maneuver to externalize his conscience. This developmental characteristic will be brought into the adolescent's relationship with his therapist, since it is universally present in the adolescent's interactions with all significant adults. This propensity is commonly expressed by the strategy of acting up provocatively to seduce important adults into meting out sadistic punishment. The therapist, as an important environmental figure, must be constantly alert to the danger of being drawn into this kind of relationship with the adolescent patient. The unavoidable technical requirement to limit defensive acting out automatically places the therapist in a precarious position from which he can all too easily slide into a superego alliance.

A 13-year-old boy's easygoing amiability was successfully interpreted as a resistance against his inner feelings. The boy's father was an angry, harsh, competitive man who frequently struck the youngster whenever he challenged any of the father's rules or statements. The youngster was able to discuss some of his anger in a session during which he was able to recognize that his excessive deference and compliance toward the therapist was a defensive continuation of a pattern that he utilized with his father to cover his inner feelings of rage.

In the next session, however, he was silent and sullen. Near the end of the session, he suddenly stated that he was "going" and headed for the door.

The therapist, rather surprised, tried to keep him in the room, and a mild shoving contest developed. The therapist recognized his error and was not surprised to encounter a very negative youngster in the next session.

He discussed the boy's need to "pick a fight" and indicated his interest in understanding how the boy felt about remaining in the office. The youngster was congratulated on the honesty he was demonstrating in his relationship with the therapist and was assured that his anger could be discussed.

Of course, the adolescent does need to externalize superego issues in order to find ways to modify his harsh conscience while using the external agent as a temporary protection against the unwise expression of impulse. The adolescent therapist can expect to be used in this way and can be helpful by tolerating some distortion of his intentions. An almost daily example occurs around the question of continuing therapy during difficult periods. Some version of the following conversation is a periodic commonplace during the therapy of many adolescents.

Adolescent (in anger): I never did need to come here. I sure as hell don't need you, and I'm not coming back in here for any more of these silly talks.

Therapist: That's not too surprising. We both know you have a tendency to run away from things when they make you too nervous, but you're strong enough to stay and talk about your feelings.

Adolescent: Why should I sit through this? Do I have to come back?

Therapist: You know that you need therapy. That's not the question. What are you really up to with all this quitting talk?

Adolescent: Okay, I'll be here next week. I should have known you wouldn't let me quit.

Therapist: Why do I have to stop you from doing something that wouldn't be good for you?

Adolescent: Aw, forget it. I'm not going to quit your precious therapy.

Therapist: Sorry, I can't forget it. Just not quitting won't cut it. We need to look at how you're trying to set me up.

Adolescent: God! Even my parents aren't this hard to get along with.

Therapist: Maybe they're mainly interested in how you behave—what you do. I'm interested in why you do things and how you feel. Sometimes it's easier to do what you think I want than to look at your feelings. The only reason that it's any of my business whether you quit or not is that it would interfere with your therapy.

Adolescent: Very funny! But you did say that I need to stay in therapy. You are telling me what to do!

Therapist (laughs): Yeah. Simon Legree rides again.

Adolescent: Aha! You admit it!

On it goes as the adolescent forces the therapist into a super-ego role. Still, the therapist must resist the temptation to criticize the adolescent for his provocation, to threaten him, or otherwise behave in a punitive way. This does not mean that the therapist avoids superego issues. Later, we consider the methods of dealing with material in this area in a way that encourages emotional growth.

The immediate point is that only the observing ego is a dependable ally in therapy with the adolescent. Even when a superego alliance produces a diminution of acting-out behavior, there is little true gain in maturation. The surface improvement tends to be ephemeral in most cases. In other instances, it is maintained through an ascetic constriction of personality that chokes off spontaneity and the capacity for pleasure—a terrible price to pay for superficial socialization. There has been no gain in independence and autonomous control in either case.

RECOGNIZING THE ALLIANCE

If the therapist is able to avoid unholy alliances and to respond with appropriate empathy, tact, and precision to the adolescent's defensive operations, evidence of a therapeutic alliance begins to appear. It is important to recognize and acknowledge this important new skill in the adolescent without implying a paternalistic endorsement of "good" behavior. Perhaps, the most meaningful acceptance of the alliance is a comment that merely recognizes its value in the therapeutic process. Its value is purely "instrumental." It is a tool that permits more effective therapeutic work.

In order to credit the adolescent with his discovery, however, it is necessary to recognize its appearance. The alliance may show itself in various forms, depending on the style and personality of the adolescent patient. One recognizes its presence primarily through a subtle change in the tone of the sessions. The atmosphere is somehow no longer totally adversarial. The therapist recognizes intuitively that he can relax somewhat, since his patient has at least become interested in observing and understanding the frightened, wary, guarded, and devious styles of relating that have characterized him in earlier sessions. In short, the therapist no longer feels that he is working totally alone in opposing the patient's resistances.

CHECKPOINTS FOR THE ALLIANCE

This general "feel" for the situation can be checked against some behavioral specifics that usually attest to the development of an alliance.

1. *The client expresses an interest in introspection.* For example, the youngster occasionally says, "I'm not sure I know why I did that," or "I think I understand why I got so upset," or "Can you understand what I really was upset about?" In other words, the client demonstrates a tendency to reflect on his affective experience, or at least a willingness to allow the therapist to suggest an underlying motivation for an intense feeling state. This is particularly meaningful if the affective experience in question directly involves the therapist, as "I think the reason your comment made me so angry is—."

2. *A switch from threatening actions to discussing thoughts and exploring their origins.* Instead of "I'm not coming back here," a change to "When you say things like that, I get so angry at you I feel like quitting."

3. *Paradoxically, the development of the therapeutic alliance may also be indicated by a more tolerant attitude toward episodes of loss of impulse control.* These episodes are discussed with moderation and objectivity, rather than withheld, bragged on, or criticized with an air of self-loathing. The attitude is not merely intellectualization, however, since the accompanying affects are not

isolated but are discussed. The adolescent can say, "I lost a battle, but overall I feel I'm winning the war."

4. *A recognition and discussion of affects appearing during the session.* The patient is able to comment, "I don't know why, but this discussion makes me very nervous."

5. *A recognition and acceptance of ambivalence as an internal reality.* No longer "My parents treat me like a baby," but rather, "Sometimes I want to grow up, but at other times it scares me to death."

6. *A reflective, curious response to appropriate confrontations and interpretations rather than a defensive, critical reaction.*

All of these attitudes may appear as isolated occurrences without signaling the arrival of a therapeutic alliance. They represent merely some specific behaviors that may serve as checkpoints for verification of the general air of cooperation described above. Without the overall sense that the therapist has been accepted as a working partner, these behaviors mean nothing.

MAINTAINING THE ALLIANCE

The therapeutic alliance is a delicate structure that is constantly threatened by the anxiety that results from its operations. The successful functioning of the alliance leads repeatedly to upsurges of aggression and erotic feelings that are threatening to the working coalition, especially since these feelings frequently become directed toward the therapist. The adolescent, with his constant search for real objects, has great difficulty in understanding the meaning and nature of transference. We discuss the overall management of transference in adolescent psychotherapy in the next chapter. It is mentioned in this context merely to note that it is a major force acting against the maintenance of the therapeutic alliance.

The fluctuations that characterize ego functioning during adolescence are themselves a threat to the steady maintenance of a therapeutic alliance. During periods of marked regression, the rational therapeutic alliance may be scuttled along with other reality-oriented ego functions. The adolescent therapist must be flexible and adapt himself to the startling changes in level of functioning and defensive patterning that the adolescent shows from one session to the next. The adolescent patient himself often does not view these "moods" as changeable reflections of aspects of the self. He tends to see each new ego state as the way he "really" feels and the way life "really" is. The therapist must try to utilize the therapeutic alliance to assist his patient in accepting his complexity and variability. It has been suggested that when the adolescent seems to ask "Who am I?" the therapist can often be most helpful by replying, "Many people. It depends on circumstances inside you and conditions around you." The therapist assists the adolescent to maintain a sense of "wholeness" and personal continuity despite rapid and puzzling changes in mood and attitude.

EXTERNAL THREATS TO THE ALLIANCE

In addition to internal dangers, the alliance may also be threatened by external events. Parents may unknowingly or consciously sabotage the alliance for a variety of motives. Possessive parents may be threatened by the affectionate tie between the therapist and the child. Controlling, hostile parents may view the therapist as an agent of their control and convey this image to their youngster. Other parents may actually be threatened by the improvement they observe in the adolescent if these changes interfere with family patterns that are important to neurotic stability. Some ideas regarding the management of these problems are presented in chapter 8, dealing with the parents of the adolescent patient.

Other external occurrences may produce such intense affects that the adolescent is forced to erect rigid defenses that cannot be explored for a period of time. These occurrences may be the illness or death of an important person in the adolescent's world or an overwhelming defeat or disappointment in the adolescent's personal struggle for competence and acceptance. During these periods, the adolescent needs to withdraw and mourn. The therapist must recognize the legitimacy of this need and accept a role of passivity and empathic sharing until the adolescent is prepared to work again. More active intervention during such a period may permanently impair the therapeutic relationship. These instances do permit the therapist to observe the adolescent's style of dealing with loss. When the mourning process goes awry or is avoided by the adolescent, the therapist may act to encourage the appropriate expression of grief and the constructive adaptation to loss. However, when the adolescent's grief and mourning are appropriate, the therapist should remain unobtrusive and grant the necessary time for the work to be completed.

WHAT TO DO UNTIL THE ALLIANCE COMES—AND WHEN IT DOES NOT

The therapeutic alliance may simply never materialize. This can result from the failure to respond accurately or effectively to early defenses or affects in a particular patient. In these instances of therapeutic error, an open discussion of the problem may permit a new start. If this is not possible, transferring the patient to a different therapist may be considered. Before carrying out transfer, however, it is worthwhile for the therapist to examine his decision closely to be sure his plan does not merely represent a rejection of the adolescent based on countertransference. Even when this proves to be the case, a transfer may still be in order. However, the therapist and the adolescent will benefit if the real reason for the transfer is recognized and discussed.

The problems are somewhat different when the patient was simply never a candidate for outpatient psychotherapy. No matter how carefully the diagnostic process is conducted, some errors will occur. When this is recognized, one must present the problem and the new recommendations to the patient and his family without undue embarrassment or apology. This situation is discussed further in the chapter on termination.

WHY DOES THE ADOLESCENT STRIVE FOR THE ALLIANCE?

After surveying all these problems, one might wonder why the therapeutic alliance ever survives the vicissitudes that it meets. These negative forces we have just enumerated are countered by two positive effects that tend to balance them. The first of these is the sense of freedom and release that usually results from increased self-awareness. The adolescent is motivated to persevere because of the sense of mastery that accompanies therapeutic gains. This rational advantage is bolstered by the adolescent's pleasure in the identification with the therapist. The frequency with which adolescent patients develop the ambition to be a psychotherapist reveals both the identification and, at least very often, the defensive fear of passively losing identity unless they turn passive into active and "go the therapist one better." In our opinion, this defense should not be challenged. Instead, the adolescent should be permitted to regard himself as a junior partner and eventual peer so long as he does not use his psychological insight destructively toward himself or others. After all, when the therapeutic alliance is functioning properly the adolescent is literally functioning as his own therapist much of the time. Even when the adolescent uses his newfound skill destructively, the perversity of such a practice can be interpreted without attacking the identification.

Sarah, the 15-year-old girl with the symptom of promiscuity described earlier, had many preoedipal problems with her mother. In the middle course of therapy, she had developed considerable expertise in observing and interpreting her behavior and feelings. During this time, she related an interchange with her mother. The mother saw the patient's kittens, already quite large, nursing the mother cat. She reacted with anger and disgust that such large kittens "would not leave their mother alone." Sarah interpreted her mother's disapproval of libidinal pleasure and associated to her mother's negative statements about sexuality. She then told of accusing her mother of being chronically unhappy because of neurotic self-denial (a correct interpretation, by the way). She told the mother she really should see a psychiatrist. The mother became quite angry and criticized Sarah for needing psychiatric help, since that revealed her lack of "true Christianity."

Sarah was initially indignant at her mother's reaction "when I was only trying to help her." The therapist noted he had been unable to detect much sympathy or understanding in Sarah's comments. Could it be that Sarah was angry and critical of her mother, simply using her insight as a more effective weapon of attack?

Sarah was able to accept the interpretation and turn to an exploration of the origins of her overreaction to her mother's attitudes toward the cat. She eventually recognized her identification with the aggressively demanding kittens and her guilt because her mother acceded to her wishes but then induced guilt through an air of sadness and martyrdom.

Later in therapy, she came to a sympathetic and affectionate understanding of her mother. She was able to support and encourage the mother to find community activities in which the mother's dependency needs could be met comfortably and without shame or disgust.

EVIDENCES OF A FAILING ALLIANCE

The recognition that the therapeutic alliance has collapsed usually comes from the same intuitive grasp of the total therapy situation that was mentioned as the best evidence of the presence of the alliance. One senses a new tendency toward opposition, not so much toward the therapist but toward the work of therapy. Again, the therapist senses that he is struggling alone in his efforts to utilize the therapeutic session to aid the process of self-understanding. The adolescent is no longer manning one of the oars, and the therapist must row the boat upstream without assistance.

There are isolated events or checkpoints that help to confirm the overall impression:

1. *An absence of any evidence of self-observation and exploration.*
   The adolescent is again immersed in experience and shows
   little interest either in understanding his role in creating his
   personal emotional experiences or in dealing effectively
   with these experiences.
2. *Subtle or gross actions directed toward the therapist that are dismissed as unimportant even when they are noted.* Examples would
   include coming late, missing sessions, interrupting the therapist, frequently misunderstanding the therapist's words, and
   other manifestations of hostility, but also bringing gifts, prais-
   ing the therapist, and other seductive behaviors.
3. *The reappearance of defensive attitudes that were previously interpreted, understood, and discarded.* Again, this is accompanied
   by a bland disregard of the implications of the behavior.
4. *A return of manipulative behavior and attitudes toward the therapist.* Stated differently, there is a return to neurotic interpersonal interaction with the therapist expressed in action
   rather than verbalized for exploration.

REESTABLISHING THE ALLIANCE

If the therapist identifies a disruption of the therapeutic alliance, he can then work to repair it. The therapist should recognize that no other work will be useful until the alliance has been
reestablished. No matter how much inherent interest the content of the sessions may hold, the therapist should utilize only
that portion of the material that may help to rebuild the therapeutic alliance. In the absence of a working alliance, the therapist's intervention will be ineffective or even antitherapeutic.

How, then, can the therapist reestablish the alliance? The first
step is the identification of the cause of the disruption. As mentioned above, the most common sources of disruption are the
anxiety and uncomfortable affects released through the activity
of the therapeutic alliance itself. One very honest 13-year-old,
confronted with her resistance, stated the problem succinctly:
"The trouble with looking at yourself is that it doesn't feel
good."

Of course, this is the very stuff of which therapy is made. The therapist should accept the inevitable fact that properly conducted psychotherapy produces pain and all people try to avoid pain. The adolescent patient has every right to complain about this and to expect his therapist to sympathize. Mankind has always chafed under the painful demands of reality. Surely, we can be sympathetic and supportive when the adolescent frets at these nettles. Of course, the therapist's sympathy is directed at helping the adolescent to bear this realistic fact of life, not toward shielding him from it.

When confronted with a break in the therapeutic alliance, the therapist needs tactfully to acknowledge with his patient the change in their relationship. Often, the therapist will have to explain to the adolescent that his change is not viewed as "goofing off," obstinacy, or rebelliousness. The distinction between resisting the therapist and resisting the therapeutic process often needs extensive clarification if the adolescent is to learn how to observe this interaction objectively and without feeling criticized by the therapist. It is essential to help the adolescent to understand that his interactions with the therapist will be treated in the same objective, curious, nonjudgmental way with which the therapist responds to his other affective experiences.

Tammy, an attractive 17-year-old girl, requested psychotherapy one night in the midst of a family row over her poor school performance. She told her therapist that her real reason for wishing to be in therapy was a feeling that life was passing her by and that she was unable to form close friendships that were meaningful to her. Over the first few psychotherapy sessions, Tammy formed a warm relationship with the therapist and utilized her capacities for introspection with some success in understanding her relationship to her hard-working, intense, and somewhat driven mother. She was able to recognize that her poor academic record reflected both a repudiation of her mother's anxious way of life and a fear of competing with the mother.

Throughout this time, she periodically complained that she did not seem to be popular. Although she first blamed this unpopularity on her moral standards, which she felt were higher than those of most of the girls at her school, she gradually recognized that she was somehow "turning off" the boys who showed an initial interest in her. As this became a focus in therapy, the therapist commented on the fact that Tammy did not seem to take her femininity seriously and seemed in many respects to treat relationships between boys and girls as though they were a game that did not involve any intense feelings. Tammy's response at the time was to distort the comment somewhat and to state defensively that she has engaged in some necking and that she was not afraid of sexuality.

However, in the next interview Tammy was visibly anxious and found it difficult to talk. She fidgeted in her chair and regularly pulled at her skirt. She tended to avoid the therapist's direct gaze and frequently blushed whenever she would try to speak. After a few minutes of this, she was able to become somewhat comfortable, but seemed to be talking at a very superficial level and showing none of her characteristic curiosity about her own feelings, thoughts, and behaviors.

When the therapist commented that it seemed Tammy had lost a good deal of interest in exploring her feelings, Tammy felt that she was being criticized. After the therapist clarified that this was not the case and suggested that feelings about therapy and the therapist could be openly discussed, Tammy was able to say that she was feeling somewhat annoyed with the therapist when she left the previous session and was aware that she was quite upset. She stated further that she could not remember the topic of discussion from her previous session and volunteered that this was unusual for her, since as a rule it was quite easy to remember her sessions. The therapist supported her honesty in this and encouraged her to continue talking about any reactions that she might have had toward the therapist.

Initially, she spoke with some timidity, but gradually this

diminished as Tammy began to complain that the therapist was "finding problems" that she did not know she had. Because of this, she could not be sure whether therapy was helping her or making her worse. She noted that generally she enjoyed a good mood most of the time but that she has been rather depressed for the entire past week. At this point, the therapist reminded her that he had commented that she sometimes treated life as a game and refused to take it seriously and suggested that perhaps she found this necessary because of some tendency toward depression, which she was attempting to avoid. The therapist supported her honesty in facing up to some of these sad feelings and wondered with her which course of action held the greatest promise in the long run.

"Well, if you can stand a blubbering idiot, I guess I can weep my way through it. I suppose I've known this all along myself," Tammy replied.

It seemed that Tammy's discomfort was related to sexual feelings toward the therapist that were activated by his direct recognition of Tammy's femininity. However, in the absence of a therapeutic alliance strong enough to deal with this kind of material, the appropriate response was in the direction of dealing with the uncomfortable affects stirred by the therapy process in the interest of reestablishing a therapeutic alliance. The techniques of management of sexual transference in adolescents are discussed in the next chapter.

If the disruption of the alliance arises from some unfortunate event in the adolescent's life, a period of unobtrusive and undemanding support will need to precede any attempt to reestablish a therapeutic alliance. As mentioned above, the therapist must allow the adolescent to take the initiative in indicating an interest in continuing the exploratory work of the treatment unless the grief reaction itself is seriously distorted. More likely than not, the adolescent will indicate his readiness to go back to work by complaining, "We don't seem to be getting much done in here lately!" The complaining adolescent may be quite surprised to see his therapist, somewhat worried during the mourning period, suddenly smile and say, "Man, I can't tell you how relieved I am to hear you say that! Let's get with it."

Parental sabotage of the alliance must be recognized and differentiated from stresses arising from the therapy itself. Often, parental interference is signaled by comments that disavow previous areas of conflict with the parents. The adolescent, on the contrary, reports "therapeutic sessions" with the parents and may imply that they can help him more than the therapist. Especially if such periods coincide with or follow anxious phone calls from the parents, the suspicion of parental sabotage is justified. These problems are discussed more fully in a later chapter, but it is well to recognize that the problem cannot be handled unilaterally with the adolescent patient once it has reached this level. The parents themselves must be helped either through a collaborative therapist or directly by family conferences.

THE ALLIANCE IN PERSPECTIVE

The therapeutic alliance is not only essential to any psychotherapy; it coincides with an important developmental task of the adolescent period—the emergence of the observing ego. Therefore, the development and maintenance of a therapeutic alliance with the adolescent patient assume a double importance. We have explored some of the particular problems and pitfalls in establishing a therapeutic alliance during this phase of psychosexual development. We have also tried to point out that the maintenance of the alliance is inextricably linked to various other aspects of therapy, especially the transference tendencies of the adolescent and the problems of the adolescent's parents. The capacity to establish a therapeutic alliance is an essential skill for the therapist of the adolescent.

At this time therapists are struggling to treat increasing numbers of adolescents whose problems make it extremely difficult for them to develop a classical therapeutic alliance. Because of severe defects in their sense of self they cannot even grasp the concept of growing through honest self-scrutiny and often cannot understand the therapist's role as a separate and helpful human being. In the next chapter we will try to understand the subjective experience of these youngsters and to explore techniques for helping them.

CHAPTER 4
malignant defenses, malignant resistances, and atypical alliances

Although the model of the therapeutic alliance described in the previous chapter is one that the therapist should always strive for, it cannot always be achieved. In some ways it must be regarded as an ideal since many adolescents in psychotherapy will utilize the therapist as a real object in their psychological development. Some youngsters, particularly psychotic and borderline youngsters, youngsters with severe narcissistic pathology, and youngsters with severe character problems exaggerate the adolescent tendency to force the therapist to play a role in their lives that is quite different from the image of a neutral, objective guide.

It seems evident that many of these adolescents cannot tolerate the degree of distancing and neutrality implied in the traditional therapeutic alliance. Their sense of self is so fragmented and distorted that they cannot develop the degree of relatedness to a real person in a specific role that would allow an even-handed and nonjudgmental discussion of their psychological functioning. From a pragmatic clinical viewpoint, however, it seems that many of these youngsters benefit materially from a psychotherapeutic interaction in spite of the absence of a therapeutic alliance dominated by observing ego functions.

Progress in the absence of an ideal alliance is a psychotherapeutic process that is still poorly understood and relatively unexplored. Many therapists are very uncomfortable when they are pressed into a role in the adolescent's life that seems at variance with their own professional identity as a psychotherapist.

DEVELOPMENTAL FACTORS: THE CONCEPT OF COMPETENCE

The forces that produce a sense of hopelessness in the adolescent include all those that afflict adults—including unresolvable internal conflicts, significant losses, major physical illnesses, and the like. The adolescent faces, in addition, major developmental strains that probably account for the high rate of emotional disability during the adolescent years in spite of generally robust health, massive increases in drive energy, and an appropriate future orientation that generally would allow for some discounting of current difficulties and discouragements. The adolescent's problem is that he or she is sufficiently mature and well informed to become acutely aware of a need for self-confidence, problem-solving skills, adequate educational background, interpersonal effectiveness, and a whole range of coping abilities that we will lump together for ease of communication into the word competence. The adolescent knows that these skills are prerequisite for adult success—and knows that he or she does *not* have them. These are abilities that will only gradually take shape during the course of adolescent development and will reach their fullness in early adulthood with continuing refinement, if all goes well, until senility or death intervenes.

Since it is very difficult for adolescents to wait, this awareness of inescapable skill requirements compared to current ineptitude produces anxiety for the most normal of adolescents. This anxiety is typically expressed in the erratic adaptational level shown by many young people that includes periods of disavowed dependency and helplessness alternating with periods of unrealistic grandiosity. In the relatively normal adolescent, both of these extremes are subordinate to more extended periods of limited and focused dependent learning relationships coupled with peer and adult support. The entire process is sustained by the optimistic expectation that the goals of adulthood are achievable.

Still there are periods of concern. At times during this adaptation the adolescent will consider anxiously some identities and lifestyles that would lower the complexity and intensity of his anticipated adult adjustment. The very bright and academically capable adolescent may think of living quietly on a farm somewhere, communing only with nature and perhaps the county agricultural extension agent.

Searching criticism of the adult culture is common not only because the adolescent needs to find values and objectives worthy of sacrifice and effort but also because he hopes there might be a lighter load, an easier path.

Fortunately—given the inner strengths developed through childhood and latency, a reasonable degree of support and training from the current adult population, peer friendships, and the major positive developmental thrust provided by nature—most adolescents arrive rather successfully at the same kind of flawed but generally productive and enjoyable adulthood that most of us have achieved.

However, our concern is with the sizable group of adolescents who encounter significant problems in reaching this realistic and highly desirable endpoint. We need a little more discussion about how normal development proceeds in order to orient ourselves to the basic differences in the problems that our adolescent patients encounter.

MORE ON THE CONCEPT OF COMPETENCE

Obviously the development of a sense of competence is a highly complex series of conscious and unconscious mental operations. We would like to artificially simplify that complexity in order to focus the discussion. We suggest that competence—the inner confidence that one can cope successfully with people, learn new skills, and master challenges—grows out of an ongoing interaction between the development of individual personal skills coupled with positive and helpful interactions with other people.

The relationship between personal experimentation and the use of help is most obvious in the young child where the joy of mastery and the widening scope of exploration and experimentation are periodically interrupted by frustration or anxiety that is allayed through temporary supportive contact with a trusted and empathic adult. This sequence of events is at its peak during the stages of the toddler's effort to gain separation and individuation and especially during that period of life so aptly designated by Mahler et al. (1975) as the period of rapprochement.

During this alteration between adventuresomeness and retreat to psychological home base, we can assume that there are corresponding internal variations in the subjective sense of competence. The toddlers who are venturing forth to try new things, explore new areas, and test new skills surely must have a sense of positive expectation that can evaporate rapidly if they encounter unexpected setbacks or frightening events. In their tearful rush back toward their mothers one can observe no evidence of their previous self-confidence and hopefulness.

However, as the mother provides appropriate support while encouraging and accepting the movement away from her at the child's own rate, we can observe a gradual increase in the youngster's ability to tolerate greater uncertainty, overcome larger obstacles, and explore ever more unfamiliar terrain and events. We must assume that youngsters in some way build within their own minds a capacity to comfort themselves. There must be an internal prospective image that recognizes a growing ability to comprehend and problem solve and also an expectation of the reliability of help from others when individual effort is not sufficient. In short the toddler gradually develops a competence based on recognition of personal mastery skills coupled with trust that when these skills and abilities are not sufficient alone, appropriate help and support will be provided from a basically kindly and supportive world of others.

Along with these developments there is a simultaneous growth of emotional depth, an ever widening capacity for empathy, and most important, an ability to develop affectionate attachments. These emotional developments allow an increasing openness to intimacy that leads over a lifetime to a degree of self-affirmation and consolidation of identity that carries marked resilience to stress.

Unfortunately in clinical work, therapists are involved primarily with people who have encountered serious problems in successfully developing this sense of competence. Oversimplifying again for the purposes of discussion, there may be advantages to thinking of patients as being from two groups. The first group is made up of those adolescents who have progressed to the point of accepting personal competence as a reasonable goal even though they may doubt their ability to achieve that desirable endpoint. This group was just considered in the chapter on the traditional therapeutic alliance. The second group is constituted of adolescents who do not accept competence as their psychological objective, indeed who cannot even conceive of achieving that status.

Many of the concepts used here are quite similar to the traditional notion that clients may have either genital or pregenital sources of their difficulties. Yet, it is worthwhile to consider the issues from this slightly different perspective for clinical reasons. Conceptualizing the issues in the ways that we will be suggesting may be helpful in planning therapy and particularly in understanding transference reactions and the nature of the therapeutic alliance.

The influences of Kohut (1971), Masterson (1981), and Kernberg (1984) will be obvious although we do not pretend to the careful theoretical discipline that they bring to their writing. Our comments should be considered purely in a clinical framework.

YOUNGSTERS WITH BENIGN DEFENSES

Let us begin with the group of patients who develop an acceptance of competence as a goal that they desire but despair of achieving. These are individuals who usually have not had major biological or constitutional defects, have enjoyed "good enough" mothering in their earlier years, and who are accepted by their parents as separate, reasonably intact human beings. They develop difficulties in achieving an accurate and positive view of themselves because something about them causes one or both parents excessive fascination or anxiety. In other words the adolescent either "seduces" or threatens one or both parents through characteristics that the child actually or potentially possesses, such as masculinity, femininity, intellectual potential, or the like. In other instances it is not so much that the parents react in this way as it is that external events such as divorce, death of a parent, illness in the parent, illness or injury to the child, or other happenings are interpreted as though they reflected parental displeasure, disappointment, or lack of affection for the developing youngster. Obviously we are talking about the broad range of neurotic adolescent problems and adjustment reactions serious enough to cause the adolescent to be referred for therapy.

Adolescents who come for treatment with a background like this usually see themselves as the problem. They suffer from various fears about themselves, fears that might be characterized as irrational but not unreasonable. They worry, for example, that their thoughts and feelings are bad or shameful or silly or childish. They worry that they themselves are inadequate, too little, too dumb, too ugly, too thin, too fat. Probably most of them do not really believe that the fears are true. These are concerns that they are supposed to believe and that indeed do trouble them. With careful listening, however, one can usually hear an almost playful air of pretense in the neurotic fears. These adolescents are presenting us with a gravely important drama but the tragedy is only tentative; the hero may still save the day. Deep down these adolescents know that they have the capacity for competence. They think in some dim and hidden way that they have been placed under a curse that forbids them to express their abilities and enjoins them from enjoying their capacity to love and be loved.

Such adolescents come to therapy searching for a seer who will understand the truth of their situation, solve the riddle of the Sphinx, and release them from their maledictions. The trials they assign to us to prove ourselves have been described in the previous chapter. They test our integrity, intelligence, and benevolence with inventive and sometimes frightening challenges to see if we can be trusted to face their inner demons. Understanding these tests and avoiding carefully set traps are the basic skills that add an extra dimension to psychotherapy with adolescents. Once the bewitched adolescent is satisfied that the therapist is trustworthy, friendly, and reasonably able, therapeutic work tends to unfold in a rewarding and interesting manner within the framework of a therapeutic alliance. Although appropriate family work and reasonable attention to educational and other developmental needs are always a part of treatment, the important and central event is the dyadic re-creation within the transference relationship of those encounters and misunderstandings that led the youngster to believe he or she had been jinxed. Since the therapist has no wish or motive to diminish the youngster's competence and no fear of adolescent attractiveness, vigor, and adequacy, many of the previous distortions can be resolved and the youngster leaves therapy with capacities unleashed.

Because this positive outcome is very frequent for this kind of adolescent patient, we can think of their defenses as benign defenses, and their resistances as benign resistances. This is not to deny that treating them takes skill and sustained effort. There are no easy adolescent patients. The problems of this group are only *relatively* benign.

Before considering the second group of adolescents, it is necessary to talk about family dynamics in a little more detail. As mentioned earlier, the youngsters with benign defenses have encountered a need to distort their true natures because of their interaction with their parents or at least their perception of this interaction. Yet, most of the families of these youngsters retain a strong respect for reality and a capacity to internalize conflict even while they confuse their children regarding their true value and capabilities. These parents do not act out themselves though they have neurotic discomfort. They transmit similar neurotic problems to their children while in most other respects training them well for functioning in the world. They do not use their children directly to satisfy their own needs although they may use them to buttress their defenses. Of course, they

still damage the child by projecting their fearful and constrict-
ing vision of the child's nature.

There is a second group of families strong enough to fill the
developmental needs of the child up to a point of genuine
individuation who nonetheless have problems in their own relationship with reality. These parents, though basically neurotic,
do transmit to the youngster permission for ego regression and
at least for certain specific areas of acting out. This is the concept of superego lacunae (Johnson, 1949; Johnson and Szurek,
1952).

     Marilyn, 14 years old, came to a residential treatment
program because of uncontrollable acting out. She was involved in total rebellion against her parents, promiscuity,
alcohol and drug abuse, and absolute belligerence toward
all adults and all of society's rules. Yet, given a residential
staff offering consistent limits, positive attention, and a
reflective exploratory attitude toward her behavior, Marilyn quickly demonstrated her basic strengths as well as her
neurotic distortions about her sexuality and her capacity to
function as an individual. As one might expect the past
history gave many clues that Marilyn indeed was healthier
than her presenting picture might have suggested. She had
had a stable childhood; in fact there was evidence of overattachment and excessive dependency on the mother with
some separation problems in early latency. Difficulties began only when secondary sexual characteristics appeared
in early adolescence. In this instance a long-term follow-up
revealed that Marilyn's mother had been struggling with
intense antisocial impulses at the time of Marilyn's early
adolescence. These tendencies later erupted in a series of
extramarital affairs and an arrest for shoplifting even
though the family was quite wealthy.

The point is that not every neurotic adolescent presents with
an internalized problem and a positive desire for psychotherapy. On the contrary there is usually at least some effort
toward an external rather than an internal solution. In the case

of families where behavioral resolutions are accepted, there may be a considerable overlay of acting out behavior. One must also consider the important distinction between fixation and regression, considering the best level of development achieved by the child and recognizing that, in a panic over failure to move forward, the adolescent often shows both instinctual and ego regression. The degree of regression can be considerable, particularly if drugs are added to the problem mix.

Many adolescents who present in extreme rebellion against the world, reality, adults, and conventional expectations are not just going through a phase, are not disguised neurotics, and are not benign in their defenses, resistances, or their treatment outcome. Their problems are malignant, very destructive to any opportunity for emotional development, and very difficult to treat successfully. Unfortunately, they now comprise a large percentage of the caseload of most adolescent therapists.

The early history of these adolescents often reveals evidence of basic defects in the ego apparatus. Many of them have suffered learning disability, severe attention-deficit/hyperactivity disorder, residual effects of fetal insult or prematurity, or other difficulties that have compromised the basic apparatus for modulation of affective and motor discharge and development of cognitive skills. Often in addition to these disadvantaged emotional beginnings, there is evidence that the nurturing environment was deficient, frequently to a tragically extreme degree. Stories of early neglect and abandonment, child abuse, and sexual molestation are not uncommon. Even when there is not such active ill-use of the child, there is still clear-cut evidence of marked family system pathology. This pathology usually includes severe distortions of generational boundaries, active and direct use of the child to meet parental needs, a bewildering muddle of communication, and a general readiness to distort aspects of reality when these are uncomfortable or inconvenient for family members. The impact of these forces on the developing child is predictable and devastating. To varying degrees in each of these children the effort to gain a sense of competence is undermined by two factors: personal ego skills are deficient and the development of trust in the dependability of helpfulness of surrounding adults is sabotaged.

That success is necessary to encourage and support skill development is obvious to both our common sense and our observations of children. Youngsters tend to simply stop trying if they encounter repeated failure. Severe stunting of skill development will follow since all ego skills require success and practice. The youngster is reluctant to try new environmental challenges, senses the environment as a threat, and does not develop an inner conviction of mastery. This can be reversed or at least ameliorated through careful support and handling by the parents. If this help is not available, however, the negative spiral into disordered functioning accelerates.

We have discussed earlier the need for reliable dependency support to promote a youngster's acceptance of challenge and to forestall a paralyzing fear of the environment. The absence of this support, especially when coupled with personal deficiencies in coping skills, leads to a sense of helplessness, panic, and a fearful dread of real world challenges. These terrified youngsters cannot move beyond infantile omnipotence as their primary system for feeling safe in the world. Tentative efforts to cope realistically are doomed to failure since they lack both skill and persistence, so the child regresses to omnipotent defenses again and again.

As these youngsters grow older they enhance omnipotent fantasy with both the motor and intellectual skills that develop in the course of maturation. Ingenious arguments, manipulations, and distortions obscure the basic irrationality of their world view to themselves and to others. The families' lack of commitment to reality further supports this pseudosolution. Indeed, if the particular family system pathology needs an ill or deviant youngster, the family may directly and indirectly promote, support, and even *require* continuation of the unrealistic world view. The therapist is faced with a conspiracy to confuse the issue, avoid the important questions of life, and preserve the magical world view.

Since these children do not anticipate successful mastery of challenges, they avoid those developmental tasks that would point up their areas of vulnerability. As a result their developmental skills lag steadily further behind their age mates. As their inner sense of helplessness and incompetence increases, their need to delude themselves and others grows and their efforts to maintain a myth of omnipotent control over themselves, others, and their external world becomes ever more desperate. Because of this series of events, by adolescence their defenses are often malignant and if they come for therapy the resistances they bring are malignant also.

The omnipotent defenses are usually action-based to a degree far beyond the normal tendencies of the adolescent to externalize. Not only do these youngsters act out, their acting out is energetically directed toward changing the world around them in ways that are clearly unrealistic. For example, severely delinquent adolescents act as though there is no need to follow rules, as though all needs can be met immediately, and as though the goodwill and support of others is unnecessary. They pretend that everything can be obtained by cunning, intimidation, or simple theft.

It is important to remember that these behaviors are active, coherent adjustment efforts, not simply the chaotic and random breakthrough of impulses. For example, careful observation of any severely antisocial youngster shows that much acting out is done to buoy a flagging sense of omnipotent control rather than because the youngster is upset or out of control. The delinquent youngster needs the "fix" of conning someone, successfully pulling off a caper, or simply intimidating someone in order to maintain a sense of self-esteem. Paradoxically, this need can be intensified by a friendly or supportive interaction or anything else that threatens the defensive stance. If these youngsters looked at themselves objectively, in the real world, they would see a lonely, insecure, unsuccessful child perpetually pursued by anxiety and depression. However, in the gangland fantasy of an all-conquering, daring macho man or gun moll fearlessness, there is a sense of safety and strength. Unfortunately, since the youngster is not omnipotent at all, there is an ever recurrent need to re-project the flickering outline of this fragile mirage.

However, no matter how unsuitable this solution appears to us, it is the only possible solution the adolescent can imagine. It is not possible to learn or to gain in skills without facing areas of inadequacy and vulnerability. You can't learn what you don't know that you don't know. These youngsters are unable to entertain such a frightening vista and must view themselves as all-conquering know-it-alls at all times. Obviously then, these youngsters do not present themselves to a psychotherapist with a sense that they are troubled. They may admit that things are messed up but if so they place the blame outside themselves and complain of unfair teachers, harsh law enforcement personnel, unreliable friends, and, of course, stupid psychotherapists. In other words, what we see as their problems are all that they have going for them. Their pathology is ego-syntonic to say the least.

Even at those times when these adolescents cannot maintain this self view, there is still no entree for the therapist. When the omnipotence is shattered and the youngsters recognize their destructiveness to self and others, that awareness causes a massive helpless depression that cannot even conceive of solution and that eventually must lead to suicide or another effort to reinstate the omnipotent defenses. Yochelson and Samenow (1976) have called this the "zero state."

These adolescents do not view their defensive structures as problematic; in fact, they actively look for people who will support these distorted life views. If they cannot find friends who share their view of the world, they will avoid human contact. Anyone who tries to relate closely to them while questioning their unrealistic lifestyle or, heaven forbid, espousing a more realistic approach to life's difficulties, very rapidly becomes an enemy, subject to active attack. Their motto might be, "Love me, love my illness."

Naturally, this presents some difficulties for the prospective psychotherapist. By the very nature of our profession the circumstances that lead to our contact with these adolescents set the stage for a very negative encounter. They wouldn't be in our presence if everything were as wonderful as they want to believe. These adolescents do not approach the therapist with the sense of playful curiosity about themselves that can be developed through a therapeutic alliance with youngsters with benign defenses. The universal initial adolescent negative reaction to therapy tends to continue in these cases of malignant defense. These youngsters are not won over by fairness, objectivity, and benevolence. Indeed as these adolescents see things, these characteristics in the therapist pose a serious threat to maintenance of their only possible emotional safety. They try to cure the therapist of dangerous tendencies such as benevolence, honesty, and objectivity. The patients actively try to corrupt, intimidate, enrage, disgust, or in some other way invalidate the therapist's stance as a friendly and helpful adult. They do not want a kindly and wise seer since they have actively concocted—with a little help from their parents and friends—an illusory self, and truth about this is the last thing in the world they want to hear.

Although the character pathology in these youngsters is malignant, it is neither untreatable nor unavoidably psychologically terminal. If these adolescents are not able to let us be involved with them in an intimate dyadic exploratory relationship, some other approach may permit them to see us as a potentially useful adult.

Perhaps we can begin to explore an approach by considering a metaphor. If the youngsters with benign defenses were in search of a benevolent seer, *these* youngsters are looking for the Wizard of Oz. Aware that they are lacking in heart, brain, or will, these boys and girls hope to find a magician who can grant them their wish for wholeness that they believe will provide a grandiose and omnipotent success. This hope for magic solutions takes them to cults, gurus, and gangs who are always ready to exploit their dreams. How can we, who pride ourselves on being scientific (or at least empiric) and nonexploitive, follow the old therapeutic truism and meet *these* patients where they are?

Obviously we would not suggest that we promise magic solutions since we cannot deliver them. On the other hand we may need to accept these patients' need to distort our function in order to tolerate therapy with us. Also, we may have to become comfortable with the fact that we actively influence patients. We have not always been willing to acknowledge that we utilize our positions of perceived or real power and authority in ways that are subtly or not so subtly coercive. The following clinical vignette illustrates this point. We have chosen Ralph because he is a transitional example, if you will, a somewhat milder, eventually verbal version of malignancy.

Ralph was referred for psychotherapy as a 16-year-old near the middle of his sophomore year in high school. The referral was initiated by Ralph's mother over Ralph's protest and with only lukewarm support from the father. The mother requested to speak with the psychiatrist before Ralph was seen and was given an appointment.

She explained that she had been quite concerned about Ralph for two or three years. She stated that Ralph had never been an outstanding student but had accomplished an acceptable performance in elementary school. She also noted that in the earlier grades Ralph was friendly, socially accepted, cheerful, and "resilient." When Ralph was in the sixth grade the family moved and Ralph had to enter a different school. The mother felt that this experience was very hard on the boy although he did make some new friends and appeared to be adjusting to his new situation. The seventh grade also did not present problems, but in the eighth grade Ralph began to have significant problems with the other youngsters. He stated that he was not liked and began to be more reticent at home. He began to have difficulty getting to school on time in the mornings, and his grades began to deteriorate.

The mother felt Ralph was worried about his masculinity. A friend of his once told her that Ralph gave up too easily in making friendships with girls. The friend indicated that Ralph had called one girl for a date but when he received a negative reply he withdrew and refused to call any more girls. Ralph said at the time that he would never have a girl friend.

The mother stated that she felt Ralph was extremely depressed. He had recently said to her, "You think life is great and wonderful. I hate it." When the mother wept in response to hearing this despairing comment, Ralph became angry with her and shouted, "Stop that, that's what made me such an old lady." The mother felt that Ralph looked depressed almost all of the time. She was very worried about him and seemed particularly concerned about her relationship with the boy. She and Ralph had had excellent communication until about two years ago. He had told her during the time when they were closer, "You're proud of me, but I'll never make father proud of me." The mother said that she and the father had argued a good deal during Ralph's early life. She admitted that she might be somewhat indulgent and overprotective but felt that the father was unreasonably demanding of precocious independence from Ralph. The father was especially strict regarding table manners and total obedience to rules when Ralph was a young child.

During this interview the therapist asked to speak to Ralph's father. The father was a very handsome man, noticeably younger in appearance than his wife though they were approximately the same age. He was cooperative and stated, "Ralph's having a lot of problems with his own feelings about himself." When asked to expand on that, the father replied, "The problems I fasten on depend on my mood. I'm moody and I reflect a lot." In his opinion the family had "normal family frictions" and probably "doesn't communicate too well."

The father focused a great deal on Ralph's performance difficulties, admitting that Ralph's poor school achievement bothered him. It bothered him even more that Ralph was difficult to get up in the mornings and customarily went late to all scheduled activities. The father admitted he was extremely annoyed by Ralph not seeming to care whether he was on time or not. He noted that Ralph's one ambition was to be a guitarist in a rock group but that in fact Ralph had demonstrated no musical talent.

Both parents indicated that Ralph had told them that a traumatic event occurred during his eighth grade year that he could not discuss with them. This secret, Ralph stated, was the cause of his depression and continuing problems.

An interview with Ralph was scheduled although both parents had some concern that he would not keep the appointment. They asked if there was any point in "forcing" Ralph to come to the interview. The therapist told them that Ralph should come to the appointment if they had to drag him there. In fact, Ralph came reluctantly but voluntarily. He was overweight, unattractive, clearly depressed, and just as clearly sulky and petulant. His long hair was lank and appeared dirty and his dress was somewhat sloppy and disheveled. He spoke reluctantly and there was considerable conscious withholding, but in addition there was genuine psychomotor retardation. Though there was no apparent thought disorder, it did seem that Ralph occasionally became confused and had some difficulty in maintaining his train of thought. He stated rather early in the interview in a somewhat challenging way that he was not going to talk about his real problem. The therapist elected to pursue a friendly cross examination since Ralph's manner somehow suggested that that was what he expected and needed. This interrogation gradually revealed the following points:

- Someone had let him down in a very serious and painful way but Ralph could not talk about this.
- Ralph had a secret too embarrassing and painful to disclose.
- "Half the time" Ralph felt hopeless and thought that his problems were insoluble.

- The effort to solve his problems was too much trouble anyway.
- He could not trust the therapist because the therapist might use information against him or simply not understand him or both.

Ralph said that both parents irritated him, especially his mother. She irritated him first of all by being too nice and explaining too much and secondly by singing nursery rhymes and "acting like a kid sometimes." Ralph thought that at times he blamed his parents for his problem. His blaming did not take any definite form, "just the way they are. They raised me." Ralph stated that he had never told his mother that he was angry at her because she was very sensitive and "it would hurt her." When asked how he would know she was hurt, he stated that she would cry. Ralph was unable to say anything specific about how his father irritated him but with some prodding said, "bugging me like waking me up or sometimes treating me like a little kid."

Ralph quickly seemed uncomfortable about these complaints toward his parents and added, "It's probably all just my fault, I don't know." He stated that he did not have any friends but that he would like to have some if they were "the right kind." When asked what sort would be the right kind, he stated, "Someone who doesn't hurt me. Someone I can trust, and someone who is popular."

The therapist formed a diagnostic impression of an extremely narcissistic boy with a severe depression. The presence of multiple neurotic traits of compulsive rumination, phobic tendencies, and a suspiciousness that verged on the paranoiac suggested poor ego structure and the possibility of a borderline personality organization. Both the parents and Ralph were told that Ralph's problems were extremely serious. When Ralph stated that he still did not wish to have therapy, he was told firmly that he had only two choices, either to come in for individual sessions or to be part of family therapy. He was told that he did not have a right to refuse therapy in view of the pain and concern that his unhappiness was creating in his family. The effect of this comment seemed to be more supportive and face-saving than upsetting to Ralph. He was able to accept individual treatment on this basis.

The first few months of treatment with Ralph were characterized primarily by long silences and an extreme dearth of material. He seemed to be relaxing, however, and occasionally would enter into brief discussions with the therapist. The therapist maintained an extremely active, cheerful, and chatty manner although Ralph's sullen silence and unresponsiveness sometimes caused the one-sided happy chatter to sound a bit like the babblings of a good-natured idiot. After about four months of treatment Ralph announced that he would like to describe the traumatic events that happened to him in junior high but that he was not sure he could. The therapist took this as permission to prod, pry, cajole, and actively pursue this material. Three or four sessions later Ralph described the events that happened in the eighth grade. Basically they involved a competitive run-in with a youngster who became his enemy. This youngster had considerable skill at teasing and was able to get groups of youngsters to laugh at Ralph on a few occasions on the school grounds. The ultimate upset occurred when this enemy drew a caricature of Ralph on the school wall with spray paint, particularly emphasizing Ralph's somewhat oversized nose. All the kids laughed and thought the picture was funny. Ralph was humiliated.

Over the next few sessions Ralph continued to discuss the impact of these events on his attitudes and thinking. It became clear that he had developed an almost paranoid attitude toward other youngsters that at times approached "ideas of reference." For example, if Ralph would see two youngsters laughing together he would wonder if perhaps they were talking about him and laughing at him. He also came to feel that school work was not important. He dreaded attending school each morning and could hardly force himself to go, thus accounting for his chronic tardiness. He became more and more seclusive and did not wish to talk with his family since he felt sure they would not understand his problem. He was concerned that his father would criticize him for not dealing more effectively with the situation while his mother would be overly sympathetic and excessively supportive. Specifically he felt that his mother would tell him that he was a handsome and likeable youngster when he felt convinced that he was ugly, obnoxious, and unlikable.

Several months were spent dealing with Ralph's reaction to these events in early adolescence. The therapist focused particularly on the absence of any memory of overt anger, desire to retaliate, or obvious competitiveness in Ralph's response to his peer problems. Initially Ralph flatly denied having any such feelings but gradually began to recover some memories of anger and competitiveness. These bothered him a great deal and he confessed them with tremendous guilt. At the time of entry into treatment Ralph was an avowed pacifist who stated that he had strong moral opposition to violence in any form. Violence for Ralph included many behaviors normally regarded as appropriately aggressive and competitive. For example, he felt that one should never criticize another person even for constructive reasons since that might inflict pain on the other individual.

At this point in treatment the material shifted slightly and Ralph began to talk about his difficulty with girls and his intense desire to have a girl friend. As he described the relationship he wished for, it became clear that his fantasized goal was a symbiotic union with an adored girl friend against the rest of the world. It was crucial to Ralph that his girl friend be absolutely beautiful not only in his own eyes but in the consensual evaluation of the entire world. In connection with the discussion of his sexual development and his attitudes toward himself as a male, Ralph gingerly approached another secret. He was never able to confess it on his own, but when the therapist suggested that he had many guilt feelings about masturbation, Ralph wept and admitted that that was the subject he had been alluding to.

Ralph argued that the habit of masturbation could be overcome if only the therapist would help him. Ralph demanded explanations as to why the therapist would not join him in this effort. He was extremely reluctant to accept the reality of the sexual drive and felt that he should rise above it in much the same way that he insisted he should be able to overcome any feelings of anger or competitiveness.

These complaints were merely specific instances of Ralph's general dismissal of the value of therapy. Although he now attended regularly and without protest, he maintained a sullen grumbling attitude toward the treatment effort, frequently noting that it had not helped him. The therapist's attitude toward all these complaints was to accept them without comment even though the family reported that Ralph's behavior had improved considerably and Ralph himself admitted reluctantly that his report card had improved dramatically during the last marking period. He assured the therapist that it was because he had easy courses and in any event it was of no importance to him.

At this point in therapy Ralph presented another obsession that he stated was virtually exhausting him. In describing the development of this obsession, Ralph inadvertently revealed that his social contacts had increased considerably. In these interpersonal situations Ralph would predictably become anxious at times and would feel he had to get away and be alone so he could "think about the world." What Ralph meant by "thinking about the world" was devising his own mind solutions to all human problems. He felt that if he could solve racial prejudice, poverty, war, and general human suffering so that everyone in the whole world could be happy, then he himself could be content and happy also. If he failed in these mental gymnastics, happiness would be impossible for him. He was convinced at times that with enough perseverance and time, he could succeed at this grandiose undertaking. At other times he recognized the obsession as "a ridiculous mind game" that was serving a defensive function in containing his interpersonal anxiety and his fear of the new situations occurring in his life.

Shortly after this, Ralph found another solution to his dilemma. He announced to the therapist that he was quite sure that the therapist was somehow contacting the youngsters and teachers in his school to "put in a good word for him." He admitted that this seemed impractical and when pushed said that possibly it was only a feeling or thought that he had, but nonetheless he felt "pretty sure" most of the time that the therapist was actively interceding to cause people to treat him better. The "delusion" was particularly interesting in that it was accompanied by a great increase in Ralph's social activity and his comfort with it. He began to date and his parents reported that he now had several friends who frequently called him and came by to visit. Ralph's attitude toward this benevolent interference in his life was somewhat mixed. He was pleased that the therapist wanted things to go well for him but stated that he felt bad that he could not do it on his own. At no time, however, did he ask the therapist to stop interfering nor did he seem angry or resentful about the fantasized intrusion into his personal life.

This phenomenon persisted for approximately four months and then was abruptly dismissed as "a silly idea." During these four months Ralph solidified his social situation and his academic performance converted to almost straight A's without much apparent effort on Ralph's part.

Ralph's case is more clear cut than many involving youngsters with malignant problems. Ralph's solutions to his conviction that he could never be competent were mental and psychological. Therefore they were closer to the neurotic patients that we understand so well than those defenses encountered in many of the more violently acting out youngsters. Ralph did use drugs and massive withdrawal, but these were never totally embraced. In addition, since Ralph had some capacity for reflection, it is somewhat easier to follow the inner experience of the transference. However, the same kind of absurd idealization and unrealistic expectation of help that Ralph brought to therapy can be observed in the antisocial youngster who becomes attached to his or her therapist. Overhearing "my therapist can whip your therapist" conversations on a residential program for antisocial youngsters can be quite enlightening.

The basic point is simply that Ralph and his more aggressive counterparts will view their therapists differently than the neurotic patient. Our readiness to accept unrealistic and even outrageous temporary roles in these patients' lives is important, particularly early in therapy. Some of these roles may offend our identity as scientifically oriented, democratic, liberal, objective, and realistic permissive helpers. We may at times have to assume active postures, promise results, demonstrate and even remember and recount the patient's progress for them, and finally, gradually accept their demystification and humanization of us.

Kohut (1971) described a process of normal development characterized by a gradual disillusionment with the narcissistically invested idealized parental image. This disillusionment occurs without any direct verbal disavowal of omnipotent powers on the part of the adult. The unavoidable frustration of unrealistic hopes regarding the adult leads to gradual relinquishing of unrealistic wishes. In the psychotherapeutic relationship, relinquishing this illusion is, of necessity, telescoped in time and tends to be enormously painful and regularly accompanied by alternating periods of depression and rage directed toward the therapist.

Davy, a 16-year-old boy, was admitted to a psychiatric hospital because of a suicide attempt. In the hospital setting he appeared markedly inhibited, frightened of his age-mates, and often nearly psychotic in his fearfulness of the environment and in his capacity to drift into long periods of reverie during which he seemed totally uninterested in his surroundings. The developmental history revealed that Davy had always been extraordinarily dependent on his mother who regarded him as an extremely sensitive, intelligent, and a "very special human being." He had never had good peer relationships and had tended to be the scapegoat in his classes throughout his school experience.

In his individual sessions Davy spoke very little to his therapist regarding personal matters. He was quite willing to discuss his hobbies that included sports (though he did not participate personally), literature, and music. In all of these areas Davy was unusually well informed and showed a quick and incisive logic that was quite impressive for his age. When pressed to discuss his personal difficulties including the suicide attempt, he would become evasive. If the pressure was continued, Davy would simply clam up.

In family therapy, however, Davy began to express his concern about being overly dependent on his parents and began to ventilate feelings of frustration and anger when his mother's behavior seemed to him to be infantilizing. He also began to rebel against being the scapegoat in the peer group and twice became involved in physical fights when he felt he was being "pushed around."

As his general functioning improved, it was decided that Davy could be discharged from the hospital and followed in outpatient treatment. This decision was maintained even though Davy quickly reverted to his social isolation on his return home. Although he continued to decry his inability to relate to people outside his family, he could not bring himself to make any active efforts to change that state of affairs.

In his individual treatment, Davy began to speak more freely about himself and his ideas. At the same time he seemed overly interested in the virtual "honor" of being a patient of his therapist. He was preoccupied with the therapist's national reputation, complimented the therapist on the brilliance and subtlety of his simplest statements, and sang the therapist's praise to his family and anyone else who would listen. During this period he confided a variety of grandiose wishes and fantasies about himself and also recounted some embarrassing and frightening daydreams and wishes. He was particularly concerned about some homicidal fantasies and admitted that his suicide attempt was partially an effort to "rid the world of a potential murderer."

As the months went by, the unqualified admiration of the therapist continued but a new theme of identification with this power and Davy's self-adulation became increasingly clear. For example, Davy would develop complex, imaginative metapsychological theory systems and present them in detail to the therapist. The manner of presentation suggested that he was attempting to earn the admiration of the therapist through emulation of the therapist's area of interest. Although there were some undercurrents of competitiveness, these seemed much less important than the desire to be praised by a "hero" figure.

Gradually, however, Davy began to look for clay feet. He devised situations, such as refusing to attend school, that created crises in which the therapist was powerless. He also showed a wry humor directed at the exalted image of the therapist that he had created. Usually Davy reacted with open anger and disappointment when the therapist had to cancel appointments. During this period, however, Davy suddenly accepted an absence with cheerful indifference. When asked why he wasn't upset this time, Davy replied, "I've come to accept that it's just part of having a semi-famous psychiatrist."

Davy was quite depressed during this period. The disappointment of recognizing the therapist's human limitations and lack of magical power was clearly painful. Davy varied between grief and rage toward the therapist. Only gradually was he able to begin to struggle realistically with his own life. After two and a half years of therapy Davy grudgingly admitted, "I guess I'm a lot less crazy than I was two years ago and I suppose you had something to do with that." For the therapist this was quite a comedown from his previous grandeur in Davy's eyes, but for Davy it was a significant improvement in his ability to recognize the genuine value of another human being.

Kernberg (1984) described in detail the primitive defenses that the borderline youngster uses. He comments particularly on the defense of splitting that is often employed in varying combinations with the unrealistic idealization just described. It is important that the therapist listen attentively to the negative feelings of rage and frustration expressed toward others during the period when the therapist himself is idolized. It can be safely assumed that this hostility and depreciation will eventually be expressed in the transference also. Other youngsters may begin therapy by presenting the negative side of their tendency to split. These youngsters may continue to idealize their parents or other adults and utilize the therapist as the target of their negative projections. This is particularly likely because of projective identification, commonly utilized by these youngsters, which leads them to fear that the therapist is harboring those destructive impulses that are, in fact, struggling for expression in their own minds.

It is important to remember that these styles of relating are not "defensive" in the usual sense. They are more akin to "acting-in"—a demonstration within the treatment situation of serious deficiencies in their previous relationships with parenting figures. They require a gradual living through of these primitive ways of attaching to another human in order to repair damaged or undeveloped intrapsychic personality structures. The self-object patterns of relating in therapy may take several different forms.

THE THERAPIST AS A CORRECTIVE SUPEREGO FIGURE

Another atypical relationship that frequently proves constructive without actually measuring up to a genuine therapeutic alliance occurs with some youngsters who present with superego pathology. Johnson (1949), writing about the treatment of youngsters with superego lacunae, has provided important guidelines in this area. She felt that a major aspect of the treatment relation with these youngsters is concerned with the search for an incorruptible adult model. In treating youngsters with superego defects, the therapist must remain comfortably alert to the inevitability of efforts to corrupt her conscience. One can be sure that the patient will, with varying degrees of subtlety, try to get the therapist to join him in breaking rules or at least in condoning the youngster's asocial or antisocial behavior.

One therapist described a situation with a patient who was being interviewed in the course of a stroll. The adolescent was drinking a soda and as the therapist and patient passed a fence with a large sign that said "NO TRESPASSING," the patient casually tossed his empty can over the fence. The therapist was briefly in a quandary since any action on her part seemed to be corrupt. If she said nothing, the patient could assume that she countenanced the littering. If she allowed the patient to climb the fence in order to retrieve the can, that would involve defying the clearly posted sign. Fortunately, she had the presence of mind enough to stop and reflect out loud on the dilemma. She said that though it was hardly the end of the world, she preferred to follow rules even in this somewhat trivial matter. She considered the possibilities open to her and the patient's interpretation of them. She carefully avoided suggesting that the patient had deliberately put her in this moral bind. Her demeanor made it clear that she did not intend to move on or continue the discussion until a solution within the rules could be fashioned. After a few minutes of this the patient said sarcastically but with an undertone of respect, "Oh, if you're such a goody two shoes, I'll get you out of this one." He picked up a fallen limb, raked the can to the fence, retrieved it, and dropped it into a trash barrel. The therapist complimented him on his ingenuity and thanked him for solving her dilemma.

Other youngsters may utilize the therapist more directly to strengthen their reality testing and superego controls. A handsome and muscular 15-year-old boy with a history of multiple juvenile offenses regularly insisted to his therapist that he "didn't give a damn" what the therapist thought of his behavior.

In spite of this avowal, he gradually began to describe his planned antisocial behavior in advance during his therapy sessions. For example, he would tell the therapist that he badly needed some material object that he did not have the money to buy. He would then talk about the possibility of stealing the object or of dealing in drugs in order to obtain funds. The patient would then state that he knew the therapist disapproved of such activities but would then challenge the therapist as to how the problem could be solved without getting into trouble. At these times the therapist would offer various alternatives such as doing extra work around the home to obtain funds or saving up his allowance. Inevitably the patient would scoff at the advice, but invariably he would follow it. The patient would then return to the next session to complain that the solution was dumb and that he preferred to do things as he had done them in his antisocial past. In spite of this constant harping and apparent hostility, the patient continued to grow and develop, not only avoiding legal problems but showing steady improvement in school work, family relationships, and socialization.

Another 15-year-old boy with strong delinquent tendencies and a history of almost homicidal rage outbursts and physical fights showed sudden and persistent improvement in his functioning shortly after he was hospitalized in an adolescent psychiatric unit. During group psychotherapy another patient asked the boy why he had stopped fighting with everyone and the patient explained, "My doctor is a champion boxer. I'm not about to tangle with that guy." The patient had learned that the therapist was a boxer from a hospital employee who had known the therapist in high school. In fact, the therapist was 10 pounds lighter than the patient and had not boxed in 20 years. In situations of this kind, the patient creates the therapist in some image that allows emergency control of his frightening impulses. It is important to recognize that although these images may be somewhat primitive and at variance with the self image of benevolent nurturing preferred by the therapist, they may be temporarily important to the patient. For a brief period the patient may need to provide himself with the fantasy of someone strong enough and aggressive enough to counter the tempestuous violence within himself. The image of this helpful authority can be gradually modified as the therapist demonstrates in his direct management of the patient a kinder, warmer, but still reliable style of impulse control.

We are on relatively uncharted ground when we accept or at least do not directly disavow such unrealistic images of ourselves. For one thing, we are much more vulnerable to countertransference errors because we are less guided by our tradition and training. Treatment relationships of this kind approach patterns described in psychodrama and go well beyond Franz Alexander's notion of the corrective emotional experience. Since the therapist at least passively takes a role in the externalized drama created by the adolescent patient, there is considerable danger that the adolescent may be used for self-gratification. For example, if the patient places one in the position of a powerful superego figure, the therapist may unconsciously enjoy exercising this power and authority over another person's life. This gratification may prevent the therapist from helping the adolescent take control of his own destiny.

It is apparent that these special relationships must be regarded as temporary stages in treatment. Aichorn (1925) stated that the therapist who assisted the delinquent youngster by permitting and encouraging narcissistic transferences could not continue the treatment at the point where the patient became more neurotic and thus available for a more intensive and dynamic treatment experience. However, Aichorn actively pursued a transference of this kind and may have thereby limited his availability as an object of other transference tendencies. In some cases it does appear that the patient can come to understand his need for a distorted image of the therapist, work through this need, and proceed to a more traditional alliance with the same individual.

The therapist must take complete responsibility for sorting out the emotional currents in these atypical treatment alliances. In the traditional therapeutic alliance, this responsibility can be shared to a greater extent with the patient. Supervision with peers or with more experienced psychotherapists is an important aid in maintaining objectivity and in preventing countertransference errors. Self-scrutiny is also very important.

In reviewing these somewhat unusual psychotherapeutic encounters, one can utilize the same questions that shed light on transference patterns with any patient.

"How does the patient seem to wish to view me?"

"What does he want from me?"

"What is this role that he is placing me in doing for his psychological functioning?"

The answers to these questions require a careful understanding of the patient's developmental history, his current level of psychological functioning, and his overall life situation. When the questions can be answered with some degree of accuracy, the therapist can consider further questions.

"To what extent is it ethical and comfortable for me to serve this function for the adolescent patient?"

"Can this style of relating conceivably lead eventually to healthier psychological functioning for the adolescent patient?"

It does seem possible in some cases to assist a troubled adolescent without ever achieving a genuine therapeutic alliance. As implied earlier, perhaps the mechanism of growth is related to the adolescent's use of the therapist as a "real object." In these cases the patient creates in the person of the therapist a particular adult image that can be internalized to complete aspects of development that had not been previously realized. As in the case of Ralph, these notions regarding the therapist may be quietly discarded when the patient no longer requires them. In other situations, as was the case with Davy, the unrealistic expectations of the therapist are relinquished only with great reluctance and pain.

BASIC TECHNIQUES IN YOUNGSTERS WITH MALIGNANT RESISTANCES

The alert reader may be asking, "Aren't you now suggesting the development of unholy alliances? Just a chapter ago you were warning us against them."

True, the therapist *did* accept, even invite, a pathological super-ego alliance with Ralph. Why is it now an acceptable technique?

1. *Probably nothing else would have worked.* A previous effort to meet Ralph with a permissive therapeutic approach aborted quickly. Besides, Ralph was so totally preoccupied with moral ruminations little else interested him.

2. *The approach was used knowingly, recognizing that there would be repercussions that would have to be handled.* In Ralph's case these appeared as a benign delusion that the therapist was helping him through an omniscient and omnipotent intrusion into his daily life. In short, the relationship developed in this form because that was the level of Ralph's internal psychological organization, perhaps the only level at which Ralph could relate in an integrated, reasonably comfortable, sustained manner. The therapist accepted this and let Ralph come to utilize him as an idealized image as a step in integrating a picture of himself as a competent person. Initially Ralph could only believe that his success was the result of the therapist's activity on his behalf, but with this imagined safety, Ralph could experiment even more actively in the world.

There are a few changes in attitude that insight-oriented psychotherapists need to make in order to treat youngsters with malignant defenses.

1. *It is usually necessary to assume active control of the youngster's life to some extent.* With Ralph the control was merely verbal, but in other cases it may be necessary to use the power of the juvenile court, overt parental pressure, or residential placement. This active stance is almost always necessary in order to interrupt the youngster's effort to maintain omnipotent defensive maneuvers. A creative variant of this active role is the use of a "bogeyman" as described by O'Connor and Hoorwitz (1984). Obviously, many therapists do not enjoy taking direct and coercive action with the patients and need supervision and support in order to tolerate the patient's resulting anger and efforts to intimidate.

2. *Related to taking control is the need to function without a traditional alliance.* It is difficult to accept the distortions the patient

makes of the therapist's true role. This is especially true when the patient acts to discredit the therapist's role as a healer. This is often the case for an extended period. Remember that the patients are threatened by the possibility of disclosure to a much greater extent than are neurotic patients. To exaggerate, the neurotic youngster has an inferiority complex; these youngsters *are* inferior—at least that's the way it feels to them. They aren't just princes under an evil spell, they have never seen or even imagined their kingdom. Since they always feel the therapist is a threat to their illusions, they do not move toward a more trusting bond until much later in therapy. For a long time the therapist is viewed as an enemy to their basic security.

3. *The alliance, even when it is friendly and functional, tends to make the therapist something other than what he or she actually is.* The youngster uses the therapist as a "self-object," a replacement part in their own psychic machinery and often this means the child will focus on only a portion of the therapist's personality and attributes.

4. *The therapist needs to accept and learn to manipulate a "cast of thousands" rather than the intense dyad that we experience in psychotherapy of the neurotic.* The youngster with malignant defenses mobilizes friends to defend important emotional pretensions, populates the world with villains and heroes, and often manages to bring much of this into the therapy in very direct ways. These patients don't just talk of such things. The therapist gets irate phone calls, concerned visits, critical letters, and more. Efforts to collaborate with parents, school officials, probation officers, and even co-therapists turn into frustrating battles as the youngster's splitting and manipulating has each helping individual worried about the competence, motivation, and even intentions of the others. This is why team treatment in some form is necessary with these youngsters. As the youngster projects elements of his or her fragmented self onto different team members and then sees them harmonized as the team somehow reaches consensus, there is an opportunity for internalization, integration, and growth in the patient.

5. *The therapist must take responsibility for ensuring success experi-*

ences for the patient. This includes providing appropriate remediation and academics or social skills; taking an active, even inspirational and exhortative, educational role in treatment; and then serving as the patient's memory and "scorekeeper" so that successes are noted and recalled by the patient.

6. *The therapist must accept limited goals even after great efforts.* These youngsters do not tend to "get well" in the sense that many neurotic youngsters do. They often improve and show growth as Kohut has described by becoming more creative, wiser, and more able to laugh at themselves and others but without moving beyond a basically narcissistic personality and lifestyle. They also remain vulnerable and often need periodic brief contact with the therapist during periods of stress even after formal therapy has ended.

SUMMARY

Adolescent therapists are encountering many adolescents who do not respond well to traditional psychotherapy. Our challenge is to treat these youngsters with sensitivity to their special needs without being drawn into antitherapeutic pathological interactions. In this effort we do not yet have the clear and time-tested guidelines that exist for treatment approaches to the neurotic and therefore we are at greatest risk for countertransference error, especially since, in order to be effective, we often must be more active. Our best protection is always supervision, peer supervision, and personal therapy when necessary. Gradually our skills in using ourselves as instruments to help these "malignantly" disturbed adolescents will improve.

We cannot adequately discuss the various forms these "malignant" action defenses may assume. For example, many youngsters with severe eating disorders including anorexia nervosa and some cases of bulimia probably have similar basic psychopathology. In their case, control of food intake and weight becomes the narrow, artificial world in which they try to exercise an omnipotent control. Many of them have borderline personality organization but their effective treatment is complicated by the nutritional and medical complications generated by the symptom. There is considerable controversy at this point about effective therapeutic approaches and the reader is advised to carefully study a broad range of the recent literature in order to prepare for effective treatment of these difficult young people.

CHAPTER 5

the problems of ongoing psychotherapy with the adolescent

GOALS AND TECHNIQUES OF PSYCHOTHERAPY WITH THE ADOLESCENT

Most, if not all, therapists would agree that even the neurotic adolescent patient is not a candidate for a total resolution of psychological conflict through psychotherapy. The goal, instead, should be to assist the adolescent to achieve an ego synthesis that would permit him a moderate degree of gratification within the limits of social reality. This synthesis may include many areas of unresolved conflict managed, bound, and partially neutralized by productive, growth-oriented compromise character formations. After all, the proper concern of adolescence is the construction of a viable and sustaining identity. The further refinement of personality is the task of young adulthood.

The basic tool in the psychotherapy of the adolescent is the youngster's relationship to the therapist, with the opportunities that this permits for new emotional learning experiences and the more effective utilization of emotional systems existing in the patient. It is within this interaction that the adolescent can gradually recognize his emotional needs and learn which of them must be modified and which can be gratified safely in interaction with other human beings. He may also learn that he is more capable and effective than he thought.

UTILIZING THE THERAPEUTIC ALLIANCE

The Therapist As a Trusted Adult Friend

The very existence of a comfortable therapeutic alliance has substantial inherent and immediate value to the adolescent. It permits the adolescent to be dependent without the dangers involved in his dependent ties to his parents. The adolescent needs a trusted adult outside his family group, but may have few opportunities to find such a relationship in a society characterized by isolation of neighborhoods and lack of social cohesion. It is a necessary and valuable function of therapy to provide this kind of relationship.

The therapeutic alliance allows a moderate degree of psychological support, guidance, and reassurance to the adolescent. Most adolescents seek and will utilize advice and opinions from their therapist, especially if the therapist shows no special interest in controlling them or in demonstrating his adult superiority. In many adolescents, marked psychological growth follows merely from the opportunity to speak freely with an adult who quietly demonstrates his interest and respect.

Closely related to the supportive function is the educational role of the therapist. Often, the adolescent longs for an adult who can offer factual answers to troubling questions. Adolescents still worry that they may be sexually abnormal despite the increase in sexual sophistication in our time. The questions are more refined, and often more disguised, since few modern teenagers consciously fear that masturbation will drive them to insanity or cause hair to grow on the palms of their hands. Fear of homosexual impulses, concern about the size and appearance of genitals, worries over sexual attractiveness, concerns about body size or shape, unrealistic self-expectations in the dating game, fears of being hypersexed or hyposexed, and the like are commonly brought to the therapist. Although these questions can rarely be settled by education alone, since they often are partially rooted in unconscious conflicts, the adolescent deserves truthful answers. This at least helps the adolescent to distinguish those concerns that are realistic from those that are related to his personal problems.

A 16-year-old boy finally was able to drop his bravado and confess his feeling that girls did not like him. He felt that he was ugly, even grotesque. He said that this bitter conviction was a major cause of his multiple delinquencies. The therapist asked how he knew that girls did not like

him. As the boy discussed his interaction with girls, it became clear that he treated them in a haughty and superior
manner to avoid being rejected.

The therapist encouraged him to try being friendlier to a
few girls in his class and to report his results. He returned
discouraged. He had tried friendliness, but nothing happened. The boy was further encouraged to ask one of the
girls for a date. The therapist explained that the boy
looked like a regular guy to him. He should take a chance,
even though there was always the possibility that his offer
would be rejected. The boy was told that girls expected to
be pursued and that he could not expect them to show
interest in him if he did not woo them. The therapist even
helped plan an evening that a girl would enjoy and appreciate. Along with the practical advice, the youngster was
openly encouraged and supported. The invitation was accepted, and the evening proved at least a partial success.
The boy began dating fairly actively. His emotional reactions to dating experiences opened the door to exploration
of the boy's sexual conflicts. Among other things, it soon
became clear that the virtual delusion that he was ugly was
related both to his "ugly" (that is, sexual) thoughts about
girls and his perception of his mother's view of men and
her early reaction to the sight of his penis.

Without the practical help and advice on dating procedures, which barely stopped short of dialing the telephone
for him, the work of therapy could not have continued.

Dating is only one social reality that the adolescent may not
understand. Some have a poor concept of how families, schools,
communities, and governments function. The disillusionment
that often follows the loss of childish belief in the perfection of
hallowed institutions may lead to a bitter cynicism. After some of
this disappointment is worked through, extensive reeducation
regarding many aspects of the social and political facts of life may
aid in the process of maturation. Although the therapist should
not present himself as a fount of wisdom on all subjects, he can
raise questions and cite experiences that broaden the adolescent's view of his world. Since honesty is the cornerstone of the

therapeutic relationship, this implies a willingness to admit that institutions are considerably less than perfect. As a rule, these discussions are much more valuable after the adolescent's superego can permit him to admit that he is not perfect either. He can then use knowledge of society's faults and problems as a guide to productive adaptation rather than a defensive self-justification.

In the case of the more seriously damaged and deficient youngsters we discussed in chapter 4, the therapy must often be more actively educational. Often the assistance of expert educators in special areas is necessary. The adolescent may need remedial education; methodical, detailed social skills training; or organized and formal help with values clarification. As mentioned earlier, this introduces the "team" into the therapy experience and often provides many opportunities for splitting that have to be recognized and utilized constructively. Since these teams have historically functioned mainly in inpatient settings, much of the useful literature on the subject is found in discussions of inpatient treatment (Zinner, 1978; Schwartz, 1984; O'Connor and Hoorwitz, 1984).

The Therapist As Guide in the Search for Self-Understanding

These pedagogic and supportive roles, however, are secondary to the primary therapeutic goal of increasing the adolescent's insight into his own emotions and their effect on his attitudes and behavior. The therapist tries to teach the interested adolescent everything possible about his physical functioning and the world in which he lives, but this information is less valuable than those things that the adolescent learns about his own wishes, attitudes, and style of relating to other people. Information of this kind, however, cannot be taught at the level of intellectual discourse. It emerges almost as a byproduct of the experiential interaction between the adolescent and the therapist. The adolescent gradually reveals his emotional makeup in the interplay with his therapist. It is through the exploration of this living, vital experience with another individual in the here and now that the adolescent may be helped to know himself.

TALKING WITH THE ADOLESCENT—ON BEING NATURAL

In order to have a relationship of suitable intensity with the adolescent, the therapist must learn to conduct psychotherapy in a reasonably relaxed, conversational style. Most adolescents cannot tolerate a silent, totally passive "blank screen" technique or a stiff and stilted style of therapy, especially not early in the treatment process. For a variety of reasons, including their tender narcissism, their distrust of adults, and the expectation of moral criticism, they usually react to silence and formality with intense anxiety and increased defensiveness. The difficult technical dilemma is to be reasonably talkative and responsive without being directive or intrusive. Once the adolescent gets unwound and comfortable, the therapist's silence is viewed as a positive willingness to listen. This recommendation to "chat" with the adolescent does not imply an awkward attempt to speak "hip talk" or to act like an adolescent. The adolescent is usually turned off by an adult who does not conduct himself like a grownup. What is appreciated is an openly friendly, quietly cheerful manner designed to make the adolescent as comfortable in the office as his inner feelings will allow him to be.

It is sometimes possible to use humor with adolescents in order to create rapport, communicate a sense of mutuality, and even to interrupt the assumptions that the teenager is bringing to the evaluation or therapy meeting. Sometimes it works to inject a bantering or teasing comment into a conversation, as long as it is done in a way that communicates that the therapist accepts and cares about the client (Bernet, 1993; Salameh and Fry, 2001).

LET'S FIGHT IT OUT

Arguing with adult psychotherapy patients is generally discouraged and even recognized as an indication of countertransference. Adolescents, on the other hand, expect to argue. They spend a great deal of their time arguing with parents and friends. In these arguments, they are often learning and changing, although they rarely admit it at the time. Frequently, an adolescent patient ends one session fiercely defending some viewpoint against his therapist and opens the next session by emphatically stating the very opinion he was battling only a few days before. The adolescent usually does not bother to credit the therapist for those ideas and insights that he appropriates. Naturally, the wise therapist leaves well enough alone and does not demand a credit byline. Although the adolescent himself may push an argument to the bitter end, he expects his therapist to be able to admit when he is wrong. The adolescent therapist cannot afford the appearance of arrogant certainty and pompous self-assurance. If he uses his knowledge too forcibly, the therapist may find that he has won an argument but lost a patient. In fact, whenever possible, the therapist should admit areas of ignorance, especially when the adolescent is knowledgeable on the subject. Since adolescents are always being taught by adults, they appreciate the opportunity to demonstrate their knowledge. Usually, it is easy to find areas in which the adolescent knows more than the therapist if the therapist is comfortable enough to accept this reversal of roles. Often, these occasions develop around the discussion of dynamics and motivations. When the adolescent realizes that his opinions and ideas are respected and considered on their merit even when they conflict with a statement made by the therapist, the therapeutic relationship is strengthened. Since many adolescents find it almost impossible to admit it when they are wrong, they admire the adult who can do so without a loss in self-esteem. Since they often feel that they "know it all" while actually fearing that they know nothing, they can relax with an adult who easily admits areas of ignorance and imperfection while demonstrating a comfortable self-respect.

THE ROLE OF CONFRONTATION AND INTERPRETATION

Confrontations and clarifications involve showing the patient what he is doing either without knowing it or without recognizing its importance or its connection with other behaviors and attitudes. In interpretation, we address ourselves to why the patient performs certain actions or expresses certain thoughts. Interpretations are often further distinguished as interpretations of defense or resistance and interpretations of content or impulse. These distinctions have some value in organizing a discussion of interventions, but within the reality of the psychotherapy process, they often merge and overlap. In our example of the youngster who smoked in his therapy session, the confrontation (what the youngster was doing) led quickly to a consideration of the why of his behavior. This is the proper sequence of effective interventions, since they must concern observable behaviors or attitudes that are important to the patient in the here and now. This is especially important in adolescent psychotherapy, since the adolescent typically encodes his most important messages in behavior rather than words. Effective confrontations that decipher these loaded behaviors often lead to anxiety and the emergence of powerful affects. Often, the impulses behind these affective storms are extremely apparent to anyone who has some understanding of unconscious motivations. The adolescent may reveal rather directly impulses and fantasies that are seen in adults only in states of extreme regression whether these are pathological or deliberately induced through careful psychoanalytic work. These impulses should not be interpreted. Nothing can be gained by pointing out the adolescent's homosexual, incestuous, or homicidal wishes even when these seem virtually conscious.

This kind of awareness is not useful to the adolescent and can only further compromise an already overburdened ego. The therapist instead extends himself to support the adolescent's ego, encouraging healthy defenses and emphasizing the adolescent's control over unacceptable impulses. One of the most important jobs for the adolescent therapist is to recognize those times when the adolescent is fearful of losing control. The therapist then offers help by recognizing the anxiety and by trying to assist the adolescent to find ways in which he can deal with the emerging impulses.

DEFINITIONS RELATED TO PSYCHOTHERAPY

Transference is the projection of the client's feelings, thoughts, and wishes onto the therapist, who has come to represent an object from the client's past.

Countertransference is the projection of the therapist's feelings, thoughts, and wishes onto the client, who has come to represent an object from the therapist's past.

* * * * *

Ego-syntonic refers to ideas, impulses, or behaviors that are acceptable to the ego and compatible with its principles.

Ego-dystonic refers to ideas, impulses, or behaviors that are not acceptable to the ego and are rejected. A synonym is ego-alien.

* * * * *

The ego is the part of the mind that mediates between the person and reality. Ego functions include perception, self-awareness, motor control, memory, affects, thinking, synthesizing external and internal experience, and mental creativity.

The id refers to the unconscious part of the mind that consists of sexual and aggressive drives.

The superego is the part of the mind, largely unconscious, that represents the person's moral principles and ideal aspirations.

* * * * *

Primary narcissism refers to the omnipotent feeling of infants that is disproved by experience and frustration. Longing for this lost feeling remains as narcissistic needs.

Secondary narcissism refers to the good feelings derived from the affection and admiration of parents and others.

The *Psychiatric Dictionary* (Campbell, 1996) is a good place to look up unfamiliar terms that are related to psychotherapy.

A large, aggressive, 16-year-old borderline youngster was regularly confronted with the fact that much of his behavior suggested a need to intimidate and compete with his therapist. This led to extensive discussion of his father's worship of his athletic prowess that was accompanied by excessive physical affection that verged on homosexual seduction.

In one session, the boy became extremely excited, anxious, and agitated as he compared himself with the therapist. He shouted that he was more intelligent, stronger, and "more of a man" than the therapist. The therapist agreed that he was a fine young man, but also noted that he seemed worried that he would misuse his capacities or only use them to show up other people. The therapist expressed his confidence that the boy would make constructive use of his abilities. The youngster calmed down somewhat and recognized that he had been saying, in effect, that he had a "super-penis." He laughingly asked, "I guess I made it sound like it was long enough to pole-vault with, eh?"

In the next session, he reported a wild session of joking fantasy with a male friend in which they carried the idea of penile size to more and more ridiculous extremes. They had collapsed in hysterical laughter over the recognition that the man with a "super SUPER penis" would not be able to wear normal clothing or even drive a car for fear of an erection. The homosexual nature of the fantasy was implied as the patient and his friend joked about the insoluble problems that the girl friend of such a man would face.

The therapist accepted the joke and joined in the laughter. Later, he added that the youngster seemed also to be making an important and serious point about manhood, namely, that there was much more to being a man than physical attributes or even intellect. Although positive potentials were important, their constructive utilization was of even greater consequence. This episode seemed to be a turning point, and gradually the youngster was able to apply some of his competitive energy in more productive pursuits.

In short, confrontations are commonly used in the psychotherapy of the adolescent. On the other hand, interpretations of
unconscious content are rarely indicated. When such impulses
must be mentioned, as in our example above, the emphasis is
properly on the fear of their expression. Such interpretations of
fear of loss of control are accompanied by acceptance and support of any defense that is adaptive (or even just harmless) that
the adolescent can muster to regain his sense of self-mastery. It
should be noted that defenses suggested by the therapist are
rarely useful to the adolescent. In fact, suggesting specific activities to handle an anxiety and replace acting out behavior usually
interferes with the therapeutic alliance. The adolescent reacts as
he does to well-meaning adults who counsel, "Instead of running all over town with those weirdo long-haired friends of
yours, why don't you stay home and read a good book?" Only
the adolescent can really feel his itch, and only he can figure out
where to scratch himself.

Although we feel that this basic approach holds generally
with adolescent patients, there is an exception to the rule. This
occurs with adolescents who are painfully aware of wishes,
ideas, or fantasies that they regard as insane and terrifying.
These youngsters need open discussion of their fears of homosexuality, incest, or murder in order to learn that these ideas
need not lead to action or to psychosis, but may be treated as
uncomfortable but harmless thoughts. Confusions of this kind
frequently develop in youngsters with limited intellectual ability
or borderline ego function.

Mark was a good looking, husky boy of 16 who had a
tested Full Scale IQ of 87. His academic performance was
extremely poor in the highly competitive school setting
that his ambitious parents forced on him. In addition, he
showed an intense and unreasoning contempt for his
mother despite all her efforts to show affection and concern for him. This antipathy was pushing Mark toward
delinquency.

Gradually, the therapist began to recognize that Mark
was terrified of being alone with his mother. Over a period

of several months, a therapeutic alliance developed and the therapist felt that he must approach the matter directly with Mark.

"Mark," the therapist said one day, "I get the feeling that your mother scares you."

"Naw," Mark said. "But she is trying to ruin me."

"I'm not sure I understand what you mean by that."

"Well, it ain't something I can tell you, but she's trying to ruin me."

The therapist considered his choices. From a number of things Mark had said, he felt sure that the boy's fears of his mother were generated primarily by incestuous wishes. He also knew that Mark's thinking was extremely concrete and that he would probably misinterpret his mother's hysterical mannerisms. He decided to take the bull by the horns.

"Mark," he said, "have you ever had the feeling that your mother wanted you to fuck her?"

Mark hardly hesitated. He seemed relieved that things were out in the open.

"Yeah. She does want me to. It's not just something I think. She doesn't sleep with my dad. I don't think she ever has. She wants me to screw her."

The therapist knew that since Mark was adopted, it would be impossible to prove to him that his parents, in spite of separate bedrooms, did have intercourse. Instead, he elected to focus on Mark's direct perceptions of family reality.

"When did you first get the idea that she wanted you to have sex with her?"

"When she used to take nude sunbaths outside my window. I'd watch her and get a hard-on."

The therapist explained that any teenage boy would react with excitement to the sight of a nude woman whether it was his mother or not. He assured Mark that his feelings were perfectly normal under the circumstances.

The next several sessions were devoted to convincing Mark that if he acted on his idea that his mother was seducing him it would lead to much trouble for him. The therapist patiently explained that some women, including Mark's mother, had a strong need to be admired and loved. They did not know how to meet these needs except by sexually teasing men, even including their own sons. However, they were not really aware of what they were doing and would be horrified and frightened if the men responded to their sexual provocation. Mark was told flatly, "Boys do not screw their mothers, no matter how things may appear."

Following this period of therapy, Mark began to make a few friends outside of the home and even attracted a girl friend. He continued to be somewhat cautious and distant around his mother, but did not constantly criticize her as in the past. He came to refer to his incestuous wishes as "those dumb thoughts I used to have."

GENERAL MANAGEMENT OF TRANSFERENCE WITH ADOLESCENTS

Younger adolescents feel intensely and use projection with abandon. They often are totally unaware that their picture of another person is constructed within their own mind. Their transference feelings usually seem totally real to them. This holds not only in therapy, but in their relationships with other adults and peers. We have discussed the narcissistic needs that give rise to this style of relating in the chapter on the dynamics of adolescence. Because of this characteristic, the primary problem in managing transference in adolescent therapy is simply to convince the adolescent that the projection originates within his mind, not in external reality. This undertaking is, like much of life, easier to describe than to accomplish.

First of all, there is the adolescent's compelling need to be right in his opinion of others. He is struggling to construct a world that makes sense to him and within which he can live. Marked distortions are desperately defended, since to relinquish them would expose him to a confusing external world and to confusion within himself. He would be left without confidence in himself as one who can see life, including other people, clearly. Part of his desperate defensive structure designed to control his sexual and aggressive drives is founded in this obsessive concern with "being right" and being in control.

For most adolescent patients, considerable educational work must precede any clarification of transference distortions. The aim of this educative effort is to lead the adolescent to put his trust in a groping, gradual objectivity, rather than in an impulsive, intuitive, and subjective global grasp of interpersonal relationships. Later, when his intuitions are less defensive in origin, he can learn to trust them again and to utilize these "hunches" in conjunction with a reasoned, "secondary process" approach to life.

Many techniques may be valuable in accomplishing this goal. Often, it is wise to begin with work on those distortions produced by other people. The adolescent may describe a friend who has changed his attitude radically toward the patient or another person. The patient may be shown how both attitudes were based more on the friend's inner needs than on the characteristics of the object. It can be further pointed out that this is a common tendency in human relationships. The technique of universalization may be extensively utilized in this area. The therapist may wish to offer a benign personal anecdote if one comes to mind.

This educative groundwork will need to be repeated until the adolescent seems to get the idea. When he begins to offer illustrations of his own, concerning himself or others, these are accepted and the adolescent should be given credit for his wisdom. The simple comment, "I think you're right," from the therapist may encourage the adolescent to continue his objective scrutiny of interpersonal judgments.

A 16-year-old girl was panicky about her relationship with a special girl friend. She lived in constant fear of offending the friend. This came to a climax when the friend called and dramatically demanded that the patient bring her drugs for a suicide attempt. When the patient refused, her friend became very angry and accused her of never wanting to help!

The patient was finally able to recognize that her friend
was determined to feel rejected by others and had to engineer situations in which this would be unavoidable. Since
the patient had similar tendencies both within therapy and
with others, it was possible to use this insight productively
later in her treatment. Whenever she was angry because
the therapist had opposed self-destructive behavior, he
would say, "Now you know I dislike you, since I won't even
help you kill yourself."

THE ADOLESCENT WHO LIVES FOR POWER STRUGGLES

In some patients, there is little opportunity to build a background for acceptance of transference clarifications. These
youngsters enter therapy with a flurry of hostile allegations
about the therapist. They view the therapist as a computer, already programmed with preconceived ideas and attitudes about
them and with very definite plans for their future. Many of these
youngsters come from families in which virtually no limitations
were set by parents. Instead, the parents have relied on cunning
and underhanded techniques for influencing behavior. It is useless to deny the accusations of these youngsters, since experience
has taught them that their parents deny their intrusive control
while continuing to practice it. "We don't want to tell you what to
do; we only want you to be happy. Now here's what you must do
in order to be happy." It also does little good to ask what they
themselves want to do. Their interest is only in opposing what
they imagine to be the therapist's wishes, not in asserting their
own. If you insist that you are interested in their wishes, they
often reply that their wish is to quit therapy, run away from
home, or take some other action that any responsible adult would
have to oppose out of concern for their welfare.

It is difficult to relate to youngsters of this kind, since their
whole existence is bound up in soliciting control struggles.
Strictly speaking, their attitude toward the therapist is not an
expression of transference so much as a symptom and a way of
life. One can only empathically accept their anger and frustra-

tion while sharing in a friendly way the awareness that no therapist could please them, since they are determined to pick a
fight. Therapy is designated then as a friendly battle (at least
friendly on the therapist's side) and the therapist accepts his
adversative role with as much grace and humor as he can manage. It is important to credit the adolescent with his victories in
these sallies. Often in these cases, no true therapeutic alliance
forms, and the therapist is actually conducting supportive psychotherapy, functioning more as an unaccepted and unsung
guardian than a true psychotherapist. However, this role may
be literally lifesaving for some of these youngsters. Some of
them return, when they are older, with greater capacity to cooperate in therapy.

As mentioned in chapter 4, other youngsters form atypical
alliances that do permit genuine emotional growth if the therapist can be flexible. The transferences are basically narcissistic
with varying degrees of idealization and use of the therapist as a
self-object. The differences are mainly related to the adolescent's greater tendency to act on transference distortions. This
tendency toward action requires the therapist to have some
genuine external control of the patient's life to avoid potentially
hazardous acting out. Usually the family can provide this external support to the treatment effort but in some cases, residential
care may be necessary to make treatment possible.

Of course, therapy is undertaken only if there is a clear and
compelling need for treatment. Some of these angry, narcissistic
adolescents discover productive and safe ways to engage their
environment and may mature and mellow considerably without
therapy. This sometimes permits the youngster to seek therapy
in a more cooperative frame of mind.

GARDEN VARIETY TRANSFERENCES

The more typical outpatient youngster shows transference
attitudes that are subtle and related to the material that is emerging in therapy. Although the younger adolescents still tend to
have difficulty in recognizing the internal origin of their trans-

ference attitudes, they can be prepared educationally to explore this possibility.

It is important to recognize and clarify transference as it appears. Often, the adolescent is reluctant to voice feelings about the therapist, especially if these are negative. It is usually up to the therapist to detect the tendencies implied in behavior and to verbalize them for the youngster at the proper time. For example, the adolescent may reveal a competitive oedipal transference by describing his accomplishments, only to diminish them quickly. The alert therapist notes this and assures the adolescent that he has a right to be proud of real accomplishments, noting that he behaves as though he expected the therapist to criticize either his accomplishment or his pride in it.

As in the next example, it is usually necessary with the adolescent to point out his unspoken assumptions while simultaneously clearly disclaiming the projected distortions. Words alone are often not enough. After the transference attitudes are clearly demonstrated, one must actively show by attitude, words, and behavior that they do not accurately reflect the therapist's true characteristics. In short, the therapist tries to neutralize irrational transference distortions as quickly and totally as possible.

A 14-year-old boy was convinced that his therapist felt he was stupid. He was surprised when the therapist asked his advice about which make of automobile to purchase. The therapist asked for specific information that the youngster could easily supply from his extensive reading in this area. The youngster was especially impressed that the therapist actually wrote down the information he gave. Later, the boy expressed his amazement. The therapist said, "What's so strange about it? I know a lot about how people feel and behave. You know a lot about cars. You came to me for help; why shouldn't I ask for your help?"

In a similar way, the transference feeling that the therapist is uninterested may be offset by remembering the details of the patient's comments in a previous session or by actually offering practical help and advice.

Since the goal in adolescent psychotherapy is not to elicit

regression and a transference neurosis but to increase ego control, these active interventions are indicated. Transference is interpreted to the adolescent only to prevent interference with the therapeutic alliance. The therapist always acts to clarify the irrationality of the transference and to diminish its impact in the therapeutic situation.

This is not to say that transference attitudes are ignored or denied. The adolescent is not encouraged to pretend that his irrational feelings do not exist. These feelings are noted and brought to conscious attention. He is then helped to recognize that they originate in his own mind. Finally the patient is supported in his attempt to deal with them as creatively as possible. Every effort is made to interfere with the adolescent's tendency to deal with the therapist as a real object for libidinal or aggressive drives. It should be recognized that this is a difficult technical problem, since only the older adolescent is capable of maintaining objectivity toward intense transference attitudes. The younger patient needs a healthy dose of reality and early intervention to prevent the development of an explosive and destructive transference.

There are certain types of transference patterns that regularly appear in the treatment of adolescents. All of them interfere with the therapeutic alliance and with ego growth in the adolescent and therefore require early recognition and active management.

The Erotic Transference

Sexual transferences are common in adolescent psychotherapy. They are extremely frightening to the younger adolescent who has developed neither a comfortable acceptance of his sexuality nor the subtle ego techniques for expressing these feelings with any finesse. As a result, open manifestations of sexual transference during the psychotherapy of younger adolescents are often panicky eruptions of a rather crude kind. At other times, the feelings are held in fearful secrecy. They are apparent only in the blushing, agitated confusion of the adolescent's behavior.

Often, these youngsters simply cannot tolerate a young therapist of the opposite sex because of the overwhelming intensity
of their sexual fantasies.

Even though older adolescents are better prepared to modulate their feelings, they still must face the incestuous implications of their responses much more directly than the adult patient who can partially rationalize his feelings since the therapist
is an approximate age peer. The awakening of similar feelings
in adolescents places them in the same fearful oedipal situation
that they have been attempting to escape in their own family. If
these stirrings are not actively managed, the result is often a
precipitous flight from the danger represented by the therapy
relationship.

A 14-year-old girl squirmed and twisted in her chair
while telling her therapist of a fantasized relationship with
an older boyfriend. During the recital, she was in an intense state of excitement. Her twisting and turning resulted in extensive exposure of her genital area. Her comments were crudely suggestive and her seductiveness was
grossly evident. She seemed in a virtual frenzy of sexual
excitement mingled with intense anxiety.

The therapist commented that her mind seemed to be
more on fun than on the work of therapy. She agreed,
giggling. The therapist stated firmly and gravely that the
therapy hour was not a place for fun. She would have
opportunities for fun with her friends, but the therapist
was interested in understanding her feelings, not in having
fun with her. This firm disavowal of interest in her seductive overtures allowed the girl to gain control and returned
the emphasis of the session to therapeutic goals.

With great relief, she joked, "Boy, you're really old-
fashioned."

The therapist agreed firmly, "Yes, I am."

With older adolescents, the expression of erotic transference
feelings is more subtle and approaches that seen in adults. Still,
even the older adolescent can rarely handle sexual transference
feelings openly. It would be unwise to focus attention on their

origins or to encourage their elaboration. Instead, the therapist emphasizes their value in emotional growth and their defensive function, clearly and tactfully maintaining his unavailability as a real sexual object.

A 17-year-old girl left "gifts" for the therapist session after session. She forgot cigarettes, matches, change, and other small objects. During this time, she became more and more distant and quiet. When the therapist linked these two patterns of behavior, the girl blushed. She admitted to a fear that she might "get a crush" on the therapist. She did not want this to happen, since it would be humiliating and childish to have such a "puppy love."

The therapist assured her that she could feel friendly and emotionally close without necessarily developing a crush. He added that crushes were often expressions of liking and admiration which did not imply that the young person loved the elder in the same sense that she would someday love a person of her own age.

The therapist was attempting to offer himself as a friendly, supportive father figure who would not respond seductively to her.

The Omnipotent Transference

The omnipotent transference is even more seductive than the erotic transference with the adolescent. The expectation that the therapist will have answers to all questions and solutions for all problems bears enough similarity to some ordinary or at least fantasized relationships between the generations to be quite attractive. The therapist expects to offer some realistic advice and help to his adolescent patient in the normal course of conducting psychotherapy. It is easy to drift gradually into a relationship in which the adolescent presents as a helpless, idiotic emotional cripple, repeatedly rescued from disaster only because of the brilliance of the therapist.

As gratifying as such a situation may be to the therapist's narcissism and his own unresolved infantile omnipotence, it is catastrophic to the goals of psychotherapy. When these transference attitudes are challenged, the adolescent usually reacts with irritation or open anger. This occurs because the transference actually covers the adolescent's secret fantasy of personal omnipotence. After all, the adolescent grants the therapist his power! It is also the adolescent who enjoys its benefits. The therapist only serves as a dupe, fronting for the adolescent's defense against his fear of confronting reality without magical powers.

In adolescents with malignant defenses and basic fixation in pregenital, narcissistic psychopathology the issue is different. The transference manifestation of omnipotent expectations is not a relatively benign regressive phenomenon but rather the demonstration within the therapy of the core problem.

A 15-year-old boy who had been sexually and physically abused by his father was being treated in a residential treatment center. His father, out of his life for many years, yet technically retaining custody of the youngster, called and demanded to take the boy out of the center. The boy told his therapist he didn't want to see his father. When the therapist tried to discuss the legal and technical problems involved in keeping a legal parent away from his child, the boy began to scream and threaten the therapist.

"You hate me. You can keep him away if you want to. If you try to kill me, I'll kill you."

He was calmed with great difficulty only after the therapist promised him he would protect him against the parent.

Through the course of several years of therapy the patient only gradually gave up the feeling that his therapist had complete power over the events that affected the patient. This attitude persisted side by side with a fairly realistic recognition of the therapist's lack of omnipotence in other matters.

This kind of omnipotent transference cannot be avoided since it results not from countertransference but from the patient's personality structure. It is resolved only by a gradual process of idealization, carefully dosed disillusion, and gradual recognition of self-worth.

The Negative Transference

Adolescents, like younger children, can rarely tolerate continuing psychotherapy in the face of a strong negative transference. As indicated above, intense and pervasive negative feelings toward the therapist usually do not represent transference. They express, rather, an intensely negative attitude toward all adults in authority. Negative transference should also be differentiated from the defensive hostility that many adolescents flaunt. This "porcupine" attitude often covers painful feelings of shame, inadequacy, and anxiety. This defensive hostility often disappears when the adolescent recognizes that the therapist will respect his feelings. Some younger adolescents are so fearful of therapy that they cannot risk any positive attitudes toward the therapist. In this instance, the negativism represents an attempt to avoid therapy by forcing the therapist to reject them.

True negative transferences may appear early in therapy. This occurs when the therapist happens to resemble a disliked figure from the past. Such occurrences are rare. More frequently, early negativism results when intense ambivalence is split and the therapist is cast into the role of the bad parent. Often, the relationship with the parent improves superficially as a result of the split. If the parents cannot understand what is actually happening, they may consider the adolescent to be cured and withdraw him from therapy prematurely.

SOURCES OF NEGATIVE TRANSFERENCE FEELINGS. Later, in therapy, true negative transference attitudes are usually more subtle and disguised than the global rejection described in the patterns above. The therapist may realize he is being slyly depreciated, pointedly ignored, or craftily maneuvered into ridiculous positions. These situations are marked by the collapse of the therapeutic alliance and disinterest in the therapeutic work.

These vague, unstated negative attitudes must be brought into the open for discussion. From the therapist's point of view, they should be explored objectively to determine their origin. We have already described the normal and ubiquitous angry reaction to those interventions that cause narcissistic injury to the adolescent. Any comment that interferes with a functioning defense, thereby increasing anxiety, naturally arouses some hostile feelings toward the disturbing influence. These angry feelings are not truly transference phenomena. They are affective reactions to the reality of the therapy situation. They are tolerated by the adolescent only because both his positive feelings for the therapist and his growth experience within therapy give him hope that the overall process will be beneficial to him. Because of this positive orientation toward the future, he can accept some pain in the present. Since he has a sense of trust in the therapist's positive attitude, he can forgive some injuries to his pride.

When faced with a hostile patient, the therapist must also consider the possibility that he has actually attacked the patient. Whether the insult has been direct, as in an angry or deprecatory response to provocation by the adolescent, or indirect, as in a subtle betrayal of a confidence to the parents, the adolescent may be expected to retaliate angrily. To treat this reaction mistakenly as transference will only compound the therapeutic error.

THE THERAPIST AS FRUSTRATOR.   True negative transference reactions occur when situations in therapy reactivate earlier experiences in which negative attitudes toward important loved objects predominated. They appear whenever the therapist, as a representative of reality, is seen as opposing gratification of libidinal drives or appropriate "ego drives." They appear whenever the therapist himself seems to refuse to gratify emotional needs that appear legitimate and important to the patient. They also appear whenever the therapist is viewed as opposing appropriate drives for achievement, independence, and autonomy. Obviously, the feelings cannot be considered as transference if the therapist is in fact antagonistically opposed to his patient's wishes for pleasure and accomplishment. It is the inappropriate and incorrect projection of these attitudes originating from previous introjects which constitutes transference.

The therapist will, of course, unavoidably frustrate the adolescent. Therapy is designed to explore and investigate impulses, not to gratify them. However, the long-range goal of therapy is clearly to aid the patient to maximize gratification and minimize frustration.

The therapist may be seen as a frustrating parent when he questions the relative value of immediate pleasure as opposed to long-range goals. In the terminology of psychoanalysis, the therapist favors the reality principle over the pleasure principle. This stance is often mistaken for a generalized ascetic opposition to gratification. The adolescent has not as yet synthesized his drives with a wider appreciation of his own future survival and well-being. Often, he is willing to sacrifice prudent self-protection for the impulsive gratification of an immediate urge. Opposing this tendency frequently gains the therapist a reputation as a wet blanket with his adolescent patient.

Just as frequently the therapist can "spoil the fun" by interpreting the true motive behind certain "pseudolibidinal" activities. Pointing out that a planned seduction seems more hostile than sexual may produce intense resentment in the adolescent patient. Clarifying the destructive motives involved in helping a "friend" get drugs or run away from home can lead to rage at the therapist. In these instances, the therapist is calling attention to the hidden hostile pregenital components that the adolescent is attempting to "bootleg" under the guise of a loving act. It is this hidden hostility that is actually freed for expression toward the therapist. The therapist is accused of puritanical suppression to avoid recognizing that the rage actually belonged to the adolescent all along and was merely disguised, disowned, and projected.

On the other hand, the adolescent's anger because the therapist will not personally gratify his libidinal transferences is, from the adolescent's point of view, a justified response. The therapist is certain to let the adolescent down in this regard. The adolescent will direct many vague wishes and hopes toward his therapist. He may expect the therapist to fill various neurotic expectations magically. He may hope to become omnipotent, free of depressive feelings, or imbued with phallic power. He may hope for symbiotic nurture or libidinal gratification. Since the therapist cannot meet these needs, the adolescent will inevitably feel disappointed and even cheated. This, of course, produces feelings of anger toward the therapist, who may be viewed as spitefully withholding gratification.

"YOU DO NOT WANT ME TO SUCCEED." The adolescent patient who suspects the therapist of thwarting his ambitions is often struggling with strong destructive competitive urges. These may be oedipal or more primitive wishes to dominate or destroy the therapist completely. These urges cause guilt that may lead to fears of retaliation or to projection of the unacceptable impulses onto the therapist. These defensive maneuvers help to justify the hostile competitive feelings toward the therapist and partially relieve guilt and anxiety.

Management of the Negative Transference

In all instances of negative transference, there are basic rules that may help to restore the therapeutic alliance. First, the negative feelings must be accepted objective]y as additional experiential data for therapeutic exploration. Objective acceptance implies not only the avoidance of counterattack, but also a quiet yet firm refusal to accept unrealistic blame. Occasionally, therapists, in a well-intentioned eagerness to appear fair and open-minded, will accept excessive criticism and hostility from the adolescent without pointing out that the anger is irrational. This attempt to help the adolescent express his "true feelings" can interfere with the therapeutic process by implying that the feelings are justified by the therapist's personality or behavior. This obscures their intrapsychic and unconscious origin and confuses the patient. In addition, as Fromm-Reichmann (1950) pointed out, inviting the patient to express his hostility actually serves to prevent the genuine expression of hostility and to protect the therapist from hearing honest anger from his patients.

As the adolescent is encouraged to explore the causes of his anger (or annoyance or irritation, if the adolescent prefers to soften his terms) in the same way that he has learned to study his other feelings in therapy, some clues usually emerge that help to clarify the general origin of the anger. The therapist can begin to guess whether he is being seen as a "spoilsport," a selfish withholding parent, or a competitive bully. These transference attitudes can then be countered by the therapist's words and actions as described above in the general section on management of transference. The question of how far the transference feelings should be allowed to develop before they are actively neutralized can only be decided by clinical judgment. Older, healthier adolescents can tolerate longer and more thorough exploration of negative transferences, whereas younger and more disturbed youngsters need quick and active aid in reality testing in order to sustain the therapeutic relationship.

A successful intervention that dissolves the negative transference reaction is often followed by a period of regression and depressive affect in the adolescent. In some instances, this depression may be obscured for a period of time by a defensive elation. The depression results from some degree of awareness of the personal origin of the frustrated wishes and a dawning recognition that the wishes are incompatible with reality and must be abandoned. It is always sad to realize, even dimly, that a gratification must be relinquished. During this period, the therapist must steer a close course between excessive sympathy and cold, unfeeling objectivity. When the adolescent is mourning a lost illusion, he needs both empathic understanding of his sense of loss and help in remembering that what was lost was, after all, always only an illusion. The pleasures of reality, although sometimes dimmed by complexity and responsibility, at least have the advantage of actually existing. The therapist gently encourages the adolescent to recognize that, with all its faults, reality is the only dependable source of pleasure.

The Therapist As Superego

Clients of all ages frequently see their therapists as superego figures. This tendency is especially marked in adolescents. Indeed, the success of adolescent psychotherapy frequently hinges primarily on the skill with which superego conflicts are managed. These conflicts are strongly reflected in the therapeutic relation-

ship and produce countless complex dilemmas. It is quite difficult to guide an adolescent toward a self-respecting sense of firm
impulse control while also assisting him to relax the rigid, inflexi-
ble superego of latency.

Within the therapeutic relationship, the adolescent frequently
sidesteps this developmental task by projecting his superego onto
the therapist, as we have previously noted. All of the therapist's
interventions tend to be experienced as superego sanctions. Because of his moral preoccupation, it is difficult for the adolescent
to understand other rationales for foregoing the gratification of
any impulse.

WHAT DOES YOUR CONSCIENCE SAY?   The initial phase of the
work with the adolescent's superego conflicts consists of recognizing and clarifying the pattern of his internalized moral prohibitions. It is crucial to demonstrate that these are the adolescent's own taboos, which he is attempting to ignore, externalize,
or otherwise escape. The therapist insists, on the other hand,
that the route to real freedom demands open and honest confrontation with these internal policemen. They can be altered
only through conflict, not avoidance.

The techniques of confronting the adolescent with his own
superego vary with the particular personality structures that are
encountered. The most common pattern is the adolescent who
rebels against his own conscience and then reveals his guilt
through self-destructive behaviors. If the connection is repeatedly brought to the youngster's attention, he can gradually become aware of his sense of guilt and of the unconscious interdic-
tion that he is violating.

Other superego restrictions produce only inhibitions and personality constrictions. These may reveal themselves in therapy as
overcontrol of certain impulses or conversely as a defiant overemphasis on some aspect of life. For example, both the shy, inhibited adolescent and the brassy, insolently bawdy youngster may
be revealing strong unconscious guilt feelings around sexuality.

Some youngsters present their superego problems more
openly, clearly cognizant that their feelings of excessive guilt
are irrational. Other adolescents expect to be relieved of guilt

feelings while continuing to do things that are self-centered, exploitative, and destructive to others. There are also adolescents with defects in superego structure who require active confrontation. This is also necessary at times with youngsters who are attempting to escape superego pressures with various bribes and rationalizations.

A 17-year-old boy professed extremely high moral standards and was extremely critical of middle-class hypocrisy. At the same time, he did not hesitate virtually to blackmail his wealthy mother for money, utilizing the most flagrant and often dishonest manipulations to extort the cash that he wanted. This dishonesty was motivated by spiteful oral rage and rationalized on the basis that he had no respect for his mother and should get from her what he could. This behavior allowed the youngster to maintain a fantasy of symbiotic sustenance secretly while disavowing any sense of dependency. It gradually became clear that his secret delinquency was one source of the boy's nagging sense of inferiority.

He came to therapy one day nonchalantly planning the purchase of a new automobile. The therapist asked where he got the money, since the youngster had been complaining of being broke. The boy explained that he had told his mother that he had learned he had a terrific "inferiority complex" that might be ameliorated by driving a flashy car.

"You implied that you learned that from therapy?" the therapist asked.

"No, but if she wants to think that, it's sure okay with me. It's not my fault she's stupid."

"It isn't okay with me. I don't want to be part of your con game. Besides, you are throwing away your chances in therapy for a bunch of chrome and steel. I can't go along with that."

"What do you mean?"

"Do you have any idea of how much that lousy car is really costing you? If you want to live the life of a con artist, that's your business, but let's at least be honest about what you're doing when you come here."

THE THERAPIST'S VALUES.   It should be obvious that the therapist cannot remain completely neutral in moral questions. By
the very nature of his work and his technical operations, the
psychotherapist conveys a value system. Emotional honesty,
self-awareness, fairness in interpersonal relationships, and reasonable control of impulse, coupled with a tolerance of unacceptable fantasy and a preference for reality gratifications over
neurotic gratifications, are values that are revealed by the therapist's general approach to the adolescent. Whether these values
are derived from a scientific knowledge of the nature of man or
merely represent a personal credo that characterizes most people who become psychotherapists is a debatable point. The
therapist should be aware of the moral assumptions that he
holds, regardless of their origins.

Since the adolescent therapist is even more of a pedagogue
than his adult therapist counterpart, he should not hesitate to
admit his moral biases frankly and to defend them energetically. Since the younger adolescent tends toward a "black or
white," right or wrong view of morality based primarily on
institutional sanctions, it is useful to him to discuss some of the
more rational and informed foundations for moral conduct.
Some degree of sexual restraint has more to recommend it
than a puritanical fear of sin or a terror of the social stigma of
illegitimate pregnancy. The dangers of exploiting others or of
being exploited and the difficulties involved in accepting emotional responsibility for the sexual partner are only two of the
issues that would recommend some degree of caution in sexual
expression. It should be kept in mind, however, that the honest
expression of one's own moral stance does not mean attempting to impose that morality on the adolescent patient. The
youngster must reach his own definition of right and wrong
and live by that.

The adolescent is not only involved in a dramatic unconscious
moral upheaval; he is also learning to think out his value system. The therapist must provide not only professional help in
understanding the internal struggle, but a model as a rational
adult with considered opinions regarding the proper conduct

and meaning of life. He does not force these views on his young patient, but neither does he attempt to avoid his responsibility as an adult to offer his ethical conclusions based on a long period of considered experience and observation of human interaction. Such openness in discussion also encourages the adolescent to think about his own assumptions and to use his own powers of logic to the best possible advantage. Obviously, this kind of teaching should never deteriorate into self-righteous moralizing. The adolescent quickly loses interest when he feels that he is listening to a sermon.

Even more important than what the therapist says is what the therapist does and reports doing. Adolescents are accustomed to encountering adults who espouse high standards while not actually living them. They expect a similar corruptibility in therapists and search for it.

> A 15-year-old, rather delinquent youngster who didn't work in therapy told his therapist, "Look, Doc, this is a drag for both of us. I'm only coming because the old man says I have to. I ain't never gonna talk to you. So . . . what do you say I don't come and you bill the old man anyhow. I'll never tell and we can split the dough."

Unfortunately for us very human and imperfect therapists, the invitation to corruption is not always so blatant and recognizable. When we do perceive the invitation we need to reject it firmly but matter-of-factly. Adolescents often interpret extreme prudishness and self-righteousness as indirect evidence of temptation.

SPECIAL TECHNICAL PROBLEMS

A few special technical problems that are regularly encountered in the psychotherapy of adolescents deserve brief comment.

Embarrassment over Being in Therapy

Adolescents frequently feel intensely ashamed of their need for psychotherapy. This reaction is most common in the early stages of treatment, but may recur throughout the therapeutic encounter. The patient may complain either of a personal feeling of shame or of concern about what friends or others will think.

As we noted above, the adolescent is extremely ashamed of his dependency wishes. This developmental fact explains a large part of his discomfort in the therapy relationship. An exclusive emphasis on the normative aspect of this attitude, however, can obscure the specific meaning of the shame in particular patients.

Obviously, those adolescents who have the most intense dependency needs will tend to have the strongest feelings of shame. It is important to help them to see the wish for care that is hidden behind their fear of accepting help. This can be approached in the same way that other hidden wishes are gradually revealed, if the therapist is alert to its presence. What is important is the recognition that those adolescents who do not have marked dependency needs accept this part of therapy without undue fuss.

Some adolescents who express embarrassment are speaking for their parents. Although the social stigma associated with therapy has lessened in recent years, it has not disappeared. In addition to this cultural factor, many parents view the need for therapy as a negative reflection on their parenthood. The attitude is conveyed to the adolescent, who feels that his need for psychotherapy shames his family. Unless the parents can be helped to view the situation more objectively, therapy may be seriously compromised.

Finally, the adolescent who has marked feelings of social anxiety and inferiority may focus these on the therapy process. The youngster then blames psychotherapy for his lack of social success. One can only encourage these adolescents to persevere while gently refusing to accept total blame for their discomfort. The question of whether they should tell their friends that they are in treatment should be explored dynamically in the therapy rather than defensively answered.

Bringing Friends

Some adolescents, far from hiding their involvement in therapy, announce it widely in their peer group. This may represent, in addition to an expression of exhibitionism, an attempt to avoid serious involvement in therapy. Instead of a private and important relationship, therapy and the therapist become subjects of social chatter. However, there is some value in this sharing of the therapy experience. Often, the peer group can be helpful in lowering anxiety and the discussion may be a learning experience.

Other youngsters occasionally appear at sessions with friends whom they wish to bring into the treatment room. The motivations for such behavior vary widely, but, in our opinion, the action should be viewed as a transference behavior. If this is true, it should be treated as a communication to be examined and understood.

A 16-year-old boy appeared for his therapy session with a friend in tow. He asked if the friend could accompany him to the therapy hour. The therapist replied that the time was his and he could use it as he wished.

The two boys joked uncomfortably while the therapist watched quietly, occasionally commenting on the vaguely hostile tone of their conversation.

The patient finally asked his friend to wait for him in the reception area. When he was alone with the therapist, he asked, "Well, what do you think of my friend? My parents don't want me to run around with him."

"I don't really know him. What do you think of him?"

"I think he's fine."

"If you're sure of that, I wonder why you brought him here to get my opinion?"

The patient began cautiously to explore his feelings about his friend. He admitted reluctantly that the boy was immature, self-centered, and hostile to adults. He also began to look at similar traits in his own personality that caused him to be defensive when his friend was criticized.

In this instance, a friend was brought to therapy as a proxy. If the therapist criticized the friend, it would mean that it would not be safe to reveal certain unacceptable personal traits and attitudes in therapy.

The wish to refer a friend to the therapist, although often reflecting a positive attitude toward the treatment experience, may also express a wish for a smokescreen to divert attention from the original patient. Generally, it is wise to insist on exploring the motives behind the referral rather than to accept the new patient. If the friend clearly needs help and desires it, the patient may be directed to a competent colleague. Later in therapy, the referral of a friend may be an indication that the patient is ready to consider termination.

Requests for Special Attentions

Some adolescent patients develop intense dependency ties to the therapist. They may request extra appointments, telephone the therapist, or request extra therapeutic contacts of various kinds. There is little advantage to be gained by attempting to meet these primitive needs for nurture. What the patient does need is a quiet, undemanding therapist who can patiently allow the regressed patient to come to peace with his inner feeling of emptiness and deprivation.

In adolescents, this sense of deprivation, of having lost something central to life, often leads to delinquent behavior. The adolescent feels that he has been gypped by life and demands to be recompensed. If the therapist can avoid being caught up in the flamboyant protest toward current conditions and can focus his attention on the inner state of incompleteness, the delinquencies often stop. The therapist must avoid, however, holding out a false promise of total gratification. As we have noted earlier, adolescence is not the time for extensive remediation of early fixation points. The therapist merely accepts the deprived adolescent's complaints and anger as emotionally legitimate while quietly encouraging the adolescent to confront the problems of maturity despite his feelings of emptiness and incompleteness.

Silence

Brief silences may represent productive and creative periods in psychotherapy with adolescents. In fact, the capacity to sustain a period of silence without excessive anxiety often marks a significant growth in self-confidence and acceptance of inner feelings for the adolescent. The therapist should not be quick to fill these silences.

More often, however, silences in adolescent psychotherapy are defensive. They serve to avoid the discovery and expression of angry fantasies that might appear if the adolescent spoke freely. The management of these defensive gaps in communication is extremely difficult with adolescents. It is almost impossible for an adolescent to tolerate the tension involved in remaining silent while confined in an office under observation. This tension is blamed on the therapist, thus increasing the hostile affect and further blocking communication.

In the older adolescent, silence can often be managed within the therapeutic alliance by interpreting the patient's fear of his angry impulses. In younger or more disturbed adolescents, it may be wiser to "let them off the hook" by talking to them or suggesting some activity after mentioning that they feel too upset to talk. This obviously means sacrificing some potential depth of therapy in order to salvage a tolerable therapy relationship.

In some adolescents, silence does not represent a transference phenomenon, but rather a character defense of inhibition and withdrawal. Some of these youngsters have never learned to view emotional communication in a positive way. These youngsters require skillful and tactful education in the value and techniques of conversation. During this period, the therapist must be prepared to carry the major burden of responsibility for the therapeutic dialogue.

Utilizing Dreams and Artistic Creations

Although the focus of adolescent psychotherapy is on ego functioning, this does not rule out the appropriate utilization of symbolic productions such as dreams, stories, poems, and paintings. The adolescent often is quite creative and we can learn a great deal from the study of his productions. This need not interfere with the emphasis on reality functioning if the therapist confines his comments about the symbolic materials to their relevance in the adolescent's attempt to achieve ego synthesis.

It is true that adolescents often offer their creative products to the therapist as a substitute for themselves. The unwary therapist may be drawn into a dispassionate intellectual discussion of the "ideas" contained in the art work as though these ideas were totally unrelated to the adolescent's life. Needless to say, adolescents should not be encouraged to retreat into autistic daydreams. However, dreams and creative fiction often reveal valuable information about the adolescent's real concerns even when he is attempting to avoid them.

Jimmy was a 16-year-old youngster with marked problems in adjustment. He abused drugs, totally rejected parental guidance, had dropped out of school, and showed little interest in the future or in any sublimated interests in the present. His conscious attitude was one of nonchalant disinterest in his plight. He said that the goals of adult life meant very little to him and that he intended to live merely for his immediate pleasure.

In the tenth therapy session, he reported the following dream:

"Our whole family was flying somewhere. My parents each had their own small private plane, but I was flying a B-17. I landed it on the first fueling stop, but then I became frightened. I knew that only one man had ever landed the B-17 alone, without a copilot or crew. I was afraid to take off again."

Discussion of the dream content yielded the information that Jimmy had taken a few flying lessons in the past, but had been frightened by some near accidents on landing.

His instructor had to take over the controls to complete the landings. Jimmy felt scared and ashamed. He admitted that he had been questioning the importance of learning to fly. He easily accepted the suggestion that his loss of interest in flying was related to his anxiety about his ability to handle the plane. The therapist commented that people often convince themselves that they do not really want to do the things they are afraid they cannot do. Jimmy admitted that he really wanted very much to learn to fly.

"By the way," the therapist asked casually, "what was the name of your plane?"

"B-17," Jimmy replied.

"When is it that you'll be 17?" the therapist asked pointedly.

"Why, next month," Jimmy replied.

Then, the light dawned. "You mean you think the dream was about being scared to grow up, to be 17?"

"The prospect has been known to scare guys, especially if they feel they have to manage it completely alone," the therapist replied.

Then, he added with a grin, "Sometimes, they get so worried about it, they have to pretend they don't care at all."

Although Jimmy was somewhat skeptical, his own dream and associations were difficult to dismiss completely. Gradually, his derogatory attitude toward the goals of maturity diminished. He began to discuss plans to return to school with appropriate concern about his ability to handle age-appropriate tasks.

The therapist did not comment on the family fragmentation or the possible sexual implications in the dream, since these were not relevant to the current phase of therapy.

Similar therapeutic work may be accomplished by using the artistic creations of adolescents.

David was a brilliant and creative boy of 17. His considerable talents were severely dulled by obsessive rumination, intellectualization, and isolation of affect. He entered therapy because of chronic depression and gnawing fears of masculine inadequacy.

Although he forced the issue of psychotherapy by threatening suicide, he was initially extremely resistant to all attempts to link his behavior and feelings to his actual life situation. He was particularly opposed to any discussion of his feelings for his mother and father. He assured the therapist haughtily that he was in no real sense their offspring and that they no longer mattered to him in the least.

A few sessions later, David timidly brought a poem to his therapy session. It was an excellent literary effort. (The poem was so excellent that it was later published under the author's real name. Therefore, it cannot be reproduced here without compromising confidentiality.) The therapist told David frankly that the poem was good. David did not like the poem, however. He dismissed it as "egocentric adolescent raving."

The therapist asked David what the poem was intended to convey. After a supercilious lecture on the bourgeois mentality that sought a moral message in every work of art, David condescended to comment on a few of the "thematic images" suggested in the poem. He said that the poem "obviously" had to do with the complete solitude of the individual and his "terrifying isolation in the infinity of existential vacuity."

The therapist said that he saw a different theme. He read the poem slowly aloud, verbally underlining the numerous words and phrases in the poem that seemed to refer to birth symbols and to man's origin from his fellows rather than his isolation. The therapist stated calmly that the poet may have intended to emphasize man's separation from his fellows, but the poem seemed to say that no man sprang full formed, alone, and self-sufficient from emptiness.

David listened quietly, and then asked softly, "So I am my father's son?"

"What do you think?"

"I think that I am asserting through negation."

"Can you put that simply for me?"

"You know what I mean. He must really have a hold on me if I have to pretend I don't even know him."

The therapist's goal was not so much to call attention to the father-son relationship, but to help David move beyond his sterile autistic isolation and into affectively meaningful material. Once again, the adolescent's own words, written in a sense in spite of himself, were the agents of change.

COMPARING NOTES WITH OTHER THERAPISTS

It would be instructive and also fun to sit in on a therapy session and observe how an experienced clinician handles the twists and turns of working with an adolescent client. Ordinarily it is not possible to do that in real life, but there are many opportunities to read case histories—some of them quite detailed—that expert therapists have published. We will provide several references that relate to the process of psychotherapy with adolescents. Blos (1983) described his psychotherapeutic work with an adolescent girl. Williams (1986) illustrated how the clinician may need to be simply a trusted adult friend before becoming a psychotherapist. Anthony (1988) reported his experiences in treating adolescents who were unusually bright or creative. Massie (1988) reported the treatment of two psychotic youngsters. Galatzer-Levy (1985) described the successful psychoanalysis of a depressed adolescent. Chused (1990) presented case material to show that clinical neutrality may be the best way to avoid countertransference problems. Godenne (1995) offered practical tips on how to build a therapeutic alliance. Finally, Katz (1998) described several instances in which he cleverly initiated and maintained a therapeutic alliance with adolescent clients.

A LITTLE HELP FROM SOME FRIENDS

Individual therapy isn't always the treatment of choice. At times group therapy is useful instead of the individual approach or in addition to individual therapy. The next chapter focuses on some of the problems of using that approach and some methods of making group psychotherapy successful.

CHAPTER 6

group psychotherapy of the adolescent

There is something inherently appealing about the idea of treating disturbed adolescents in a group. The age group has a spontaneous interest in getting together and the conditions of current social reality require adolescents to spend most of their waking hours interacting within formal and informal peer groups. Developmental pressures cause these groups to hold great fascination and importance for the young person.

It has been reasoned that group therapy would take full advantage of this natural grouping in the adolescent period, converting a distraction from individual therapy into a powerful therapeutic alternative. The troublesome dependency-independency-authority conflict with adults would be diluted by the presence of other young people in the treatment setting. Prompted by friendship and mutual concern, group members would recognize and confront maladaptive behavior in one another, including self-destructive pathological clashes with authority figures. These interventions would have great impact since they could not be dismissed as "uptight adult hassling." Theoretically, group psychotherapy should lead to effortless success.

In practice group psychotherapy with adolescents often does not unfold in that way. Group members do not settle into a friendly acceptance of one another. Instead they approach each other with silence, suspicion, and defensive affectations. They may not approach at all. Many groups disintegrate after a meeting or two.

If the group survives, perhaps because of external pressure to attend, the authority conflict is not diluted. In fact, instead of struggling with a single snarling youngster, the therapist is confronted with an angry and disruptive mob. Therapists have been known to disband groups out of fear for their own safety or at least their reputation in their clinic or private office building. Naturally, this extreme is unusual, but there are plenty of frightening war stories around to alarm the uninitiated.

Some therapists have succeeded in corralling their groups, only to find that their reasonable, cooperative patients expect them to do all the work. The therapist is clearly accepted as a powerful leader and is besieged with requests for advice, practical help, and infantile support. These unfortunate experiences follow from a failure to consider all aspects of adolescent development, psychopathology, and the dynamics of group formation during adolescence as they affect the formation and function of therapy groups.

There are many youngsters who need psychotherapy who will either fail to respond to the group approach or who may even be damaged by this technique. These youngsters can be screened through careful evaluation prior to group placement. If diagnostic study suggests that the presenting complaint results from ego depletion with panic and disorganization barely contained, the youngster is not a candidate for outpatient group therapy, at least not before a period of individual therapy. In individual work, youngsters of this kind can utilize an extremely dependent transference to gradually strengthen and widen their defensive skills and to partially resolve the primitive conflicts that are dangerously near eruption. At that point they have the potential to utilize interaction with peers constructively. Earlier they would have merely experienced a lively, challenging group as another stress to an already overburdened coping system.

A second category of youngster who cannot benefit from group therapy includes those who are fixated at a level of development that does not value the opinion or support of peers. Such adolescents often present with psychosomatic or self-destructive behavior that seems clearly motivated by a need to coerce nurture from adults. They require an infantile feeding relationship with a caring adult to maintain marginal functioning.

Ann, a thin, tense, 14-year-old, had been in psychotherapy with three different therapists since age eight when
her multiple neurotic symptoms of school phobia, abdominal pains, vomiting episodes, and multiple phobias first
became evident. Her mother was a narcissistic, infantile,
and extremely unhappy woman who had been in psychoanalysis for eight years. She made no secret of the fact she
experienced Ann as an unlovable burden. Ann's father was
distant and rigid, confining his family interactions to occasional outbursts at his daughter when she interfered with
any of his plans and criticism of his wife for not coping
better with the children's management and control. Ann's
problems had been variously diagnosed as an anxiety neurosis, borderline personality disorder, and childhood schizophrenia. Psychotic diagnoses had been considered because
of Ann's general disorganization and because some of her
phobic concerns were quite bizarre. For example, she
feared she might wet herself at school but responded to
this common worry by wearing four to six layers of undergarments. She also was periodically fearful that her hair
was falling out, that she had cancer, or that she had performed acts that she had only thought about. Reality testing clearly was shaky.

After a year and a half of therapy with her latest therapist
she had stabilized markedly and was symptom free. She
began to move toward adolescent concerns and behaviors,
but complained chronically that she had no friends at
school. The therapist tried to explore her role in this state of
affairs with very little success. Motivated more than a little
by countertransference annoyance, he pushed her to join
an adolescent group where her ways of relating to agemates
could be directly observed. She agreed reluctantly, insisting
on continuing individual sessions concurrently (though she
complained constantly that they were valueless).

In the group Ann was paralyzed with anxiety, developed
a blind hatred for the female cotherapist, and alienated the
other group members with her childish and demanding

behavior. In one active session while being confronted by another group member, her eyes rolled back in her head and her neck muscles went into spasm so that she literally could not "see what was being said." She had to leave the meeting. The support of extra individual sessions allowed her to recover quickly and, after some ambivalence, she decided to return to the group where by subduing herself, she was able to attain a degree of acceptance. However, it was the therapist's opinion that she had only survived the group experience, not that it had benefited her. She remained in individual therapy after the group was terminated, and maintained her symptomless but constricted adjustment even as the frequency of appointments was gradually reduced to one a month.

Similar failures, more dangerous to the group than to the patient, may occur with unsocialized acting-out youngsters. Of course, many adolescents who present with antisocial behavior are basically well socialized and are handling neurotic or developmental problems by acting out. They work out quite well in group therapy. However, those youngsters who have never shown evidence of adequate object relations and the capacity for affectionate attachment will not respond to group pressure and cannot adapt to group expectations.

Fortunately, most youngsters who should not be in group have some awareness of this fact. They, like Ann, resist the plan for psychotherapy. Although some youngsters who do well in group resist the idea initially, strong reservations should lead the therapist to review his diagnostic thinking carefully before pressuring the youngster to enter group psychotherapy. As a rule, the appropriate group candidate is anxious about the prospect of group work but is also fascinated and intrigued by her fantasies of what may happen.

WHY ADOLESCENTS WANT TO BELONG

Some consideration must also be given to the nature of spontaneous adolescent groups. The developmental pressures that drive the adolescent toward his peers and the emotional needs that he hopes to satisfy in peer groups strongly affect the readiness with which adolescents will relate to one another in a therapy setting and the style of communication that will tend to occur. These developmental factors also influence the reception the therapist can expect as the therapy group's leader. For a recent discussion of the importance of peers in shaping the development of personality and attitudes, see Harris's (1998) *Nurture Assumption.*

In early adolescence the youngster turns toward peers under the pressure of his need to emancipate himself from his family. It is more of a panicked flight than a positive quest. As the parents are rejected and devalued, their utility as sources of narcissistic support is weakened or lost. The youngster does not yet have a suitable substitute internal mechanism for maintaining his sense of worth. The peer group provides a temporary emergency support system. This means, however, that the adolescent's friends must be people he can view as equals or superiors and that they must offer him a primarily positive reflection of himself. Naturally, he is willing to conform slavishly to group norms in order to obtain this acceptance. The adolescent is very particular in choosing his associates. His ties are somewhat fickle, since he will drop any friend who falls from favor with the remainder of his gang. It is the rare 14-year-old who will maintain an open friendship with a youngster whom "everyone else" regards as "weird" or "queer."

As the youngster grows older, the peer group increasingly becomes important as a support system in the task of modifying the superego. The group shares guilty secrets with bravado and even encourages previously unacceptable behavior, particularly actions that defy adult authority. However, group members are not merely "partners in crime," as they also offer one another limits based on the human rights of other members of the group. They may also persuade individuals not to "go too far" because certain behaviors may be dangerous to the individual or may threaten the continued existence of the group. Therefore the group serves both to loosen the constraints of the latency conscience and to provide an alternative, reality-based system of controls.

As these developmental tasks are mastered, the adolescent becomes increasingly interested in his peers as real people. Relationships become less narcissistic and attachments are based on positive attraction rather than flight from the family of origin. Bonds are still somewhat tentative and there is considerable role playing, but relationships are warm and enduring over relatively extended periods of time. Even friction and controversy are accepted as necessary and valuable aspects of a rounded experience in the group.

This progression is often interrupted or uneven in the troubled adolescent. Many patients, even in late adolescence, are still more invested in the search for "psychic band-aids" than in learning from an honest give-and-take relationship. This fact creates two kinds of problems in the early stages of adolescent group psychotherapy.

First of all, the troubled adolescent is reluctant to accept his fellow group members. It is difficult for the patient to idealize people who are gathered with him because they too "have problems." He is frightened by the prospect of losing self-esteem through accepting membership in a group of "misfits." If some group members have strikingly different defenses, social styles, or socioeconomic backgrounds, the patient's certainty that he is in the wrong place grows exponentially. Some patients are often lost to the group at this point. As those who remain begin to find some group members who seem acceptable as "friends," there is a strong tendency for the group to fragment and develop cliques and scapegoats. It is a trying time for the therapist whose goal is to promote total group cohesion.

A second problem is created by the narcissistic vulnerability of the adolescent. Because of the need to use peer relationships for narcissistic confirmation, the adolescent tends to hide his problems and to cooperate fully with the same defensive strategy as it is utilized by the other group members. The patients want to avoid criticism and are understandably reluctant to throw the first stone. Each patient pretends to offer what he hopes to receive—total acceptance and admiration. Any confrontations that occur tend to be directed toward scapegoats and are hostile and distancing. It is easy for the therapist to become the only one in the group who "hassles the kids who are okay." He must be careful also to avoid being the only one who "takes up for the dopey ones."

The adolescent's use of peers to assist in the modification of his conscience also carries a threat to the successful formation of a therapeutic group. Most groups will test the therapist in this area. In more subdued groups, the discussions of forbidden thoughts and actions will be carried on initially before the therapist enters the group. Sooner or later, however, some group member will be either brave or nervous enough to broach the topics in the therapist's presence. Other groups are much more bold. In either case the group must know the therapist's stance. Will the therapist encourage acting out or will he come across as a parental-superego figure? Will he be corruptible, seducible, and manipulatable or repressive and rigid? Of course, the opportunity of therapeutic exploration is lost if the therapist is drawn into an unholy alliance with either the id or the superego. This problem has been considered earlier in regard to the development of the therapeutic alliance in individual psychotherapy and the principles of management are the same in groups. However, the countertransference pressures of facing a group involved in externalizing superego issues are greater than those encountered with individual patients, particularly when the group seems in danger of transforming itself into a vicious, salacious street gang before one's eyes. Skilled group therapists have managed to navigate this risky period spontaneously, but many problems may be avoided by utilizing some of the technical structuring patterns suggested later in this chapter.

This brief discussion of developmental issues that influence the achievement of group cohesion underlines the fact that the natural tendency of adolescents is indeed to form groups, but not groups that are inclined to explore the meaning of behavior. Of course, groups can be helpful, even therapeutic in the broad sense, without investigating the meaning of behavior. One successful strategy of group therapy with adolescents is to simply accept the basically narcissistic, supportive patterns of spontaneous groups and to harness these forces for constructive goals. This technique does not encourage introspection and will be described briefly. A second approach that utilizes structural techniques intended to encourage introspection, investigation of motives, and scrutiny of the emotions which underlie interpersonal transactions will be discussed in greater detail. Many groups actually develop some characteristics of both types of group structure.

THE OPEN-ENDED SUPPORTIVE GROUP

Therapeutic groups that focus on changing self-destructive behavior by embracing and manipulating natural patterns of adolescent behavior in groups have been rather successful in a variety of settings (Berstein and Duquette, 1995; Corder, 1994; Siegel, 1987). These groups have certain characteristics in common although there is considerable variation in their membership, specific procedures, and goals. Initial membership is often compulsory and enforced by outside agencies such as probation agencies or the officials of a residential treatment institution. The groups are open-ended and, in fact, often define the addition and successful assimilation of new members as their primary function. Members are selected primarily on the basis of their symptoms or because of their presence in a particular institution. The group, then, is rather homogeneous, either for symptom (drug usage, delinquency, etc.) or through common experience in daily living circumstances. The work of the group is oriented toward fairly circumscribed goals, usually either altering the common symptomatic behavior or improving the adaptation to the common living situation.

The basic force for change in these groups is a core of committed "old members" who have been converted from a prior involvement in the symptomatic behavior to an alternative lifestyle. They credit the group and its leader for their success in changing. They are familiar with the gratifications and temptations of the negative behavior and recognize immediately the common defensive patterns and attitudes that insulate the new group member from awareness of the destructiveness of his maladaptive symptoms. Since they have decided that the symptomatic behavior is unwise and self-destructive, they are quite willing to confront the new member. Their self-esteem now depends on maintaining the wisdom of their decision so the new member's defense of the rejected behaviors represents a personal threat and is vigorously attacked. Since they have also "been there, done that," the old members tend to temper their assault with empathy, support, and open confession of their own shortcomings.

The technical devices utilized by leaders in these groups are primarily inspirational, supportive, and directive although group members may actively pursue hidden motivations. Exploration is primarily directed toward subtle manipulations of the group and its leader by the unrepentant new member. Interpretations and confrontations are mainly aimed at unmasking the new member, helping him to "shape up" and stop "playing games." On the other hand, extended discussion of personal genetic and dynamic material tends to be viewed with suspicion since such material may be used as a justification for the unacceptable behavior, an excuse to avoid essential change, a "cop-out."

In many ways the leader of these groups serves primarily as a consultant and support to the old members who carry the main thrust of the rehabilitative work. The leader is there to help if the old members become discouraged or if they are manipulated into an unnecessarily punitive or overly permissive position in relation to a particularly difficult new member. The leader assists the group in maintaining focus on its tasks and values. Usually he or she does this without commenting on the motives or problems of the older members. The leader points out that the old members may temporarily lose sight of the purpose and correct procedures of the group because their task is difficult. Leaders avoid criticism or discussion of the old members' psychopathology since this might weaken their loyalty to the group and lessen their influence on the new members.

The narcissistic values of being "right" and "cool" are usually sufficient reward for the old members' work in the group, especially as these values are continually reinforced by the successful conversion of new members to the group ethic. The group provides an opportunity to obtain admiration from a peer group that is acceptable (i.e., the members are streetwise, tough, know the drug scene) without engaging in behaviors that are dangerous and self-destructive. The group also provides a reasonable new superego model divorced from childhood and the parents. The almost evangelical drive to help other youngsters provides an important sense of worth and mission which can substitute for the need to prove one's self in daring and illegal actions.

Although these groups are powerful agents for change, there are many limits to their application. It may be that some environments are so brutally unfair and destructive that adolescents subjected to their viciousness are unreachable. However, skilled workers with honest commitment can ameliorate some of the damage in the worst environments. The difficulty of finding therapists with sufficient empathy, skill, toughness, and concern to activate the group and form the original pro-therapy core of "old members" is an important limitation. Many are called, but few succeed and persevere. Yet, when these groups function well they can be heaven-sent to many of the youngsters with "malignant defenses" discussed earlier. The narcissistic support of a well-functioning group can make it possible for the youngster to give up destructive omnipotent defenses and learn human and constructive alternatives. The amazing treatment record of Alcoholics Anonymous and other similar group treatment organizations can teach us a great deal about the value and power of this approach.

Still, some youngsters cannot respond to any form of group therapy. Those so socially immature as to be immune to group pressure and group rewards cannot respond to a therapy based on these factors. Open-ended support groups are also relatively ineffective in correcting symptomatic behavior that is grounded in severe neurotic conflict, particularly when the behavior is part of a generally masochistic pattern.

Even with an appropriate leader and members who fit, there are potential problems. Failure to influence one or more new members is demoralizing and can erode collective self-esteem. Trusted old members can relapse in response to increased stresses in their lives with an even greater disruptive impact on the group. Charismatic new members may tempt the entire group to return to old value systems. In short, the group ties are basically narcissistic and therefore somewhat unreliable when pressures mount. The group leader's own charisma, flexibility, and clinical wisdom will be severely tried as he attempts to maintain a positively functioning group entity over time.

THE EXPLORATORY THERAPY GROUP

The developmental impediments to adolescent group work may also be circumvented by altering the structural characteristics to encourage the development of a group ethic of emotional openness and exploration. The model described here does permit the addition of occasional new patients at infrequent intervals, but is designed for a group with constant membership and a reasonably prolonged existence. It is basically designed for outpatients. Under these circumstances, further modifications are necessary to ensure continuing parental cooperation in the group work.

The open-ended group described above can afford to neglect parental involvement since the group and the residential setting basically substitutes for the family. In contrast, the dynamically oriented group is virtually certain to consider in detail the impact of family problems on the attitudes, feelings, and interpersonal quirks of its members. These discussions will tend to activate latent family conflicts and may lead the parents to sabotage treatment or even terminate the adolescent's group membership. The needs of the parents must be considered if the group structure is to be successful. This parental involvement in the group will rarely substitute for specific therapy directed toward their marital or personal problems. Although some parents benefit personally, the primary goal is to enlist their enlightened support for the work of the adolescent group.

We can now turn to a description of the model. As in the remainder of the book, the procedures will be described explicitly with the clear recognition that other therapists have utilized other techniques successfully. Models must be altered to fit treatment conditions and personal preferences.

GROUP SELECTION

Members must be chosen carefully for outpatient dynamic group psychotherapy with an eye to both the needs of the individual youngster and the overall composition of the group.

The criteria of group selection are hardly scientific, but some principles seem clinically sound. We have already mentioned some youngsters who should be excluded from groups. Additional criteria should be mentioned. It seems important for the prospective member to have parental permission and, preferably, parental encouragement to join the group. Good group work produces anxiety and resistance. If the parent is poised to support flight from the experience, it is unlikely that most adolescents will be able to resist this invitation to escape immediate pain in the interest of long-term benefits.

The youngster himself should have at least a modicum of positive motivation for the group experience, perhaps limited initially to a mixture of interest and anxiety with an agreement to try the group for a month or two. The youngster's motivation will be evaluated in more depth during the evolution of individual treatment contracts, a process that will be described later.

Some attention should be given to choosing a group population that will be socially compatible within broad limits. Early impressions of other group members are important and adolescents are often harsh in their judgment of superficial characteristics. For example, a psychotic youngster with the same style, vocabulary, dress, and social experience would probably be less threatening to an adolescent group than a healthier youngster with a disfiguring physical defect or a background and lifestyle that seemed "weird" to the other members.

An adolescent group jelled with surprising rapidity except for Bill, a 17-year-old who remained withdrawn and uncomfortable through the first four meetings. He requested an individual interview where he told the therapist the group wasn't helping him. The other kids seemed strange and unfriendly and he intended to quit. When pressed about his discontent his complaints were vague. The therapist commented on Bill's uncharacteristic silence in the group meetings and wondered if he could really assess the other members' friendliness without being more open.

Bill responded with angry tears.

"I can't."

"Why not?"

"You're stupid. Why did you put me in a rich kids' group?" Though the therapist hadn't realized it, every member of the group except Bill came from very affluent families. They spoke casually of their cars, going out to dinner, and elaborate vacations. Bill's father was a university professor who couldn't afford such luxuries.

In this case, Bill's educational and social background was actually quite similar to those of the other group members. They were quite prepared to accept him although he felt very "different" from them.

Bill was able to resolve his discomfort and work successfully in the group. His reaction is described merely to illustrate the adolescent's exquisite sensitivity to superficial social differences.

Some attention must also be given to the "balance" of the group. Passive and silent members must be offset with some "talkers." Youngsters inclined toward "acting out" solutions to conflict should be placed in groups which include some youngsters who reflect or even ruminate on their feelings before acting. Mostly one must depend on an intuitive sense of how the group will fit together. This sense is never infallible, but the chances for success are increased by knowing the individual youngsters reasonably well. This kind of knowledge can only be obtained through fairly prolonged pre-group individual evaluation.

The diagnostic advantages of pregroup evaluation have been mentioned but these sessions are central to group success in other ways as well. The early stages of group therapy are extremely anxiety producing for many adolescents so it is important for each group member to have a stable, trusting relationship with the therapist prior to the first group meeting. Many youngsters should be started in group only after a period of individual psychotherapy with the therapist. Others may be referred by therapists who do not do group work themselves but believe the patient would be helped by a group experience. If the colleague's assessment is correct, these youngsters may require only a few individual sessions to get acquainted with the therapist and learn something of the pattern of group work he follows. Of course, the group therapist also uses these meetings to assure himself that the youngster is ready to function constructively in the group. If he does not think so, the patient can be referred back to the original therapist for further individual work.

If the group will have cotherapists, they can divide the evaluative work between them. This has practical advantages since most therapists do not have group evaluation time in their normal schedule and are somewhat overburdened by the extra work involved in preparing to begin a group. The procedure does produce some technical problems since group members may resist group involvement and cling to their individual relationship to the cotherapist who evaluated them. However, this problem is preferable to the risk of early group dissolution. In any event, this excessive attachment to the therapist quickly diminishes as the group members become acquainted and form attachments to one another.

Pregroup meetings also allow patients to elaborate their anxieties and fantasies about group therapy. The therapist can correct frightening misconceptions and explain the goals and procedures of the group. The ground rules of the group—such as prohibitions against physical contact, the desirability and limitations of confidentiality, the need for regular attendance, the procedure for quitting the group and the expectation that each group member will formulate a treatment contract for the group—can be discussed fully. The youngster has the opportunity to consider his treatment goals and to solicit the therapist's help in shaping a treatment contract that he would be comfortable in sharing with the group. This is important since many youngsters wish to discuss very sensitive topics in the group, but would be understandably reluctant to disclose these fully in an initial meeting of the group. For example, the 15-year-old boy who has never had a date and is terrified of girls may need permission to limit his first treatment contract to "I would like to improve the way I get along with girls." At the other extreme from youngsters who might say too much are those who require pressure and assistance to come up with any personal treatment goals. The pregroup individual sessions provide an opportunity to explain that comments like "I'm only here because my parents sent me" or "I was just curious about what happens in groups" will not suffice.

Pregroup meetings also permit the therapist to clarify his expectations about how the group will proceed. Comments such as "when a group really gets going, you get pretty involved with the other people" both explain the importance of regular attendance and set the expectation that group members should comment on each others' absences, consistent lateness, or precipitous desire to quit the group. The therapist has defined these behaviors as evidences of concern rather than meddling in someone else's business. Similar double duty is accomplished by predicting some of the problems the youngster may expect in the course of the group experience. "If this group really works like others I've had, there will be pretty open talking about how people feel about one another. Sometimes you may not like what people say about how you're coming across." "You know, there may be things about people in the group that annoy you. Now at school you might just avoid that person, but in a group it's important to talk about how you really feel even if you're afraid the other person may get mad or have their feelings hurt. Do you think you can do that?" Of course, these comments are tailored to the dynamics and relating style of the individual youngster. The diagnostic evaluation often allows a fairly accurate prediction of the types of group interaction which a given youngster will find most uncomfortable. Naturally these structuring comments do not guarantee that the group will actually move toward confrontation, emotional openness, and exploration of interpersonal processes, but it begins that process by presenting the possibility for such interactions and implying that the therapist expects these possibilities to occur.

Once the therapist has determined that the youngster seems appropriate for the group that is being formed, the therapist may want some form of commitment that the patient is truly interested and will actually show up for the first meeting. Also, these youngsters are usually quite curious about who are the other prospective members and what is wrong with them. "Are they nerds or retards or geeks?" is implied, if not stated directly. It is usually possible to be reassuring by mentioning some of the psychosocial strengths of the other group members, while acknowledging that they all have problems of one kind or another: "One guy in the group used to play football until he broke his leg. There's a girl who did a solo in her school musical." Another technique is starting a sign-up sheet, a formality familiar to every high school student:

Group Therapy Sign-up Sheet

I want to be in the therapy group that will be on Thursdays, 4:00 to 5:15, starting October 15.

Name	Grade	School
Jimmy D.	11	Brentwood
Alyce B.	10	Hume-Fogg

What this sign-up sheet does is communicate to the prospective group member that there are other real kids who are going to be in the group. It tells a minimal amount of information about the other patients and the information that it does tell has been volunteered by the youngsters involved, since they know that the sign-up sheet is going to be seen by other patients who are interested in being in the group. The process also creates a sense of commitment on the part of the patients who do sign up on the sheet.

The therapist predicts the patient will be emotionally accepted in the group and also states a rule when he explains, "The reason we make a fuss about someone stopping is because a lot of times the group wonders why someone quits, maybe even blames themselves. If you decided to leave the group— let's say you got your problem worked out—it would be important to explain that. The rest of the members would probably hate to see you go and they might wonder if it happened because of something they said or maybe they weren't interesting or good enough. So we ask anyone who thinks about quitting to bring that up at the start of a meeting and to tell why they're thinking of leaving the group. The other good thing about this is for you, the person who's thinking of quitting, it gives you a chance to hear what the other people think about your reasons for quitting and gives you a chance to think it over. And that's good, because stopping the group is a pretty important decision and you'd want to think about it pretty seriously."

OBJECTION! Your Honor, the doctor is leading the patient. You bet your sweet id.

And that's only the beginning.

THERAPIST ACTIVITY

The leader of an adolescent group must work actively at promoting spontaneity and intimacy. The therapist's activities include structuring group tasks and procedures and the usual group leader's activity of conceptualizing and verbalizing the group experience (group process) as it unfolds, but these professional activities are not enough. The therapist must also be active as a person, alive and involved in the group. He needs to share his own feeling responses to the meaningful emotional interactions that develop between group members.

Obviously this activity poses potential dangers of encouraging excessive dependency in group members. The therapist may be seen as a guru, a teacher, a good parent. These developments need not be unhealthy if they are recognized and discussed openly. If the therapist is alert and free of excessive needs for power or status, there will be plenty of chances to support emerging leadership in the group. The therapist's overt and explicit interventions can often decrease as the group's momentum grows, but he must remain an actively interested and emotionally invested observer.

In the seventh session of an adolescent group the therapist confessed his discomfort.

"I don't know. It seems like I'm talking too much in here. I don't think I'm giving other people enough chance to talk and that's really bad, because I'm not even getting to know you guys well enough to know whether I'm saying the right things."

Alan, a previously silent 16-year-old, said, "You're not. I'm sorry, but we need to get the kids talking. Me too, I guess. I haven't said much myself. I think we ought to interview each other, like take turns being the patient. Everyone could ask three questions—course if you don't think . . .

"Sounds great to me, but maybe you'd better ask the other kids.'"

"Okay, but Alan has to go first." Everyone chimes their agreement that Alan had to be the first "patient."

Everyone has their own style of activity. The important point is that passive, detached, dispassionate scrutiny may have great value in some scientific settings. The adolescent psychotherapy group is not one of them.

THE GROUP CONTRACT

The group contract or the rules of the group are nothing more than a set of conditions that group members agree to follow in order to achieve treatment results they desire. This quality of informed consent and mutual commitment needs to be emphasized to offset any fantasy that group contracts are made in heaven or in the therapist's head. The anticipation of possible control problems in adolescent groups may lead the therapist to focus on a long list of prohibitions as the primary content of the group contract. The adolescents correctly perceive this as a frightened insistence on a superego alliance and respond according to their particular pathology. Overly inhibited youngsters slavishly obey the rules and youngsters in rebellion fight them. Neither group becomes involved in treatment.

The fundamentals of the group contract have already been discussed with each youngster during his pregroup individual sessions. Each therapist must decide the basic working conditions under which he or she can conduct meaningful group therapy. Many would consider most of the following rules important for the reasons given.

1. *No hitting in the group.* The therapist explains the obvious fact that people cannot speak honestly with one another unless they are assured that the therapist and the group will neither permit them to hit or be hit. Some therapists extend this rule to "no physical contact" to rule out physical expression of positive feelings (kissing, sitting on laps, etc.) along with the expression of aggression. This may be questioned on the grounds that it introduces some confusion by including "hittin' and huggin' " in the same category as though they were somehow interchangeable or related to the same emotional origin. Secondly, the vagueness of the general rule suggests that the therapist is reluctant to confront adolescent sexuality directly. Finally, from a practical viewpoint, some physical contact (i.e., embracing a crying fellow member) may be decidedly constructive.

2. *Regular attendance is expected.* If it is totally impossible to

attend a session, it is the patient's responsibility to contact the therapist and explain why the absence is unavoidable.

The therapist explains that the members need to get to know one another very well in order for the group to be helpful. This requires very regular attendance. In addition, the unexplained absence of a member wastes valuable group time as the present members speculate on the reasons for the absence. Some members may even inhibit their group participation out of concern that some interaction with the absent member drove him away.

3. *Any member who considers leaving the group should announce his intention at the beginning of a group session and permit full discussion of the decision.* The reasons for this rule have already been discussed. Some therapists require a group notification of two sessions or more. Theoretically this makes sense; however it may invite passive aggression if some group members perceive the rule as a disguised attempt to force members to remain in the group when they have definitely decided to quit.

4. *Each group member will be expected to make an individual treatment contract.* This expectation will be discussed further in this chapter.

5. *The group is told that the group will function best if there is no discussion of the group proceedings with others.* Some therapists feel that this rule is impossible to enforce and add, "If you must discuss something that occurs in here with your parents or anyone else, at least don't use names."

6. *The therapist or cotherapists may also wish to explain their position regarding confidentiality,* namely, that they will not discuss things that occur in the group or information revealed there unless, in their judgment, a group member is in danger of harming himself or others. Some therapists also reserve the right to answer parental questions regarding treatment progress. Most adolescents seem to accept their parents' right to know if the youngster is utilizing treatment appropriately, but some therapists feel uncomfortable with "sending home report cards."

7. *The group is told that any contact between members outside the group sessions should be reported in the next group meeting.* It is explained that important group issues may be missed if group

members have discussions that exclude the remainder of the group.

8. *Some therapists forbid outside contact, but there are serious difficulties in taking this position.* It is a rule that cannot be enforced, seems artificial, and invites rebellion. Also, many therapists have observed that much extra-group contact is supportive, pro-therapy, and conducive to the development of group cohesion.

These conditions are not presented as a list of dogmatic regulations. They are discussed with the group as important issues that require resolution. This does not mean they are totally or even primarily negotiable. For example, few therapists would consider working with a group that could not agree to refrain from striking one another. The therapist must press for the conditions he needs, attempting to convince the group of the therapeutic necessity of each rule. There is no reason to avoid "sales talk." The resulting contract is designed to benefit everyone, especially the group members.

THE INDIVIDUAL TREATMENT CONTRACT

The practice of requiring each group member to formulate a personal treatment goal and to verbalize the goal to the group has several advantages. It is not an unreasonable expectation when the adolescent receives assistance with the difficult job of thinking through his contract in the pre-group individual sessions. It is probably true that any youngster who is suitable for outpatient group work is able to make this degree of commitment. However, the therapist must be willing to permit some face-saving reservations. For example, it is probably acceptable for the adolescent to say, "Well, the *real* reason I'm coming to the group is because my father says I have to, but since I'm here, I might be interested in learning more about how boys should treat girls."

The group presentation of individual treatment contracts is taken up as soon as the group completes consideration and acceptance of the group contract, often in the first session. The therapist introduces the topic by saying, "Okay, since we've agreed to those things, let's get on to people's individual contracts. Remember we said everyone would tell the group why they're coming here and what they hope to accomplish in the group. Who wants to go first and get it over with?"

Usually someone will volunteer, but if not, the therapist can ask a member to begin. Each contract is open to discussion by the group and the therapist and may be accepted or rejected as inappropriate. Generally speaking, any serious goal that seems neither destructive or foolishly grandiose is accepted. One does not expect or need psychologically sophisticated contracts at this stage in adolescent group work.

The two primary purposes of requiring contracts in the initial sessions are to open problem areas for group discussion and to provide the therapist with legitimate, neutral instrumental authority. Since each member has asked for help with a specific problem, the "mutual protection pact" of denial that often characterizes adolescent groups during their formative period is less likely to develop. The open admission of difficulty and the request for help give both a focus and permission to the other group members as they consider commenting on a fellow member's verbal or nonverbal behavior in the group. For example, if a youngster has stated that he is coming to the group because he wishes to learn how to make friends, the group feels more free to confront him with his silence, sarcasm, or egocentricity without feeling they are intruding or merely being hostile. "Maybe the reason you have trouble making friends is that you're always cutting people down. At least you do here."

The therapist is also in a better position to avoid the unholy alliances with either id or superego. The process of making individual treatment contracts defines him as a consultant to the group. He becomes an expert given the responsibility for guiding the group toward behaviors that will permit the individual members to accomplish their chosen goals. If it becomes necessary to set limits on group behavior, the therapist does this as a leader exercising his duty to help the group accomplish its aims, not as an offended uptight parent figure. His function is executive and oriented toward promoting better ego functioning with the group.

Any contract that is sincere will accomplish these two purposes. As the group work continues, contracts may be altered and refined. The therapist may suggest changes, or new definitions of the problem may be offered by the patient or other group members. For example, the therapist may comment to a patient, "I would like to suggest a change in your contract now that I know you better. I don't think you exactly have a problem in making friends. I think you should consider working on your tendency to expect too much of friends and the way that causes you to be disappointed in people and overly critical." Later yet the contract may evolve to, "Trying to stop setting people up to prove they don't like me and that I'm better than they are."

The treatment contract is only a tool so its value will depend on the skill with which it is used to further the group work. Some therapists are worried that adolescent patients will not accept this condition of group work. They might consider the possibility that a group so resistant to the treatment process is unlikely to be successful in any case. Perhaps it is better to dissolve an unworkable group early in its course so that more suitable treatment approaches can be attempted. In actual practice, most adolescent groups will accept this condition of treatment. Naturally some of the more resistant members will hold back, but as more and more group members commit themselves to a treatment contract, the pressure to "get aboard" grows. The contracted members point out that it is only fair that all members reveal their problems and aspirations to the group.

THE PARENTS

Many patterns of parental involvement have been utilized in group work with adolescents. Some therapists conduct concurrent treatment groups for the parents or arrange for such groups to be conducted by a colleague. Attendance at these groups may be required as a condition for accepting the adolescent in the group. These groups are sometimes quite difficult and unsatisfactory because the parents are unmotivated and do not recognize a need for treatment. However, a skillful therapist can often make these groups effective by permitting the parents to focus on their youngsters initially, gradually using common themes and problems to build group cohesion and a capacity for personal therapy work.

Another successful approach involves periodic family meetings, basically an adolescent group meeting with the parents invited. The adolescents may also be seen individually with their families. These approaches are effective and are well received by the parents. The only potential disadvantage is that family work closely linked to the group may dilute the intensity of the attachments formed within the group. If the aim is to maximize group intimacy so that the group can serve as a microcosm of emotional life, this may be a disadvantage too serious to accept.

Another alternative is to approach the parents as collaborators in the group process, leaving any direct therapy they may require outside of the group involvement. A parents' meeting is called just prior to beginning the adolescent group. The therapist or cotherapists present the aims and methods of the group didactically, explaining all aspects of the group procedure in detail. The parents are told that their youngsters' individual problems will be approached indirectly through the creation of a human relationships laboratory experience in the group setting. The parents are offered examples to demonstrate how this experience serves to develop the capacity for self-awareness and skill in relating to other people in a fair and honest way.

The parents are told of the problems and disadvantages of this approach. The therapist admits that this kind of work creates considerable anxiety that may cause their youngster to express desires to leave the group. They are warned that youngsters often attempt to manipulate their parents to support their flight from the group by suddenly claiming all problems have been solved, being amazingly cooperative in the home, expressing concern about the morality and mental health of other group members, or trying to imply that the therapist is hostile toward the parents.

The parents are assured that they are not expected to force their youngster to remain in group. The desire to quit may be appropriate. The therapist merely wants their support in asking the youngster to discuss his decision and the reasons for it in the group setting. The parents are asked to refer any complaints their adolescent may have about the group or the therapist to a group meeting, encouraging the open expression of negative feelings in the group setting so that the youngster's emotional experience within the group can be as complete as possible. The parents are told that if they have any questions about the group or the therapist's behavior, these should be discussed directly with the therapist.

The importance of confidentiality is discussed so that the parents can understand why the therapist cannot fully disclose the happenings of the group to them. The therapist also explains why he needs their permission to talk openly with their youngsters about any contracts the parents and therapist may have. Parents are encouraged to call the therapist with any questions or information but to inform their youngster that they are calling. They should also tell their adolescent the general content of what they intend to say. Group fees and policies about absences are discussed along with an explanation of the importance of regular attendance.

The parents are encouraged to ask questions and to be sure they understand and agree with the plans for the group. The therapist tries to discourage intensive discussion of individual problems except when these lend themselves to illustration of general group concerns and techniques. Some questions may be referred to the other parents and some worries, such as fears that a particular youngster may not speak in group, may be generalized. The therapist can then talk in a general way about the way the problem will be handled in the group.

Similar meetings may be held periodically during the life of the group. They are always announced in advance to the adolescents. The parents develop considerable camaraderie and an atmosphere of mutual support for the adolescents' group work as these meetings continue. Some group interaction often develops among the parents. Frequently this is of both diagnostic and therapeutic value. In all meetings the therapist maintains the confidentiality of the group, but permits the parents to share information they may have regarding the progress and behavior of group members including their own youngster.

THE WORK OF THE GROUP

Once the tasks of developing cohesion and open communication are achieved in an adolescent group, the observed interactions are very similar to those seen in adult groups. The words and issues differ, of course, but the work of recognizing, confronting, and resolving interpersonal blocks to group progress is technically similar to adult work. The therapist gradually becomes less of an active structuring agent. and moves toward a more reflective, interpretive stance in the group.

There are two rather common patterns in adolescent group work that do differ somewhat from the typical adult group. The first concerns the frequency and intensity of direct competition with the therapist. Of course, similar interactions occur in adult groups, but the adult patient is usually less frightened by his effrontery than is the adolescent. Often the adolescent can express his new strength only in the context of totally discounting the therapist's importance to him. Frequently he announces his desire to leave the group. The persistence of occurrences of this kind in adolescent groups is related to the adolescent's need to utilize adults as identification figures. With the support of the group the adolescent goes through a cycle of testing the therapist, accepting (or even idealizing) him, challenging the therapist and testing him again at a less dependent level, and then accepting a new relationship on this more egalitarian basis. No special group techniques are necessary in the management of this pattern of behavior. The cycle merely needs to be recognized as a natural growth experience that is basically constructive for the adolescent involved. If the group therapist can com-

fortably accept the challenge and support new strength in the
member, the remainder of the group can usually remind the
challenger of remaining problems and prevent his precipitous
departure from the group.

The second problem results from the adolescent's relative
lack of conceptual skill with which to describe the subtle and
intricate nuances of interpersonal transactions. This deficiency
can usually be countered verbally if the therapist can develop
the capacity to describe complex social phenomena in words
and images familiar to the adolescent. This kind of translation is
sometimes insufficient or unconvincing. In these situations, judi-
cious use of psychodrama and gestalt techniques to make the
impasse tangible may be indicated. These experiments often
permit the group to comprehend the emotional factors beneath
surface behavior and to feel the power of hidden forces operat-
ing in the group.

Pat, age 15, was silly and disruptive in a group that had
decided to work seriously. He fended off efforts of group
members to engage him in serious talk with clowning and
flippant remarks. The group was angry and wanted Pat
ejected since he was "just goofing off."

Pat had made an individual treatment contract but had
described considerable anxiety about joining the group
during pregroup individual sessions. The therapist was
sure that the clowning reflected this anxiety rather than
lack of motivation, but comments to this effect did not
decrease the group's anger at Pat or change his defensive
style.

The therapist proposed a "psychological exercise" that
he said "might help the group members to understand one
another better." One member (a popular boy) was blind-
folded. He was asked to choose someone to lead him
around the room. Without hesitation he chose one of the
attractive girls in the group. After they had traversed the
room without incident, they were asked to describe their
feelings. The boy laughed and said it was fun—"A good
excuse to hold hands with Cathy." The girl said she'd wor-

ried a little that he was walking too fast. Once or twice she thought he might bump into things and blame her.

"Okay, we'll talk some more about how you reacted later. Right now let's try someone else. How about you, Pat?"

"No siree, you're not gonna put that snot-rag on my face. Germs. Germs!"

"Yes, come on, Pat."

Pat ambled up slowly, rolling his eyes in mock terror. "Stop clowning, Pat," a member said.

Pat ran his hand over his face as though to wipe off a smile and pulled a solemn expression. The handkerchief was tied in place and he was asked who he wanted to lead him. He named the female cotherapist. She declined and told him he had to ask a group member. Pat began to look tense and worried beneath the blindfold as the silence lengthened.

"Come on, Pat, who do you pick? Hurry up."

Pat abruptly tore off the blindfold and rushed to his seat, clearly troubled and upset.

"You look scared," the therapist commented.

"They'd run me over something. They hate me anyway." Pat was obviously serious.

"God, he's really scared," a member said.

"Yeah, he doesn't trust anyone but the doctor."

Pat continued to have problems in the group, but the members were more sympathetic and were able to sense and explore his very real fear of people his own age.

TERMINATION

The issues involved in termination of group psychotherapy differ from individual work because group members are at various points in their development, yet the group must stop at one moment in time. In practice, termination of group therapy can occur because of clinical progress for the individual, but entire groups are usually terminated because of external events. Many therapists designate the life of the group at its very outset. A common pattern is to start groups in September and terminate them in June since many adolescents are unavailable in the summers. Individual decisions are made at termination as to whether a youngster should return for another group in the fall, continue in individual work, or leave treatment entirely.

Regardless of how this practical issue is handled, it does seem important for the group to have a clear and definite point of cessation. If the group is permitted to merely drift apart the therapist deprives the members of the opportunity to face and learn from their idiosyncratic responses to separation. There is also considerable value in the process of reviewing the group's progress and assessing its benefits to each member. This can be organized around the individual treatment contracts of each member. The opportunity to address both the triumphs and failures of the members and the therapist offers both a chance for consolidating gains and for identifying areas that require further attention, in or out of formal therapy.

ADOLESCENT GROUP THERAPY IN PERSPECTIVE

It seems that therapists are increasingly eclectic in their choice of treatment techniques. This would appear to be a reasonable development in a field where no single treatment approach has been demonstrated to have clear superiority. One benefit of this eclecticism is that it permits various combinations of treatment approaches tailored to the individual needs of a specific adolescent and his family.

The combination and integration of individual and group therapy with the same therapist enjoys popularity among adolescent therapists. The two forms of treatment appear to catalyze movement in each. For example, a youngster may be hesitant or unsure how to bring up a particularly touchy subject in group. The therapist could use the individual meeting to plan and rehearse how the client will discuss the topic in the next group meeting. In some circumstances, a youngster may need to debrief an unusually difficult group experience in her next individual therapy meeting. Also, a group experience may provide a transition between a successful but extremely dependent individual therapy relationship and termination.

Group work may also be combined with family therapy or utilized to assist in dealing with a specific problem in ongoing therapy. Placement in a group may help an adolescent who is excessively enmeshed in his family to emancipate during the course of family therapy.

In short, group psychotherapy is a technique that can be helpful or disastrous to the troubled adolescent. Careful initial and continuing diagnostic evaluation should dictate when it is used and which other techniques need to be combined with it for maximum benefit.

The method of beginning and conducting group therapy described here is only a skeleton. It is useless, even dangerous, without training and experience both in group therapy and work with individual adolescents. There is no substitute for supervised experience in a live encounter with real adolescents.

MANUALIZED FORMS OF GROUP THERAPY

This chapter has discussed two forms of group psychotherapy for adolescents, the open-ended supportive groups that typically occur in residential treatment programs and exploratory group therapy that typically occurs with outpatients. There is another form of group therapy with adolescents that is sometimes used with specific, homogeneous populations (for instance, depressed adolescents or substance-abusing adolescents) or with youngsters who need a very specific intervention (such as social skills training or anger management). The therapy technique has been manualized, which means that the therapist follows a specific curriculum over a certain number of meetings. Usually there is a workbook for the group members to use during the meetings, to complete as homework assignments, and to eventually keep as a reminder for what they learned during the course of therapy.

Although this form of group therapy is not addressed in this book, the reader may be interested in these references. Fodor

(1992) edited a handbook that describes specialized techniques for teaching social skills and anger control and other topics. Another example is Jaffe's (1998) manual for teenagers who are participating in a chemical dependency treatment program.

There is a good deal of literature available on both theoretical and practical aspects of group therapy with adolescents. Irving Berkovitz's (1972) book, *Adolescents Grow in Groups*, is a classic. S. R. Slavson was the father of group therapy for children and adolescents. He and his colleague, Mortimer Schiffer, wrote many books on this topic (for example, Slavson and Schiffer, 1975, and Schiffer, 1984). Meeks (1973, 1974) wrote early articles on technical aspects of group therapy with adolescents. More recent books on group psychotherapy with adolescents were written by Azima and Richmond (1989), MacLennan and Dies (1992), Kymissis and Halperin (1996), Malekoff (1997) and Stoiber and Kratochwill (1998). In addition to discussing the general principles of group therapy with adolescents, some of these authors (such as Berkovitz and Azima and Richmond) have chapters that address specific issues and populations, such as group therapy with minority teenagers, group therapy with delinquents, or group therapy with alcohol and drug addicted youngsters. In addition, Berkovitz (1995) has written extensively on the use of group therapy in high schools. The history of adolescent group psychotherapy was chronicled by Rachman and Raubolt (1984). Bernet (1982) described the technique of verbal games, which is useful in group therapy with younger adolescents. Oldfield (1986) pioneered a specialized style of group therapy called The Journey. Oldfield employs a rich variety of technique, including guided imagery, role playing, and mask making. In The Journey, teenagers recapitulate the steps through adolescence, which have been captured over the centuries in myths, legends, and folktales.

PSYCHOTHERAPY AND THE ADOLESCENT'S PARENTS

Psychotherapy with the adolescent has an additional complexity that so far we have mentioned only briefly. Even when the therapist has a clear grasp of the therapeutic alliance, considerable skill at conversing with adolescents, and the ability to recognize transference and handle it therapeutically, he may still run into difficulties related to the adolescent's family. We turn now to two chapters that address the technical problems raised by the complex interrelationship of the adolescent and his parents.

CHAPTER 7

family therapy

Family therapy has come of age during the past two decades as an important treatment modality in the management of troubled adolescents. An early neglect of the developmental and intrapsychic aspects of family therapy has been rectified by the involvement of many child psychiatrists and analysts in family work. The intricate play of developmental pressures, family structure, and family communication patterns has added both theoretical and clinical richness to our understanding of personality development. An early emphasis on the form of family therapy (for example, narrow insistence on having every family member present in every session) has matured to a recognition that the essence of the family therapy approach is a clear conceptualization of emotional disorders within their family context. The most effective family intervention at a given point in therapy may consist of an individual interview with an adolescent child or that youngster's placement in group psychotherapy. Frequently it may be separate interviews with the parents to strengthen the husband-wife relationship.

The family therapist appreciates the fact that these direct therapy contacts with individuals or subgroups of the family have great effects on the entire family structure. For example, the therapist makes a strong statement supporting the importance and legitimacy of the husband-wife relationship apart from the couple's parenting function merely by scheduling an interview that will focus exclusively on this subgroup and role relationship within the family. This message will reverberate throughout the family, influencing or perhaps threatening previous configurations of family priorities, alliances, and status distributions. The family-oriented therapist attempts to anticipate these repercussions, arranging those interventions that will accomplish the family alterations that further family growth, flexibility, and effective communication.

This brief introductory comment is intended to convey a sense of the increasing clarity of therapeutic conceptualization in family therapy. The first practical step, however, is diagnostic. There are two very different types of families who need family therapy and it is very important to make this distinction. The first type is a family whose family member is indeed suffering from a catastrophic mental illness or is adjusting to a catastrophic life event such as terminal illness, rape, or loss of a loved object. In these families family therapy is performed to enable the family to look at the catastrophic event, to educate them about its effect on all family members, and to mobilize the strengths of the family to recover. A combination of crisis intervention, psychoeducational and supportive problem-solving approaches will be utilized (Lantz and Thorward, 1985).

For example, parents who have just discovered that their handsome, bright 17-year-old son has bipolar disorder or schizophrenia must have help to mourn the loss of the healthy son, education regarding the illness, and help to plan effectively for his future needs. In most instances the parents should not assume responsibility for the development or maintenance of a primarily organic illness. Parent and family advocacy groups such as the Alliance for the Mentally Ill are of great assistance to these families. These experienced self-help groups object strenuously to the mental health profession's tendency to reframe the illness to include the family in the pathology.

In the second type of family the identified patient's psychopathology is interwoven with the psychopathology of the family. This chapter will focus on this type of family in which the identified patient suffers from a symptom that is, in fact, affected by and perpetuated by the behavior and attitudes of other family members. These families are emphasized because they often are the most difficult and confusing families encountered by the beginning family therapist. Special problems are also raised by special family constellations such as single parent families and "stepfamilies." These situations will be addressed in chapter 15.

The treatment of the pathologically intertwined family has become fairly well defined. The therapist proceeds methodically through several steps in his approach to the family. First he works to obtain acceptance as a temporary and yet important member of the family group. Minuchin (1989) has referred to this crucial step as "joining." Its successful accomplishment is necessary to the next step of redefining the "emotional illness" in an individual family member as instead a family problem, a problem in family functioning that is partly manifested through the symptomatic behavior of the designated patient. This step is quite difficult in some families. Certainly it is rarely accomplished by mere theoretical insistence. The family must be shown, not told, that the family system, not the symptomatic member, is in need of help and change.

Once these two steps are accomplished, the therapist is able to use his special role in relation to the family to block maladaptive patterns of relating within the family and to encourage exploration and experimentation with the styles of interaction that may be more satisfactory. In this effort he may utilize the entire range of psychiatric interventions, perhaps emphasizing interviews with the entire family, but certainly not restricting himself to this format. The choice of interventions is guided by a tentative diagnosis of the family patterns and pathology. This conceptual framework is constantly revised and refined to include the data that are revealed by the family's response to those interventions that the therapist attempts.

This process is quite complex. In many ways it is a more difficult skill to master than is individual therapy, since it requires greater activity on the part of the therapist and is therefore more prone to induce errors, both because of countertransference and the ease with which subtle verbal and nonverbal cues can be missed in the turmoil of an active family session. The family therapist is truly a participant observer and very busy at both jobs. These statements should not be construed as a warning against the dangers of doing great damage through family therapy. Family systems are very resilient and, in fact, hard to change. Still, effective work in the area requires careful study and supervised experience. One of the best introductory texts is *Families and Family Therapy* (Minuchin, 1989) which is clear and concise and highly sophisticated. The purpose of this brief chapter is merely to whet the appetite of those adolescent therapists who have not considered the positive applications that family therapy offers in adolescent psychotherapy. Family therapy as a formal approach has some particular indications that will be considered now, followed by a more complete explication of the steps in family therapy mentioned earlier.

INDICATIONS FOR FAMILY THERAPY

Conjoint family therapy with the entire family seems to be the treatment of choice in certain situations and for certain kinds of emotional disorders. Crisis situations in adolescence, including runaways, suicide attempts, and illegitimate pregnancies, often are best approached through family interviews. These sessions are of value in encouraging the family to find more adaptive ways of responding to the immediate problem and, in addition, may reveal the chronic family problems that resulted in the eruption of symptomatic behavior in the adolescent. In many of these families, for example, the underlying excessive closeness of the adolescent to one or more family members may be the cause of a runaway or delinquent action that represents an ill-advised attempt at emancipation. Unfortunately, many families do not seem motivated to continue in therapy once the immediate crisis is resolved.

PROBLEMS OF ENMESHMENT

Even in the absence of crisis, the adolescent whose difficulties seem primarily related to problems in separating from his parents is probably best treated in conjoint family therapy. These youngsters may present with clear developmental immaturities including social anxiety, academic difficulties, and overt cling-

TYPES OF FAMILY THERAPY

There are several forms of family therapy—so the serious student can investigate the different theories and techniques and develop a style that best suits herself.

Integrative family therapy, based on psychodynamic principles, was the term used by Nathan Ackerman (1958, 1982), considered the father of family therapy.

Structural family therapy is represented by Salvador Minuchin (1989, 1993). His approach is to join the family in searching for the structures, patterns, or rules that are the foundation for the patient's or the family's symptoms. The therapist actively teaches the family how to engage each other more constructively.

Strategic family therapy is exemplified by Jay Haley (1971, 1980), who thought that symptoms of the individual patient were manifestations of dysfunction within the family. The individual could not change unless the entire family changes. The therapist may give the family explicit instructions about how to change their behavior.

Experiential family therapy was practiced by Virginia Satir (1983), who encouraged communication and facilitated the family's search for its own solutions.

Family systems theory of Murray Bowen (1978) focused on the person's family of origin rather than the person's nuclear family. The therapist shows the client how to collect and understand information regarding parents, grandparents, etc., through detailed multigenerational research.

Analytic family therapy or object relations family therapy has been described by David Scharff and Jill Savege Scharff (1991). They help family members recognize unconscious material by interpreting, developing insight, and making use of transference and countertransference phenomena. They would not actually try to shape or instruct the family.

ing, childish behavior. They may disguise their excessive dependence, with the family's collusion, as psychosomatic illness and complaints of illness. Of course, this family pattern may be precipitated and potentiated by the presence of actual physical disease, particularly chronic illness, in the child. As mentioned earlier, these families may come to therapy only at the time the adolescent tries to extricate himself from the excessively close family bonds. Occasionally the family is pressured into therapy by external agencies such as the school who detect the adolescent's social immaturity.

The basic problem in many of these families is an unsatisfactory marital relationship leading to inappropriate utilization of the adolescent to satisfy parental affectional needs or to provide a buffer between the parents. Therapy efforts are directed to strengthening the husband-wife subgroup if possible. If this seems impractical, the dissatisfactions can be rendered more explicit and the parents can be assisted to meet their needs outside the family while the adolescent's desire to separate is strengthened and supported. The therapist needs honest empathy for the "holding-on" parent in these families in order to keep the families in treatment and permit the eventual release of the adolescent. It is very easy for therapists with a special interest in adolescents to overidentify with the youngster. Merely blaming the parent and lecturing about the adolescent's right to a life of his own will only increase anxiety and perpetuate the frightened clinging pattern in the family. Many of these parents know at some level what they are "doing wrong." They need help in discovering alternatives.

The first step in altering excessively close bonds in a disturbed family is to understand the origin of the enmeshment. Very often the explanation is to be found mainly in the emotional history and needs of the parent. In other instances, however, the origin of the overattachment is mainly in the child. For example, children who are especially vulnerable due to constitutional or organic deficits in ego apparatus may subtly pull their parents into initially appropriate protective relationships that only gradually deteriorate into destructive bonds. Another example is the patho-

logical bond that develops in the families of chemically dependent patients as a result of the addictive process. We will discuss
that specific problem in chapter 17, but the point is that we need
to carefully evaluate situations of family enmeshment since each
has its own history and family function. In addition it is wise to
remember that all families faced with serious emotional problems tend to regress and this may exaggerate the apparent degree of excessive dependency and enmeshment actually present
in the ongoing family system. Family interaction is just that—
*inter*action—and there is often hidden complexity and more wisdom than we suspect at first glance even in families with serious
problems.

EXTERNALIZING FAMILIES

Another group of adolescents who may be assisted through
family therapy are those who live in families who externalize
problems. In these families each member is preoccupied with
the shortcomings of various other family members, and tends to
feel that whatever unhappiness and adjustment problems he is
having actually result from shortcomings of another family
members. If individual sessions are held they are dominated by
complaints directed against other members of the family. If the
therapist sees two family members separately and discusses a
recent upset with each, he is often left wondering if the two
people were actually involved in the same event. There is virtually no introspection and the capacity for self-observation seems
as limited as the skill in finding faults in other family members is
hypertrophied. Diagnostically, adolescents from these families
often present as behavior disorders or personality disorders.
Usually the pathology is relatively ego-syntonic and the adolescent rejects designation as a patient. However, since he clearly
sees the pathology in other family members, he may accept
family therapy as necessary.

Family therapy in these cases is difficult and trying for the
therapist who is constantly being sought as an ally against other
family members. With patience and dogged perseverance, how-

ever, it is possible to gradually require these families to communicate in ways that diminish the need for cycles of recrimination and blame. For example, the therapist, after assuring himself that he has effectively "joined" the family, may prohibit critical statements between family members. All communications must be translated into personal requests and statements of personal need. For example, if the father wishes to complain that his wife is not affectionate, he must say, "I feel lonely and I need affection. Is there any way I can help you show me more warmth?" In previous family discussions he probably would have said, "Our trouble is that you're a frigid bitch." The therapist may also require the parents to sit together and even request that they hold hands. The purpose of these maneuvers is not to forcibly graft these new behaviors on the family. The goal is merely to block previous stereotyped interactions that serve to avoid awareness of internal feelings by displacing them on other family members. Of course, many other techniques will be utilized in the tedious and prolonged effort to change destructive relationship patterns. The examples offered are merely illustrative of the way in which the therapist actively moves to alter family tradition.

FAMILIES WITH A SCAPECOAT

Another adolescent who may be best treated through family interviews is the youngster whose pathology is required to maintain a neurotic family homeostasis. This includes youngsters with "superego lacunae" but also a variety of other situations in which the adolescent is made into a scapegoat by his family. In some of these cases it is necessary to provide a period of individual therapy to the scapegoat, in order to raise his status in the family group and to discover and activate personal goals that lie outside the scapegoat role. Without this special assistance, the scapegoat is often unmotivated to give up his central role in the family. Like the man who has been ridden out of town on a rail, he feels the procedure is uncomfortable but more of an honor than merely walking like everyone else.

The family therapist is interested in assessing family functioning in a number of interlocking dimensions. The first of
these considers the family boundaries. The therapist tries to
determine if there are clear generational boundaries, boundaries between individuals in the family, clear boundaries between the family and the surrounding society, and clear sex
role boundaries. Pathology may result from excessively rigid
boundary definitions or from boundaries that are vague or
capriciously changeable.

The second structural feature of the family that is observed is
the nature of the subgroups within the larger family. For example, a common dysfunctional subgrouping consists of mother
and children allied against the father. The result is that the
father is rendered ineffective in the parenting role and is lost to
the wife as a gratifying husband. In normal families subgrouping occurs in a variety of patterns determined by the emotional
or practical issues that occupy the family at the moment. There
is flexibility and shifting alliance patterns without strong family
efforts to resist the changes. The therapist also studies the family patterns of communication, noting both the conceptual clarity and the affective range. Normal families have relatively open
communication that tends to be clear and determined by present needs rather than defensive maintenance of family myths or
the need to deny particular affective states. Some disturbed
families cannot permit the expression of angry feelings. When
these threaten to emerge, communication may be blocked by
irrelevant expressions of mutual concern or warmth. Other
families block expressions of tender feelings. In very disturbed
families communication may be unintelligible.

During the diagnostic period of family therapy the parenting
skills and styles of the family are also delineated. Do the parents
provide appropriate nurture? Are they able to set limits? Can
they provide information in a form that is usable and accurate?
Can they deal openly with husband-wife conflict or do they
utilize the parenting function to fight one another? Have they

relegated parenting, particularly the emotional components of the parenting role, partially or wholly to one of the children? These and many other questions must be answered if one is to plan an effective treatment approach for the specific family. Another whole arena of investigation is opened by studying the family "missions" that adolescent children may be assigned by parents or even grandparents or other powerful members of the extended family (Stierlin, 1977).

Finally the therapist observes the family's style of problem solving. He is interested in seeing whether the family permits wide involvement in reaching decisions and planning actions or depends on one autocratic leader. If there is a single leader, is he or she supported or is there implied rebellion and contempt behind the apparent passivity of other family members? The therapist will encounter other families who seem incapable of reaching a decision. In these families there is no leadership or the process of problem solving is so contaminated by raging affective conflicts that it becomes chaotic and inconclusive.

FAMILY TREATMENT

After diagnostic evaluation it is possible to arrive at treatment goals for a specific family. These goals may have levels of priority although the therapist considers the entire picture in all his interactions with the family. For example, the therapist may decide that a family's confusing style of communication is a basic problem that must be actively confronted early in treatment. At the same time, however, he may be aware that one purpose of the disjointed communication is to disguise the fact that the overtly respected father is actually powerless in the family. He may choose then to focus on the communication problem by utilizing the father as his ally, thus simultaneously attempting to improve the father's status and to reveal the family's use of confusion to block the father's competence.

As the therapist intervenes to change the family, his approach must constantly respond to the countermeasures the family mobilizes to prevent change. The process is not static but interactive.

TECHNIQUES OF FAMILY THERAPY

The techniques of family therapy were summarized by Josephson and Moncher (1998). The following examples of therapy techniques are useful for family problems commonly observed in clinical practice.

Joining refers to the clinician joining the family as an agent of change. That includes communicating that the therapist understands each person's views.

Reframing is a verbal intervention in which the therapist provides an alternative way to perceive a behavior. The therapist may take a problematic behavior and give it an adaptive, positive connotation.

Circular questioning is a way to explore or track patterns of communication within a family without directly confronting the symptomatic individual.

Family enactment refers to the technique of asking family members to do or say something within the therapy meeting. Enactments expose a family problem and also assist the family to find healthier, alternative responses to the problem.

Prescribed tasks or "homework" are behavioral interventions in which families are instructed to approach a conflicted area and master it away from the therapy session.

Paradoxical interventions are unusual or contrary demands that the therapist makes of a family. For instance, asking a family to exaggerate a symptomatic or maladaptive pattern of behavior.

Realigning boundaries involves identifying and changing family boundaries that are too rigid, too permeable, or otherwise misaligned.

Facilitating attachment involves redirecting the family's attachment behavior, encouraging either engagement or disengagement with caregivers.

Throughout the treatment contact, the therapist focuses primarily on family strengths and skills. Even behavior that must change is usually relabeled positively even while it is questioned and blocked. An intrusive, domineering mother may be told that she is taking too much responsibility and pressure in the family. Her husband may be asked to take over some of the work, "to give your overburdened wife a little rest from all her worries." A general expectation that family members will help one another is regularly voiced by the therapist. The value position that mutual support is the function of the family is clearly enunciated, even when the needed support is a limit. "Johnny has a problem in that rules sometimes make him angry. Now you need to help him with that by making rules clear and not arguing about them or trying to explain them when he's angry. It might really be a help to him to know that he can talk with you about the rules later, when he's calmed down."

Needless to say, the focus in family therapy is on the present, although the content of sessions may have many references to past events. When the family begins to recount past history they sometimes do so in order to refocus on the individual designated patient as the "real" problem in the family. Talk of the past is sometimes, therefore, defensive—a countermeasure aimed at neutralizing therapeutic activity. There are at least three exceptions to this general rule. Occasionally, the family will bring up the past in order to reveal a family secret to the therapist. Of course, this is not defensive, but a step in opening the family interactions to the work of therapy. The clear difference from defensive use of the past is that these past occurrences continue to have a strong impact on the entire family in the present and knowledge of them helps to clarify current issues and conflicts.

A second exception tends to occur late in family therapy when an individual family member has dropped his defensiveness and has accepted personal responsibility for his role in the family problems. At that time, a member may focus on experiences from his past that serve to distort appropriate responses to present family reality. It may be useful at this point to refer the family member for individual therapy.

The third exception relates to those situations in which the patient is reenacting important past events. These may include family secrets, family myths, or turning passive into active as when a victim becomes the victimizer. A common example, of course, is the multigenerational recurrence of child abuse.

SUMMARY

Family therapy offers much as the primary therapy in certain kinds of adolescent problems and may be useful as a temporary adjunct to other treatment methods in many other cases.

It differs somewhat from other intensive therapy approaches in that it depends less on introspection and insight to achieve lasting change than does either individual or group psychotherapy. The family therapist, in his direct interactions with the family, is more of an orchestra conductor and participant than an interpreter of events. He does not aim merely to help the family understand itself. He acts to change the family so that it no longer blocks the understanding and growth of its members. Understanding—true, deep emotional understanding—often accompanies these changes as an important byproduct.

Therapeutic activity, however, is not random or dictated by countertransference. It is carefully planned following a careful diagnostic study of family pathology. Family therapy is not anti-intellectual and intuitive in its conception. Although the therapist may reveal more of himself than is customary in more reflective therapies, this revelation is directed only partly by his subjective experience of involvement in the family. This spontaneity must be tempered by a precise understanding of the purposes for which he is utilizing himself as a living instrument. Arriving at this understanding will require the best intellectual and professional skills one can command along with a painstaking multigenerational assessment of the many dimensions and capabilities of each family member as created and revealed in their history together. Achieving the goals of family therapy will require a combination of activity and restraint that equals the most challenging demands of any form of psychotherapy.

CHAPTER 8

the parents of the adolescent patient

Many parents would agree that adolescence is the most trying period in the experience of rearing a child. For the parents of the disturbed adolescent, this phase of growth may be virtually unbearable. Problems that have been latent become menacingly overt. Dependency problems blossom into pitched battles as the adolescent invites parental involvement and help by his maladaptive behavior, and then vilifies the parents for babying him and trying to live his life for him. Competition becomes vicious as the adolescent's overdependence on intellectualization and grand sweeping generalities lead him to view the parents as narrow, dull, and ineffective. Superego externalization causes the parents to be viewed as harsh and joyless on some occasions, as immoral and self-indulgent on another day. Any parental defensiveness, self-justification, or counterattack provokes a vengeful rage and a sullen sense of martyrdom.

There are basic elements of duplicity in both generations during this developmental phase. The adolescent is actually struggling against intensified dependent ties to his parents. At the same time, he wishes to gain autonomy and independence. This combination of increased emotional investment coupled with the urgency to escape the family is hardly conducive to openness and honesty in the adolescent's interactions with his parents.

On the other hand, many parents of disturbed adolescents are dishonest in their relationships with their children. Although consciously claiming to desire independence and maturity for their youngsters, they unconsciously undermine growth because of their neurotic needs. They act to prevent separation,

213

heterosexual maturity, or self-sufficiency in their child when these would threaten their own tenuous adjustment or result in an unbearable sense of loss to them. The degree of tenacity with which the parent clings to the adolescent varies with many factors including the extent of parental psychopathology and the realistic sources of substitute gratification available to the parent. The widowed mother, living alone on meager funds, obviously faces greater problems in relinquishing her last son than a happily married woman in comfortable financial and social circumstances, although both must deal with some sense of loss. Both the adolescent and his parents have reasons for obfuscating the terms of the unwritten contracts that regulate their interchange.

The tendency for the family to regress if the adolescent has serious emotional conflicts adds to the problem for the adolescent psychotherapist. Parents often present with their "worst foot forward" because of the pain they feel over frustrated efforts to help the adolescent. Often they treat the therapist as the child treats them, making unrealistic demands, rejecting help, and being unduly critical. This can lead the therapist to exaggerate the parental pathology and, sometimes, to identify with the adolescent and minimize the youngster's contribution to the family distress.

ENTER THE THERAPIST

The therapist who ventures into this devious and supercharged intrigue as a catalyst to emotional growth can expect to become embroiled with both parties. In order to work successfully with adolescent patients, one has to accept this involvement with the parents. Even when the parents are referred to a colleague for therapy, they will usually still insert themselves directly or indirectly into the adolescent's therapy. This involvement should be expected and utilized. Attempts to avoid it or deny its occurrence are at best futile, at worst tragic. The probabilities of a successful treatment are increased by planning a constructive reaction to the welter of emotions between parent and child. Ignoring the certainty that these forces will be expressed in the therapy can only leave the therapist blindly reacting to the manipulations of both his patient and the patient's parents. Although the technical approach may be individual psychotherapy of the adolescent, the therapist must remember that the entire family is the real patient.

This does not mean that the therapist adopts a tough and pugnacious determination never to be "sucked in" by neurotic family patterns. It does mean that the therapist is alert to the multiple determinants and implications of the communications that he receives from the parents or from the child about the parents. It means that this awareness is utilized to promote growth and independence and to protect the vulnerable and crucial therapeutic alliance with the adolescent. If this bond is sacrificed in order to pacify immediate strains in the parent-child relationship, the therapist has lost the effective foothold necessary to help the family. All attempts to influence and manipulate the therapist, whether they originate from the adolescent or his parents, must be received with the same respectful, objective, exploring attitude that is accorded all other relevant material. This analysis of underlying meaning determines whether the therapist reacts to the manipulation with interpretation, firm limit setting, or temporary acquiescence. The therapist tries to choose the response that offers greatest promise of promoting the long-range goals of the therapy.

THE PARENTS AND THE THERAPEUTIC CONTRACT

The effort to develop a workable therapy contract with the parents of the adolescent begins in the postdiagnostic family conference. The most common roadblock at this early stage is the therapist's failure to insist on the necessary conditions for an effective psychotherapy. This reluctance to "drive a hard bargain" may often be a response to parental ambivalence about the proposed psychotherapy. Their conscious or unconscious fears that the family homeostasis may be jeopardized lead parents to threaten, offer deals, or otherwise attempt to influence the conditions of therapy. These efforts will not be difficult to manage if the therapist keeps the minimum requirements of outpatient psychotherapy clearly in mind.

Basic Conditions of Outpatient Individual Psychotherapy

1. *The patient must have a real choice about beginning and continuing therapy after clearly understanding its nature and purpose.* Of course, several interviews may go by before the adolescent has finished testing the therapist, sending up trial balloons, and generally "casing the joint." Only then does he have any real understanding of the nature and purpose of therapy. Simply telling him what therapy is all about accomplishes very little. It is sometimes useful to offer a negative adolescent a definite number of interviews in which to decide whether he wants to involve himself in therapy. Even if his decision is positive, his willingness to accept and to continue therapy may be evidenced only by his appearance at his sessions. If he comes without being threatened, bribed, or physically coerced, this may be accepted as prima facie evidence of an interest in the treatment process even if he grumbles constantly and regularly questions the need for therapy. On the other hand, if he must actually be forced to attend the sessions, it is unlikely that progress is possible. Some modicum of responsibility for his own treatment must be assumed by even the very young patient.

2. *The adolescent must be allowed to come to therapy for his own problems.* A psychotherapy program explicitly or even implicitly undertaken to shape adolescents to some parental expectation or to persuade or dissuade them in regard to a particular action is doomed before it begins. Adolescents must be in therapy for themselves. Their reasons for coming must be accepted and therapy must begin with their concerns. Of course, in the long run, successful therapy may produce some or all of the results that would please the parents, but this happy circumstance must only be a fortunate byproduct of autonomous choices made by the emotionally maturing adolescent. The adolescent must separate and individuate. His goals must be his own, neither arising

from passive compliance to parental wishes or based on blind rebellion against those wishes.

3. *The patient's communication with the therapist must be confidential unless or until the therapist feels that a clear danger to the patient or others exists.* The parents can expect to be told whether therapy is progressing satisfactorily, but not the feelings, fantasies, and concerns that the adolescent voices in treatment. They have a right to know "how things are in treatment," but not "what is going on in treatment."

4. *The therapist and the patient must have an honest relationship.* The therapist cannot agree to lie to the patient. Although he will not "tell all" to the parents, he must feel free to inform the patient of the occurrence of each contact with the parents and the content of these interactions at any time that this information seems therapeutically relevant or at any time that the adolescent wants to know. The therapist will "keep secrets" from the parents, but will, if it seems indicated, feel free to "tell all" to the patient.

5. *In matters that pertain directly to the treatment process, there can only be one therapist.* If the adolescent verbalizes feelings about the therapist at home, these should not be evaluated by the parent, but should be referred back to the next therapy session. If the adolescent expresses uncertainty about continuing therapy, he should be told to discuss this concern with the therapist as he would discuss any other idea or feeling. If the adolescent asks parental opinions regarding a comment or a procedure employed by the therapist, the parents should ask the adolescent what he thinks and whether this has been discussed with the therapist directly. If the parent feels the therapist has behaved inappropriately, the parent should discuss this feeling directly with the therapist.

These requirements may sound autocratic, stringent, and unrealistic. Many parents react to them as if they were just that way. They feel that the therapist is intruding into the sanctity of their home to dictate their management of their own child. As a matter of fact, this is precisely what the therapist is doing. However, it must be recalled that the therapist is assuming this authority at the request of the family. The therapist has been hired to lead the family members in their effort to improve family functioning. This position as therapeutic leader is untenable unless the parents grant authority in matters pertaining directly to the psychotherapy.

If the therapist is so passive, nondirective, or timid that he fails to explain the role that must be played, the therapist is in no position to confront the parents when they trespass into the expert's area. If he does not assume firm therapeutic leadership, he may soon find himself being utilized as the family scapegoat. The family members may handle their hostilities, anxieties, and depressions by turning them on the therapist. That poor mortal may soon feel like the bystander who tried to break up a marital argument and ended up being attacked by the husband and wife, now comfortably united in their rage at the outsider.

Even more frequently, the adolescent will attempt to avoid limits and feelings of guilt by playing the parents against the therapist. The parents can avoid being drawn into such manipulations if they have a clear conception and acceptance of the therapist's temporary leadership role.

The parents are likely to become angry when the therapist sets limits on them, just as the adolescent reacts with anger when his acting out is questioned and opposed. This should not deter the therapist from doing the job. If the family is treatable, the parents will come to respect the therapist for courage and determination to assume responsibilities. If they intended all along to employ the therapist only so long as he did not really interfere with the status quo, it is better to get that fact out into the open.

Of course, it is not necessary for the therapist to be belligerent or combative. The therapist must remember that he serves purely at the family's pleasure. He is never in a position of telling the family what they must do, only what must be done if therapy is to succeed. Even in this, one must humbly remember that even therapists may be wrong! However, it has been said that wisdom consists of acting on the basis of incomplete information. The therapist must be a decisive leader even though he cannot claim absolute certainty. If there is good reason to believe that a request for a vacation, a schedule change, or a family discussion about the therapist interferes with therapy or represents resistance, it is the therapist's duty to convey this opinion frankly and with conviction. If parental behavior continually interferes with therapy, it is his duty to explain that treatment will be impossible unless the parents are able to understand and change their disruptive actions.

Function of the Treatment Contract

The contractual terms discussed are intended as a guide for the therapist in making arrangements with the parents for treatment. A rigid demand for absolute compliance with these conditions would stifle the parents' interaction in the treatment process. The list of conditions is not presented as a binding package deal during the postdiagnostic family conference. Generally, only those points that are raised directly or indirectly by the family need to be emphasized. The others are merely mentioned in a brief, matter-of-fact manner. Even though parents agree to this contract, they are likely to break one or more clauses under the pressure of emotions stirred in the course of treatment. The previous explicit or tacit agreement, however, allows the therapist to highlight the motives involved in the breach, since the parent cannot claim simple ignorance of the proper helpful role in regard to the treatment process. The parent who cannot accept the contract, as well as the parent who accepts and then complains that the agreement is unfair, also reveals his family-bound pathology directly to the searchlight of therapeutic curiosity. It must be emphasized, however, that parents do deserve education regarding the goals and methods of psychotherapy. If they do not understand these goals and methods and their own proper role in facilitating their achievement, they may interfere with the therapeutic undertaking out of simple ignorance, which may be misunderstood as neurotic meddling.

The real importance of guidelines is to help the therapist to avoid falling unknowingly into unsatisfactory agreements. By holding firm ideas regarding the working conditions that he needs, the therapist is alerted to recognize those parental anxieties that lead to unwillingness to allow their youngster every possible advantage in the treatment situation. When parents begin to negotiate for unworkable contracts, the therapist has an alarm system that warns him not to defeat himself in his therapeutic efforts before he even gets underway.

Enforcing the Terms of the Contract

Actually, the therapist has no power to enforce any of the clauses of the therapeutic contract with the parents. Their cooperation depends on their understanding of the reasons that the therapist makes certain requests and the extent of their trust in his professional competence and his benevolence toward the entire family.

In a very real sense, the therapist not only must maintain a shaky therapeutic alliance with the adolescent, but also must maintain one that may be even more tricky with the parents. The alliance with the parents is partially cemented by their mature wishes for their youngster to improve and attain self-sufficiency. Therapy cannot be conducted if the parents are totally devoid of this healthy desire. Fortunately, this bleak condition rarely exists in parents who seek treatment for their adolescent. Usually, this hope for successful maturation is present, but is opposed by a variety of anxieties, neurotic ties, and cultural expectancies. The therapist must appeal to the best in the parents in an attempt to strengthen the healthy portion of the parental tie with the adolescent.

> Mr. and Mrs. Jones brought Janet, their 13-year-old daughter, for psychiatric evaluation because of poor school performance, a dawdling, passive refusal to perform household chores, and general "emotional immaturity." Mrs. Jones particularly complained of Janet's clinging, demanding attitude toward her.

A most cursory evaluation of the family relationships revealed serious strains and blatantly neurotic accommodations to many hidden conflicts between family members. Mr. Jones was an extremely successful television executive. Because of the pressures of his job and a poorly defined "heart condition," he expected and received remarkably solicitous treatment from all family members. Nothing was expected from him in the home. Janet and her sister understood that they must remain absolutely quiet when he was in the house. Mr. Jones's heart condition was especially sensitive to any angry sounds. The mother threatened the children with the responsibility for their father's death whenever they argued or fought while he was within earshot. Even if the mother became annoyed with them and shouted she blamed them for this threat to the father's health.

In fact, the mother nagged the children and especially Janet, the older, constantly. She hovered over their every move and was preoccupied with the fear that they might be kidnapped due to her husband's prominence.

Janet was a timorous, anxious child. Her manner was obsequious and pollyannaish to a degree that suggested conscious caricature of her mother's expectations. She spent her diagnostic interview explaining her many academic and social problems, besieging the therapist with demands for advice and instant help.

After diagnostic study, the therapist told the parents that Janet needed psychotherapy. The parents' role in the problem was approached warily and counseling was recommended for them. Mrs. Jones spoke for them and stated that she did not wish to have treatment. She explained that a friend of hers had become overly dependent on a therapist and that she felt therapy might "ruin" her. She also felt that therapy might be upsetting and "too much for Mr. Jones's delicate health." The therapist wondered if the couple had similar fears about Janet's therapy. Mrs. Jones admitted that she did, but expressed confidence in the therapist, whom she felt "seemed to understand what Janet needed."

Somewhat reluctantly, the therapist decided to try to work with Janet. His diagnostic hunch that Janet had considerable hidden strength proved correct. She moved rapidly into an active therapeutic alliance and made remarkable strides toward an increased maturity.

The parents were very pleased with Janet's initial changes, since they discerned a new openness and sense of responsibility at home coupled with considerable improvement in her schoolwork.

However, when Janet suddenly made friends with Dolores, a mildly rebellious and sexually aware girl, the mother's attitude toward therapy underwent a rapid and drastic change! She telephoned the therapist to tell him coldly and firmly that she thought Janet no longer needed treatment and, in fact, was afraid treatment was making Janet worse. With some difficulty, the therapist convinced her to come to his office to discuss the reasons for her change in attitude.

Mrs. Jones had calmed down by the time she arrived for her appointment. She said she recognized that it had been silly for her to say Janet should quit treatment. If she had stopped to think, she would have realized that Janet was mistaken in her notions that the therapist approved of the friendship with Dolores! Mrs. Jones was sure the therapist would clarify the matter and show Janet how harmful the friendship was to her.

The therapist agreed that this was one possible course of action. He wondered, however, what Janet's reaction might be if the parents and the therapist took over the responsibility of choosing appropriate friends for her. Would she perhaps be tempted to return to her old pattern of irresponsibility and total dependence on adults? Might it be better to permit her some freedom in this area, maintaining safeguards by structuring the time that Janet and Dolores spent together in a wholesome manner? The therapist admitted that this approach represented a calculated risk.

Dolores might have a negative influence on Janet. However, if the parents and the therapist maintained a friendly relationship and showed respect for Janet's good judgment, she might discuss her interactions with Dolores openly and allow them to help her utilize the relationship constructively. The therapist empathized with Mrs. Jones's wish to help Janet avoid danger. He pointed out that he and Mrs. Jones were in total agreement on this point and need only discuss the best techniques for achieving this goal without causing excessive dependence. He also told Mrs. Jones quite frankly that he understood that it frightened her when she did not know exactly what Janet was thinking and doing.

Mrs. Jones began to cry. She confessed that she knew the therapist was correct. In fact, she knew all along that he would suggest this approach and that it was the proper one. She recognized that she had wanted to remove Janet from therapy to avoid discussing the emotions and family problems that caused her to want to "treat Janet like a two-year-old." Then, she said, "I realize I'm going to need to study that whole mess. Oh, well, I knew if I came here today, I'd leave with a therapist's name in my hands."

Mrs. Jones meant that she had finally decided to accept referral for psychotherapy.

Preserving the therapeutic alliance with the parents frequently requires both encouraging the healthier aspects of the parent-child relationship and sympathetic acceptance of parental anxieties and needs. This combination of factors must also be utilized in helping the parents to involve themselves in collaborative therapy or counseling.

REFERRING PARENTS FOR TREATMENT AND COUNSELING

A purist might argue that all troubled adolescents come from troubled families and that therefore all parents should have personal therapy in conjunction with their child's treatment. In practice, however, many parents do not consciously recognize any relationship between family problems and the symptoms of their disturbed adolescent. A fierce resistance is the only result if these parents are arbitrarily forced into a treatment relationship. The most important factor to be considered in deciding whether to refer parents for psychotherapy or casework is whether such a step is really necessary.

Do the Parents Need Treatment?

The presence of a clear relationship between parental attitudes or marital patterns and the psychopathology of the adolescent does not necessarily mean that it is crucial for the parents to have treatment. Some parental problems are the result, not the cause, of adolescent difficulties. It is hard to grow up, and there are enormous variations in the adaptive equipment that each child receives through the accidents of heredity, prenatal and neonatal illnesses, and uncontrollable environmental experiences.

Over and above these considerations is the fact that parents often grow over the years, whereas their children may carry some precipitates of earlier difficulties in the form of character defenses or symptoms. The father who was anxious and unsure of his competence at age 24 may be a much more relaxed and accepting father at age 36. His 16-year-old son may still need therapy because of defensive patterns that he developed at age 4 in order to deal with his father's excessive oedipal rivalry. Treating the father in the present would not necessarily assist the adolescent to resolve his (now internalized) problems with male authority.

Some adolescents may even be encouraged to evade responsibility for their own problems if the parents' need for treatment is overemphasized. It is obvious that many young people manage a satisfactory adjustment despite fairly marked psychopathology in their parents. Since effective psychotherapy with parents may well require two to three years and extend beyond the adolescence of the young patient, the therapist certainly cannot demand complete parental mental health as a prerequisite to the successful treatment of his young patient. Generally, it is wise to encourage the adolescent patient to accept his parents as "givens" and then to assume the responsibility for managing his own life productively. If the parents become healthier, with or without therapy, so much the better.

When Parents Must Have Help

Still, there are family situations that are incompatible with psychotherapy of the adolescent. The youngster who lives in a family that maintains itself by encouraging the adolescent to assume a role inappropriate to his age (such as an infantile or, conversely, an adult role), an inappropriate sex role, or a role that is clearly destructive (such as a criminal or "stupid" role) can rarely utilize a therapeutic approach that permanently excludes the parents. Curiously, these youngsters are often surprised by the recommendation that their parents receive therapy; in fact, they often oppose treatment for the parents. This observation may be useful in diagnosis and planning. The adolescent who shrieks, "Why don't you treat my parents? They're the ones who need it," may not be the youngster whose parents have drawn him into a comfortable neurotic impasse.

Those parents who do need treatment must often be brought gradually to a recognition of their need by their child's therapist. Careful preparation is often necessary if the parents are to utilize a therapeutic experience constructively. Therapy that is undertaken without a felt need is rarely successful. Some parents arrive for the diagnostic evaluation with a vague recognition of the family's involvement in the adolescent's problems. Others readily come to such an awareness during the diagnostic process in the postdiagnostic family conference. Still others, like Mrs. Jones in our earlier example, can recognize their enmeshment only after improvement in their child disturbs the family homeostasis. Because of this third group, it is often necessary to plan treatments that begin with only the child in psychotherapy, but with clear knowledge that eventually the parents will need direct help. This help is offered when the parents are ready to use it. They are led to recognize their need through their contact with the child's therapist. These early contacts are discussed more fully below.

It should be noted that a valid recognition of involvement in a youngster's problems must be differentiated from the defensive offer to "do anything that will help our child." This passive offer to be "worked on" does not imply any usable awareness of the family pathology. The current sophisticated, "I know we must be doing something to cause all this," may also mask an unspoken blithe attitude of, "But I don't have the slightest idea of what it could be, nor do I really care to know!"

Needless to say, the task is far from completed when a successful referral for therapy is accomplished. The skillful cooperation of two therapists in a collaborative treatment arrangement is a complex topic in itself. The therapists must depend on mutual respect, open communication, and emotional honesty to avoid being manipulated into overidentification with their respective patients to the extreme detriment of the overall goals of therapy. When a collaborative therapist treats the parents, the interactions with the parents described below are kept between the parents and their own therapist whenever possible. In the following section, these interactions are presented primarily as they occur when the adolescent's therapist is working alone.

THE PARENTS AND THE ONGOING THERAPY OF THE ADOLESCENT

The Telephone Contact

During the therapeutic work with the adolescent, some continuing contact with the parents is necessary to ensure their cooperation and support. The telephone is a useful instrument for much of this contact. The parents may be instructed to call if they have information or questions. They are told that they should let their adolescent know when they call and the general topic of discussion. Experience shows that most parents do not abuse this opportunity to contact the therapist ad libitum. Early in the therapeutic contact, the calls may be frequent; however, these calls usually decline fairly rapidly. If the therapist reserves a specific period in his day for returning phone calls, the arrangement need not be burdensome. The parents who do call with extreme frequency make up one group of parents who require direct treatment. In the course of these telephone contacts, along with occasional interviews, the therapist has the opportunity to create a trusting and understanding relationship with the parents. This will allow him to make referral for personal treatment a positive and meaningful recommendation. The parents often come to recognize their need for help through their relationship with the therapist and are more accepting and motivated for treatment. Although some difficulties may arise around transferring their therapeutic relationship, this gap can usually be bridged through the cooperative efforts of the two therapists. The parents' therapist must accept the early allegiance to the adolescent's therapist and avoid competitive responses and professional jealousy. The adolescent's therapist must respect the parents' therapist and assist the smooth transfer, tactfully resisting the parents' efforts to cling to the original therapist. Joint sessions involving the parents and both therapists may help to convey the mutual respect of the team and aid the parents to accept a team concept and approach.

Parents Who Never "Bother" You

It was mentioned that anxious, uncertain, or controlling parents, who tend to telephone frequently, make up a portion of those who need referral for treatment. Without this assistance, they find it difficult to provide the living area of maximum freedom and personal responsibility safely surrounded by firm boundary lines of acceptable behavior that the adolescent needs if he is to reap the benefits of psychotherapy.

Those parents who never call the therapist may need help even more. Most of them are so frightened of "doing the wrong thing" that they exclude themselves from their child's life. Some of them are merely displaying a lack of interest in the youngster or outright rejection of the child. Some of the parents have brought their adolescent for psychotherapy only as social insurance so that no one can ever accuse them of not "doing everything possible to help the child." Involving these parents is difficult, if not impossible. Even if the attempt is unsuccessful, it helps the adolescent to see and accept the reality of his family situation. It is difficult enough to grow up in a rejecting home without the additional burden of being deluded about the facts of the matter. Telephone contact with the parents, then, has both therapeutic and diagnostic value.

If the contacts between the therapist and the parents are handled openly with the adolescent, these contacts should not interfere with the therapeutic alliance between the therapist and the child. It is possible, of course, to create problems through the inappropriate management of the relationship with the parents. Parents usually call for advice on the management of adolescent behavior, for recommendations for dealing with family crises, or in order to seduce the therapist into an alignment with them in the neurotic family conflict. The motives for contact must be evaluated, not only with each family but in each individual instance, in order to respond appropriately.

The Value of Advice and Education

Often, the appropriate response is to provide the advice or information that is requested. Many parents have only the vaguest notion of what behavior to expect from an adolescent. They may be deeply concerned over one piece of behavior that is age-appropriate while blandly accepting other behavior that evidences severe distortion of normal development. The therapist should provide the parents with information regarding the developmental phase. This can be done directly and also by suggesting reading materials that may assist the parent. Our recognition of the central role of emotional factors in shaping parent-child relationships often leads to an excessive depreciation of the value of the intellect. In past generations, knowledge of normative child behavior was disseminated informally through the extended family and the cohesive wider community. Since this effective casual instruction is largely unavailable under current social conditions, it must be replaced by more formal educative

American Academy of Child and Adolescent Psychiatry (AACAP) (www.aacap.org) provides information for mental health professionals and for the general public. The popular "Facts for Families," which can be used as handouts for parents, are available in several languages.

American Psychological Association (APA) (www.apa. org), the professional organization for psychologists, also provides extensive resources for the general public.

American Society for Adolescent Psychiatry (ASAP) (www .adolpsych.org) is a professional organization for psychiatrists who have a particular interest in treating adolescents.

The Arc (formerly Association for Retarded Citizens of the United States) (www.thearc.org) is the country's largest voluntary organization committed to the welfare of all children and adults with mental retardation and their families.

Aspen of America (www.asperger.org) provides information, support, and networking for individuals with Asperger's disorder and their families.

Association for Children and Adults with Learning Disabilities (ACLD) advances the education and general well-being of children and adults with learning disabilities and attention disorders.

CHADD (www.chadd.org) represents children and adults with attention-deficit/hyperactivity disorder and offers education, advocacy and support.

National Alliance for the Mentally Ill (NAMI) (www .nami.org) engages in a wide range of advocacy efforts that benefit individuals with mental problems, their families, and their communities.

efforts. Parents need models of family interaction and child behavior, not to adopt blindly, but to utilize as guidelines.

It is helpful for the therapist to have a firm grasp of normal adolescent development in order to be comfortable in educating parents. The young therapist, who is recently out of graduate school or medical school, may feel intimidated that an average set of middle-aged parents may know a lot more about day-to-day life with teenagers than he does. The beginning therapist usually knows more about normal adolescence than he realizes, but he needs a way to organize and articulate his wisdom. In addition to learning from teachers and from textbooks and other professional sources, the beginning therapist can draw on his own life experience. He also might have the opportunity to get in touch with his own ambivalent and otherwise complex feelings about adolescent issues through his personal therapy or psychoanalysis.

Therapists can learn about normal adolescent development through professional literature as well as reading handbooks that are intended primarily for parents. The modern literature on normal child and adolescent development started with Stanley Hall (1904) and continued through classic authors such as Gesell et al. (1974) and Inhelder and Piaget (1958) and, of course, Erikson (1963). More contemporary books on this subject include works by Elkind (1997), Gemelli (1996), Greenspan and Pollock (1991), Hauser et al. (1991), and Ponton (1997). Some reference books have chapters on normal adolescent development, such as Kagan and Gall (1997) and Richter (1997).

Many books on parenting are available, some of which are listed in the separate "Bibliography for Parents" at the end of this chapter. These books deal with emotional interactions within the family, the importance of communication, discipline, fostering self-esteem, and timely issues such as alcohol and drug abuse. The therapist should take a look at any book that he recommends to parents—for his own edification and also to be sure he agrees with its general philosophy. A knowledge of the book's contents will also allow the therapist to spot any parental distortions and discuss them with the parents.

The therapist also advises freely about matters that directly concern the psychotherapy. He is the expert on the subject and should not expect the parents to know whether the child can safely miss sessions, reduce their frequency, change therapists, or terminate. In these matters, he needs the observations and opinions of the parents to assist him, but the final decisions are his.

Advice to Avoid

There are traps to avoid in advising parents directly. These mistakes may be generally described as any intervention that accepts the "cookbook theory" of child rearing, that is, the overemphasis on parental behavior rather than parental feelings and attitudes. Specifically, this problem frequently arises around requests for advice on "discipline." The parents who need support in this area often are unable to use it wisely. If they are extremely unsure of their prerogatives, they may counter their youngster's angry reaction to limits by announcing that the limit was recommended by the therapist. This appeal to "expert opinion" has the effect not only of completely negating the adolescent's respect for his parents, but also of interfering with the nonauthoritarian therapeutic alliance. This devious exercise of authority merely causes both parent and therapist to appear frightened of direct communication with the adolescent. If the therapist must assume a limit-setting function with his patient, he should do so in a direct, person-to-person manner.

Other parents who ask advice regarding discipline merely want the therapist to join them in their effort to dominate the adolescent. Dispensing explicit advice on techniques of controlling the child is rarely in harmony with the therapist's goal of increasing the adolescent's autonomy and independence, regardless of the motive that drives the parents. It is wiser to explore the goals and aims of parental discipline, leaving the methods completely up to the parents.

Many parents do need help in understanding the purposes of limit setting. Fuller knowledge allows them to evaluate the complex reactions of their adolescent to family rules and to use these reactions as information that will help them to understand the teenager's real needs. They should be assisted to see the plea for control and structure that may be hidden in flagrant rebellion. Some of them can understand the ways in which their youngster may utilize "crime and punishment" to deal with his guilt. They are also helped to see that their anxiety about granting reasonable freedom to an adequately functioning youngster may represent envy of his vitality or fear of being deserted. The management of limits is a delicate barometer of the emotional climate between adults and adolescents. It should be fully utilized in the therapeutic effort, not closed off by rigid directions from the therapist.

Parent Support Groups

Some parents are extremely isolated from other families in the community—perhaps because they have frequently moved and have not had time to establish new friendships or because of a perverse family tradition of aloofness or because both parents work and there is little time for socializing in the neighborhood. Single parents may be so busy working and raising their children that they don't save time to stay in touch with their own peers. In any case, parents find themselves dealing with their teenagers in a social vacuum and winging it from one crisis to the next.

Parents benefit tremendously from neighborhood networking, which basically means that they stay in touch with the parents of their own children's friends. Since teenagers spend much of their day checking with each other on how to beat the system in one way or another, it makes sense for teenagers' parents to have some form of informal but regular communication. Parents can be a tremendous support to each other and can learn from each other's experiences. Parent support groups are organized through local high schools, perhaps as part of the antidrug program at the school; by community mental health centers; by social service agencies; and by organizations such as Toughlove. In addition to parent support groups, some agencies offer parenting education. One example of organized parenting education is called Parent Effectiveness Training.

Probably the most effective parent support group is the kind that arises spontaneously out of a felt need within a neighborhood:

> Mr. Collins was a single parent who unexpectedly came to have custody of his 14-year-old son. The boy's mother had died, so he suddenly came to live with the father in a way that was difficult for everybody. Mr. Collins felt overwhelmed by the magnitude of his situation, suddenly having to deal with school arrangements, suspicions of drug and alcohol abuse, discipline, medical care, and all the other details of full-time parenthood. Mr. Collins sought help from a therapist because of his own feelings of confusion and panic and he took the opportunity to get some tips on how to raise a young adolescent. The therapist gave some suggestions on how to address some immediate issues regarding the son and he gave Mr. Collins another appointment in two weeks.
>
> At the second appointment Mr. Collins announced that he had the situation under control. In the meantime, he had organized a meeting of four or five sets of parents in his neighborhood, who all had sons of about the same age. The parents found it extremely helpful to compare the "policies and procedures" that they had in their own households. They decided to establish a few rules that would be consistent through the neighborhood, such as no phone calls before 8 a.m. or after 9 p.m. They also agreed *not* to agree on other issues, such as whether to allow their sons to wear earrings! The therapist congratulated Mr. Collins on being both innovative and industrious in assuming his role as a new parent.

Helping Parents to Manage Crisis

Any therapist who accepts the responsibility of treating adolescent patients must expect parental telephone calls announcing crises within the family. Parental anxiety is high, not only because of the adult's tendency to project and expect the worst from the adolescent, but because of the adolescent tendency, based on impulsivity, to deliver the worst. Many emergency calls from parents are disguised requests for support, muted complaints about the course of therapy, or subtle attempts to lure the therapist into a family intrigue. These can generally be recognized for what they are by the obvious disparity between the level of parental anxiety and the magnitude of the behavioral problem described. The therapist, of course, insists on a leisurely exploration of the questions raised; if necessary, he schedules a full interview for this purpose.

Mrs. Smith called her son's therapist in the evening. She apologized for bothering him, but rushed ahead breathlessly.

"I don't know what I can do with Jeff! He refuses to study for his midterm. I know I should let him handle this, but you can't just stand aside and watch them ruin their lives! What should I do? Should I force him to study?"

"How would you do that?" the therapist inquired.

"That's why I called you. What can I do?"

"I'm not sure you need to do anything. Jeff's been doing pretty well in his work lately, hasn't he?"

"Yes, but he's going to ruin it all. You must tell me some way to get him to work."

"What does your husband think?"

"Oh, he isn't here. He's out of town this week. I'm so mad at him! He's never here when I need him."

"Have you been feeling pretty alone?" the therapist asked.

"Yes," said the mother, crying. "I sure have. And now Jeff won't even let me help him with his work. He ordered me out of the room and said he'd study like he wanted to. I only wanted to help him!"

"I know that, Mrs. Smith. I guess some company would be nice for you, too. I think your loneliness and need for company when your husband is away are things you ought to discuss in your next therapy session."

"What about Jeff?"

"I believe it would be best to respect his wish to work alone. After all, you and your husband have just put a lot of work into helping him to take responsibility for his own work—sink or swim."

"Well . . . I guess you're right. I may just call up a friend and visit a while to relax myself."

"That sounds like a pretty good idea to me. I do think this is something you ought to explore pretty carefully with Miss Jones [her therapist] next time you see her."

There are some situations, however, that do constitute bona fide crises. Most of these are discussed in Part Two of this book, which deals with special problems in adolescent psychotherapy. Suggestions for dealing with the parents involved in such emergency situations are offered there.

When confronted with crises of any kind, the therapist often feels that he is walking a thin line between overinvolvement in the situation and a failure to assume appropriate helpful responsibility. It is obvious that a realistic emergency situation such as a suicide attempt or a runaway cannot be met with excessive therapeutic aloofness and cold objectivity. At such a time, parents need very direct emotional support and explicit advice on handling the problem. At the same time, the therapist must be careful not to be stampeded into an antitherapeutic action by parental anxiety and manipulation. It is wise to ask for full information before taking action. One does not wish to advise that the police be called in order to protect a runaway when the actual situation is merely one of the adolescent being out of the home for three or four hours without notifying the parents of his whereabouts.

The therapist also attempts to avoid usurping parental responsibility or permitting the parents to dump a trying situation entirely into his lap. An example might be the therapist's personal participation in a search for a runaway. Only in extremely rare

and unusual situations would such a departure from the therapeutic role into direct care for the adolescent be appropriate.

This wavy and indistinct border between directing the therapy and directing the adolescent's daily life is the line of demar-
cation between parental responsibility and therapist's responsibility in all matters pertaining to the adolescent. The adolescent
patient himself should assume as much responsibility as he can
on both sides of the line. When he is not able to take care of
himself, the parents assume responsibility temporarily until he
is able to handle the job again. When the lapse in responsibility
directly affects his psychotherapy, the parents should defer to
the therapist and be guided by him.

The therapist should never permit himself to be maneuvered
into taking greater responsibility than he can realistically discharge. If the patient is suicidal, homicidal, or otherwise in real-
life danger, the therapist must inform the parents and insist that
they assume ultimate responsibility for their child. Of course, the
therapist offers all possible assistance to them in this undertaking. Some explicit approaches to managing these situations are
suggested in Part Two of the book.

TALKING WITH THE ADOLESCENT PATIENT ABOUT HIS PARENTS

Just as the parents of the adolescent need help in understanding and assisting their youngster through this turbulent phase,
the adolescent needs direct assistance in dealing with his parents. The typical adolescent has many complaints about his parents that may be presented so convincingly that the beginning
therapist is tempted to identify with the apparently victimized
youngster, viewing all his difficulties as understandable reactions to parental unfairness. With greater sophistication, the
therapist comes to realize that many of these complaints are
unjustified in reality and represent primarily projected adolescent pathology. This focus, true as far as it goes, overlooks the
interactional nature of family pathology. Although the adolescent may be entirely incorrect in his accusations, his basic sense
that his parents are actively contributing to his psychopathology

may be entirely accurate. Parents do have emotional needs and emotional conflicts and these are often inappropriately expressed in the parent-adolescent interaction. Sooner or later, this portion of the adolescent's problem must be faced in his psychotherapy. It is unrealistic to ask the adolescent to face and accept painful realities about himself, his society, and his friends while protecting the parents from similar honest appraisal. In his role as guide, the therapist will be drawn into this exploration of parental personality and motivation. Often, he will have to accept or reject interpretive comments offered by the adolescent, and at times he will need to share his own impressions of unconscious family pathology.

It should be obvious that the therapist is on dangerous ground whenever he deals with any material that cannot be directly verified with his own patient. With the adolescent and his parents, the therapist runs the additional risk of being manipulated into taking sides in a neurotic power struggle. The adolescent may use therapeutic comments as ammunition to attack his parents. This misuse of information is more common early in therapy before the adolescent is able to face his personal responsibility for his problem, his conflicts, and the course of his life. The therapist should be sure of the therapeutic alliance and confident of his patient's growing maturity before verifying parental psychopathology to the adolescent. Even then, the adolescent must be helped to see that the existence of psychopathology in his parents does not excuse him from responsibility for managing his own life. To blame his parents for his failure and unhappiness may merely allow the adolescent to continue being miserable. To understand why his parents may have had some problems in parenthood may permit the adolescent to forgive them and concentrate on making the most of his own assets and liabilities.

The greatest hazard to the successful resolution of the adolescent's resentment toward his parents is the countertransference of the adolescent's therapist. There are some therapists who relate well to adolescents but who fail therapeutically with them because of their own unresolved (and often unrecognized) resentment of their own parents. These therapists are still locked in a chronic state of adolescent rebellion themselves. They often overtly or covertly encourage their adolescent patients to wallow in their refractory rage toward their family. The therapist and the adolescent may then avoid facing the inevitable need to accept the burdens of maturity. Unfortunately, they also forego maturity's gratifications and pleasures.

Perhaps, the core dynamic behind such prolonged spite is the stubborn refusal to accept the bitter fact that no one is omnipotent and that each human being must face the struggles of existence without a magically powerful parent. As long as one can mesmerize oneself with complaints about "how it could have been if only my parents had been different," one can hold onto a dream of a nirvana that might have been.

Of course, there are other factors that may interfere with this therapeutic step. The therapist may overidentify with his patient, especially if the parents are hostile, rejecting, or irresponsible in their behavior toward the adolescent. It is helpful to remember, however, that these parental attitudes are shaped by the parents' endowments and experiences. If the therapist adopts a deterministic, causal view toward his adolescent patient's psychopathology, he should allow the parents a similar objective acceptance. All parents are doing their best with their children. There are no bad parents, only some who are unequal to the demands of parenthood. The therapist may need to offer firm restraint on some of the parents' destructive floundering, but he cannot permit himself the luxury of casting them in the villain role. His adolescent patient settles for this easy way out on pain of perpetual psychological invalidism. Some parents make it quite difficult for their adolescent to grow up, but this does not change the nature of reality. The adolescent must grow up anyway, or live with the misery of a lifetime of emotional infantilism. The therapist must help the adolescent to accept this difficult fact. He can be very gentle in this confrontation, but he must also be very firm. A widespread reluctance to force this issue is suggested by Masterson

(1967) as one possible reason for poor long-range therapeutic results in his study of treated adolescents.

Rebellion Versus Freedom

The adolescent also needs help in seeing that his perception of himself as a younger child and his wishes to enjoy a more dependent relationship with his parents frequently lead him to overreact to their expectations and wishes for him. Even when the parents are controlling and push the youngster toward preconceived goals, the adolescent must learn to be free to reject or (even more difficult) accept these goals according to his own needs and abilities. Often, the adolescent mistakes rebelliousness for freedom. He cannot choose any goals that happen to coincide with parental desires, even when the goals are identical with the adolescent's own ambitions. Obviously, under these circumstances he is not free to do what he wishes. The adolescent can sometimes grasp this through an allegory: "It seems to me that if you were ravenously hungry and your parents commanded you to eat a beautiful and delicious meal, you would refuse!"

The adolescent also needs help in recognizing that the parental tendency to "treat him like a child" does not actually make him childish. He is only in danger from his own childish wishes. The immature adolescent takes umbrage if his parents dare to remind him to drive carefully. The mature adolescent recognizes the concern and anxiety for his well-being implied in the warning and responds reassuringly to the parents. Even if he suspects that the overconcern has roots in suppressed hostility toward him, he still realizes that the hostility is not expressed because the parents also love him and are fearful that their anger will harm him. He is aware that he is a separate person with ambivalences and defenses of his own. This complex understanding is eloquently expressed in his simple explanation, "Aw, they're good parents. They're just worrywarts. Hell, I'm not perfect myself."

"If Only I Could Get Away from Them"

Frequently, adolescents express the desire to leave home. This wish is part of the fantasy that they could be mature if only they did not have to live with their parents. In some cases, there is a degree of truth in this idea. There are parents who undercut healthy adolescent independence. However, even in these families, geographical distance will not resolve the adolescent's ambivalence. Sooner or later, the adolescent must be willing to give up the regressive gratifications that the family offers in favor of maturity and independence. In other words, the adolescent's most dangerous opponent in his struggle for independence is his own wish for dependency. Some adolescents can understand the clarification, "Could it be that you want to run away from home quickly to avoid thinking about really growing up and leaving home?" This paradox can be expanded by pointing out that a poorly considered, precipitous departure from home may actually be designed to ensure failure, a parental rescue, and continued dependency. As Blos (1967) has commented, these youngsters are "doing the wrong things for the right reasons." In these adolescents, this conflict is often reactivated with the therapist as termination approaches. They are tempted to "quit" treatment prematurely to avoid openly facing the pain of separation that would appear during a planned termination.

SUMMARY

In many respects, the management of the complex relationships between the youngster and his parents and between the parents and the youngster's therapist is the most important and delicate task of psychotherapy during adolescence. The therapist must obtain and keep the trust and cooperation of the parents without compromising the adolescent's movement toward independence from the family. The parents must be mobilized to accept and support the eventual goal of the young person's emancipation. Often, they will need the support of their child's therapist, if not personal therapy, to bear the pain of releasing the adolescent and reestablishing family homeostasis without him.

After the qualified therapist has performed an adequate diagnostic study, chosen an appropriate candidate for outpatient psychotherapy, formed a therapeutic alliance with parents and child, and effectively responded to the ongoing problems of psychotherapy, he still faces one final crucial task. He must effect a termination at the correct time and in a constructive manner. Some of the issues and techniques involved in this phase of the therapy are considered in the next chapter.

BIBLIOGRAPHY FOR PARENTS

There is no individual book that will be suitable for all parents. Among other issues, the choice would depend of the treatment style of the therapist; the strengths, weaknesses, and values of the parents; and the particular situation within that family. These books do not all say the same thing—in fact, they flatly disagree on some aspects of raising teenagers.

This Bibliography for Parents and the list of advocacy groups on page 229 may be copied and reproduced without specific permission from the publisher.

Foster W. Cline and Jim Fay. *Parenting Teens with Love and Logic: Preparing Adolescents for Responsible Adulthood.* Colorado Springs: Piñon Press, 1992. This book was written by a child and adolescent psychiatrist (Cline) and an educator and principal (Fay). They build on basic principles such as responsible teens feel good about themselves; owning up to problems and solutions; and empathy plus consequences equals success.

Charlene C. Giannetti and Margaret Sagarese. *Parenting 911.* New York: Broadway Books, 1999. This book pertains to early and middle adolescents. The authors give practical advice for common problems of teenagers—drugs, sexuality, mood changes, extreme sports, school failure, and violence.

Don Dinkmeyer and several other authors. *Parenting Teenagers: Systematic Training for Effective Parenting of Teens.* Circle Pines, MN: American Guidance Service, 1998. The Systematic Training for Effective Parenting (STEP) program has taught over two million parents how to encourage mutual respect, cooperation, responsibility, and self-reliance in their children.

James Dobson. *The Strong-Willed Child: Birth through Adolescence.* Wheaton, Illinois: Tyndale House, 1992. Dr. Dobson is a psychologist with a Christian orientation. His message has been expounded on a radio show and several videos, that parents should have deep love and affection for their children, but should also exercise their authority through appropriate discipline.

Don Fleming and Laurel J. Schmidt. *How to Stop the Battle with*

Your Teenager: A Practical Guide to Solving Everyday Problems. New York: Simon & Schuster, 1993. Dr. Fleming is a psychologist who believes in "firm discipline coupled with caring." The book is organized in a directive, cookbook approach, which includes precise, step-by-step solutions to a large range of adolescent issues.

Thomas Gordon. *Parent Effectiveness Training: The Tested New Way to Raise Responsible Children.* New York: New American Library, 1990. Dr. Gordon is a clinical psychologist who developed the P.E.T. system, an educational program for parents that has been taught in thousands of cities in every state. The book describes the technique of "active listening" and the use of negotiation to arrive at solutions that meet the needs of the youngster and the parents.

Michael Gurian. *A Fine Young Man: What Parents, Mentors and Educators Can Do to Shape Adolescent Boys into Exceptional Men.* New York: Jeremy P. Tarcher/ Putnam, 1998. Several books were published recently regarding the special needs of teenage boys and this is an example of that genre. Dr. Gurian continues in this book where he left off in his earlier work, *The Wonder of Boys.* This book gives detailed descriptions of what boys are like during early, middle, and late adolescence.

Jane Nelsen and Lynn Lott. *Positive Discipline for Teenagers: Resolving Conflict with Your Teenage Son or Daughter.* Rocklin, CA: Prima Publishing, 1994. The authors have also written several other books involving "positive discipline." This book, which goes far beyond the topic of discipline, addresses communication with teenagers, healthy relationships, and many other topics.

George H. Orvin. *Understanding the Adolescent.* Washington, D.C.: American Psychiatric Press, 1995. Dr. Orwin's central theme is that family relationships form the context of adolescent development. This book, which is intended for both parents and professionals, discusses both normal adolescent development and adolescent problems.

Philip Osborne. *Parenting for the '90s.* Intercourse, Pennsylvania: Good Books, 1989. Dr. Osborne is a psychologist who has an eclectic approach, in that he takes part of the James Dobson approach and part of the Thomas Gordon approach and part behavior modification. He emphasizes the importance of the "No Problem Area," which are the times "when parent and child are together and neither one is upset."

Lynn E. Ponton. *The Romance of Risk: Why Teenagers Do the Things They Do.* New York: Basic Books, 1997. Dr. Ponton, a child and adolescent psychiatrist, explains why some teenagers take bad risks and also offers suggestions for how to encourage good risk-taking. The book includes 15 case histories of adolescents who were unable to avoid dangerous risk-taking.

David B. Pruitt, editor. *Your Adolescent: Emotional, Behavioral, and Cognitive Development from Early Adolescent through the Teen Years.* New York: HarperCollins, 1999. This book was written by a committee of child and adolescent psychiatrists. It gives advice for the common problems of family life with teenagers, as well as guidance for addressing more serious issues, such as emotional disorders, disruptive behavior, eating disorders, and substance abuse.

Paul W. Swets. *The Art of Talking with Your Teenager.* Holbrook, MA.: Adams Media Corporation, 1995. Rev. Swets is a Presbyterian minister who teaches communication skills, such as how to converse with a reluctant teenager. This is an upbeat book that focuses on the details of effective communication, such as the interplay of the personality traits of the parent with the temperament of the teenager.

Phyllis and David York and Ted Wachtel. *Toughlove.* New York: Bantam Books, 1997. Toughlove is a national movement, with the basic principles that parents should assert themselves to stand up to their unruly adolescents and that they can derive support from parent groups within their community. Toughlove is intended for "young people whose outrageous behavior requires unorthodox responses."

CHAPTER 9
termination of psychotherapy with the adolescent

In an earlier chapter, we suggested that the technically necessary process of forming a therapeutic alliance with the adolescent has the additional beneficial effect of strengthening the adolescent's observing ego. This therapeutic instrument, therefore, has a curative value of its own because it promotes a developmentally crucial task. The proper management of the termination of adolescent psychotherapy is perhaps even more important, since the basic function of all adolescent development is to complete a "second individuation" (Blos, 1967). The separation from the therapist, both physically and psychologically, is an integral part of the entire psychotherapeutic process. Many of the earlier gains of psychotherapy may be lost through unskilled management of the issues and technical problems raised in the termination phase. It is equally true that this part of therapy provides the opportunity for observing and partially resolving many adolescent dilemmas that may remain latent until the adolescent is confronted with termination. The series of decisions concerning the methods of ending an important personal relationship arouses important developmental conflicts. Often, the actual leave-taking in therapy comes to symbolize the process of loosening the bonds to internalized parental images and giving up the magical omnipotent and passive expectations that go with them. When the termination of psychotherapy becomes the microcosmic representation of this accommodation to young adulthood, it is indeed a momentous event in the adolescent's life. This is often the case in the treatment of youngsters in middle and late adolescence, especially the latter.

One may expect a wide gamut of defensive and regressive maneuvers as the adolescent attempts to deal with the anxieties that accompany the important psychic restructuring related to termination. Emotional upheavals, symptom recurrences, and episodes of self-destructive fantasies and even behavior (often calculated to provoke rescue and reinstatement of dependency) may alternate with wishes to flee prematurely or deny the importance of therapy and the therapist, to "run away from home to avoid leaving."

Youngsters with "malignant" defenses and major fixations in pregenital positions will experience the greatest difficulty in terminating. In a sense they are actually not ready for termination even after fairly successful treatment. Often, even late in treatment, they still need the therapist to test reality, support their self-worth, and focus their psychic energy. We will discuss these youngsters, including those who cannot be terminated, later in this chapter.

It follows from these developmental considerations that the termination of psychotherapy with the adolescent must be correctly timed, sensitively related to his particular needs, flexibly managed, and conducted with maximum alertness to complicating countertransference issues.

DECIDING TO TERMINATE THERAPY

In our opinion, successful psychotherapy contracts with adolescents tend to be unnecessarily prolonged. This may result in a blunting of the developmental thrust toward independence, which partially nullifies the positive impact of the therapy. Individuation, the goal of adolescent development, is best served by assisting the adolescent toward a workable character synthesis and then quickly moving aside so that the adolescent's new strengths propel him toward real and available objects outside the sheltered therapy office. The problem of course is to have reasonable confidence that the synthesis is stable enough to permit continuing individuation in the real world. It is our impression that the therapist frequently withholds this confidence too long from youngsters who have clearly found the right path to maturity out of an anxious desire to walk along and guard the adolescent all the way to the goal. There are other motives for unduly delaying termination that are discussed below. Even if the therapist accepts the premise of early termination, he still has to establish some guidelines for deciding when to consider its initiation.

General Patterns That Suggest that Termination Should Be Considered

In the adolescent, as in the adult, one looks for symptomatic improvement, a heightened capacity for nondestructive pleasure (especially in interpersonal relationships), greater comfort with the acknowledgement and appropriate expression of a wide range of emotions in herself and others, a capacity to laugh at herself, and other quasi-objective phenomena that Hiatt (1965) has listed in detail. In addition, one expects a more objective attitude toward the therapist. Intensive transference reactions leading to expansive overevaluation of the therapist's skills, capacity to nurture, or wisdom, as well as hostile devaluation and belittling of her abilities, should be minimal and should be recognized as distortions by the adolescent client when they do occur.

NORMAL COMPARED TO WHAT?—THE NEED FOR DEVELOPMENTAL NORMS

The problem of deciding when termination should be considered is complicated in the adolescent by the need to measure the characteristics mentioned in the above section against a scale of developmental norms. For example, some tendency to mild depressive episodes, interpersonal touchiness, and a slightly shy and coquettish treatment of the therapist are expected behavioral characteristics of the 13-year-old adolescent girl. They do not indicate a need for further therapy. Older adolescents gradually approximate the young adult model and consequently signal a readiness for termination with general behavioral patterns that resemble those described for adults. Reasonable levels of expectation for adolescents of various ages may be developed by observing the behavior of normal adolescents (every therapist should make the effort to become acquainted with some), reading descriptive studies of normal adolescent behavior, and to some extent by recalling one's own adolescent behavior and feelings.

If you want to be a little obsessive in comparing your adolescent client with a group of normal teenagers, try informally assessing him with the "Autonomous Functioning Checklist." This instrument, described by Sigafoos et al. (1988), is usually completed by parents to measure behavioral autonomous functioning in adolescents. It is divided into subscales, including routine personal care and family-oriented functions, the extent to which the adolescent handles his interaction with the environment, the ways in which the adolescent chooses to use free time, and social involvement and pursuit of vocational directions.

There is another point that is obvious, but which may be forgotten in the heat of therapeutic ambition. It is impossible, even with the most skillful psychotherapy, to resolve emotional conflicts that are related to developmental tasks beyond the youngster's years. The 13-year-old girl described above cannot be expected to achieve final resolution of her oedipal attachments, since this maturational step normally occurs later in life, often not until young adulthood. She would be ready for termination when she could show a dawning appropriate interest in boys her own age (or slightly older), a budding capacity to identify with her mother's positive female traits without total fear of a homosexual bond, and a capacity to move in and out of regressive pregenital positions with relative comfort. The absence of paralyzing rigidities and inhibitions or defensive pseudoadult behaviors would indicate that she had "gotten back on the developmental track." One does not try to accompany the adolescent on her entire developmental journey, only to guide her off sidetracks and back to her age-appropriate station on the main trunk of the developmental line.

At times, the therapist must point out the limitations of therapy to the adolescent client herself. Despite the inner thrust toward independence, the youngster may find a comfortable therapeutic alliance hard to relinquish. The client recognizes that the collaborative work with the therapist has helped her to free herself from many inner terrors. She naturally hopes that the same device can help her resolve other dilemmas, even when these are desirable "growing pains." The therapist must gently and firmly prevent the adolescent client from using psychotherapy as a magic talisman to ward off or delay necessary developmental struggles.

Naturally, not all adolescent clients will be able to reach ideal goals even when these are corrected for developmental variation. Adolescents who have severe ego defects on the basis of constitutional or organic pathology, severe emotional deprivation, or grossly disturbed family relationships will always show some distortions in personality functioning related to these basic defects.

Treatment in the above cases aims at establishing a workable synthesis that will probably include defensive patterns that are partially crippling. One attempts to work to a point where personality functioning provides some pleasure and sense of identity to the adolescent without seriously infringing on the rights of other people. If the underpinnings of the adolescent's personality have been crushed in early life, she will probably always move with a psychological limp. The therapist only hopes that he can help her learn to get around and take care of herself despite the disability.

Some Checkpoints for Termination

The only reliable basis for a decision to terminate therapy is a careful consideration of general behavior (in and out of the therapist's office) in comparison with developmental norms. When this global and partially intuitive assessment suggests that the adolescent is ready for termination, this impression can be checked against some specific behaviors that often appear in

conjunction with an inner readiness for greater independence.
The hunch that termination is near is reinforced when:

1. *A growing appropriate involvement with peers results in a friendly* and *nonprovocative decrease in interest in therapy.* The genuine gentleness and warmth toward the therapist that accompany this "drifting away" clearly differentiate it from the defensive avoidance of dependency relationships that one often sees early in therapy.

2. *The adolescent wants to discuss the "hang-ups" of a friend without relating these to herself*—that is, these problems are discussed without contrasting them with her own problems in an attempt to minimize her difficulties, divert attention from herself, or show her own plight as more serious or deserving of sympathy. In short, the adolescent appears to have the necessary emotional energy and comfort with her own identity to concern herself about another person with reasonable objectivity and clarity of ego boundaries.

3. *The adolescent suggests that the therapist could help this friend.* When the expectation of what the therapist could offer the friend is reasonable, this often signals a willingness to share the therapist. Often, we suspect, it is also an unconscious attempt to deal with guilt feelings engendered by the wish to "abandon" the therapist by offering a replacement.

4. *The adolescent shows a capacity for more objective evaluation of her parents, considering both their assets and their liabilities as human beings.* She is able to accept their strong points as identification models while rejecting some of their weaknesses.

5. *The adolescent uses fewer superlatives.* Hiatt (1965) noted this change in adults, and it seems to hold for adolescents. However, it should be remembered that the normal adolescent may use more superlatives than the sick adult. In adolescents, one expects not a total avoidance of superlatives but a greater capacity for moderation than noted earlier in treatment.

6. *The adolescent rarely acts out in regard to the therapy.* She comes

on time, does not battle over scheduling hours, does not haggle over stopping on time, and rarely needs to "play games" by teasingly withholding information, feelings, and ideas. There is a sense of simple forthrightness that is age-appropriate.

7. *The adolescent inquires about the possibility of termination in a frank and comfortable manner.* This is an especially good indicator of approaching readiness for termination if it is accompanied by appropriately mixed feelings delivered with typical adolescent sentimentality. "I really think I'm about ready to split this scene. Damn trouble is, I'm so used to you nagging me to look at why I draw every breath, I'm gonna miss you. Man, I never thought I'd say that!"

8. *The adolescent's use of externalizing defense mechanisms is less frantic and more realistic and shows greater consideration for the complexities of human needs and motivations.* It would be neither reasonable nor desirable for the adolescent to give up her efforts to change herself or her environment. It would be detrimental to our development as a society and a personal dereliction for the adolescent to accept the social status quo with all its defects calmly. Efforts to change malevolent social conditions, even if the efforts are disruptive and unpleasant, do not necessarily suggest that the adolescent is emotionally ill.

The healthy adolescent may even remain somewhat utopian and naive in her plans for social change. It is the single-minded demand that the environment accommodate completely to the idiosyncrasies of the adolescent that suggests a defensive utilization of social activism or cultural philosophy. A reasonably mature compromise in the choice between internal modification and alteration of outer reality is an acceptable point for termination. It is especially encouraging if the adolescent shows some recognition of both her capacity to change things and her limitations as an agent of social change, succumbing neither to grandiosity nor apathetic withdrawal.

On "Letting Go"

Adults have many motives for emphasizing the inadequacies of adolescents. There are both conscious and unconscious sources of envy that may lead to underevaluation of adolescent abilities. These generational factors, which may include protective and competitive elements in varying degrees, contribute to the therapist's reluctance to let his young clients handle things on their own. Of course, the adolescent client can also lead the therapist to kick her out angrily and prematurely with an open or veiled prophecy that her attempted independence will fail and she will come crawling back. This, of course, is not really "letting go."

In addition to these generational distortions at the time of termination, the therapist faces the discomfort that every human being feels when he relinquishes a valued relationship. At the ending of a successful psychotherapy with an attractive adolescent, the honest therapist must often admit to a "forgotten parent" element in his complex of feelings. This aspect of his reaction might be stated as, "Now she wants to leave me, just when I get her grownup enough to be useful and enjoyable to have around." The frequency of this countertransference attitude may be part of the reason that many adolescents seem slightly guilty and apologetic about their appropriate wish to terminate and handle their own affairs.

The therapist's problem in letting go probably explains the frequency with which final sessions are taken up with Polonius-like lectures and advice. Fortunately, the now-healthy adolescent is usually indulgent and forgiving of the therapist's lapse into pomposity. If the adolescent were not, the therapist might undo much of his good work in ego building by this effort to reassure himself of his importance to the adolescent.

Of course, there is one very practical reason that the therapist has some reluctance to terminate successfully treated cases. Since the therapeutic alliance with these youngsters is firmly established, he anticipates their sessions with comfort and even pleasure. When they are terminated, who will take their place?—probably an angry, devious, defended, difficult youngster who will carry little of the load of the therapeutic work for some time to come. Small wonder that the therapist is tempted to hold onto his comfortable and cooperative youngster past the time when the adolescent really needs him.

On "Kicking Out"

We have emphasized the factors that tend to prolong therapy unnecessarily. Countertransference problems may also lead to errors in the other direction. Hostile feelings toward an adolescent, especially if these feelings are unconscious, can lead the therapist to exaggerate the client's progress in order to rationalize an angry rejection as an appropriate termination. A narcissistic or omnipotent need to achieve quick results may tempt the therapist to skip over important and necessary therapeutic work. Parental pressure based on realistic financial problems or emotional needs may hurry the insecure therapist. Fear of erotic urges stirred by closeness to the client can cause a panicked wish to withdraw and terminate in the interest of self-protection.

On both sides, the therapist must rely on his intellectual and emotional honesty, accepting the fact that he will invariably err in both directions on occasion.

TECHNIQUES OF TERMINATION

The key word in termination of the adolescent is flexibility. Rarely can the adolescent terminate smoothly and with finality in one try. The "open door" policy is almost mandatory for the adolescent client. No matter how carefully one approaches the emotional reactions that termination stirs in the adolescent, it is usually necessary for the client actually to experiment with physically leaving therapy, returning briefly, and going away again. One reason for this is the expected continuation of developmental storms that may trigger temporary regressive episodes that the adolescent knows the therapist can help to clarify and resolve. More often, however, it seems that the adolescent merely needs to visit home briefly. The purpose of these visits is considered below.

Introducing the Idea of Termination

Often, the adolescent will verbalize an appropriate interest in termination. When she does, Menninger's (1958) suggested reply, "I think you could finish up soon," is useful. It introduces the issue of termination in a definitive way without committing the youngster or the therapist to any set time. The answer also implies that the adolescent and the therapist have further work to do within a finite time limit. It also maintains the focus on the adolescent's responsibility for finishing the job.

Many adolescents will not suggest termination in a direct manner. Many of them are too comfortable in a helpful dependency relationship, which is not inappropriate to their stage of life. Normally functioning adolescents still need understanding adult friends, adult listeners, and adult advisors. When all these characteristics are combined in a trusted adult who has stood by them through many very difficult periods, it is easy to see why they are not eager to give him up.

Although it is important to avoid the appearance of kicking the adolescent out of therapy or shaming her for her dependency wishes, it is also important to introduce the topic of termination as soon as the adolescent is emotionally ready. This need not be done abruptly or tactlessly. The client will present numerous opportunities for the therapist to introduce the idea of termination in a positive light. The therapist's attitude should imply the calm assumption that he and the adolescent share a pleasant anticipation of a healthy, warm, and constructive parting of the ways, although both may have some mixed feelings about it.

The teenager's pride in her independent functioning and her constructive use of object relationships that she has developed on her own are supported and approved as they begin to appear in the course of therapy. More and more, the adolescent says, in one way or another, "And here's another thing I handled well without your help." The therapist replies, in one way or another, "That doesn't surprise me or hurt my feelings. You're a rather competent person and I'm glad of it."

Very gradually, the adolescent is encouraged to rely on her own resources with less help from the therapist. It is often useful to introduce brief discussions of one's own limitations and dilemmas in therapy hours. This does not imply a discussion of deeply personal problems or conflicts the therapist may encounter, since the adolescent is unprepared to face and deal with the full impact of adult problems in living. The goal is merely to help the adolescent realize that the strengths of maturity derive from skill at problem solving and the acceptance of reasonable personal goals. The therapist must be careful not to overwhelm the adolescent or to suggest that the therapist himself finds life too difficult.

Terminations of this kind may be rather prolonged. The therapist should not succumb to pressures or temptations to rush things.

Sarah, the 15-year-old with problems of promiscuity, academic difficulty, drug use, and poor interpersonal relationships who has been mentioned previously, had a long and difficult termination phase.

Strong dependency yearnings that were violently denied early in therapy came to be centered on the therapist. It became necessary to point out repeatedly Sarah's tendency to play at helplessness in order to elicit a supportive helping response from the therapist. When Sarah was able to see this clearly, she joked, "You know if you told me I could solve a problem by holding my breath five minutes, I'd try it, turn blue, and swear it worked!"

Although she gradually came to utilize therapeutic help more realistically, she showed little indication that she regarded her arrangement with the therapist as anything less than lifelong.

Around the end of the second year of treatment, Sarah was symptom-free and enjoying moderately good social relationships in and out of her family. Her first indication of an awareness that therapy would have an end came when she reported angrily that her father had asked her when therapy would be over. She regarded this as evidence that he wished to undermine her treatment (actually this had been a problem early in therapy). The therapist wondered if her father's present comment might be seen rather as a compliment, an indication that she seemed well to him. Sarah asked if the therapist thought she was ready to stop treatment. The therapist replied that he had not thought too much about it before, but, since she had brought it up, she had been handling things very well and if she continued to work hard, the idea certainly would not seem totally unreasonable within the near future.

Sarah didn't say anything more about it in that session, but came to the next interview loaded with problems to discuss. "Everything," she declared, "is falling apart. I'm all strung out!" She then recounted a series of concerns that sounded rather trumped up. The therapist commented that perhaps she was feeling a need to work out all of her problems in a hurry, since the idea of termination had come up in the last hour. He added that he really suspected that Sarah herself was quite capable of dealing with most of the problems she had mentioned.

Over the next few months, Sarah vacillated between feeling that she was ready to "quit" and a panicked feeling that she could not deal with life without the therapist's help. The therapist confronted her with her tendency to confuse herself and tied this to her invariable use of the word "quit" to describe termination. He suggested that perhaps it was difficult for her to imagine two people parting in a friendly way. She seemed to have a need to "go away mad" or to imagine that the other person was angry with her, which tended to interfere with her comfort in functioning independently.

This interchange led to a more direct expression of a variety of ambivalent fantasies about termination. At times,

Sarah accused the therapist of being tired of her and disgusted with her inability to handle her own life. At other times, she was sure that the therapist would not let her "quit—I mean stop. Oh, dammit, why do I always say 'quit?' "

Even the issue of the fee was raised again, although Sarah was able to decide she was glad the therapist was paid to see her. "I guess it keeps it all straight and on the up and up."

Again and again, the therapist discussed the concept of voluntary separation based on a mutual agreement that it was time for new kinds of relationships. Often, it was possible to universalize about the adolescent's wish to leave home, not because she hated her parents or they hated her, but because she was ready for another phase of life. The distortions and conflicts around this issue in Sarah's real family were discussed rather fully during this time.

A full six months after termination was first mentioned, Sarah took LSD again for the first time in over a year. She came to her next session a bit sheepishly, but approached the exploration of the "slip-up" (as she called it) with a determined air. She mentioned that she realized she had no real desire to "trip." The experience was unpleasant and she felt annoyed with herself under the drug and could not achieve the state of pleasant "boundlessness" that she had previously experienced with LSD.

"I kept thinking, 'I'm only doing this for X's [her therapist's last name] benefit.' It was pretty lousy. I'd really feel silly except I know I'm trying to figure out how to stop coming here without being mad about it."

She continued to explore her behavior objectively and with skill for several minutes, and then said angrily, "Well, aren't you going to say anything?"

Genuinely surprised, the therapist spontaneously replied, "Gee, I'd be glad to, but you were doing so well yourself!"

Somehow, this seemed to reach Sarah more than the

voluminous explanations the therapist had offered earlier. She shook her head in wonderment.

"That's all there is to it, isn't it? You really don't mind helping me. You really believe I don't need it any more."

"Yeah. That's it exactly. Wish I could have told you sooner."

"Oh, that's okay. I think you did. I just listen slow." She paused for a moment, and then said softly, with tears in her eyes, "I'm ready to stop seeing you now, but don't expect me not to miss you."

Needless to say, the therapist did not escape the session dry-eyed either. Sarah terminated in four more sessions, utilizing them primarily to talk of her feelings of sadness that were accompanied by a quiet sense of excitement. She was especially looking forward to leaving home for college and talked a good deal of her plans.

In the ensuing three months of high school and the summer vacation, Sarah did not contact the therapist. She wrote from college after three months to report that things were going well and that she had many friends. She said that she also liked her dormitory "mother" and occasionally liked to talk with her.

". . . but," she added, "I don't lean on people totally any more. I can always use help, but mostly I lean on me."

The therapist returned a brief note congratulating her on being happy and stating that he enjoyed hearing from her. She did not write again.

Sarah's case illustrates many of the issues that tend to appear around termination of therapy. These include anxiety over separation, fears of rejection, anger over relinquishing omnipotent expectations of the therapist, and a desperate struggle toward personality integration. In adolescents who have needed a less intense attachment, the conflicts are often briefer and more easily resolved. Some of these conflicts may be fleeting and hardly visible. They are all usually there in some form, however. In adolescents with a less sound therapeutic alliance, more may be acted out. Instead of talking about "quitting" as Sarah did, these youngsters may actually quit, with a need to return later and deal with the issues more directly when they learn that the therapist will neither condemn them for bolting nor pursue and rescue them from their impulsive folly. Some adolescents also show a greater need to "return home" in order to relinquish lingering hopes that the therapist is omnipotent, the perfectly desirable sexual partner, or the source of unlimited gratification.

Mike was a 16-year-old who handled termination by denying his dependency and feelings of loss. He insisted on leaving therapy only two sessions after the therapist had agreed with his assertion that he had "pretty well worked out his problems."

Two months later, he called, insisting on an interview on that very day. The therapist said that he would be glad to see him, but did not have an opening for two days. Mike angrily accepted the appointment. He used the session to express his sad feelings over breaking up with a girl friend he had been dating for six months. The therapist agreed that partings were sad, but indicated that he felt Mike was handling his feelings quite well. He added that he saw Mike's capacity to cry and feel sad about the breakup as evidence of emotional health and a necessary and appropriate preparation for dating again.

Mike seemed relieved. He expressed thanks for the help that the therapist had given him during treatment. When he left, he shook hands with the therapist, smiled with some wistfulness, and said, "Thanks again. You're really okay." He seemed somewhat sad and left the office rather slowly.

Therapy—Interminable

Some adolescents cannot be totally terminated. Despite the best therapeutic efforts, they are unable to manage their dependency needs without indefinite support from the therapist. This may be due to an inability to see the therapist's insistence on separation as anything other than a rejection. These clients are so convinced that they are unlovable that any attempt to terminate them is seen as a wish to be rid of them. They cannot believe any explanation of termination as a vote of confidence for them and as a bittersweet separation experience for the therapist. Dewald (1965) described the catastrophic reaction of a patient to his announcement that he was terminating her because of a move to a different city. The amazing thing was that his only contact with her in quite some time had consisted of intermittent brief telephone calls designed to monitor her medication! It is also interesting to note that the patient was able to accept the termination and to reconstitute psychologically after an interview in which she expressed her intense feelings about being left.

Schizophrenic clients, many borderline and narcissistic clients, suicidal adolescents, and other adolescents who actually have no dependable family seem especially likely to prolong therapy indefinitely. Many of these youngsters fall into the pattern we have described earlier as clients with "malignant defenses."

The therapist may elect to reduce the frequency of therapy sessions gradually with these potentially interminable clients without pressing the issue of finalizing termination. If holding the therapist in reserve, as it were, allows the client to make a more successful adaptation, there is no compelling need to withhold this support. It is a relatively inexpensive and harmless addiction. However, it would seem wise to reevaluate the overall situation periodically. If the client's life situation or ego strengths improve sufficiently, it may be possible to bring her back into more frequent therapy sessions for a brief period in order to effect a true termination.

Unfortunate Endings

There are two situations in which termination cannot be handled as constructively as one might wish. These are the termination of unsuccessful attempts at treatment and those terminations that are caused by external events.

TERMINATION OF UNSUCCESSFUL ATTEMPTS AT THERAPY

In the termination of unsuccessful treatment contracts, those in which it has been impossible to establish a therapeutic alliance, one attempts to salvage as much as possible. Hopefully, these terminations will not be abrupt or come as a surprise to the adolescent client. The honest therapist will have commented on the absence of a true alliance periodically during his contacts with the youngster. As we have seen earlier, the formation of the alliance is a necessary condition for dealing with other material. The therapist should avoid "going through the motions" of the therapeutic work before completing this essential task.

The client's inability to form a therapeutic alliance should be approached sympathetically and in a spirit of benevolent inquiry, but the therapist should still make it clear that no useful work can occur without this alliance. If the client's mistrust of others, defensive structure, or living situation makes an alliance impossible, it is preferable to admit that and suggest termination. Often, the adolescent is as frustrated as the therapist and has mentioned interruption of treatment several times herself. One can only try to make the dissolution of the therapy effort as constructive as possible. If a different treatment arrangement such as inpatient care appears indicated, this recommendation may be made to the adolescent and her parents. If the youngster's problems are less serious, it may be more advisable to part as amicably as possible, hoping that the youngster will be able to return later in a more accepting frame of mind.

Martha was referred for psychotherapy against her will when she was 13 because of poor school performance, lack of friends, and passive-aggressive behavior toward all authority figures expressed by forgetting, procrastinating, and other techniques that tormented her energetic, domineering, and compulsive parents.

Martha was the family scapegoat. Her mother persisted in efforts to organize Martha's life completely despite her inability to counter Martha's passive opposition effectively.

Martha's father was openly contemptuous of her and either avoided her or slashed at her verbally. Martha preferred this treatment to her mother's worried nagging.

Martha was impossible to involve in any meaningful therapeutic alliance. She seemed terrified that she would be controlled by the therapist and defended herself by denying that she had any inner motivations and feelings. She was, she said, "a very simple person." She made fun of the therapist's comments by caricaturing them into ridiculous pseudo-Freudian nonsense. If the therapist asked about an episode of forgetting, Martha would say, "Oh, yeah. I forgot my glasses because I detest glasses. You see, I was frightened by a pair of glasses when I was a little child."

In spite of this attitude toward the work of treatment, Martha seemed to like the therapist personally and rather enjoyed her hostile bantering with him. During the few months that she was in treatment, she made some improvements in her social relationships and in getting along with her parents. Martha herself tended to deny that things had changed, and when she could not deny the changes, she made it very clear that she did not feel they were related to her contact with the therapist. Martha continually protested that she did not need treatment. The therapist finally decided that it would be wiser to accept the symptomatic improvement and stop therapy. This was done with the statement that the therapist felt Martha still had unsolved problems.

Almost three years later, the therapist was called to see Martha because of an impulsive suicide attempt. Martha had ingested poison and was in real medical danger for several days. During this time, the therapist visited her regularly in the hospital. He noted that Martha seemed less frightened of him, more relaxed, and able to be genuinely appreciative of his attention during this trying period.

Psychotherapy was reinstituted at Martha's request. Although she remained rigidly defensive, she showed some interest in understanding her emotions and was less condescending toward the therapist. Some useful therapeutic work was possible under these circumstances.

Other adolescents return to therapy much less dramatically than Martha. Often, it appears that the therapist's willingness to release them allows these youngsters to return of their own volition.

Of course, some do not return. Sometimes, one hears that they found another therapist with whom they can work more comfortably. Sometimes, one hears that they have been through several therapists without success. This may happen when the parents remain too involved in dictating the goals of therapy. It also happens when the youngster has insufficient trust and interest in other people to allow the development of any enduring human relationship.

FORCED TERMINATION

At times, therapy must be terminated because of the therapist's illness, death, or change of location. Adults and adolescents have similar reactions to these losses. The response is one of grief. Anger is expressed toward any new therapist until the feelings toward the lost therapist are accepted and resolved. The client works through her ambivalence toward the old therapist gradually and only then is able to form an attachment and a therapeutic alliance in his new treatment relationship.

SOME FINAL COMMENTS ABOUT TERMINATION

Do Not Expect a Rose

Adatto (1966) described the narcissistic investment of the adolescent that prevents total analysis of transference during the adolescent period. From his patients who returned for analysis as adults, he also learned that he had been introjected to a surprising degree and had served as an important internal figure in the intervening years. "Analytic associations in the adult phase indicate that I not only became an object of transference

but was also introjected as a new object who acted as a transition
between the old and the future, growing 'organically' from the
past, and actively used in restructuring and synthesizing the
psychic apparatus."

We feel there is a valuable lesson for adolescent therapists in
Adatto's observations. The therapist often helps his adolescent
clients toward health without knowing it and certainly without
their explicit acknowledgment. He is often much more important to them than they can let him know!

The adolescent does not wish to admit dependency. Still, she
often takes the therapist's comments, reflective stance, and noncritical, exploratory attitude home with her. She may ignore,
kid, and even deride the therapist in the office, but at home she
secretly mulls everything over.

When the therapist is able to see the growth and development
that may continue even after psychotherapy has officially ended,
he is amply repaid for his efforts.

At Last!—The Payoff for the Therapist

As valuable byproducts of his therapeutic efforts with adolescents, the therapist may collect a broadening sense of involvement in social conflict and social change as well as a more
wholesome grasp of the mutual interdependence of the generations. The need to recognize and retain the enduring human
bonds that transcend cultural change and social upheaval challenges the therapist's wisdom as the searching adolescent forces
him into the problems of the immediate present. Ossification
and ivory tower isolation are at least delayed, if not prevented.
Treating adolescents may not keep one young, but it tends to
discourage the worst features of aging—the impoverishment of
thought and constriction of viewpoint.

As the therapist reflects on what the adolescent has given
him, perhaps he will even be able to find the strength, enthusiasm, and faith to prepare himself for the next adolescent client.
And who will replace his departing young friend? As noted
earlier, the new client will probably be an angry, devious, de-

fended, difficult youngster who will carry little of the load of treatment for some time to come. In short, in many respects and for everyone concerned, termination is always a new beginning. The adolescent begins again, more completely self-reliant. The therapist begins again, not only with a new client but with a new impetus to the development of his own "ego integrity." As he moves toward this goal, he avoids despair and the fear of death. To the extent that he succeeds, he may be able to help his adolescent clients to avoid the fear of life.

Part
Two

introduction

This section of the book deals with special problems that may be encountered in the psychotherapy of adolescents. These topics are discussed separately to allow elaboration of the technical complications introduced by extreme behavior patterns. The suicidal adolescent, for example, requires particular precautions and introduces unique countertransference issues. These were largely omitted in Part One in order to avoid tangential excursions that might have detracted from the continuity of the presentation. Despite the separation of syndromes in Part Two, the basic techniques described earlier apply in these special cases as well as in the more "average" case.

Part Two is intended primarily as a beginning reference source for the therapist when she is confronted with a case involving one of the symptom complexes that are covered here. The chapters are self-contained and may be read independently from one another.

As in Part One, we have generally recommended a specific approach as the best method of dealing with each clinical situation. In treating these difficult and complicated problems, suggesting that one technical method is best is even more risky than in the discussion of general techniques. As in Part One, the suggested "right" approach should be viewed as an orienting statement. Each therapist must think out her own philosophy and technique, utilizing only that portion of the approach described here that seems comfortable and useful in her own work. If our "orientation" serves to catalyze this thinking process in the individual therapist, it will have served its intended purpose.

CHAPTER 10

the adolescent at school

School, with all of its academic, behavioral, and social ramifications, is the adolescent's work world. For better or for worse, his life at school is the single most important parameter that defines the youngster's intellectual ability, physical skills, social competence, his ability to separate from parents, and his finesse in coping with rules and adult authority. The adolescent's sense of self-esteem depends on his success at school and the things related to school, such as sports and activities with peers. The school experience is so encompassing that it touches on countless facets of the adolescent in psychotherapy. We are addressing a few of these, focusing on school performance evaluation as a diagnostic tool; school refusal; learning disabilities; and attention-deficit/hyperactivity disorder in adolescence.

SCHOOL AS MICROCOSM

It is easy to start an evaluation of an adolescent by asking him about school—his grade; his schedule; his teachers; extracurricular activities; athletic accomplishments. What does he consider his best subject and why is it the best and what are they studying right now in that subject? What does he consider his worst subject and why is it the worst and what are they studying now in that subject? Is there a drug problem in his school? How does he get to school? Whom does he sit with on the bus?

School is a good topic with which to initiate the evaluation process for several reasons. First, the youngster sees this as a natural line of questioning. Since school is such a big part of his life, the examiner seems like a normal person to want to get that information first. Maybe, the youngster thinks, shrinks aren't so weird after all!

271

Second, most adolescents find these questions easy to deal with. Even if school happens to be an area of great difficulty, it is still relatively easy for a teenager to answer matter-of-fact questions about his daily schedule and his likes and dislikes about high school.

The third reason that school is a good initial topic is the most important: a discussion about high school can be an extended in vivo projective test. The examiner can learn a lot from what the adolescent says about his fellow students because he may project his own opinions and feelings onto them. When he describes his teachers or the school's administrative staff, he may be displacing feelings about his parents. When he tells you how he reacts to the frustrations of plane geometry, he is revealing a little piece of his world-view and his style of responding to challenge.

Another approach is to talk about movies or television shows. Most adolescents will discuss the human relationships between fictional students with comfort and enthusiasm.

It is easy to guide the initial interview from the topic of school to almost any other subject. With a little imagination the therapist can find a transition from some aspect of school to a discussion of drugs and alcohol, sexuality, depression, family issues, or whatever. The therapist may want to come back to the subject of school and education toward the close of the interview. At that point it may be good to inquire about the future, what the client is going to be doing after graduation, what his aspirations may be for employment or for college. This is not only a nice way to tie up an evaluation interview and to move on from the immediate imbroglio to thinking about the promise that the future holds, it also gives valuable information about your client. Does he have a vocational ambition? Can he imagine himself as an adult? . . . as a husband? . . . as a parent?

This chapter addresses several clinical aspects of the adolescent's life at school. We will discuss school refusal. We will consider the adolescent who has a learning disability or attention-deficit/hyperactivity disorder. We will discuss the role of alternative schools and will refer to the relationship between the therapist and school personnel.

"School refusal" is simply a phrase that indicates a particular piece of behavior, i.e., nonattendance at school. It is not a diagnosis and it is not a syndrome. It is a symptom that warrants a diagnostic evaluation and it turns out that there are several possible causes. Although we generalize reluctantly, the underlying explanation or the dynamics of the school refusal are frequently related to the developmental level of the child.

Young children in elementary school have trouble going to school because of separation anxiety, which has been called school phobia. They are afraid of the insecurity associated with being away from the parents.

Early adolescence is approximately the years of junior high school, the seventh and eighth grades. These youngsters stay home from school because they are afraid of what will or what they fantasize will happen at school. They are usually afraid of the challenges of peer relations that arise in early adolescence. They usually have expanded mundane early adolescent concerns into major problems: that other kids won't like them, that they will be picked on, that something is wrong with their bodies, that they will be exposed as mentally and physically incompetent.

Middle adolescence is approximately the years of high school, especially the ninth to the eleventh grades. When these youngsters refuse to go to school, it may be necessary to sort out whether the school refusal is simply truancy, which has a delinquent bent to it, or is phobic in nature. The truant adolescent avoids both school and home and is usually out in the neighborhood with friends. The phobic adolescent avoids going to school and stays home by himself. Truancy often comes as a surprise to parents, while they are usually well aware of their youngster's fears and phobic concerns.

Phobias and Fears

While "school refusal" usually implies only a piece of behavior, the term "school phobia" refers to a particular syndrome with its own pattern of symptoms, individual dynamics, and family pathology. In papers that are now classics, Coolidge et al. (1960) and Coolidge and Brodie (1974) at the Judge Baker Guidance Center in Boston described many children and adolescents with school phobia. They felt that the fundamental dynamics in all the age groups were basically the same. That is, the children and adolescents were comfortable when close to the parents, especially the mother, and they were reluctant to give up their dependence in order to advance along the line of separation and psychological autonomy. This symptom in a younger child was frequently an acute impasse and yielded to active treatment. In fact, the long-term outcome was related more to the depth of the counseling with the mother than it was to the nature or duration of the treatment of the child. However, Coolidge found that the occurrence of school phobia in an adolescent was more ominous because these clients had more fixed personality traits and were resistant to treatment. In the case of adolescents, the client and the parent may conspire for years to avoid true emotional separation, but this pathological collusion may not be recognized until overt symptomatology occurs in adolescence. The term "school phobia" is not an official diagnosis; usually these youngsters have the diagnosis of separation anxiety disorder.

Mogul (1969) used the symptom of school refusal to show that a particular piece of behavior may have been determined by completely opposite dynamics. He presented four adolescent boys, all of whom avoided school or refused to attend school. "Yet in two of the four cases, this behavior signified the failure to relinquish infantile object ties resulting in failure of further growth or in regression. In the other two cases, the same overt behavior had just the opposite significance: it was directly in the service of freeing these adolescents from early object ties and dependence to create an identity as an independent adult." For instance, one of the boys avoided going to school and stayed home with his mother and played with his younger brother. On the other hand, another youngster refused to continue school in a college preparatory program because he wanted to move on with his own nonacademic ambition of becoming a forester or a farmer. Mogul pointed out that it would not make sense to provide the same therapy for both of these adolescents. In the case of the first boy, who had the traditional form of school phobia, the goals of therapy would be to help him achieve psychological independence and also to stay in school. In the case of the second youngster, who was in the process of achieving psychological independence, the goal of therapy would be to help the parents accept that their son might not be going to college.

The person with a phobia is afraid of something in his mind; the person with a fear is afraid of something in the real world. In addition to being phobic, there are other reasons why an adolescent may manifest school refusal. He may simply be afraid of real bullies who control the day-to-day life at that particular high school. He may have an unrecognized learning disability, which has convinced him over the years that school is a perpetually frustrating and disheartening experience. He may be experiencing prepsychotic confusion and is protecting his fragile ego from any stimulation he can avoid.

Outpatient Treatment of School Phobia

The treatment of school refusal first requires the therapist to consider some or all of the possible patterns described and to make a specific diagnosis. The treatments for drug abuse, conduct disorder, psychosis, and other causes of school avoidance are discussed elsewhere in this book. In this chapter we will focus on the treatment of the dependent adolescent who is overly anxious about dealing with the tasks of adolescence and fearfully overattached to home and parents.

The ideal therapy regimen for these youngsters includes family therapy, individual therapy, and an adolescent therapy group. The family meetings allow the therapist to observe first hand what happens among the family members and also provide an opportunity to make sure that everybody understands the priorities in the treatment process. It may be helpful to use the family meetings to discuss changes in the parents' roles. For instance, suppose the client's mother is easily manipulated or easily swayed by the adolescent's demands for dependency. It might work for the father to be more involved with the youngster's school attendance. That is, it could be the father who drops the client off at school in the morning and it could be the father who takes the calls from the school nurse when the client feels ill.

In individual therapy, the youngster and the therapist can explore the details of the student's ambivalence about growing up. Participation in a well-functioning therapy group can be very helpful. The group members can give the school-phobic youngster a good deal of support and helpful advice about how to cope with the real-life difficulties of high school life as well as a model for more independent functioning. In the process, the school-phobic client may use the group to learn how to develop sincere and mutually satisfying peer relationships.

The therapist will need to consider other aspects of treating the school phobic adolescent. It is almost always important to maintain a dialogue with the high school guidance counselor. The counselor will be delighted to hear from you and will be able to give you some valuable information. For example, if the teenager has been telling you that her third period French teacher is an intolerant and sadistic person, the counselor may be able to give you a second opinion. Also, it may be helpful to work out a "back-to-school" program for the phobic adolescent in which it is clear that the client absolutely must go to school every day, but at the beginning will only go to two class periods. After a week or so, the expectation would be to attend three periods, and so on. At the beginning it may work better if the adolescent is told that all she has to do is show up and sit in the classroom and that the teacher will not have any expectation of her to perform. As the youngster accommodates, the expectations are raised. In order for any kind of program like this to work, it is important to have a clear understanding between the guidance counselor, the teachers, the student, the parents, and the therapist.

Many phobic clients and their parents ask that the student be put on homebound teaching, in which the city or county school system sends a teacher to the student's house for several hours each week and the student is thereby excused from attending school. That is usually not a good idea, since it simply makes it easier to avoid addressing and resolving the underlying issues. Some schools do arrange for "homebound instruction," but that means that the student is tutored individually in a separate room at the school itself and not really at home.

Some school phobic youngsters become extremely anxious, to the point of having the symptoms of a panic attack. They are certainly unhappy and frequently chronically depressed. The depression is derived from realizing that they are not functioning to the level that they should and also that they are being asked to give up the comfortable and comforting tie to the mother. Both the panic attacks and the depression may respond to antidepressant medication.

The therapist should have a sense for timing and for setting priorities in treating school phobic adolescents. In the initial phase of therapy it is desirable to try a crisis intervention approach. That is, convey at the outset that it is important for the youngster to be back in school. It is his "job" to be in school every day and it is important to keep up with the assignments, whether or not he is attending class. Point out that it will be good for his sense of self-esteem and will give him a feeling of mastery if he overcomes his fears and stays in school. In a later phase of therapy, while the client is attending school at least part of the time, you can explore what makes it so hard to be at school and the underlying reasons for the anxiety.

Alternatives to Outpatient Treatment

Other treatment interventions should be considered, if there is no progress with outpatient therapy or if the clinical situation is especially difficult:
- inpatient treatment on an adolescent psychiatry unit that has a good school program, if the youngster has been out

of school for several weeks and is resistant to outpatient therapy;

- a psychiatric day treatment program, if both the parents and the client are motivated for treatment, but the youngster is too disabled to continue at his regular school;
- transfer to another high school or a private school or an alternative school, if it seems clear that the school refusal was caused by the students or the teachers or the circumstances of the original school. Students who refuse school may say that all they need is a fresh start in a new school, and sometimes they are right.
- referral to a residential treatment center, if further evaluation reveals that the youngster will need prolonged physical separation from home in order to accomplish true psychological separation.

School Refusal in Other Syndromes

The behavior of school refusal may not represent school phobia at all, but may be the top of a totally different iceberg. For instance, it may be learned through clinical evaluation that the school refusal is a manifestation of incipient psychosis. In that case the therapist would not be encouraging the youngster to return to school immediately, but would be considering psychotropic medication and perhaps hospitalization. If the school avoidance is a result of continuing drug and alcohol abuse, the therapist should consider referral to an adolescent chemical dependency program. If the problem is chronic truancy and the parents are unsuccessful at disciplining their child, the therapist should think about involving the legal system, in the guise of a probation officer.

ADOLESCENTS WITH LEARNING DISABILITIES

Concern for children and adolescents with learning disabilities is one of those issues that has touched many professional disciplines. The first person to describe these syndromes in a systematic manner was a neuropsychiatrist, Samuel Orton (1937). Another prominent individual in this field has been a pediatrician, Melvin Levine, who spent a career studying learning disabilities and educating the public about them. Levine (1987, 1998) has organized a comprehensive and elegant summary of the neurodevelopmental functions which need to interact effectively for a child to learn. A child psychiatrist, Larry Silver (1989), has insisted that professionals must think holistically in order to understand fully clients with learning disabilities. He states that it is necessary to consider many variables, including the constitutional and neurological substrate, the youngster's intrapsychic and interpersonal dynamics, learned behaviors, and family interactions. In other words, the basic neurological problem alone cannot explain the entire symptom picture in these youngsters and treatment may need to be multifaceted.

DSM-IV-TR (2000) uses the following categories and terminology for learning disabilities and related disorders:
- Learning disorders
  - Reading disorder
  - Mathematics disorder
  - Disorder of written expression
  - Learning disorder not otherwise specified
- Communication disorders
  - Expressive language disorder
  - Mixed receptive-expressive language disorder
  - Phonological disorder
  - Stuttering
  - Communication disorder not otherwise specified
- Motor skills disorder
  - Developmental coordination disorder

In general, the first criterion in *DSM-IV-TR* for a learning disorder is that the achievement level, as measured by a standardized, individually administered test, is substantially below the expected level, given the person's chronological age, measured intelligence, and age-appropriate education. The second criterion cited in *DSM-IV-TR* is that the disturbance significantly interferes with the person's functioning in that specific area.

CAUSES OF ACADEMIC UNDERACHIEVEMENT

Academic underachievement is the single most frequent reason that adolescents are brought for psychological and psychiatric evaluation. Sugar (1987) outlined and discussed the many causes of underachievement.

Hereditary: mental retardation; dyslexia; impulsive temperament.
Congenital: fetal alcohol syndrome; complications of labor and delivery; poor vision; poor hearing.
Developmental: learning disabilities; speech and language disorders; Asperger's syndrome.
Infections: encephalitis.
Metabolic and Hormonal: cretinism, phenylketonuria, iron deficiency anemia.
Toxins: high lead levels; substance abuse, especially inhalants.
Trauma: concussion, one big one or several small ones.
Tumors: not just brain tumors, but also leukemia.
Neurological: seizures; Tourette's disorder.
Nutritional Deficiencies: that's the reason for school breakfast and lunch programs.
Cognitive: failure to achieve abstract thinking or formal operations; attention-deficit/hyperactivity disorder.
Emotional: subtle psychosis; depression; separation anxiety; posttraumatic symptoms; reaction to pregnancy; obsessive-compulsive disorder.
Family: children of divorce; family violence; illness, death, or absence of a parent; extremely pushy or successful parents; parents who discourage or disparage education.
Educational System: unsympathetic or untrained teachers; poor communication between parents and school personnel.

Learning disabilities may also be classified according to the nature of the dysfunction. These include perceptual problems (that is, an impairment in the processing of sensory inputs), cognitive problems (an impairment in the integration of these inputs), memory problems, language problems, and motor problems. Some recent texts on this subject have been edited or written by Hallahan et al. (1999), Kavale and Forness (1995), Myers and Hammill (1990), and Wallach and Butler (1994). Silver (1998) published a book that is primarily intended for the parents of learning-disabled children and adolescents. It summarized the laws that pertain to educational placement. The American Academy of Child and Adolescent Psychiatry (1998b) has published practice parameters for the assessment of adolescents with language and learning disorders.

Case Example

Learning disabilities are usually first noticed in elementary school, because the child's academic achievement is below what would be expected from his overall intelligence. School personnel do screening tests to see if the child's actual achievement is at least two years below his expected level. As appropriate, more detailed tests are performed to determine if a specific learning disability is handicapping the child. It is unusual for a learning-disabled youngster to reach adolescence before his condition has been evaluated, but sometimes it happens. One problem is that special education teachers are trained to work with younger children and some may not know what to do with the learning disabled teenager.

Jack was a 14-year-old ninth grade student who was underachieving and was very unhappy. His parents were very frustrated because of what they perceived to be chronic, willful disobedience. The father was a businessman who was transferred frequently, so the family traveled and Jack had been in several schools, including two that were overseas. He was never in any school long enough to be both noticed and evaluated.

Jack was brought for psychiatric evaluation because his extreme passive-aggressive behavior was interfering with his school work. Jack would sit quietly in class, but would flatly refuse to respond to the teacher's questions or do any written work. Some days he would spend his time in class reading quietly to himself—not magazines or comic books, but novels. He occasionally did homework, but would not turn it in.

Jack also refused to participate in the psychiatric evaluation. After his mother parked the car, Jack bolted from the parking lot. He did agree to be in an adolescent therapy group, which he perceived as less threatening, and he later became willing to see the therapist individually to complete the evaluation. Although Jack was friendly and tried to be cooperative, he frequently withdrew into passivity. When he spoke, he had trouble expressing himself in a smooth, fluent manner. He enjoyed reading and listening, but it was hard for Jack to communicate verbally, whether orally or in writing.

The psychiatrist referred Jack and the parents to a tutor who specialized in evaluating and teaching children with learning disabilities. The tutor's evaluation clearly demonstrated Jack's handicap in expressive language. The tutor continued to work with Jack and she became the first person to really understand how to communicate with him. In a sense, the psychotherapy became adjunctive to the educational therapy.

What the Therapist Can Do

The therapist can begin helping the youngster with a learning disability in several ways by helping him understand his cognitive strengths and weaknesses. One way to do this is to obtain a copy of the educational testing and go over it with the client in some detail. This can start the process of helping the adolescent accept and understand how his own style of perceiving, organizing, and expressing information is different from the way other people do it. It is hard for a teenager to understand a deficit when he never experienced the function in the first place. Once understood, it may also be hard to accept. Denial can be very powerful. For example, one adolescent who was color blind refused to believe that there really were other colors until he was informed that he could not enter naval pilot school because he could not read the numbers on the Ishihara cards.

Once there is an alliance, the therapist can help the youngster find ways to compensate for his areas of weakness. When it gets down to the details of designing an educational strategy, this needs to be done by an educator who understands learning disabilities. But it is within the realm of the psychotherapist to make some suggestions: that the youngster who has impossible handwriting should be allowed to type his reports; that the dyslexic teenager should use a program that automatically checks the spelling; that the youngster with poor memory should always write his assignments in a notebook. The therapist might also help the adolescent plan for his future in terms of his strengths, rather than his weak areas. A person with really poor fine motor coordination should think about becoming a psychiatrist rather than a dentist.

Therapy with youngsters who are learning disabled usually is supportive and somewhat didactic. These adolescents may need extra help to learn information that other teenagers come by automatically. For instance, these boys and girls may have a tendency to be out of touch in many ways, including their awareness of sexuality. They tend to be naive and do not pick up incidental information the way most teenagers do. These youngsters need extra help in learning social skills—how to act, talk, and dress. The learning disabled adolescent may become lonely and depressed because he is uncertain about these matters.

The therapist plays a crucial role in helping the adolescent work through the narcissistic injury inherent in accepting anything other than perfection. This is aided by finding ways to enhance self-esteem, which usually takes the form of identifying and then capitalizing on the youngster's God-given abilities. In the case of Jack, the boy with the severe impairment in expressive language, it came to the therapist's attention that he was within three merit badges of becoming an Eagle Scout. He obviously had some sense of ambition and perseverance which needed to be encouraged.

Another way to give a youngster permission to think positively about himself is to mention important or popular people who have also had learning problems. We don't know if Albert Einstein had a learning disability—but he did fail to receive his diploma from secondary school because he did so poorly in history, geography, and languages. Some contemporary examples of individuals who have done very well, despite having some form of learning disability, are Cher, Tom Cruise, and Magic Johnson.

The therapist needs to establish liaison with the school to be helpful to the child. It is also important to mobilize the family and community around the child to support the effort to learn. Some concrete suggestions and approaches are described by Meeks and Dupont (2003) in their book, *The Learning Alliance: A Handbook for School-Oriented Psychotherapy*. The book is mainly focused on the school-based therapist, but includes a chapter for the office practitioner.

ATTENTION-DEFICIT/HYPERACTIVITY DISORDER

What becomes of hyperactive children? What happens to all the children with attention-deficit/hyperactivity disorder when they grow up? Some hyperactive children who are treated with medication and other interventions, such as behavior modification approaches, do well. As they mature physically, the attention deficits seem less of a problem and they are able to continue into adolescence without any further treatment. On the other hand, many hyperactive children grow into problematic adolescents and eventually into irascible adults. See Wender (1987) for a thorough discussion of these topics.

It is important for therapists who work with adolescents to appreciate the long-term course of attention-deficit/hyperactivity disorder. In order to understand why we say that, think of yourself seeing an adolescent for an initial assessment who is impulsive and not goal-directed and unhappy with his accomplishments. It is one thing if those symptoms have developed over the last few months because of some external stressor. It is altogether something different if the adolescent has been distractible and impulsive since early childhood. If that is the case, he has come to believe that he is not able to be as successful as other teenagers.

The natural history of attention-deficit/hyperactivity disorder has been studied by Gabrielle Weiss and her colleagues (Hoy et al., 1978; Hechtman et al., 1981; Weiss et al., 1985; Weiss and Hechtman, 1993). These references represent three stages of the same longitudinal study. That is, a group of hyperactive children were reevaluated at early adolescence, during late adolescence, and at young adulthood. The first follow-up occurred when the cohort of hyperactive patients had reached a mean age of 14. At that point they were still having many difficulties. Although they were less hyperactive than previously, they continued to be more restless than controls, distractible, emotionally immature, unable to maintain goals, and had developed poor self-esteem. Compared to matched controls, the hyperactive youngsters had failed more grades and had lower ratings in all subjects on report cards. The hyperactive teenagers continued to be impulsive rather than reflective. About 25% were involved in antisocial behavior, which was higher than matched controls.

The second follow-up occurred when the cohort of hyperactive children had reached a mean age of 19. At that point the research team found that there were three categories of outcomes. Roughly 30–40% of the research subjects had a fairly normal outcome, in that they were working or in school full-time; they had an acceptable work history; enjoyed stable friendships; and did not feel unusually lonely or isolated. Another 40–50% of the subjects had significant social, emotional, and impulsive problems. This group reported an unstable work history; disagreements with peers or supervisors; frequent moves, which were often sudden and impulsive; and they lacked long-standing, close relationships with either sex. About 10% of the original subjects were seriously disturbed at this follow-up during late adolescence. Their disturbance was manifested by either psychiatric disturbance or antisocial behavior. They reported much unemployment; jail terms; admission to psychiatric hospitals; a lack of intimate friends and sometimes even a lack of acquaintances; and serious depressions with suicide attempts.

The use of medication such as Ritalin (methylphenidate) should be considered on an individual basis. Some adolescents and also adults with attention-deficit/hyperactivity disorder continue to respond to these medications. Care should be taken because of the possibility that an adolescent patient or his friends might abuse these medications. Medication should not be prescribed unless the therapist believes that the patient will use it responsibly and will accurately report its effects.

Fred was a 16-year-old high school junior who came for psychiatric evaluation because of academic underachievement. He was failing several courses. Although he claimed to study hard, he just couldn't perform well enough to please his parents, especially his father. Fred's father was a successful business executive who expected his family members to operate in a timely and efficient manner. There was a continuing battle between Fred and his father. In fact, this family dynamic was so striking that the therapist concluded that Fred was asserting himself and rebelling in the safest way available, by pretending to study but by not accomplishing anything.

The therapist developed this formulation and explained his observations and interpretations to Fred, who listened politely but remained doubtful. The therapist held family meetings in order to help Fred and his father understand each other better and to collaborate in finding a solution to the problem of Fred's underachievement. In the course of these family meetings Fred tried to explain his subjective experience when he was in class and when he tried to study at home. He described how he simply couldn't stay on the task, that extraneous details would intrude on his concentration. It eventually dawned on the therapist that Fred was describing one form of attention-deficit/hyperactivity disorder.

The possibility of a trial of medication was discussed with Fred and his father. They both were intrigued by the notion that the psychiatrist might be on to something and they agreed. Ritalin was prescribed and the result was dramatically positive. Fred found that he could concentrate and began to enjoy reading and assimilating the material that he had been studying so hard. His grades improved significantly and continued at a satisfactory level through his junior and senior year. Fred's achievement in chemistry went up so suddenly that his teacher thought he was cheating.

The ongoing battle between Fred and his father was the result, rather than the cause, of his underachievement. As they stopped arguing about his poor grades, Fred and his father became able to respect each other and enjoy their relationship.

ALTERNATIVE SCHOOL PLACEMENTS

There is no easy way to predict exactly which students are going to do well in different school programs. In this chapter we will express some general guidelines, but in practice it becomes necessary to talk to school personnel and to know something about their educational goals and philosophies. Some therapists are good at matching up a specific client with an appropriate educational program, especially if the therapist has taken the time to visit and become familiar with the schools available in her community.

Public Schools

City and county school systems are responsible for providing an appropriate education for all students in their jurisdictions, including the handicapped children. The United States laws defining that responsibility are the Individuals with Disabilities Education Act (IDEA), which formerly was known as the Education of the Handicapped Act, and Section 504 of the Rehabilitation Act of 1973. These laws are the basis for the rules and regulations that the various states have established. IDEA requires the integration of children with disabilities into the public schools to the maximum extent appropriate; requires public schools to create an individualized educational plan (IEP) for each child with a disability who needed special education; and gives parents of children with disabilities the right to appeal public school actions to the state and federal courts. Section 504 prohibits discrimination against individuals with disabilities by public schools that receive federal funds.

The selection of the special education services for a particular child depends on the nature and severity of the problem. For instance, an adolescent with a relatively minor learning disability might be placed in a resource room for one or two of his class periods each day, where he will receive individualized help with basic skills and with homework assignments. A youngster with a more profound learning disability will spend less time in the mainstream classes and more time in a self-contained program for students with similar disabilities. Likewise, a student with a serious emotional problem may be placed in a self-contained program for children with emotional disorders. Since learning disorders and emotional disorders frequently occur in the same group of students, some school systems have large special education programs that deal with both learning problems and emotional problems. In any case, school personnel are responsible for identifying the students who need a special program, for evaluating these students, and for placing them in appropriate educational settings. Most school personnel are happy to receive any input that the youngster's therapist may wish to offer regarding this decision.

Special education programs for youngsters with fairly severe academic problems need to be multidisciplinary. Teachers in these programs should be trained in remedial education techniques but also need to understand some of the emotional side effects of poor school performance. As noted earlier, the young person's sense of self-esteem and his attitude toward peers and adults are strongly colored by his success or failure at school. In addition to trained educators, schools that hope to ameliorate the academic and emotional problems of these youngsters also need therapists. The tasks of creating motivation and rekindling hope has several steps that usually require therapeutic skills. These steps have been designation by the acronym AIM (Meeks and Dupont, 2003, pp. 4–9).

A—Aspiration. This refers to the therapeutic techniques that help the student understand that education has a positive value.

I—Inspiration. This refers to helping the student have confidence that he or she can succeed academically.

M—Mobilization. This refers to the process of helping the student develop attitudes and work habits that will lead to academic success.

Private Schools

Sometimes parents wonder if their child would do better in a private school or a parochial school. There are many reasons why a family might want to choose a private school, most of which do not have anything to do with emotional or psychological issues.

The parents may feel that their child will have a more rigorous education at a private school and then move on to a better college. They may feel that it would be less likely that their child would be exposed to drugs and violence and sex at a private school. The parents may be motivated by social reasons or geographic convenience or by family tradition.

Some private schools have features that are particularly helpful for adolescents with certain psychological needs. For instance, a youngster who is quite timid might do better in a school that is small and where virtually every student is automatically included in recreational and social events. A student who is on the lackadaisical or even irresponsible side might do well in a school with small classes where the teachers are able to keep on his case. A student with a learning disability, but not severe enough for the public school system to notice, might do better in a private school where faculty members are interested in disabled students and have a reputation for creative teaching.

Boarding Schools

In a similar vein, there are a number of reasons why normal parents might want to send their normal children to boarding school. Most commonly, they feel that there are academic and social advantages. Also, many boarding schools offer a sense of discipline and mission and comradeship that may be hard to find in the local community high school.

There are also clinical situations where the best treatment is to go to a good boarding school. For instance, consider a youngster in an enmeshed family who is not addressing any of the issues and tasks of adolescence because he is so tied up in a hostile and dependent relationship with his parents. In his heart, that boy is going to want to stay home and argue with his mother and will be able to come up with numerous reasons why home is best for him. In his head, however, the same youngster will be able to understand on an intellectual level that he needs to find some way to grow up. The therapist may want to promote the client's psychological growth by recommending a good boarding school. It might be possible to continue seeing the client during vacations to monitor and encourage the process of separation and individuation.

Another reason to consider a boarding school is to get the youngster out of a contentious, inflammatory situation at home. That is what happened with Tyrone:

Tyrone was a 16-year-old tenth grader, whose mother dragged him in for a psychiatric evaluation. Tyrone was almost out of control. He was furious at his mother and verbally abused her. Some of his anger had a paranoid quality to it. He refused to follow any form of reasonable discipline. He was accomplishing nothing at school.

Tyrone's parents had separated and were in the midst of an extremely angry divorce. The parents made endless accusations against each other. The father came in to participate in the evaluation. He was a dogmatic, opinionated, and physically overwhelming man. He expressed the opinion that he could successfully supervise and discipline Tyrone if he were just given a chance. Tyrone insisted on living with his mother and told the therapist that he had plans to run away to another state if he had to live with his father.

The psychiatrist recommended intensive therapy for Tyrone and counseling for the parents, in order to help the parents leave the boy out of their battle. The psychiatrist advised the family that hospitalization would be necessary if Tyrone were not able to control himself. At that point the parents precipitously and unexpectedly agreed on one thing, that Tyrone should go to a boarding school. Tyrone seemed relieved at the prospect of getting out of the war zone. The psychiatrist was skeptical about that plan because he doubted that the boy's anger and mental disorganization would be cured by a simple change of environment.

Several months later Tyrone was home for Christmas vacation and saw the psychiatrist. Tyrone was doing fine. He described the rigid, no-nonsense school in glowing terms. His mother confirmed that the staff at the school were quite complimentary about Tyrone's behavior and school work.

Tyrone spoke most highly of his track coach, whom he idolized. Tyrone was introduced to long-distance running and he had become a fanatical runner. He became the best cross-country runner in his school and he competed successfully in regional and state events. He suggested that the psychiatrist take up running as a way to get a healthy, nonchemical high.

Tyrone was lucky. His "referral" to boarding school allowed him to get out of an extremely stressful situation. The school provided good role models and a chance to sublimate his major emotional conflicts.

For an adolescent, school can make you or break you. School can be the best part of your life or the worst part. The therapist can take a school history as one indicator of the student's success at the basic tasks of adolescence. The therapist should make sure that the treatment plan includes helping the adolescent be successful at school and at work. Succeeding in a good school can help the adolescent compensate for losses or defects in other parts of his life.

CHAPTER 11

depression, suicidal threats, and suicidal behavior

Suicide is an important cause of death during adolescent years even without counting those "deaths due to accidental cause" that may be consciously or unconsciously suicidal. The suicide rate among adolescents, especially white male adolescents, increased markedly over the last 30 years. During the 1950s about 4 out of every 100,000 adolescents (ages 15 through 24) committed suicide each year. During the 1980s the incidence of suicide among adolescents rose to more than 12 per 100,000. The rate among white male adolescents and young adults was even higher, over 20 per 100,000. Some groups of Native American adolescents also have a disproportionately high rate of suicide. During the late 1990s the adolescent suicide rates plateaued and then fell slightly.

A number of theories have been advanced to explain the increase in adolescent suicides but none has been definitely proven. The most commonly mentioned factors include the demographic increase in numbers of adolescents; the general emotional state of the culture; the increase in drug and alcohol abuse among adolescents; and factors such as greater mobility and divorce, which interrupt effective family functioning and therefore the nurture of the adolescent. When population cohorts are studied, it seems that there is a greater incidence of adolescent problems (violence and suicide) when the proportion of adolescents is higher in the overall population. That is, not only are the absolute numbers higher, but the incidence is higher. This seems to apply to the baby boom generation (Klerman, 1989) and also to the population cohort constituting the children of the baby boomers. Using a demographic model, Holinger

(1989) predicted that the suicide rate among adolescents and also the juvenile crime rates would level off or fall during the 1980s and 1990s. Another theory relates the increase of legal abortion in the U.S. in the 1980s to the fall in adolescent violence and suicide in the 1990s. The idea is that adolescent violence and suicide occurs more often among youngsters who were unwanted, neglected, and abused. Since the introduction of legal abortion presumably resulted in fewer unwanted children, that meant less adolescent violence and suicide 15 to 20 years later.

FACTORS THAT INCREASE OR DECREASE SUICIDE POTENTIAL

It is perhaps surprising that the rate of suicide attempts and successful suicides is as low as is estimated. The threat of object loss and punitive superego pressures, two important dynamic factors in suicidal behavior, are virtually endemic to adolescence. Suicidal ideation and fantasies of glorious death are extremely common among young people. Possibly, many adolescents are protected from their self-destructive impulses by a combination of felt parental concern and the relative ease with which new relationships can be formed during this period.

Another factor that contributes to suicidality is the adolescent's avoidance of depressive affect. The tendency toward depression is probably basic to many of the emotional disorders observed during adolescence. Certainly, it plays a major role in many delinquent behavior disorders, drug abuse, running away, and learning problems. This depression is related primarily to the state of object deficiency that accompanies the necessary decathexis of parental introjects. Often, the delinquent behaviors that serve as defenses against depression are clearly self-destructive "little suicides." Very frequently, they are accompanied by a conscious sense of self-loathing. The adolescent says, "I don't care what happens to me," but his behavior suggests that the unspoken conclusion of the statement is, "but I hope it's something terrible."

Suicide attempts are the most frequent reason for referral of adolescents to emergency services. Adolescents who are re-

ASSESSMENT OF SUICIDALITY IN ADOLESCENTS

This outline of important issues to consider in assessing suicidality was adapted from Godenne (1997) and Pfeffer (1998).

Consider Risk Factors: serious depression; psychotic disorders; recent discharge from psychiatric hospital; past suicidal history, including suicide attempt or suicide in family; substance abuse.

Situational Factors and Precipitants: breakup with girl friend or boy friend; significant disappointment, such as failure to be accepted by preferred college or fraternity; recent discipline by school personnel or arrest by police.

Severity of Intent and Lethality of Act: whether the youngster truly intended to die; whether the act was lethal, such as hanging, gunshot, large overdose; whether discovery was likely or unlikely.

Don't be Shy. Directly ask if the youngster is thinking about self-harm; if he has any definite plans to kill himself; if he owns firearms or other weapons; if he has access to a large quantity of drugs; if he drinks heavily when depressed.

Identify Support Group. Find out if the youngster has a best friend or associates with a group of peers; whether he is willing to communicate with his friends and family members. Interview the parents to collect history and to size up their ability to support the adolescent.

Look for Sense of Future. Ask the teenager about his plans for that same evening or the following day. This may be especially helpful with youngsters who look depressed but deny suicidal thoughts.

Observations in Interview. Notice whether the youngster communicates on a personal level, allows eye contact, smiles in response to a humorous comment.

ferred to emergency rooms because of suicide attempts have a multiplicity of other symptoms. That is, school refusal and truancy, sexual promiscuity, withdrawal, a variety of physical symptoms, compulsive hyperactivity, threats of physical assault, running away, and substance abuse are associated with depression in adolescents.

It is important to remember, however, that not all acting out is "masked depression." Depressed youngsters may show their discomfort by acting out but other youngsters act out for different reasons. In any case, even youngsters who present primarily with behavioral symptoms may have clear cut depressive symptomatology that can be discovered by appropriate evaluation when depression is actually the basic problem.

Depression in adolescence is frequently associated with disturbed family interactions (Shapiro and Freedman, 1987). For example, depressed individuals consistently report greater parental rejection than nondepressed individuals. Children and adolescents who are depressed reported less family cohesion, which is the emotional bonding that family members have toward one another. Many depressed adolescents have parents who are clinically depressed, and the relationship is probably both genetic and psychosocial. Finally, depressed adolescents frequently have at least one parent who manifests "communication deviance," which refers to vague, unfocused, and distorted verbal communication patterns.

MOTIVATIONS FOR SUICIDAL BEHAVIOR

There are many paths—both conscious and unconscious—that lead to suicidal behavior. In some cases suicidal behavior and runaway behavior is a "call for help," in that it can be a constructive attempt to manipulate parents.

In many cases, however, the secondary gains sought through suicidal behavior seem less important than their relationship to primitive internal conflicts. Some combination of factors, usually including a chronic history of dependency deprivation, reversal of child-parent roles, and threatened abandonment, gives

DIFFERENTIAL DIAGNOSIS OF SUICIDAL BEHAVIOR IN ADOLESCENTS

Katz (1995) created an elaborate outline of the psycho-dynamic reactions, interpersonal situations, and biological or psychopathological factors that lead to adolescent suicide, including the following.

Reunion Fantasies: having a strong wish to join a dead friend or relative.

Attack on the Parent-Owned Body: a desperate method to take control of one's body from the mother.

Identification with a Suicide: the wish to be the same as the family member, relative, or friend who committed suicide.

Reactions to Traumatic Experiences: a way to escape traumas such as rape, sexual abuse, severe physical abuse.

Guilt: blaming oneself for real (trouble at juvenile court) or imagined (someone's death, parents' divorce) faults.

Reactions to Loss of Romantic Attachments: this can be a great loss for both narcissistic and insecure youngsters.

Reactions to Acute or Chronic Disease: feeling abnormal, embarrassed about dependence on parents.

Family Hopelessness: family may convey that suicide is only way out of unacceptable life situation.

Failure to Achieve Family Standards: youngster is humiliated, feels like a failure, is full of self-hatred.

Contagion: an adolescent commits suicide, which gives permission to friends and acquaintances.

Depression: characterized by anhedonia, self-loathing, and anger at oneself.

Schizophrenia: influenced by paranoid delusions and auditory hallucinations.

Alcohol and Drug Abuse: substance abuse gives a person a gloomy outlook on life and increases inpulsivity.

rise to a sense of hopelessness, helplessness, and worthlessness. The suicide attempt then serves as a "trial by ordeal" or "gamble with fate" whose positive verdict is (at least temporarily) accepted. Since fate (the primitive superego) allows life to continue, the youngster is reprieved. Both the idea of the gamble and the rescue by fate are magical notions aimed at attaining irrational goals. This pattern has a tendency to repeat itself so that recurrences of suicidal behavior are not unusual, especially if the response of important loved ones is not supportive.

Suicidal behavior in adolescents is often related to a history of unsuccessful romance, conflict over incestuous feelings toward parents, and the like. In our experience, closer investigation usually shows that the romance failed because of over-possessive, demanding behavior and that the incestuous ties interfered with a previously satisfactory dependency relationship. The block to moving comfortably into heterosexual roles in the depressive adolescent is the unresolved primitive tie to the mother.

It is important to remember in evaluating any suicide attempt or suicide gesture that the suicidal behavior seems to the adolescent to be a solution. Although we may regard suicidal behavior as a problem, our young clients often view it as the only possible solution to a variety of chronic and immediate problems in their lives. Suicidal ideation and suicidal activity are ego states that are often felt as somewhat pleasurable by the distressed adolescent. This is true in depressive disorders where the suicidal behavior promises relief from the psychic pain but it is also true in situations where there are major manipulative elements in the suicidal behavior as may occur in behaviorally disordered adolescents. Shame or anticipated shame can also lead the adolescent client to see suicide as the only honorable response.

MANAGEMENT OF THE SUICIDAL ADOLESCENT

The management of suicidal behavior depends on the evaluation of a complex set of factors. One must first consider the seriousness of the suicidal behavior. If the youngster utilized an extremely lethal method (shooting, hanging), it may be that the attempt aborted by purest chance. If the attempt was planned without provision for discovery, it is clearly more malignant than an attempt carried out with built-in arrangements for being rescued. The clinical diagnosis is also important, since some studies suggest that successful suicide may be related to the nature of the psychiatric disorder. Pertinent diagnoses include major depression; schizophrenia, which is more lethal than depression, but occurs less often because of a lower base rate; and bereavement, when adolescents who have lost a parent through death seem driven to "join the loved one."

The growing recognition over the last few years of the frequency with which major affective illnesses have their onset during adolescence requires careful diagnostic evaluation of any youngster presenting with depressive or suicidal symptoms. The evaluation includes a careful history of behavior and symptoms with particular attention to cyclic swings in mood and level of activity; the family history of affective disorder; the question of whether symptoms and aberrant thoughts fit the client's mood; the presence or absence of drug abuse; and the presence or absence of overt evidences of primary depression such as crying spells, sleep disturbances, and disturbances in energy level or food intake. Of course, it is very important to interview adolescents carefully regarding their moods. One needs to keep in mind that adolescents will sometimes minimize the degree of depressive symptomatology they are feeling, particularly if they are using drugs or delinquent behavior in an effort to avoid a depressive collapse. Observing the youngster over time and inquiring about mood again after a trusting relationship is developed may be necessary in order to discover even fairly major dysphoric moods.

Most adolescents who survive suicidal behavior did not fully intend—fortunately—to kill themselves in the first place. Still, there are marked variations in the extent to which the adolescent must stack the cards against himself in his gamble with fate. He may need to make his odds so poor that a completed suicide is virtually a certainty.

In addition to assessing the adolescent's inner drive to self-destruction, the therapist must consider the extent of environmental stress, especially family disintegration. The possibility of family collusion with or even encouragement of suicidal behavior should be investigated. Finally, the adolescent's wider social environment should be evaluated. Social isolation, poor school performance, parental loss, and disruption of important friendships and romantic alliances increase the likelihood of repeated suicidal attempts.

Children and adolescents learn from somewhere that people leave letters before they kill themselves and even before they threaten to kill themselves. Parents and teachers sometimes find these notes and ask therapists to assess their significance. Of course, such a note could give the therapist valuable insight into the youngster's sense of desperation and depression. Ordinarily the therapist would want to discuss the note with the client himself. Any suicide note by an adolescent is a very important signal and should be taken very seriously. We are not aware that this issue has ever been researched systematically, but perhaps it is possible to characterize some suicide notes as statements of true suicidal intentions while others are "merely" cries for help. The two notes reproduced in this chapter illustrate this point. One note was written by a boy who was quite depressed, but did not commit suicide—it has an angry, complaining, demanding quality to it. The second note was written by a girl who immediately afterwards walked in front of a train—this message is extremely sad and has an apologetic tone. We are not suggesting that these are hard and fast criteria that determine suicide potential, but the content and tone of the suicide note are data that should be considered.

Hospitalization of the Suicidal Adolescent

After weighing the multiple factors involved, the therapist must make a decision regarding the advisability of hospitalization. Often, this decision must be taken on very incomplete data distorted by the chaotic and charged emotional atmosphere that surrounds suicidal behavior.

NOTE BY A DEPRESSED BOY,
WHO DID NOT ATTEMPT SUICIDE

This note was written by a 15-year-old boy, who then left it in his room where his mother was sure to find it. He clearly was requesting and even demanding help from his parents. This note, like all the clinical information in this book, has been modified and disguised.

Would someone please help me? I'm so lost. I want so badly for my life to end. No one understands my problems. No one, except Hanna. My one and only true friend. Can't someone bring Hanna and have her straighten me out? I want to talk to her. I need help badly. Bring he to me. Let her talk to me. I want to talk to her. You people don't give a damn if I kill myself, but she does. No one loves or cares for me. Hanna is the only one in the world who listens to me. Please—for one time—listen to me before it's too late.

J. S.—class of '89

Certainly, the therapist cannot afford to take undue risks with the life of his young client. Most therapists agree that, if the client appears to be actively suicidal, he must be protected through immediate hospitalization. However, one must remember that hospitalization itself is not free of risk. The therapist must consider not only the routine risk involved in hospitalizing any adolescent, but the particular problems associated with the suicidal client. For instance, it has been observed that there is an extremely high risk of suicide during the period immediately following discharge from the hospital. In spite of these realistic warnings, hospital treatment is frequently essential at least in the early stages of therapy of the actively suicidal adolescent.

The purpose of the inpatient phase of treatment of the suicidal adolescent is to stabilize the clinical picture, find the appropriate medication and proper dosage, and support the client's

NOTE WRITTEN BY A GIRL
WHO COMMITTED SUICIDE

This note appeared in an article in the *Washington Post* several years ago. Melissa was 14. After she wrote it, Melissa stepped in front of a train and was killed.

To my dear Mom,

You always asked me if there's anything wrong. I said, "No, I'm OK." Mom, I wasn't telling the truth. I was never OK. I was very depressed. I ran away from all of my problems. I am taking the easy way out. I am admitting to myself that I am a weak person not able to handle the weight of life.

I am very sorry to put you all through the troubles. I think everything I have to do is done. I drank some wine and took some pills. But before I did all that I prayed to my father God in heaven. I asked him to forgive me but he won't. I don't blame him for that. Please pray that I don't be sent to hell, because then I won't be able to come back and watch over you and help you. I want to do that.

Mom, please don't have a nervous breakdown and be crying all the time. I don't want you to. I want to live forever and ever, the way you want to and I will always love you very much. Please try and forgive me.

I love you always and always.

Love,
Melissa

transition into ongoing outpatient psychotherapy for underlying personality and emotional problems.

Outpatient Treatment of the Suicidal Adolescent

If the suicidal risk is not considered to be seriously imminent, treatment of the suicidal client can sometimes be initiated in an outpatient setting. Even when inpatient treatment has been necessary, it is usually important to follow that treatment with ongoing outpatient psychotherapy. This home management of the suicidal client requires attention to three areas. These are:

- "sterilizing" the physical home environment
- parental involvement in the treatment
- psychotherapy of the adolescent
- medication management

STERILIZING THE HOME.   Although people may point out that a determined suicidal client can always find a way to kill himself, there are many advantages in clearing the home of all easily available lethal materials. The parents and the adolescent are told, separately or in a joint session, that suicidal feelings come and go. Confidence is expressed that eventually the adolescent will be glad that he is alive. Because of this, he will be offered all possible protection to allow him the opportunity to reach this attitude toward himself. The therapist explains the necessity of making the home as safe as possible to decrease the possibility of impulsive suicidal behavior. All potentially lethal medications, poisons, firearms, and razor blades (electric razors are quite satisfactory) should be removed from the home. The suicidal adolescent client should be restricted from driving automobiles or motorcycles alone until the therapist feels it is safe. Although the adolescent may protest these measures, they represent tangible proof that his parents and his therapist want him to live. This reassurance may play a larger role in the preventive value of the "sterilization" than the relative absence of the means for suicide.

It is wise to advise against prolonged parental absences during the early phases of therapy with the suicidal adolescent.

Youngsters who are struggling with suicidal thoughts should not be burdened with excessive solitude. In addition, separations from the parents are potent precipitants of suicidal ideation and behavior in these vulnerable adolescents. Anecdotally, one is surprised at the frequency with which suicide attempts occur shortly before parents leave on a planned trip. Perhaps more surprising, the parents often ask the therapist if they should go ahead with their plans!

PARENTAL THERAPY. Many parents of suicidal adolescents are themselves extremely depressed, even suicidal. Many are overtly or covertly rejecting of their child. These problems are often associated with and intensified by severe marital conflict. Suicidal behavior has been found to be a response to unconscious dynamic issues within some families. Even when the parents do not appear seriously disturbed, they need extensive support and help because of the intense anxiety engendered by the suicidal attempt and the difficulties of parenting a potentially suicidal child (Katz, 1998).

The relationship between the teenager's depression and the family dysfunction is a two-way street. In some cases, the family dysfunction causes or contributes to the depression and suicidality in the youngster. In other cases, the mental problem of the youngster may cause or aggravate the parents' depression or family dysfunction. Or, both processes can happen at once.

The treatment approach for parents of suicidal adolescents is basically supportive, since unmet dependency needs are common determinants of the rejecting attitudes toward their own child. In those who are clinically depressed, antidepressant medication may be a valuable adjunct. As with the adolescent, hospitalization may be necessary to initiate treatment.

Often, it is wise to provide these parents with a therapist of their own. Despite themselves, they may tend to feel envious and rivalrous of their youngster if all share the same therapist. If collaborative therapy is arranged, the adolescent's therapist must remain alert to any evidence that the family is withdrawing from his client. This suspicion must be quickly conveyed to the parent's therapist, whose active steps to reestablish family reintegration and at least minimal support of the adolescent may be literally lifesaving. In practice, many families with suicidal children can accept help only during the immediate crisis, lose interest quickly, and do not follow through with treatment.

It is sometimes helpful to provide informational material to parents. Not only is it educational, but it also helps the parents sense that there are many other families that are in the same boat. The American Academy of Child and Adolescent Psychiatry (www.aacap.org) has a series of informative handouts, including one called "Teen Suicide." The American Foundation for Suicide Prevention (www.afsp.org) has extensive material available online. The American Psychiatric Association (www.psych.org) has material on adolescent suicide that is appropriate for clients, parents, and peers.

PSYCHOTHERAPY OF THE SUICIDAL ADOLESCENT.   The key to the long run success of therapy in the suicidal adolescent is the provision of understanding, acceptable dependency gratification, and a gradual opportunity for emotional growth within the therapeutic relationship. In a world which the adolescent views as chaotic, unreliable, and uncaring, the therapist must offer the youngster a consistent, corrective therapeutic relationship. Even in cases of clinical bipolar affective disease, psychotherapy is necessary to assure acceptance of the illness and the need for mood stabilizing medication.

The initial task in the psychotherapy of the suicidal adolescent is to establish a dependency relationship that the adolescent can accept without losing face. Many of these youngsters are extremely threatened by their intense dependency wishes. The therapist must often utilize humor, extreme tact, and vigorous support of independent behavior to help the adolescent tolerate being helped. Philip Katz (1995) said, "In dealing with suicidal adolescents, a therapist must take an active role; he or she cannot be a blank, passive, noninterventionist therapist. It is essential that the therapist throw a lifeline to the patient, that he give the patient hope."

When the dependency relationship is established with the adolescent, the problem becomes one of gradually assisting the youngster to become more self-sufficient without stirring fears of abandonment. The pace of therapy is characteristically slow and the intense needs of these clients exert a drain on the therapist. It has been suggested that suicide attempts during psychotherapy often follow a perceived rejection or negative prognostic comment from the therapist. The therapist must be alert to countertransference hostility toward the demanding suicidal client. It is imperative that the youngster not become "expendable" again.

There are a number of reasons why therapists may tire of the suicidal adolescent. This youngster has little capacity to assume responsibility for himself and often indulges in a great deal of whining and complaining. He continually sees other people, including the therapist, as withholding and unfair. No matter how giving the therapist may be, it is never enough. The therapist often begins to feel that he is trying to fill a bottomless pit. At other times, he begins to blame himself for his inability to meet the client's insatiable demands. Some suicidal adolescents add to the countertransference problems by continuing periodically to threaten or attempt suicide. Often, they use the veiled or direct threat of suicide to extract special considerations from the therapist such as dramatic late-night phone calls or extra appointments. The therapist senses that if necessary many of these youngsters would play their trump card—real suicide.

The combination of sympathy for the client's real despair and emptiness, competing with frustration and anger over the youngster's emotional blackmail, makes for a turbulent and uncomfortable countertransference. The therapist is in fact walking a tightrope in many cases. If he capitulates totally in the "suicide game" and guarantees to meet the adolescent's unrealistic, nonnegotiable conditions for continuing to live, he can actually drive the adolescent to suicide. On the other hand, if he refuses to negotiate at all, insisting that the adolescent must decide whether to live or die himself, his client may commit suicide in pique and dejection over losing the game.

The therapist must remember that these youngsters manipulate and demand because they are unable to meet their needs in any other way. They are convinced that no one will give them anything freely. They also believe that without "gifts" they are nothing. They feel that all good things come from others and that they are hollow and bad. They must blackmail, threaten, and coerce others. For them, this manipulation is literally a matter of life or death. Only gradually can they come to see themselves as possessing any inherent strength and worth.

In the management of crisis periods with suicidal youngsters, consultation with a colleague is of inestimable value. The objectivity of an uninvolved fellow therapist helps to prevent any mismanagement of the case which might result from the primary therapist's emotional discomfort. Decisions of whether to hospitalize the client, how to respond to one of the "life-and-death" deals that these clients often propose, and whether to allow the client to take a trip or go away to college are better shared than made alone. The practical advantage of consultation in medicolegal terms is also apparent. There is an obvious additional dividend for the client if consultation allows the therapist to be comfortable about his legal liability and his ethical responsibility.

In the later stages of psychotherapy, after the development of a reasonably stable therapeutic alliance, it may be possible to deal more directly with the client's dependency needs and masochistic defenses. Premature interpretation of the adolescent's active role in creating his own misery tends to be felt by these clients as criticism: "Rather than giving me the understanding and sympathy that I need, you too say that it is all my fault." Feeling abandoned, the client may again become suicidal. Some of these depressed and empty youngsters require almost indefinite support with the frequency of therapy sessions only slowly and cautiously diminished. As mentioned in the chapter on termination (see the section "Therapy—Interminable"), this arrangement should be periodically reviewed with an eye to the possibility of actually completing the work.

—And If You Lose

Sadly, even the most skillful therapy cannot always prevent the suicidal adolescent from killing himself. The therapist is then faced with the task of dealing with his feelings of grief, guilt, and inadequacy. Therapist responses in this situation range from defensive denial and rationalization to virtual refusal to accept a suicidal client ever again. It seems that therapists who succeed in mastering their feelings generally do so by presenting the case to professional colleagues with an attitude of trying to learn something about preventing a similar occurrence in the future.

MEDICATION MANAGEMENT

With the advent of the newer generation of antidepressants, including the selective serotonin reuptake inhibitors (SSRIs), the outpatient management of depression has become more practical and safe. The SSRIs are fairly rapid in onset and have very low lethality even if taken in an overdose. They also seem to have a higher success rate than previous medications. This book addresses the pharmacological therapy of depressive illness in adolescents in only the most superficial way. This treatment approach is not only of great importance, it is also changing quite rapidly. The adolescent therapist needs to read the current literature and remain updated on appropriate treatment approaches as new data is gathered. Medication is important not only for the treatment of the immediate episode but plays a major role in the prevention of recurrences (American Academy of Child and Adolescent Psychiatry, 1998a).

PREVENTION AND POSTVENTION OF SUICIDE

When the incidence of adolescent suicide increased in recent years, many professionals became alarmed and sought to create programs for the prevention of these deaths. Shaffer et al. (1988) developed an elaborate and scholarly assessment of these programs. He criticized the didactic school-based suicide prevention programs for following a "low risk strategy." That is, "given the low base rate of teen suicide, very few of the adolescents receiving the programs are likely to attempt or commit suicide." It may be, however, that some of the youngsters who participate in these programs do identify themselves as being emotionally troubled and desiring further counseling or professional help. Many communities have established suicide hot lines, but it is not known whether these efforts have actually affected the incidence of adolescent suicide. Shaffer pointed out that it would make sense to focus one's efforts at prevention at the population of adolescents who are known to be at the highest risk. If that were done, professionals and school personnel would direct most of their interventions to teenage boys who have made a previous attempt or who are depressed.

Rosenberg et al. (1989) made recommendations regarding adolescent suicide prevention after surveying 29 professionals who had many years of experience in this field. After considering a number of possible interventions to prevent adolescent suicide, the ones that were thought to be most effective in reducing adolescent suicide were finding ways to restrict the access of adolescents to firearms and the identification of high-risk youths. School personnel should not rely on classes for high school students that simply teach information about suicide without providing access to clinical assessment. There is some evidence that these classes actually perturb previously suicidal adolescents (Shaffer et al., 1990).

In some communities the media, especially television news and newspapers, have made a very big deal out of adolescent suicides. In some cases reporters have attempted to interview family members, friends, and classmates of the youngster who has died. Television cameramen have been known to use telephoto lenses to shoot through school windows at the peer survivors of a deceased student and to enter a church and attempt to film the funeral. News reports tend to glamorize the suicidal behavior—the mere fact of putting it on the front page makes suicidal behavior seem exciting, extremely special, and attractive in some strange way. It certainly would make parents and professionals wonder if their own children and clients might try to copy the suicidal behavior that has been idealized and romanticized. One would also wonder whether the suicide clusters that have occurred in some communities have been facilitated by local news reports.

Attempts have been made to study systematically the effect of newspaper stories on suicide rates (Blumenthal and Bergner, 1973; Phillips et al., 1989); the effect of television news stories about suicide on the adolescent suicide rate (Phillips and Carstensen, 1986); and the effect of television movies on adolescent suicide (Gould and Shaffer, 1986; Phillips and Paight, 1987). Some studies and anecdotal accounts suggest that some adolescents are influenced to commit suicide by what they see on television and read in newspapers. Other studies do not support that conclusion. Even if there were a relationship, it would mean that only a small number, perhaps 5 or 10%, of adolescent suicides occur because of the influence of the media. The vast majority of adolescent suicide is a result of other causes mentioned in this chapter, such as severe depression, profound disappointments, serious family problems, and substance abuse. But even if the effect of television and newspapers on the adolescent suicide rate is slight, it would still behoove the editors to maintain both good taste and ethical principles. For instance, it would seem proper that a newspaper would not emphasize or highlight an adolescent suicide; would not glorify or romanticize the behavior; and probably would not mention the specific method that was used.

Postvention refers to the steps that are taken following a suicide, to support the survivors and to reduce the possibility that another person will follow the example and also commit suicide. It would seem that group and individual meetings with family members, close friends, classmates, and certain other acquaintances can be very helpful. It gives the survivors a chance to share their grief, to address their guilt at not preventing the suicide, and to ventilate their anger and frustration at the deceased. It also gives the professionals involved an opportunity to identify other youngsters who are at greater risk for committing suicide and following up with them on a more individualized basis. If this is done in a thorough and sensitive manner, it hopefully would interrupt the tendency for further suicides to cluster around the first one.

Some school systems have gone overboard and created extremely elaborate suicide prevention and postvention programs. It would seem a better balance to include suicide awareness as part of a broader health curriculum, which also includes drug awareness, sexuality awareness, AIDS awareness, etc. Following a suicide in a high school, we do not think it is useful or appropriate for the principal to get on the intercom and announce to the entire school that one of the students killed himself. Nor do we think it necessary for the entire school to divide up into discussion groups to meet with visiting mental health professionals or for half the school to go home for the rest of the day because they are too upset. What does make sense is to hold discussion groups for adolescents who are at greater risk, such as friends and acquaintances of the deceased student; adolescents who have previously threatened or attempted suicide; and young people with serious emotional problems or substance abuse problems. The school staff could also let it be known that anybody else is also welcome to attend these meetings. It also seems healthy and generous for the parents of the suicide victim to include the youngster's friends and classmates in the funeral activities. Finally, the school might want to channel the intense feelings of the surviving students into something positive, like planting a tree or creating some other kind of memorial. See Mauk and Sharpnack (1998) for details on how to organize a postvention program.

SUMMARY

It is a frightful responsibility to become involved with a youngster who is struggling with the question "to be or not to be." The drama and finality of suicide conspire with the personality traits of suicidal youngsters to make treating the suicidal adolescent one of the psychotherapist's most exacting experiences. The wise therapist will recognize his limitations and refuse to treat more of these youngsters than he can manage. Most therapists find that two or three potentially suicidal adolescents are the upper limit that they can effectively treat. Therapists with depressive tendencies of their own may find it best to avoid working with any youngsters of this kind.

CHAPTER 12

adolescents who misbehave

Running away from home is a time-honored American tradition. Few people reach adulthood without having angrily marched out from their home (often at age 5 or 6) with the intention of making their way in the world. Many teenagers of past generations chose this abrupt emancipation from home and made it stick. Americans, with their emphasis on early independence and self-sufficiency, have an amused respect for the plucky youngster who grimly sets out to make his fortune. We have all loved Huck Finn and a long list of other picaresque heroes.

In recent years, runaways have become much more common and much less amusing. Almost every large city has large numbers of preteens and teens who have fled from their homes and families. Some of these older youngsters are merely liberating themselves from objectively cruel and unbearable living situations. Indeed one should always consider the possibility of incest or sexual abuse in any runaway of an adolescent girl. For other adolescents, running away is almost purely a symbolic expression of unconscious conflict, a true neurotic symptom. Most often, the runaway child is signaling a family disturbance that involves both himself and his parents. The running away in this case serves both to discharge family tensions temporarily and to symbolize the conscious or unconscious wish of one or both parents to desert their family responsibility—to walk off and leave it all.

The personal dynamics of the youngster who runs away from home may center around a dependency-independency conflict. Typically, the youngster is confronted with strong feelings of helplessness and wishes for dependency in a context that makes these feelings appear shameful, dangerous, or incapable of fulfillment. The resulting sense of panic leads to a desire to escape the painful situation, to prove self-sufficiency, and yet secretly to seek out a benevolent helper. The runaway is both running from something (a disappointing object) and toward something (a fantasized gratifying object). The similarity between the dynamics of runaways and depression has been noted in referring to the act of running away as a "depressive equivalent."

Jane, a rather well-behaved girl of 15, impulsively ran away from home, leaving with a boy she knew only as a "guy with a pretty bad reputation." She convinced herself that she loved him and accepted "speed" and sexual advances, stating that these experiences were "beautiful." She maintained this view even after the boy deposited her on a street corner and failed to return for her. She was then picked up by a "nice guy" who convinced her to return home.

Jane felt that she had run away from home because she could no longer "talk to her father." She said that he treated her "like a baby." She felt that he was very unfriendly to boys who visited the home to call on her. She also complained that he was contemptuous of her opinions.

The parents acknowledged that the home was very unhappy for all family members. Both parents had frequent, strong conscious wishes to escape from a situation in which they felt trapped.

In a family session Jane wept and asked her father, "Why can't it be like it used to be?"

When asked how long things had been going badly, she indicated a time that corresponded to her pubertal development.

Jane's mother was preoccupied with Jane's brother. The father had been a major source of dependency support until the biological changes of puberty forced awareness of the sexual components within the relationship.

Parents react to runaways with varying mixtures of anger,

guilt, and shame. They cannot entirely ignore the runaway's dramatic denunciation of them as parents even when they have little honest affection for the child. The intense emotional reactions to the accusations contained in the act make it difficult for parents to respond rationally to the practical problems raised by a runaway. Some parents may also unconsciously prefer to rid themselves of the responsibility for the youngster's care. They are guilty over the runaway, but not entirely displeased.

There are many reasons why children and adolescents run away from home. The table on page 315 gives an outline of the differential diagnosis that should be considered. The method of psychotherapy and other components of the treatment plan depend, of course, on the details of the individual case.

FIRST YOU MUST FIND THE CHILD—

The therapist's task falls into two phases. The first is to assist the parents to focus on the immediate crisis. The parents' attention should be turned to seeking the child actively, since the likelihood that the youngster will engage in dangerous behaviors is quite high. The adolescent's denial of panic and dependency often results in a defensive sense of omnipotence. Under the spell of this sense of magical power, the adolescent may attempt extremely daring and hazardous activities such as stealing, sexual excesses, or drug experiments. It is wise therefore to attempt to locate the runaway as quickly as possible. This is especially important in the case of the preadolescent and younger adolescent in whom immaturity and poor judgment increase the probability of hazardous behavior.

Parents should be encouraged to contact the police as soon as they are sure that a runaway has occurred, with instructions to bring the youngster home when he is located. In addition, the adolescent's friends should be contacted since adolescents rarely run away alone. Often, these friends have no intention of revealing the whereabouts of the missing adolescent. Their statements should be taken with a grain of salt, since they usually are actually trying to mislead the parent to cover the runaway's

TYPES OF RUNAWAY BEHAVIOR

There are several patterns of adolescent runaway behavior, although one should not substitute labels for careful evaluation of the individual youngster. This outline is adapted from Stierlin (1973).

Adventurers are youngsters who run away from home for a short period of time. They seek an opportunity to prove that they can survive without the support of their parents. They return home feeling older and wiser.

Hedonists feel irritated and constricted by even the most reasonable restraints on their absolute freedom to do as they wish. Their affability depends on the adult's willingness to give them their way on all matters that affect their pleasure.

Loners run from excessively binding families that hold their children too close by gratifying dependency wishes or preventing them from becoming aware of their own wishes and desires. These adolescents run away when they experience the desire to emancipate themselves.

Throwaways run from expelling families. The parents view their children as unwanted encumbrances to their own desires and pleasures. They reject and neglect the children and force them to fend for themselves.

Abused youngsters are doing what makes sense, considering their situation. Adolescents who have been physically or sexually abused or exploited figure out that other households are not the same as their own, so they leave.

Emissaries, who are sent by their families on a "mission." The adolescents are subtly encouraged to leave the home for a period of time to engage in activities that indirectly benefit one or both of the parents. These adolescents may act out impulses that the parents are not able to express directly.

tracks. Still, instances do occur where the friend is not sure that the adolescent's decision to run away was wise. He may be willing to help the parents if he feels that it is in the adolescent's best interest. Needless to say, if the parent's call is angry and threatening, the friend is likely to conclude that any sensible person would run away from such a mean person and keep going. The parents should also contact those agencies located in the areas of the city where runaways are known to congregate.

These approaches would have little chance for success except that most runaways want to be found. They expect to be searched out and need to save face by making some effort to avoid detection. They want to come home only if the parents really want them back and will show it. Once this assurance has been convincingly demonstrated, they often return quite easily after putting up enough resistance to maintain the respect of their friends.

The parents also need explicit advice on how to treat the adolescent when he is found. Since the goal is to deal with the runaway event in a constructive manner, the parents are asked to adopt an attitude of trying to understand why running away was necessary. The parents should avoid angry, accusative, and punitive attitudes as well as apologetic, self-accusatory, guilty comments. The therapist should offer an early appointment, preferably within 24 hours, for the family to consider together the reasons for this particular attempted solution of the family's conflicts. The therapist should convey to the parents an open-minded desire to understand, neither assigning fault nor permitting the parents to finalize unchallenged any premature and oversimplified explanations that merely cast blame on the child or on themselves.

—THEN YOU TREAT THE FAMILY

When the family arrives for the emergency family conference, the second phase of the therapist's job begins. This phase includes both diagnostic and treatment-planning tasks. The therapist attempts to evaluate the factors involved in the runaway. To what extent is the child responding realistically to impossible family circumstances, struggling with a neurotic conflict, or scapegoating himself to accommodate a family conflict? The answers to these questions suggest the type of help that should be recommended. The chronological and psychological immaturity of the adolescent also plays a role in deciding on the best approach in a given case.

In some instances, it is wise to arrange placement for the child whose home is realistically unsuited to adolescent needs. This placement may take the form of psychiatric hospitalization, residential treatment, a foster home, or simply helpful relatives or family friends. Youngsters with limited ego resources will need external controls to avoid running away again when they feel stressed. In addition to treating the adolescent, the parents usually require concomitant therapy during the child's placement so that he does not return to the same psychological setting that produced the problems originally.

A few runaways can be managed as outpatients. This group includes those who see their running away as an ego-alien symptom—an inner compulsion they would prefer to overcome. Some of the cases that closely approximate the "family neurosis" model may also be included, with a collaborative or a family psychotherapy approach. However, it should be recognized that symptoms rarely disappear magically at the initiation of a therapy program. One can predict to the parents that in outpatient therapy (or even inpatient care, for that matter) some repetition of the act of running away is a very real possibility. When it does occur, most therapists as well as parents have intense affective responses to this callous abandonment and indictment by the adolescent. Predicting the possibility of such an occurrence in advance may be helpful in attempting to maintain a therapeutic attitude.

THE VIOLENT ADOLESCENT

Human aggression and juvenile violence have been pervasive issues for our world and, especially, for our country. Some aspects of human aggression differ from animal aggression since humans actively kill each other—perhaps 100 million victims during the twentieth century. Aside from killing each other during wars, genocide and ethnic cleansing was practiced in Nazi Germany against the Jews and others; in Turkey against the Armenians; in Russia against the Georgians; and in Cambodia, Rwanda, and the Balkans. In this country, homicide is the third leading cause of death for adolescent boys and young men (Osofsky, 1997).

Aggressive behavior and the roots of aggressive behavior have been described, classified, catalogued, and researched in a number of ways. For example:

- Aggression as an inborn instinctual drive.
- Aggression as a learned reaction arising from frustration.
- Affective aggression, characterized by autonomic arousal, vocalizations, and perhaps a frenzied attack.
- Predatory aggression, such as stalking behavior, which has little autonomic arousal.
- Aggression in the service of narcissistic entitlement.

Vitiello and Stoff (1997) reviewed this topic and concluded that there are two subtypes of aggression among children and adolescents. They referred to the first subtype as impulsive-hostile-affective aggression. This refers to angry, out-of-control behavior, that may be associated with specific neurological insults and substance abuse. They called the second subtype controlled-instrumental-predatory aggression. This refers to antisocial behavior that is goal-directed and purposeful. The therapeutic implication is that the first group is more likely to respond to pharmacological interventions, while the second group is more likely to respond to some form of psychotherapy or behavioral therapy (Yudofsky et al., 1989).

Perhaps the best model for our purposes is to say that aggression is an inherent human tendency that must be socialized within the matrix of a loving and nurturing human relationship if it is to be channeled into benevolent uses. Aggression is a universal potential in human beings, yet almost infinitely variable in its expression. If appropriate growth conditions are provided for the young child, the potential for aggression is detectable primarily as an anlage of constructive capacities for active pleasure seeking and problem solving within the personality. Under less perfect developmental conditions, the potential may unfold in twisted and malevolent forms destructive toward the self and others.

Hollander and Turner (1985) and Lewis and her colleagues (1976, 1989) studied violent, incarcerated juveniles and showed that the behavior of these youngsters can be understood through the complex interaction of environmental, psychiatric, and neurological factors. Kalogerakis (1998) outlined three general types of violent adolescents: the psychotic or organic; the conflict-based; and the antisocial. See the table on page 320.

The prognosis for adolescents who manifest serious conduct disorder depends on the person's history. If the onset of the conduct disorder was during adolescence, the prognosis is better. But if the onset of the conduct disorder was during childhood, the prognosis is worse, especially if the youngster was characterized as being callous and unemotional. In other words, some young children have the makings of future antisocial personality disorder, even before they become adolescents.

Perhaps the reason for so few comprehensive discussions regarding the management of the violent client is related to the behavior itself, which occurs in clients covering the entire diagnostic spectrum. Psychotic, brain damaged, intoxicated, and even severely anxious clients occasionally erupt into violence. If one excludes temperament, the range of contributing organic factors includes overt brain damage resulting from perinatal cerebral insults, infection, or injury. More subtle defects in cognitive functioning, such as learning disorders, also predispose to violent delinquency. Drug and alcohol intoxication increases the possibility of violent outbursts. Withdrawal reactions may also include violent behavior. To extend further this list of important factors, we must look to the life experiences of the adolescent. For instance, youngsters who have been the victims of violent physical abuse are more likely to show violent behavior later. Even if the violence in the home has not been directed personally toward the child, merely observing the habitual utilization of violence as

VARIETIES OF VIOLENT ADOLESCENTS

There are many causes for juvenile violence in our society. In terms of thinking about the causes within a particular individual, there are four general types to consider. This material was adapted from Kalogerakis (1998).

Psychotic or Organic Violent Act. The conscious motive of these youngsters may be paranoid, such as the destruction of an enemy. On the other hand, there may be no conscious or unconscious motive at all. The act may simply be random, disorganized explosiveness. In extreme cases, these individuals may have little control over their behavior. Afterwards, they may be unaware of what they did.

Intoxication and Withdrawal. Substance abuse accounts for many violent acts by adolescents. Youngsters who are intoxicated may become disinhibited and aggressive. During withdrawal, they may be irritable and agitated.

Conflict-based Violent Act. The conscious motive of these individuals may be expression of rage, resolution of a conflict, or revenge. There may be unconscious motives also. The victim is often a family member, friend, or acquaintance. The violence is impulsive, but also specifically directed a a particular person. Afterwards, they may experience remorse, relief, and possibly continued anger. If dissociation occurred, they may have amnesia for the violent act.

Antisocial Act. The conscious motive of these adolescents may be robbery, settling a score, racial or ethnic hatred, or turf issues. For example, gang wars. There may be an unconscious motive, such as repressed hatred toward a parent or stepparent. In most instances, these individuals have complete control over their behavior. They violence is planned and deliberate. Afterwards, they are unlikely to experience remorse.

a problem-solving technique encourages the adolescent to adopt this behavior as part of his coping armamentarium.

Clinicians are faced with an episodic event with multiple causes that we predict very inaccurately. Since the behavior is episodic rather than constant, the question is usually not how to treat a violent outburst, but how we should prevent it and modify its origins for the future. Weist and Warner (1997) have made suggestions about how to prevent violence not only on the individual level, but on the institutional level through school consultation. Pittel (1998) outlined how to interview adolescents who are at risk for violence at school and, specifically, "how to take a weapons history." This is cutting edge—mental health professionals interviewing children and teenagers about how often they carry a gun to school.

Adolescents Who Fear That They May Become Violent

Some adolescents may be threatened or frightened by their angry thoughts. Youngsters with borderline psychoses or severe personality disorders are frightened not just by the imaginary power of their thoughts, but by concern that they may be unable to stop themselves from carrying their thoughts into action. These youngsters require a sensitive and supportive recognition of their fear of losing control. They are terrified of the damage that they might do and of the retribution that would follow. Some of them can be reassured by the symbolic promise of external assistance, whereas others need concrete evidence that they will not be permitted to run amok. In both cases, the youngster's capacity and responsibility for self-control are underlined as necessities. The working defenses against hostile discharge should be respected and supported.

The therapeutic emphasis should be placed on recognizing and discussing the fear of loss of control rather than on the anger itself. The efforts that the client makes to contain himself are accepted even if they are pathologic, illogical, or even emotionally crippling. These defenses should not be interfered with until it is clear that the adolescent is completely safe from the

dangers of overt expression of destructive physical aggressiveness. The therapist never focuses therapeutic attention directly
on the rage until he feels reasonably confident that the violent
impulses can be vented and considered at a verbal and symbolic
level.

Those youngsters who cannot feel safe without concrete evidence of external control may need inpatient treatment. Often,
it is difficult to decide if this is necessary without a trial period of
therapy.

Mack was a 16-year-old of sturdy build. He out-weighed
his therapist by 20 pounds and was in outstanding physical
condition, since his fears of inner feminine and dependent
strivings drove him to a herculean program of physical
culture. Mack accepted treatment because of his concern
over his inability to go to sleep without nightly calisthenics
carried on until he dropped from exhaustion long after
midnight. He worried about this symptom, since he recognized that it "wasn't good for health."

On several occasions, the parents felt that Mack was forcibly restraining himself from striking them. His mother
admitted to extreme fear that Mack might hurt her. However, Mack had never lost control.

In an early session, Mack became very angry when the
therapist commented that he seemed afraid to look at some
of his frightening feelings. Mack took this as an insinuation
of cowardice and immediately challenged the therapist.

"Can you admit that you're afraid of me?"

"Should I be afraid of you?"

"Don't give me that crap. What would you do if I came
over there and knocked the shit out of you?" Mack said.

"Frankly, I think you are strong enough to keep from
hitting me even when you're angry with me. I guess if I
were wrong and it looked like you couldn't keep from coming after me, I'd holler for all the help I could get. I don't
see that hitting me would help you. I'd try to get enough
people here to keep you from hurting me or getting hurt
yourself."

Mack relaxed visibly as the therapist spoke, but still seemed tense. The therapist continued, "Do you think I should get someone to sit in with us until you are sure that you can talk about being mad without throwing your fists?"

Mack looked at the therapist to be sure he was serious. When he was convinced, he relaxed.

"Naw, I'm not gonna hit you. You sure make me mad, though."

"Mack, I know it seems to you that I'm picking on you. That's not my aim. It's just that we've got to take an honest look at your hang-ups if we're going to get anywhere here."

"Go ahead, Doc. I'll try to behave myself."

THE HOMICIDAL ADOLESCENT

For most adolescents, violence is a feared thought or a frightening potential. Unfortunately, for others it is a very real possibility and a substantial risk. If these youngsters can be recognized prior to the eruption of homicidal behavior, tragedy may be averted. There are some clues, gleaned from the study of youngsters who have committed extreme acts of violence, that may alert the therapist to the possibility that homicidal behavior could occur.

Most authors who have studied youngsters who commit acts of murderous aggression have described a family in which open violence is a commonplace. Often, the child himself has been a target of physical abuse. If not, he has commonly witnessed brutal fights between the parents. Flagrantly seductive behavior, alternating with brutality, toward the child has been noted in many cases. Often, the child is encouraged to be violent. His aggressive assaults are not firmly limited. The parents may predict that he will eventually injure or kill someone. In some cases, the parents permitted the youngster to keep and add to a collection of dangerous weapons even after he had shown assaultive behavior. Often, there is a history of dangerous aggressiveness toward family members or pets.

Many homicidal youngsters are willing to discuss their plans or fears of violent behavior if they are asked about them. The therapist should explore violent fantasies carefully. Does the adolescent have a particular person whom he wishes to hurt or fears that he may hurt? Has he thought of particular times when he might act or the weapons that he might use? Has he obtained these weapons? Has he practiced with them? Through a series of questions, it is possible to assess the current level of homicidal intent. The history helps to clarify the danger of an impulsive and unpremeditated homicidal act by illuminating the success that the youngster has had in controlling strong feelings and delaying action.

MANAGEMENT OF THE VIOLENT ADOLESCENT

The dangerously homicidal adolescent obviously needs immediate hospitalization. The family must be informed clearly of the seriousness of the adolescent's danger to others. Confidentiality does not hold when it appears likely that the adolescent will be unable to restrain himself from injuring others. The therapist should arrange for hospitalization under circumstances that assure his own safety as well as the safety of those who will be with the adolescent during the process of hospitalization. The quiet presence of several people reassures the adolescent struggling for control that he will be prevented from hurting anyone. The adolescent should be told that the therapist is hopeful that he can control himself without help. It is important to be honest and open with the potentially violent adolescent, especially if he has paranoid tendencies. He should be told directly and firmly that the therapist feels that any eruption of violence would be terribly damaging to the adolescent himself as well as unfair to others. The adolescent should be assured that the therapist will take all possible precautions to prevent this from occurring. Of course, it is only with the extremely precarious adolescent that such elaborate cautions are necessary. In most instances, the firm statement that hospitalization is necessary will be sufficient to calm the adolescent, since it promises the early availability of external support and control. Needless to say, it is important to avoid any provocation, physical competitiveness, or unkindness toward a youngster who is on the verge of an aggressive outburst. Any individuals who are brought in to help are there to strengthen restraint and control, not to offer counter-aggression.

As a rule, the violent adolescent should not be treated as an outpatient until the threat of violence has abated. The failure of his defensive mechanisms and his fear of his own destructiveness make it difficult for him to explore his feelings without the structure and safety of an inpatient setting.

THE ADOLESCENT IN LEGAL DIFFICULTY

It is not unusual for "normal" adolescents to commit one or more delinquent acts. It is more common for disturbed adolescents to commit overt antisocial acts. These illegal activities appear in youngsters with a variety of diagnostic pictures (Miller, 1998). They may accompany psychoses and personality disorders of various types. Even basically neurotic youngsters may on rare occasions behave in a delinquent manner. Because of this propensity for delinquent activities, the adolescent therapist is frequently faced with the family crisis produced when an adolescent is arrested and threatened with possible legal action.

The therapist is often expected to assume the role of the omnipotent protector who will rescue the adolescent from the throes of the legal process. Since the legal position in regard to the adolescent offender is somewhat ambiguous, the therapist is sometimes actually offered this power by well-meaning legal authorities. Judges, probation officers, and others involved in juvenile correction are well aware of the role that family and individual psychopathology plays in many cases of juvenile delinquency. If a qualified and respected psychotherapist makes a strong plea that a particular child be managed medically or therapeutically rather than legally, charges are frequently dropped and the youngster is simply released from any legal responsibility for his delinquent behavior.

In the case of some basically normal and neurotic youngsters whose delinquency represents an isolated symbolic act, dropping legal charges in favor of psychotherapeutic intervention may be an appropriate action. Unfortunately, the youngster who is struggling with a general problem of impulse control or the specific defects associated with superego lacunae is poorly served by such a failure in legal process. His pathologic sense of infantile omnipotence is strengthened. Society seems to be too frightened, just as his parents have been, to oppose his destructive impulses firmly. The adolescent feels this timidity as hostility and secretly believes that he is being given more rope with which to hang himself. The result is often a frightened repetition or intensification of testing behavior.

Youngsters with problems of impulse control need the external limits and structure that the legal apparatus may provide. Although the psychotherapist should never encourage or support vengeful, punitive approaches to the antisocial adolescent, he must recognize the value of the law and its official representatives in helping the adolescent master his impulses. Parents must be assisted to accept a similar attitude.

Parents will often be tempted to alleviate their feelings of guilt (that may be quite justified) by interfering with the process of law. Such ill-considered "help" may prevent the adolescent from recognizing his responsibility for his own behavior. It is hard for the adolescent to come to grips with himself if the parents tell him that their past mistakes "caused" his current legal problems. It is more productive for the parents to explore carefully their past and present contribution to their child's problems with rules, accepting and dealing with any guilt in an adult and mature manner. Confessing their "failure" to the child and begging his forgiveness can only compound previous errors and problems in the parent-child relationship.

Adolescents in trouble do need sympathy and help. However, the sympathy should be for the personal problems that tempt or force these youngsters into behavior that leads to loss of freedom and a lowering of self-respect. Help should be directed at encouraging personal growth and protecting both the adolescent and society realistically until a safe level of maturity and self-control is obtained.

Often, the therapist will not have the opportunity to deal with the adolescent or his parents until after an unrealistic "rescue" has been accomplished. In this case, the implications of corruption should be actively pursued in the therapy of both the adolescent and his parents. If such subtle encouragement of acting-out behavior is allowed to continue, the eventual results are always therapeutically disappointing and often literally tragic.

THE ADOLESCENT AT COURT

There are several ways in which an adolescent and his parents could find themselves at court. These experiences range from minor encounters to extremely serious situations, with the possibility of conviction on felony charges and incarceration for many years. Teenagers who do have significant emotional problems may well come to the attention of mental health professionals through a referral from court personnel, instead of being recognized by the school guidance counselor, the pediatrician, or the parents themselves. That is not to say that every adolescent at juvenile court has an identifiable and treatable psychiatric condition, but many of them do.

In some communities parents use the local police and the intake workers of juvenile court as the "heavies" who will give their child a good talking to, perhaps scare him a little in the process, and generally set him straight. This may all be done on an informal basis, without any charges being established or filed.

The most common way for adolescents to participate in the court process is to be charged with a status offense. The term "status offense" refers to behaviors that are serious enough to involve a minor in juvenile court, but which are not crimes when committed by an adult. For instance, adolescents can be taken into custody for behaviors such as truancy, disobedience to school authorities, running away, and sexual promiscuity. Each case will be reviewed by a magistrate or other court official

CAUSES OF JUVENILE VIOLENCE

Mental health professionals are sometimes asked to comment on community issues and concerns. They may be asked, "Why is there so much juvenile violence and what can we do about it?" Juvenile violence has many causes. . . .

Insufficient Parental Supervision. Children today are raised by working parents, single parents, and grandparents, who may lack the time and energy to supervise their teenagers.

Weak Values. Many youth do not feel that they should respect the opinions and rights of other people; that they should resolve conflict through nonviolent means.

Illegal Drugs. There are frequent disagreements among the participants in the illegal drug market. Youngsters who take drugs need money. Youngsters who take drugs become disinhibited and engage in violent activities.

The Media, especially movies and television, which causes children to play aggressively and to endorse violent forms of conflict resolution. The media also idealize violent heroes.

Handguns. Teenagers who use guns to commit crimes are more likely to use handguns than other kinds of firearms.

Conspiracy of Silence among teenagers themselves. Before the violence occurs, other youngsters are likely to know that specific peers are carrying weapons; are planning a robbery; are abusing drugs in a serious way.

Societal Factors: such as poverty, unemployment, racism, and lack of education. Also demographics, meaning a higher proportion of adolescents in our society.

Family Factors: such as family violence, spousal abuse, child abuse and neglect.

Individual Factors: such as mental illness, personality disorders, and neurological conditions.

and, if appropriate, will be found to be in need of supervision or intervention. Thus, the acronym of PINS or CHINS or MINS for Person/Child/Minor in Need of Supervision. Sacks and Sacks (1980) reviewed this topic in detail and concluded that status offenders should be evaluated and treated, but should not be labeled delinquents and should not have sanctions applied to them as if they were delinquent.

An adolescent who commits a crime may be arrested and eventually tried as a juvenile in a juvenile court or as an adult in the criminal court. In general, an adolescent is more likely to be tried in juvenile court if the crime was nonviolent, if he is relatively young, and if he is thought to be suitable for rehabilitation. An adolescent is more likely to be transferred or waived to adult court if he was closer to age 18 at the time the crime was committed, if the crime was violent and he is considered dangerous to the public, and if he does not seem amenable to rehabilitation. For instance, a 15-year-old who is a first offender and stole a car is likely to be tried in juvenile court. On the other hand, the prosecutor of a 17-year-old charged with rape is going to ask the judge to waive the case to adult criminal court. Mental health professionals may become involved in this process, since the court may be interested in clinical data in order to determine whether the youngster is dangerous and whether he is treatable. This has become an extremely important decision, since adult courts hand out adult-sized sentences—a court in Texas gave a group of suburban teenagers, most of them prominent members of the high school football team, sentences of up to 20 years for participating in a string of robberies.

To push this topic to an extreme, the Supreme Court held that it is not unconstitutional for a man to receive the death penalty who was a juvenile (age 16) at the time he committed the offense. In another case, the Supreme Court said that it is unconstitutional to administer the death penalty to a man who was only 15 at the time he committed the offense.

Whether he is tried in juvenile court or an adult criminal court, the adolescent has more rights than he used to. Prior to the landmark decision of *In re Gault* (1967), juvenile proceedings were conducted in a relaxed, nonadversarial manner without the need for formal fact-finding and defense attorneys. In *Gault,* the Supreme Court held that juveniles are entitled to most of the due process rights afforded adults, such as the right to notice of charges, the right to an attorney, the privilege to avoid self-incrimination, and the right to call and confront witnesses.

In order to effectively treat the seriously violent or delinquent teenager, we must recognize his serious ego defects. Superficially this defect in ego functioning seems primarily related to a "weakness" that interferes with impulse control. However, it may be more useful to see the eruption of impulses in the delinquent as a final desperate effort to compensate for other ego deficiencies.

The ego of the antisocial youngster is highly dependent on external agents for a variety of functions including management of stimulation levels, directing and maintaining attention, modulating affects, and a whole range of subtle operations related to the regulation of interpersonal relationships, particularly those that are emotionally important. Of course, these are the skills that enable one to master the environment and to maintain secondary narcissism and a sense of adequate selfhood.

One common thread that unites the causes of violence and delinquency is their impact in the individual's adaptive skills. Generally speaking, the various etiologies of violence and delinquency act to impair ego functioning and the successful development of secondary narcissism. In various ways these conditions or events interfere with either the structures that determine coping skills or the necessary learning experiences that would encourage their proper development. It is a commonplace observation that delinquent adolescents as well as adolescents with intermittent explosive disorder and most youngsters with paranoid problems demonstrate low self-esteem and generally feel helpless and driven by the winds of fate. They do not believe that they possess the ability to control their own lives. Clinical evaluation of their capacities often confirms a deficient level of skills in interpersonal relationships, study and learning habits, and techniques of problem solving.

Given this state of affairs, the tendency to embrace life styles that permit achievement of a "pseudo-competence" is very understandable. Pseudo-competence is gained, for example, through that spurious sense of mastery that results from drug use with its artificial sense of well-being. Pseudo-competence may also be gained by joining subcultures with value systems that confer prestige and a sense of accomplishment to those who cannot gain such prizes in the more conventional world. For example, in the delinquent subculture impulsive daring and short-sighted bravado as well as physical violence may gain one a reputation for bravery and leadership. Rebellion against standard measures of success such as academic performance in this subculture would be applauded rather than condemned. In that world a prudent measuring of risk and consequence may be viewed simply as "chicken." An important component of the treatment plan is to help these youngsters identify their true strengths and improve coping skills, so they have less need to rely on pseudo-competence based on violence.

The limited adaptive skills of behaviorally disordered youngsters are reflected in their attitudes toward reality. Superficially, delinquent youngsters are clever, shrewd, and manipulative. They are often quite effective in forcing other people to accommodate to them. Delinquents often appear willful and controlling, determined to have things their own way. For example, the normal youngster is willing, perhaps after a bit of grumbling, to adjust to his teacher's assignment of the difficult project, while the youngster with a behavior disorder may expend considerable energy avoiding the task or convincing the teacher that his expectations are too high. Many times the problem youngster may avoid the task and may be viewed as someone who gets away with things while other youngsters are forced to produce. What is often overlooked in this analysis of the situation is that the healthier youngster's superior coping mechanisms allow him the luxury of accepting the teacher's demand while the behaviorally disordered youngster is forced by desperation to persist in his efforts to avoid a task that he feels he cannot master. The delinquent youngster fears change, novelty, and being overwhelmed. He develops one aspect of his coping skills, those that relate to adapting reality to his limited skills, to a fine art. Unfortunately, this emphasis on controlling others actually leads to a continuing and growing atrophy of other skills.

Most delinquent youngsters tend to view themselves as helpless and out of control. They feel that they are the victims of fate and bad luck. They have very little sense that they can control their own destiny. Frenzied efforts to control individuals, events, and situations may be recognized primarily as efforts to gain some illusory sense of impact and personal importance. From the psychological point of view, the antisocial youngster's assessment of his place in the world is correct. In fact, he is not master of his fate because of the previously mentioned ego defects. Although he misunderstands the reason for his lack of self-direction, his compensatory effects to prove that he is running the show (of his own life) are as understandable as they are ineffective in improving his situation.

Finally, it should be recognized that many violent and delinquent youngsters use their parents as ancillary ego agents while denying that their parents' interventions are desired or helpful in any way. Many of these teenagers are masters of techniques for eliciting an unusual degree of parental support, direction, and even intervention in the youngster's interaction with his environment. At times this help is requested or demanded openly but more commonly delinquents provide an indirect invitation for assistance through constant failure in adaptation and apparent lack of concern regarding their dangerous situation. Obviously, the parents feel that they must step in and save the youngster.

Often the delinquent youngster can gain a measure of success with the direct assistance of his parents, but there are other defensive advantages in involving them in his affairs in any case. If the youngster continues to fail in spite of parental aid, he can define that aid as interference, babying, or domination, all of which may then be utilized as explanations for the failure.

Specific treatment techniques may be individual, group, or family. The selection of a treatment approach or combination of approaches will depend on the specific case and the nature of the motivation for change. Regardless of the approach, however, one needs to keep in mind the basic coping defects at the core of the problem and the primary defenses that the delinquent youngster utilizes in order to avoid facing this hidden deficiency. This defensive structure will surely lead the delinquent client to act out again, to attempt to involve the therapist in a direct power struggle of some kind, and in efforts to corrupt the therapist. If one is able to patiently avoid becoming enmeshed in these defensive operations while continuing to provide affectionate acceptance coupled with reasonable limit setting, the delinquent youngster is provided with an atmosphere in which he can once again resume emotional and psychological growth.

Some delinquent adolescents do not respond to outpatient treatment, no matter how sensitive or brilliant the therapist may be. Many court-involved youngsters are referred to specialized day treatment programs and a variety of residential programs (Sarri, 1985). The residential programs include traditional residential treatment centers, training schools, group homes, and wilderness programs. Perhaps the most unusual "residential" program for delinquent youth actually traveled from place to place in the form of a wagon train. Some antisocial youngsters do seem to respond to long-term placement in a wilderness-type program. When confronted by the long, cold winter ahead and the need to build their own log shelter, some of these narcissistic adolescents lose their sense of omnipotence and entitlement. Not all delinquent youth respond to psychotherapeutic approaches and residential programs, but many do. Some future generation of therapists will probably be able to predict more accurately which interventions will succeed with particular adolescents.

CHAPTER 13

adolescents and sexual issues

Many young adolescents have sexual experiences. Even more youngsters would like their friends (often including their therapists) to imagine that they have an active sex life. The virile pursuit of girls is a socially sanctioned part of male adolescence. A similar readiness for experimentation of an overt kind has come to be expected of girls, at least in some cultural settings.

This social expectation is strongly reinforced by puberty's biological thrust toward sexual maturity. Observation suggests, however, that personal anxiety about adequacy and peer group pressure institute premature sexual behavior with greater frequency than any inner surge of lusty passion. Usually, early adolescent sexual drives are fairly well balanced by interpersonal anxiety and intrapsychic guilt, unless the anxiety is offset by a greater fear of being branded, by self or others, a sissy, chicken, wienie, nerd, or queer. Many of the adolescent boys who are seen in psychotherapy are either consciously plagued by doubts about their masculinity or driven to aggressive sexual exploitation to ward off the emergence of these doubts from the unconscious.

Some girls turn toward frantic sexuality during early adolescence to combat the regressive homosexual tie to the mother (Blos, 1962). They show more interest in scandalizing their mother and manifesting their complete scorn for her rules of behavior than in the boys that they pursue. They are not interested in any emotional relationships with the boys that they seduce. Often, they are more masculine than feminine in their aggressive conquest of males. They show virtually no tenderness toward the boys and often prefer to have many boyfriends

334

on the string. Many of these girls engage in group sex with a number of boys, the "gang bang." In all of their sexual behavior, they exhibit a swaggering, triumphant, and spiteful attitude, both toward their mother and their sexual partners. When they become comfortable in therapy, they readily admit that intercourse itself gives them little or no pleasure. They do, however, enjoy shocking people with their prodigal sexuality. They also take pride in recounting their "track record," the number of boys that they have seduced. Particular pride may be shown over success in seducing a boy who was generally considered shy, innocent, or morally upright. One gets the uncomfortable feeling that they are displaying their collection of scalps when they list their sexual conquests. Any kind words are reserved for boys who treat them with indifference and contempt. "He don't give a shit about anything" is a highly complimentary description of a male companion.

Youngsters in the drug culture are often engaged in exploitive, affectionless, and promiscuous sexual behavior. The frantic search for new pleasures with denial of long-term consequences is part of the general push for a sense of omnipotent superiority to any rules of behavior or need for temperance.

Other adolescents, male and female, utilize sexual behavior self-destructively in the service of a punitive superego. In these instances, the sexual behavior may serve more to prevent true pleasure in sexuality from emerging than to move toward its attainment. The goal of these youngsters is to elicit external control and condemnation. This censure reinforces the faltering primitive superego and reinstates its domination over the instinctual life. The overt sexual behavior of these adolescents is marked by exhibitionistic display and subtle contrivance to be caught. Often, they blame their sexual partners for "leading them astray." It is not unusual to see this pattern repeat itself in a cyclic fashion with periods of prudery alternating with episodes of complete license. In short, there is considerable counterfeit sexuality in word and deed during early adolescence.

In therapy, heterosexually active youngsters may attempt to maneuver the therapist into a stand against their sexual behav-

ior on moral grounds. If the therapist opposes their sexual involvement because they are "too young" or because they are
unmarried, the youngsters are usually satisfied to argue, relieved that they do not have to face their real problems. There
are few adolescents who would not prefer to see themselves as
precocious, daring, and immoral rather than frightened, child-
like, or hamstrung by a rigid conscience.

Not all adolescents are sexually active. One study (Ostrov et
al., 1985) reported that by their seventeenth birthdays 37% of
the girls and 53% of the boys had sexual intercourse. This was
in a suburban middle-class environment. There are many factors that seem correlated with being sexually active: youngsters
who do not live with their natural parents are more likely to be
sexually active; so are youngsters who are performing below
average in school; black adolescents are more sexually active
than white youngsters. Some youngsters are inhibited by religious prohibitions, are intimidated by strict parents, or are cautious because of concern about AIDS and other sexually transmitted diseases. It may be just as important to inquire why a
client is not sexually active as to study why he is. Current statistics regarding adolescent sexuality and pregnancy are available
from the Alan Guttmacher Institute. (See their web page at
www.agi-usa.org.) They say that 39% of 16-year-old females and
45% of 16-year-old males have had sexual intercourse.

THERAPEUTIC MANAGEMENT OF THE SEXUALLY ACTIVE ADOLESCENT

It is very easy for the psychotherapist to be drawn into a
subjective response to the adolescent client's report of sexual
activity. He may view the adolescent boy's flight into hostile
"making out" as a healthy move toward masculinity, ignoring its
defensive, sadistic, pregenital nature. Conversely, unconscious
envy and competitiveness may lead to an excessively suppres-
sive attitude toward a budding comfort with male assertiveness
of an appropriate kind. With adolescent girls, the male therapist
may panic over the possibility of pregnancy or may slip into a
subtle seductiveness. Powerful myths surround the subject of

adolescent sexual behavior and these influence the adolescent psychotherapist along with the remainder of society. When these social forces act in synergy with serious unresolved adolescent conflicts within the therapist, the result can be either an explosive unconscious sanctioning of destructive sexual acting out or, equally harmful, a stiff moralism that merely suppresses sexual strivings and stunts the adolescent's emotional growth.

On Being an Old Fogy

Considering the openness of contemporary society toward sexuality, the adolescent client will be disposed more than ever to view her psychotherapist as morally old-fashioned. The therapist usually cannot avoid revealing his values regarding sexual behavior even if he tries to remain scrupulously objective. It is probably unwise to remain morally "faceless" with an adolescent. At the appropriate point in treatment, it can be very helpful for the therapist to discuss his moral views frankly with his young client. This is especially valuable if the therapist will differentiate between those views that have some support in experience and those that "just feel right to me."

Most therapists value honesty and genuineness in human relationships, responsibility for one's behavior, avoidance of exploitation of others, and the relative superiority of long-term intense emotional commitments over casual, hedonistic attachments. Our young people do not advocate exploitation of others, interpersonal dishonesty, or self-deception. This common ground is usually sufficient for the exploration of symptomatic, pseudosexual behavior in psychotherapy. This is possibly as far as the psychotherapist should venture in evaluating and assessing the sexual behavior of our youth. At any rate, we may have to relax our pursuit of the ideal sufficiently to accomplish the possible— again, the exploration and treatment of neurotic distortions of sexual behavior.

If we accept this limitation and agree that it is not the function of the adolescent therapist to dictate or enforce moral codes, sexual behavior may be evaluated as any other interpersonal transaction. A few of the questions that must be asked in the attempt to evaluate the authenticity of any sexual activity are offered in the next section.

Evaluating the Meaning of Sexual Behavior

Do the stated goals of the behavior match the adolescent's actual management of the situation, or does the adolescent appear to be deceiving herself? Does she desire sexual gratification or punishment for sexual behavior? Is she demanding an adult prerogative verbally while clinging to childish irresponsibility and dependency? To what extent does the sexual behavior serve the defense of "misdirection?"—that is, does the emphasis on sexuality hide a depression or a hostile, aggressive attitude toward other people? Does the sexual behavior appear relaxed and integrated in the personality or forced and counterphobic? Is the adolescent leaping into sexual behavior to avoid anxiety-producing sexual fantasies? To what extent are these frightening sexual fantasies related to oedipal involvements at home or with the therapist? How closely does the adolescent's relationship to her sexual partner approximate a mature, realistic human sharing? How much is the relationship still colored by identification with the partner, projection, idealization, narcissism, and other factors that diminish the humanness and autonomy of her lover?

These questions are complex and difficult to answer. They are offered only to concretize some of the issues implied by the truism that sexual behavior is an expression of the entire personality, not an isolated phenomenon that is to be viewed only from biological and moral perspectives. A broad view of the total developmental position of the adolescent permits the therapist to respond appropriately to the relevant growth problems of the adolescent without falling into futile efforts to dictate "proper" behavior.

Usually, however, it is necessary to set limits on sexual behavior in order to deal effectively with the real concerns that are being defended and disguised in the sexual acting out. For those adolescents who are deeply regressed or flagrantly self-destructive, it may be necessary to provide temporary external control through hospitalization. In many cases, however, it is possible to establish a therapeutic alliance that is strong enough to manage the behavior. Interdictions are then based on technical considerations and are accepted because of the adolescent's wish to cooperate in a therapeutic process that already promises to provide greater benefits than those conferred by the conflicted sexual activity.

The therapist must trouble himself with one further question. Does the sexual acting out, even though it contains elements of neuroticism and immaturity, represent a progressive movement in development? The adolescent must experiment in real life. Often, she must learn by making her own mistakes, even in a potentially dangerous area such as sexuality. If the adolescent seems to be honestly evaluating her experiences and profiting by her errors, it may be unwise to emphasize prohibition. When the adolescent can decide for herself that a style of behavior is unsuited for her, she has accomplished a greater strengthening of ego functioning than when she merely desists to "please" the therapist.

It is usually possible to distinguish between acting out for purposes of learning and acting out that is defensive and regressive, although the distinction may not be easy in many cases. Usually, the therapist can sense whether the prevailing tone of therapy is exploratory or evasive. The therapeutic alliance is a useful barometer to watch during episodes of sexual activity. Its fluctuations often gauge the extent to which the flurry of activity represents a turbulent storm of change and growth, or merely more hot air.

ILLEGITIMATE PREGNANCY

Teenage pregnancy out of wedlock is a growing social problem despite improved methods of birth control and the ready availability of abortion (McAnarney and Hendee, 1989). The personal embarrassment and shame that illegitimate pregnancy causes in some families is commonly resolved by frequently ill-advised marriages. The divorce rate is extremely high in adolescent marriage; thus the original problem is often further complicated by the trauma of divorce.

Although the majority of reported illegitimate pregnancies occur in youngsters from economically and socially deprived backgrounds, teenage illegitimate pregnancies are quite frequent in other social classes. In the upper social classes, they are usually handled quietly, through precipitous marriage, abortion, or private arrangements for leaving the community during pregnancy and delivery.

The etiology of teenage pregnancy is complex, involving social, cognitive, and family forces as well as unconscious motivational forces within the adolescent girl. The conscious, intentional teenage pregnancy is usually manipulative. The usual goals are either to escape or drastically to change an unacceptable family living situation. Pregnancy may be used to force parental agreement to a marriage that is regarded as unsuitable. Other youngsters use pregnancy as a conscious and deliberate spiteful attack on the parents. Even in these adolescents, other motives may be active at an unconscious level, although obscured by the conscious design. Of course, these unconscious motives are of central importance in the cases that belong in the "accidental" category. Many times the girl's motivation was neither conscious nor unconscious. That is, there was no motivation at all because the pregnancy was the result of forced sexual intercourse.

At times, one feels that the illegitimate pregnancy serves as a device to "get the parents off the hook." The adolescent girl seems to be living out her assigned family role as the scapegoated "bad" child. The fulfillment of the prophecy that she "would come to no good end" retroactively justifies the mother's longstanding neglect and hostility toward her. In these cases, the pregnancy may actually lead to apparent improvement in family relationships. The mother, fully exonerated, may relax her efforts to force the child into actions that define her as unlovable.

One final factor that must be considered in evaluating illegitimate pregnancy is the role of resurgent infantile omnipotence in the adolescent years. This force in mental life leads the adolescent to scorn reproductive reality by taking unwarranted chances, and its collapse is a major factor in the depressions that are seen in pregnant adolescents. The fact of pregnancy is often denied for a varying period, but eventually it must be faced. The acceptance of the pregnancy completely shatters the adolescent's faith in her personal omnipotence and the omnipotence of her thought processes. This collapse adds to the adolescent's despair and heightens her sense of total helplessness. This is an obvious setting for a suicidal "ordeal" aimed at reestablishing a magical sense of unity with powerful inner and outer forces.

STUDYING TEENAGE PARENTS

Ralph et al. (1984) studied a group of pregnant African American teenagers and compared them to a control group who had never been pregnant. They found that the two groups did not differ significantly on measures of psychosocial adjustment. Although the groups differed is some sociological and demographic factors, they did not differ significantly in family or psychological disturbance. Robert Coles (1997) and his assistants interviewed teenaged mothers and fathers. He found that these youngsters were struggling with raising a baby, but also with poverty and lack of opportunity. He noted that the young fathers he met felt that the young mothers absolutely wanted to get pregnant and have a child. Foster (1999) developed a program, "I Have a Future," that addresses many of the underlying psychosocial issues, including the conscious intention of young girls to get pregnant.

Aug and Bright (1970) challenged many of the traditional views of unwed motherhood. These authors conducted a study of 24 unmarried adolescent mothers and 22 married adolescent mothers to determine their degree of psychopathology and their attitude toward motherhood. After studying them in detail, Aug and Bright divided the subjects into four groups as follows.

Group I consisted of married girls who gave a history of family stability, warmth of interpersonal relationships, clear-cut family role patterns, and a constant relationship to surrounding social and cultural norms. Familial and religious sanctions against sexual activity were marked and there had been rare premarital intercourse. These young mothers showed a high regard for their infants and a substantial amount of positive affective interchange among family members. They described the father in terms of being a provider, but also a person who evidenced love for wife and offspring.

Group II consisted of unwed girls who seemed well adjusted with reference to their particular environments. It was common for these girls to have sisters and friends with an illegitimate child and a few of these girls were consciously trying to become pregnant. None of them were using contraceptives. These girls did not report a desire to marry the putative father. Even if the putative father was pictured as kind and generous with gifts and money for the mother's expenses, he was not a serious candidate for marriage, at least at that point in time. These girls had close personal relationships with their own mothers. All of these girls kept their babies and they were pleased to have a new baby in the family.

Group III included both wed and unwed individuals who showed pronounced disturbance of interpersonal relationships. They presented a picture of deprivation of financial resources and also of practically any positive affective cues in their environment. The parents of these girls were often openly abusive verbally, physically, and occasionally sexually, toward each other and the children. The putative fathers in this group were often heavy drinkers. They were unemployed or passed rapidly from job to job and had histories of a variety of antisocial behavior. These girls were ambivalent or openly negative toward their offspring. They often expressed intense need to have children, but at the same time conveyed thinly veiled hostility toward them.

Group IV comprised married African American girls, who

also exhibited marked disturbance of interpersonal relationships. All of these girls were illegitimate children and were very sensitive about having illegitimate offspring themselves. They all married at the time when they were four to seven months pregnant with their first child. The dominant theme in these people was that of very keen social conflict. They were quite conscious of middle class values that conflicted with the mores of the environment in which they were reared. These girls came from families that were unstable and splintered rather than extended family groups.

In light of their observations, Aug and Bright criticized some of the generalizations that had previously been made regarding out-of-wedlock pregnancy. For instance, one generalization held "out-of-wedlock pregnancy to be the signal of a life gone awry. Without intervention such a girl is doomed to a 'downhill spiral' of failure." Aug and Bright also criticized the generalization that the population of pregnant teenagers is homogeneous and that the majority of problems are found in the unwed mothers and not in their wed counterparts.

It would seem clear that our understanding of the implications of illegitimate pregnancy would be greatly expanded by further objective studies of this kind. It would be particularly useful to the adolescent therapist to have comparable data on the varieties of illegitimacy encountered in girls from middle-class families.

MANAGEMENT OF ILLEGITIMATE PREGNANCY IN ADOLESCENT CLIENTS

Emotionally disturbed adolescent girls (such as those in Aug and Bright's Group III and the neurotic variety described earlier) are frequently reluctant to inform their parents of an illegitimate pregnancy. One strong motivation for seeking abortion is to avoid the dreaded confrontation with enraged or wounded parents. The therapist should not only encourage the adolescent to tell the parents of the pregnancy as early as possible, but should offer his assistance in breaking the news if the adolescent

needs and wants it. Some adolescents prefer to have the therapist tell their parents. Others want the therapist in attendance
when they convey the information.

Once the fact of pregnancy is known to the family, the therapist
needs to provide assistance in dealing with the parents' emotional
reactions as well as making practical plans for the girl. The parents can be permitted and encouraged to ventilate their feelings
of anger, shame, rejection, and guilt. The therapist must serve as
a representative of reality and of the needs of the adolescent
without condemning the parents. The parents must be gradually
assisted to accept the reality of the pregnancy as well as the fact
that their daughter has the ultimate responsibility in decisions
concerning the pregnancy. Their role is to provide support, information, and counsel. Since many families in which a teenage
pregnancy occurs have never functioned in this constructive and
helpful way, extensive parental counseling is often necessary. In
addition to this psychological help, both the parents and the
adolescent will need factual information that may be best provided by referring them to professionals who devote themselves
to the management of illegitimate pregnancy.

Abortion

The first decision that the adolescent girl and her family must
face is whether to abort the pregnancy. Naturally, the adolescent
therapist should be familiar with the laws and customs of medical practice regarding abortion in his locality. Medical and psychological opinion is divided in regard to the emotional sequelae of abortion. Some authors have suggested that serious
disturbances may follow the procedure. Other investigators
have been unable to demonstrate serious psychiatric complications in women who have had abortions. Most evidence appears
to support the premise that it is more traumatic to bear the child
and give it up for adoption than to have an abortion. In recent
years the intense media and political attention to the moral
issues in abortion have intensified the potential conflicts of the
adolescent girl.

Marriage As the Answer

If abortion is unwanted, the possibility of marriage to the baby's father is often considered. It is obvious that a forced marriage, undertaken only to avoid the shame of unwed motherhood, is rarely indicated. Usually such a decision merely expands the problem. Of course, in some older adolescents marriage is desired by the couple. Often, the pregnancy was deliberately sought to force parental consent or to overcome rational misgivings within the couple themselves, such as economic considerations. The therapist can serve only as a supportive counselor, helping the adolescent and her family to avoid a foolish decision based primarily on a panicky overconcern with public opinion.

Placement

If neither abortion nor marriage is planned, the adolescent must decide whether to place the baby for adoption or to keep the child and care for it herself. This question may be settled by circumstances outside the adolescent's control as in disadvantaged minority groups where few prospective adoptive parents are available. When a true option exists, the facts usually favor placement. By placing the baby, the adolescent girl is free to continue her education and maturation until she is truly prepared to accept the responsibilities of parenthood. As a rule, the baby is benefited, since most adoptive parents desire the child with less ambivalence than may exist in the unwed adolescent mother and her family.

Despite the above practical considerations, many adolescent mothers are reluctant to part with the baby. The need to keep the child may be based on projective identification with the unborn baby in which the adolescent fantasizes that the infant will feel abandoned and rejected, as she has. Guilt feelings about the sexual behavior that led to pregnancy may cause the adolescent to feel she should "take her medicine" by accepting the responsibility of child care. She is often strongly reinforced in this opinion by the generally punitive attitude of society toward the unwed mother. Other complex emotional patterns may make it difficult for the unwed mother to accept adoptive placement. The therapist's job is to deal with these feelings with the same exploratory objectivity that he brings to all other issues in psychotherapy. The adolescent has the right to make the final decisions regarding her child, since she must bear the emotional and practical consequences of the choice. Psychotherapy must continue following delivery, since there are difficult adjustments regardless of which plans are followed. The unwed mother and her parents need continued treatment, since there is a high probability of further pregnancies among girls who have one illegitimate birth.

ADOLESCENTS AND AIDS

The information that today's teenagers learn about sex and sexuality is quite different from what their parents learned. The content of the "curriculum" is different and the "faculty" is different for these two generations. The current generation of parents learned general information about sex from a parent— usually the parent of the same gender—and went on to get the nitty-gritty details from peers and through their own adventures. The course content mainly pertained to the anatomical aspects of sexual functioning, with a brief reference to the dangers of pregnancy, syphilis, and gonorrhea. The current generation of teenagers learns a great deal about sex at school. Today's adolescents have already been taught in elementary school the rudiments of the anatomy and physiology of sex. In some communities school personnel provide information about masturbation, homosexuality, contraception, and abortion. It is hard to say very much about any of those topics without conveying something about one's system of values. Most parents want the public schools to promote good values in their children, but disagree about what the specific values should be.

AIDS is a low-incidence, highly lethal, highly publicized, preventable disease, so in the 1980s and 1990s many school systems introduced AIDS-education programs for their students. As a result of these public health measures, many high school students learned more about AIDS than their parents. They learned the difference between being infected with HIV (human immunodeficiency virus); having AIDS (acquired immunodeficiency syndrome); and having the AIDS-related opportunistic infections. The typical approach to teaching about AIDS involves traditional classroom instruction and dramatic audiovisual material. Sometimes the videotapes include poignant interviews with individuals who are dying from AIDS. The people are diverse enough to allow every student to identify with at least one of them. They may be white, black, homosexual, heterosexual, users of IV drugs, or simply recipients of blood transfusions. At the end of the videotape, a caption may tell the viewers which individuals have already died, between the time of the taping and the time it was edited and released.

The Centers for Disease Control (1988) surveyed high school students to see what they already know about AIDS and HIV. Although the great majority of the students knew that HIV infection can occur through IV-drug use and through sexual intercourse, these youngsters had many misconceptions about HIV infection. About half of the high school students surveyed thought that HIV transmission could occur through giving blood, insect bites, using public toilets, and having a blood test. Teenagers are going to be much more successful in avoiding infection if they focus their own preventative measures where it really matters (using drugs intravenously, having sex without condoms, and having multiple sex partners) than in avoiding behaviors that do not matter at all (giving blood, having blood tests, etc.).

Belfer et al. (1988) discussed the implications of AIDS in working with children and adolescents and he pointed out that the illness will have an increasing impact on the psychological lives of both infected and noninfected individuals. He said that public health measures should address adolescents because many teenagers engage in behaviors that increase their risk of infection: multiple sex partners without any form of protection against infection; homosexual behavior; and intravenous drug use. Belfer suggested that interventions should be adapted to specific subgroups of adolescents. For instance, therapists could help educate peer counselors, who would then present AIDS education in youth-conducted rap or discussion groups. Such programs should occur not just in schools, but in runaway shelters and juvenile detention centers and other likely places of contact. He suggested that youngsters who are admitted to hospital treatment programs should routinely receive AIDS preventive education. The subgroup of homosexual adolescents is very hard to reach in a specific manner because this is largely a secret population. In your everyday public high school it would be very hard to conduct a rap session for the homosexual students to talk about AIDS prevention. However, if a community had an ongoing support group for homosexual youth, AIDS would obviously be a good topic for the meeting.

Very few adolescents actually have AIDS—so far. Because of the long incubation period, adolescents may engage in risky activities and become infected with HIV, but not develop the illness itself until adulthood. Almost all individuals with AIDS are adults (who may have become infected as adolescents) and younger children (who were infected during pregnancy or delivery by their infected mothers). However, it is likely that the number of adolescent victims will increase greatly in the next few years. This crisis will involve both boys and girls, since it will be transmitted through heterosexual intercourse.

Fear of AIDS can be an issue in understanding adolescent behavior. For instance, a youngster who had been exposed to HIV infection may become scared to death, and then propel himself into counterphobic sexual behavior in order to prove to himself that no little virus is going to hurt him or kill him.

ADOLESCENT SEX OFFENDERS

A good clinical definition of the adolescent sex offender is a youth, from puberty to legal age of majority, who commits any sexual act with a person of any age against the victim's will, without consent, or in an aggressive or threatening manner.

This definition includes both hands-on offenses, such as child molestation and rape, and hands-off offenses, such as exhibitionism, voyeurism, and obscene phone calls. The vast majority of adolescent sex offenders are males. It is useful to cite examples to clarify the difference between sex offenders, adolescents with sexual disorders, and normal sexual behavior:

- A 13-year-old boy who threatened three younger boys with a screwdriver and then exposed himself to them was a sex offender.
- A 15-year-old boy who stole female underwear and then masturbated with it was not a sex offender, but had a sexual disorder or a paraphilia of fetishism.
- Two 14-year-old boys were wrestling and then fondled each other on one occasion. They were not sex offenders and did not have a sexual disorder, but were doing what some normal teenagers, although not necessarily the majority, happen to do.

In recent years there has been a tremendous increase in psychiatric programs and other specialized programs that treat adolescent sex offenders. This explosion in treatment programs has been spurred by three interrelated factors: crime statistics, which show that adolescents are responsible for a significant proportion of sexual offenses; a realization that many identified adult sexual offenders began their offending in adolescence; and a feeling that intervention early would be preventive and therefore reduce the number of future victims.

Characteristics of Adolescent Sex Offenders

Many of the so-called characteristics of adolescent sex offenders are shared with the population of delinquent adolescents who are not sex offenders and even with the general population of all adolescents. But at the risk of being anecdotal, it is possible to state some factors that seem important in the etiology of adolescent sex offending. For instance, some studies have indicated that an unstable family background and a history of witnessing family violence or being physically abused plays a contributing role in the life histories of adolescent sex offenders. Some studies show that many adolescent offenders had been sexually victimized themselves. It has also been noted that these youngsters have little skill in establishing and maintaining close friendships. They frequently described serious social isolation. These youngsters have also been described as having low self-esteem, poor sense of masculine adequacy, fear of intimacy, gender-identity confusion, poor impulse control, and lack of moral development.

Sex offenders employ the mental defense mechanism of cognitive distortion. Cognitive distortion is a form of rationalization that the offender uses to justify his behavior. For example, a 16-year-old boy who described a 3-year-old girl as being seductive and enjoying the abuse. Another example of cognitive distortion would be the statement by an adolescent who raped a peer at knife point, that "she asked for it."

The psychiatric diagnoses that are applied to adolescent sex offenders may relate either to the offense itself or to other kinds of emotional or behavioral problems. Regarding the actual sex offense, the client may meet the *DSM-IV-TR* criteria for exhibitionism, frotteurism (touching or rubbing against a non-consenting person), pedophilia, sexual sadism, or other non-specified paraphilias.

Assessment and Treatment

A question that the practicing therapist must address, in evaluating an adolescent sex offender, is whether to recommend outpatient or inpatient treatment. It is necessary to take into consideration the psychosocial strengths and weaknesses of the individual client, the amount of structure and emotional support provided by the family, and the need to protect the community. The amount of denial is important to assess. If both the youngster and the family deny that there is a problem, despite findings of juvenile court to the contrary, it is more likely that inpatient treatment is indicated. An adolescent who committed offenses that were violent or that were compulsive should usually have inpatient treatment. Youngsters who were already in outpatient treatment and who reoffended should usually be referred for inpatient treatment.

The assessment and the treatment of adolescent sex offenders has been described by Murphy (1989) and Shaw (1999). Practice parameters on this topic have been published by The American Academy of Child and Adolescent Psychiatry (1999). In addition to the usual psychosocial and family histories, the evaluator should explore where the offender learned about sex; the possibility of physical and sexual abuse; deviant or paraphiliac sexual experiences; masturbatory history and the fantasies during masturbation; and empathy toward victims. Some treatment centers are equipped to measure the psychophysiological response of sexual arousal. That is, the client looks at pictures or listens to audiotapes that depict sexual relations among men, women, and children in various combinations. At the same time his degree of penile erection is measured with an electronic device. Another method is to carefully measure the length of time the client looks at different types of pictures. In some cases it is possible to determine exactly what sexual stimuli are arousing and what are not—information that may be useful in confronting the client's denial and also in designing the treatment plan.

In treating the adolescent sex offender, the therapist will need to communicate with the parents, court officials such as probation officers, and possibly personnel from child protective services. Whether it is inpatient or outpatient, the treatment should specifically and explicitly address the sexual offending behavior. Since sexual offending is a crime, most therapists feel that the offender should be held accountable for his behavior. It usually is helpful to combine individual and group psychotherapy. The group may be particularly powerful in confronting the client's denial and providing an opportunity for learning basic social skills. The group can also tease out and confront the cognitive distortions that sex offenders practice, which become apparent when they describe in detail their offenses.

A fundamental philosophical belief for most therapists is that sex offenders cannot be cured, but the purpose of treatment is to help the youngster learn how to control his behavior. In that respect, the "recovering sex offender" is similar to the recovering alcoholic. That is not to infer that sex offending is an addiction, but that it is a chronic behavioral disorder that requires the lifelong use of compensatory coping skills.

Clinical Illustrations

Parents have their own way of responding when it is their teenager who has been caught in some sexual activity with a younger child. Some parents have heard about it or seen it so often that they simply do not allow adolescent boys to baby-sit. Some parents overreact to situations like this. Some parents do not react at all. In any case, therapists are frequently asked to evaluate adolescent boys who have been identified by younger children as perpetrators of some kind of sexual misconduct.

John, age 13, was brought for evaluation because he had been baby-sitting two young boys and he asked them to take off their pants. John had been asked to look after the boys for two hours during the afternoon and it was his first experience as a babysitter. He was considered a responsible boy, but was somewhat immature socially. In an attempt to entertain his charges, he apparently invented a game in which the loser was supposed to pull down his pants for just a second. As the game progressed, John decided that the loser should take his pants off altogether. The little boys thought this was a lot of fun and they told their mother about it when she came home.

In the evaluation interview, John was embarrassed but was able to relate what had happened while he had been babysitting. He agreed that he had gotten very silly with the boys and that he should have acted more grown-up when taking on such a responsibility. He claimed that he did not have any intention of touching or hurting the little boys in any way. When asked about other sexual issues, he had an average amount of facts, curiosity, and misinformation for a 13-year-old. John's parents were also interviewed and they were not aware of any other sexual behavior that seemed inappropriate or aggressive. To be thorough, the therapist also arranged for a battery of projective psychological tests, which were normal.

John was seen for a few outpatient individual therapy appointments. He had the opportunity to discuss early adolescent sexual concerns with the therapist. The therapist provided some straightforward answers to John's questions, but also pointed out that in the future John could get information from his parents and also by hanging around kids his own age. The therapist told the parents that John had certainly exercised some transitory bad judgment, but reassured them that he did not appear to be a future child molester. To be on the safe side and to satisfy the therapist's own curiosity about John's development, a follow-up appointment was scheduled in one year.

This case vignette and the one that follows illustrate one extreme and then another. The behavior by John would probably constitute a sex offense, since the "victims" were much younger and under the authority of the perpetrator, but it was certainly a mild form. The second case is a more serious and blatant example of adolescent sex offending.

Antoine was a 14-year-old white male admitted to an inpatient sex offender program on an emergency basis after it was discovered that he was abusing two stepbrothers and a stepsister while in outpatient treatment. During the evaluation he reported that he had begun sexually abusing at age 12 when he abused a 4-year-old half-sister. He described subsequently abusing five males and one other female. The abuse was quite intrusive—it included his being fellated by the children; performing fellatio and cunnilingus on the victims; and performing vaginal and anal intercourse on the victims. He also reported a history of obscene phone calls at age 11 and window peeping at age 13. He admitted to being sexually abused by an uncle and also described one consenting sexual experience at age 10 with a stepsister who was approximately the same age.

Antoine had experienced an unusual degree of family trauma. Four years prior to admission a natural sister had died after a lengthy illness. About two years prior to admission his mother died, at which point he came to live with his father and stepmother. His behavior reportedly had changed after his sister's death and became even more problematic after his mother's death. At the time of admission he was shy, avoidant, and socially withdrawn. He was extremely anxious and had difficulty expressing feelings. He had very poor social skills and did not participate appropriately in group activities.

During the course of inpatient treatment further family secrets began to emerge. He acknowledged that he had been abused by his stepfather during his mother's illness. He also admitted that his stepfather had sexually abused his sister, the one who later died. She had told Antoine of the abuse and the boy subsequently blamed himself for her death.

This case represents a contrast to the earlier story of John. Antoine had a history that indicated the development of a set paraphiliac pattern. He had been sexually abused, had very poor social skills, repeatedly abused children, and had engaged in other paraphiliac behaviors. Adolescents with clinical profiles such as Antoine's need treatment that is intensive and long-term.

Adolescent sex offenses cover a lot of territory. As these youngsters become more visible and are referred more often for evaluation and treatment, clinicians should be thorough in asking pertinent questions and also reasonably comfortable in pursuing topics that might be distressful or distasteful.

PARAPHILIAS

A paraphilia is a psychiatric disorder in which a person persistently experiences an abnormal sexual fantasy or abnormal sexual behavior. *DSM-IV-TR* lists fifteen different paraphilias. What they all have in common is that they involve recurrent intense sexual urges and sexually arousing fantasies that most of us would consider abnormal. What is abnormal is that the person feels sexually aroused by objects that are not human or by people who are not consenting partners.

Paraphilias that may occur in adolescents include:

- Pedophilia, which consists of recurrent, intense sexual urges and sexually arousing fantasies involving sexual activity with a prepubescent child. This has already been discussed in the section on the adolescent sex offender in this chapter.
- Frotteurism, which is the recurrent urge to touch and rub against a nonconsenting person. It is the touching, not the coercive nature of the act, that is sexually exciting. Frotteurism is usually accomplished in crowded circumstances such as subway trains.
- Exhibitionism, which is the recurrent urge to expose one's genitals to an unsuspecting stranger. The stereotypical exhibitionist is the man in the raincoat who "flashes." Another method used by an adolescent exhibitionist was to drive around in his car with his pants pulled down. When he saw a young girl he would pull over and ask for directions. After the girl saw his penis, he would drive off.
- Voyeurism, which is the recurrent urge to observe an unsuspecting person who is naked, in the process of disrobing, or engaging in sexual activity. Voyeurism is usually what Peeping Toms are up to. What the adolescent client would describe is a strong sexual urge that can only be satisfied by peeping. Although he knows it is wrong and is dangerous, he goes out after dark and wanders the neighborhood, hoping to find the opportunity to watch or listen to people engaging in sexual activities. He tries to combine peeping with masturbating, and then he feels satisfied until the next night. Sometimes the neighbors catch on and have been known to capture and even shoot at the local voyeur.
- Telephone scatologia, which is the *DSM-IV-TR* terminology for obscene phone calls. This is a fairly common activity of preadolescent and early adolescent boys. In most instances it is self-limited and ends after the thrill wears off. Other boys and men persist in this behavior and also move on to

more serious forms of sex offending. Perhaps this behavior will become less common now that the telephone companies have the technology to easily trace all incoming calls.

- Fetishism, which is a recurrent intense sexual urge and sexually arousing fantasy that involves a nonliving object, such as female undergarments. This behavior will be discussed in greater detail below, as we attempt to show that a specific piece of sexual behavior could have a number of possible etiologies.

The practical clinical issue regarding fetishism comes up when a youngster is brought for evaluation because it has been discovered that he has been getting into his mother's or sister's underwear. It is good for the evaluator not to jump to any conclusions, since there are several possible explanations for this behavior, which range from the almost normal to the seriously pathological. The evaluator should collect enough information to determine which of the following explanations seems most likely:

An adolescent boy may be quite curious about the things that women usually keep quite private, such as their bras, panties, and tampons. A youngster who is a loner and schizoid may not be able to satisfying his curiosity by the interpersonal methods that most boys use—comparing notes with his buddies—so he resorts to rummaging around in his mother's drawers to find out what he can.

One of the purposes of adolescent masturbation is to create a bridge between childhood autoeroticism and adult heterosexuality. That is, the adolescent boy may masturbate and fantasize about girls or a particular girl. That is a step in the right direction, in that the masturbation is in the service of moving toward a healthy sexual relationship with another person. The masturbation may involve looking at *Playboy*-type magazines or fondling female underwear. If that is the function that the underwear serves, it is within the range of normal behavior and is not a fetish.

It is important to distinguish between a fetish for female underwear and normal variations of sexual behavior. Some males find that heterosexual pleasure is enhanced by involving some inanimate object in the process. For instance, it may increase the man's excitement if the woman wears a particular piece of lingerie. That is not an example of a fetish, but is simply an instance of variety being the spice of life.

A true fetish for female underwear implies that the underwear is not simply an added bonus, but is a prerequisite for achieving sexual excitement and orgasm. In the case of an adolescent, it would mean that the youngster has repeatedly taken underwear from family members and from stores and that he requires the underwear in order to masturbate successfully or to accomplish sexual intercourse.

In taking the history of a youngster suspected of having the paraphilia of fetishism, it is important to ask about other sexual urges and activities, such as homosexuality, exhibitionism, peeping, and obscene phone calls. As we have mentioned several times, clients often have multiple paraphilias. In evaluating an adolescent, it would be useful to explain to him why you are asking him questions about a variety of sexual fantasies and behaviors. It is not that you necessarily think he has engaged in all these activities, but that you are simply trying to get a full understanding of what has been happening.

It would be good to find out what the youngster is actually doing with his mother's underwear. It is not so significant if he is simply masturbating with the underwear. It would seem more ominous if he is actually putting the undergarments on and even wearing them under his regular clothes. Using the underwear for cross-dressing could indicate a serious disorder of gender identity. It is also ominous if he describes any form of bondage associated with the underwear, as in the rare but dangerous sexual asphyxia syndrome.

Finally, it is important to keep in mind that the adolescent boy who takes his mother's underwear might not have any kind of sexual disorder at all. It is possible that the behavior is simply poor judgment in a youngster who is mentally retarded. The behavior could conceivably be the symptom of a completely different disorder, such as schizophrenia.

CHAPTER 14

the adolescent victim

Adolescence can be a tough time, even in the best of circumstances. It is easy to see how a significant physical or psychological trauma could sidetrack a youngster from her developmental tasks, or even derail her altogether. In every adolescent's environment is an awesome array of potential traumas—ranging from small tragedies (moving away during senior year; hepatitis epidemic that disables the entire football team) to devastating events (suicide by one's best friend; violent death of a parent; incest).

This chapter explores the way adolescents may react to several kinds of trauma. The quality and usefulness of the youngster's coping devices depend on a number of factors, including her psychosocial strengths prior to the trauma; her level of psychological development; the nature of the trauma itself; the youngster's proximity to the disaster or traumatic event; and the availability of support systems in the family and community.

For example:

- An adolescent girl who was raped by her uncle on one occasion and whose family responds promptly and appropriately to this emergency may be able to deal with the anger and embarrassment and sense of violation, and move on with her life.
- An adolescent girl who had been molested by her father on a regular basis for several years has already modified her cognitive style and her manner of relating to other people, in a desperate attempt to have the world make sense to her.
- A boy who was mugged and severely beaten, but did not sustain permanent injuries, may be able to elicit support from his friends and convince himself that he could have

clobbered those other guys if there had not been so many of
them.

• A boy who was beaten and lost the vision in one eye may
take a long time to regain his self-confidence and sleep
without having nightmares.

It is ironic that victims of violence get blamed for the horrible
things that happened to them. Not only do family members and
peers suggest that the victim could have avoided the trouble or
the disaster if only he had somehow behaved differently, but the
victim may go out of his way to blame himself. For instance, the
youngster who was beaten up by local teenage thugs might hear
his friends say something to the effect, "If only you had enough
sense not to hassle those guys. . . ." Or his dad might remark,
"You've got to learn to defend yourself. . . ." Even without these
comments from others, the boy is very likely to conclude that
there is something wrong with the way he walks or talks or
fights, that caused him to become a victim. The adolescent victim may feel quite surprised and relieved when the therapist
tells him, perhaps several times, "You are not to blame. It was
not your fault that you were mugged."

This chapter uses several forms of trauma to illustrate the
variety of coping mechanisms that are available to adolescents.
The traumatic forces we will consider are quite different. The
Holocaust was a unique experience for our civilization, but
it teaches us something about the ability of children and adolescents to survive overwhelming disaster. Another form of
trauma discussed in this chapter is incest, since sexual abuse is
reported with a frequency that is disheartening. A third topic
will be the way adolescents might cope with a serious physical
injury. Another form of trauma is discussed in chapter 15,
which is the way adolescents deal with parental separation and
divorce.

As you consider this material and the clinical vignettes, you
should be wondering about the treatment of these clients.
Should every trauma victim undergo counseling? Should it be
intensive individual therapy or would a support group at a victims' assistance program be just as helpful? If the great majority

of untreated rape victims reach a plateau of "recovery" by twelve months after the attack, do they require treatment in the first place? Is it better to let the victim repress the horrible experience or to encourage ventilation of feelings and exploration of fantasies? If the client has sustained a serious disability and then employs a good deal of denial to avoid facing his handicap, is it the best therapy to leave the client alone and let him maintain both his relative ignorance and his relative bliss? What about cognitive-behavioral therapy for youngsters with posttraumatic stress disorder (PTSD)?

It would be nice if all these questions had clear-cut answers. We will be offering guidelines in this chapter for making decisions regarding therapy. In some situations, however, the therapist will have to develop his or her own philosophy about what seems to make sense—whether to take a supportive approach that encourages repression or to actively help the client discover and experience and express and eventually integrate her feelings. If the latter course is taken, one would hope that the cure is not worse than the illness. Furthermore, it is usually possible to discuss this issue with the client herself and for the therapist and the client to decide together on how the treatment is going to proceed. A client may want to return figuratively to the scene of the trauma, as long as she knows she can trust the therapist to help her bear the pain that she will find there.

POSTTRAUMATIC STRESS DISORDER

Some of the youngsters who sustain a severe trauma develop the syndrome of posttraumatic stress disorder. It is certainly not required for the client to have that particular condition. Some adolescents may respond to an acute distressing situation with symptoms that are less serious. The appropriate diagnoses, if the symptoms are briefer and less disabling, may be one of the adjustment disorders, such as adjustment disorder with anxiety or adjustment disorder with mixed disturbance of emotions and conduct. If the symptoms become more chronic, the diagnosis might be generalized anxiety disorder or dysthymic disorder.

DSM-IV-TR indicates specific criteria that should be met for the diagnosis of posttraumatic stress disorder:

- That the person has experienced an event that involved actual or threatened death or serious injury, or a threat to the physical integrity of self or others, and the person's response involved intense fear, helplessness, or horror.
- That the traumatic event is persistently reexperienced in at least one of the following ways: recurrent and intrusive distressing recollections of the event; recurrent distressing dreams of the event; acting or feeling as if the traumatic event were recurring; intense psychological distress at exposure to internal or external cues that symbolize or resemble an aspect of the traumatic event; and physiologic reactivity upon exposure to internal or external cues that symbolize or resemble an aspect of the traumatic event.
- Persistent avoidance of stimuli associated with the trauma and numbing of general responsiveness, as indicated by at least three of the following: efforts to avoid thoughts, feelings, or conversations associated with the trauma; efforts to avoid activities, places, or people that arouse recollections; inability to recall an important aspect of the trauma; markedly diminished interest in significant activities; feeling of detachment or estrangement from others; restricted range of affect; and the sense of a foreshortened future.
- Persistent symptoms of increased arousal, as indicated by at least two of the following: difficulty falling or staying asleep; irritability or outbursts of anger; difficulty concentrating; hypervigilance; and exaggerated startle response.
- Duration of the disturbance of at least one month.

PTSD is probably the manifestation of both psychological and physiological processes. The occurrence of PTSD and its severity may depend in part on the life experiences and the personality traits that the individual had prior to the trauma. In addition, however, Kolb (1987) proposed that the symptoms of PTSD have a neurological basis. He suggested that excessive emotional stimulation stresses and perhaps damages neuronal synaptic structures in the temporal-amygdaloid complex of the brain. His idea was that the symptoms such as affective blunting, startle reaction, hyperalertness, intrusive thinking, repetitive nightmares, etc., are caused by neurophysiological changes. Perry (1994) proposed that large increases in brain neurotransmitter activity associated with severe and prolonged stress in children may compromise the later development of the brain, placing the children at risk for developmental disorders. Pfefferbaum (1997) recently reviewed the topic of PTSD in children and adolescents and the American Academy of Child and Adolescent Psychiatry (1998c) has published practice parameters for the assessment and treatment of children and adolescents with PTSD.

GROUP EXPERIENCES

Natural disasters and man-made brutalities occur which affect groups of people or entire populations—such as floods, earthquakes, hijackings, and wartime experiences. In some cases it has been possible to study the child and adolescent victims. The purpose of this research has been to document the effect of the trauma on these youngsters; whether there is a particular pattern that emerges; and whether some children are more vulnerable and others seem to be protected from the trauma. Clinicians have also attempted to determine whether any particular treatment helps the victims cope with the trauma more effectively.

In 1972 the valley of Buffalo Creek in West Virginia was suddenly flooded when a large slag dam broke open. Several small towns were destroyed and 125 people were killed. A team of mental health professionals had the opportunity to interview the survivors and were able to describe the communities and the individuals that were affected. Newman (1976) said that the adolescents were profoundly affected by "the almost total community destruction." In terms of their reactions, "they often had to choose between rebellious predelinquent behavior or compliant social withdrawal. They suffered deeply but privately when their parents broke down under stress."

Mount St. Helens erupted in 1980. Adams and Adams (1984) studied the community of Othello, Washington, and showed that manifestations of stress in the population persisted for months following the eruption. Shore et al. (1986) also studied the community affected by Mount St. Helens and found something that was both expectable and interesting. They divided the research subjects into three groups—high exposure to trauma, low exposure, and control—and found a dose-response relationship when these groups were surveyed for psychiatric symptomatology. That is, the high exposure group had a greater degree of anxiety disorder, depression, and PTSD following Mount St. Helens.

Some authors have proposed methods of prevention, to immunize children against some future traumatic experience. For example, children and adolescents who live in areas prone to earthquakes can be educated ahead of time regarding the causes and phenomena of earthquakes. Schools can hold periodic earthquake drills. If you are dealing with a situation that allows for orderly evacuation ahead of time, such as a hurricane, it is known that children do better when families are kept together. Terr (1987) summarized her own experiences and reviewed the work of others in the area of prevention.

Chowchilla Victims, As Children

A systematic, prospective study that pertains particularly to adolescents was Terr's (1979, 1981, 1983) work in evaluating the victims of the Chowchilla school bus kidnapping. The kidnapping occurred in 1976, when 26 children were taken from a school bus by three masked men at gunpoint. The children were missing for 27 hours. During most of that time they had been buried underground in a truck-trailer. They survived because they rescued themselves—that is, two of the boys dug them out of the hole.

At the time of the kidnapping the victims were age 5 to 14. When they were evaluated during the following year (Terr, 1981), every one of the children manifested significant psychiatric symptoms, which followed particular patterns. During and immediately following the trauma the children experienced

fears of further trauma and disturbances in cognitive functions, such as perception and sense of time. Several of the
children identified "omens" in that they thought back to the
events prior to the kidnapping and they identified specific happenings which they then associated with the trauma. There
were many examples of repetitive phenomena, such as recurring dreams, posttraumatic play which repeated the kidnapping experience, and instances of the children reenacting frag-
ments of the kidnapping.

Chowchilla Victims, As Adolescents

What is more pertinent to this chapter was the four-year
follow-up (Terr, 1983), when most of the victims had become
adolescents. Terr found that every child in the study still exhibited posttraumatic effects. She felt that the severity of each
youngster's symptoms was related to the child's prior vulnerabilities, family pathology, and community bonding. She made
the observation that the brief treatment that these children received during the year following the kidnapping did not prevent signs of illness and subjective symptoms four years later.

What were these youngsters' symptoms after four years? At
times they still experienced the intense anxiety that had accompanied the original trauma. This even occurred in the group's
hero, the teenager who had dug them out of the hole where
they were buried. These young victims also described a feeling
of profound embarrassment regarding their victimization. That
is, they did not like for people to know about or find out about
their experience, because it was like announcing how vulnerable they had been during the kidnapping. As you would expect,
these young victims were fearful of the possibility of another
kidnapping, of strangers, and of particular kinds of vehicles
that reminded them of the initial experience. Some of them
overcame their earlier fears by repeatedly exposing themselves
to the feared objects (such as signal vehicles) or situations (such
as being alone).

In the four-year follow-up study, Terr also found that these youngsters did not manifest repression, in that each one could still give a detailed account of the experience. However, they did employ conscious suppression of thoughts and feelings because they knew they would be uncomfortable in reviving those memories. In spite of their efforts to suppress the memories, some of these children daydreamed so much about the events that their school work suffered. These youngsters still manifested misperceptions and distortions in time sense. Terr described how almost all of these youngsters showed "severe philosophical pessimism," in that they expected a short life or some future disaster. Even after four years the victims described recurrent posttraumatic nightmares and other repetitive phenomena. One would conclude from this study that adolescents who experience severe, acute psychological trauma are likely to have symptoms for a very long time.

THE HOLOCAUST

It may seem strange to discuss the events of the Holocaust in a chapter on the psychological trauma among adolescents, since the events of 1941 to 1945 are so far removed from the circumstances of today's teenagers. But we will learn something about the coping abilities that adolescents may have in dealing with extraordinary stress. Is it possible that extremely difficult life experiences may shape young people into very hardy and successful adults?

It is hard to imagine the cruelty that the children and adolescents of the Holocaust experienced. Since the Nazi government intended to exterminate Jews forever, it was necessary for them to kill children as well as adults. Children and young adolescents could serve no useful purpose to the government, so the Nazi troops threw them into trucks from rooftops, buried them alive, burned them alive, and allowed them to freeze and starve to death. It is said that children were handed over to German soldiers to use as target practice. Some teenagers survived by escaping and living in forests for several years or walking hundreds of miles to safety.

Moskovitz (1983) described 24 children who survived the Holocaust and their adaptation as adults. These were the children
who came to England after World War II and lived at the
Lingfield orphanage and were studied by Alice Goldberger and
Anna Freud. Most of them seemed surprisingly healthy and
happy as adults—Moskovitz (1985) noted "the wide range of
adaptation where there was theoretically no reason to expect to
see anything positive."

Two Jewish teenagers of the Holocaust later became
famous—one died, one lived. Anne Frank (1953) was age 13 to
15 during the two years that she and her family were in hiding
in the warehouse of her father's business. Her diary chronicled
her concerns about mundane adolescent issues, as well as her
impressive altruism. Perhaps its most quoted statement was, "In
spite of everything I still believe that people are really good at
heart." Anne's family were sent to Auschwitz. She later was
transferred to Bergen-Belsen and died there of typhus. Elie
Wiesel (1972) was age 14 when he was interred by the Nazis. He
survived, came to the United States, raised a family, and spent a
lifetime as an author documenting the Holocaust experience
and its aftermath.

Another source of information comes from two adolescents
who were victims of the Holocaust and who later became psychiatrists. Krell (1985) and Rotenberg (1985) were willing to
write about their experiences and observations about themselves and other victims. Rotenberg (1985) was a victim of the
Holocaust from 1941 until 1948. He and his family were
marched from the ghetto of Czernowitz, Romania, to an abandoned village in the Ukraine during mid-winter. After his parents and brother died of typhus, Rotenberg and his sisters survived by finding scraps of food and eating grass and leaves. As
the war ended in Eastern Europe, Rotenberg lived in orphan-
ages in several countries until he eventually emmigrated to
Canada in 1948, when he was 13.

So, how did this experience affect his adolescence, his ability
to relate to others, his ability to enjoy life? Rotenberg's experience as an adolescent was "to put as much distance as possible

between myself and my past." As a teenager in Canada he actively became part of his new culture. He learned how to get along. He overcompensated tremendously—he learned a new language rapidly and graduated from high school with the highest grades ever achieved in English in his province. He described how he found substitute parents, "to whom I could become attached and who would form some attachment to me."

What makes a person into a survivor? Rotenberg thought that he survived psychologically because he had already experienced the unequivocal warmth and affection of his family, especially his relationship with his father, before the Holocaust took away his parents and every aspect of physical comfort and safety.

Krell (1985) was also a child survivor of the Holocaust who later became a psychiatrist. He was separated from his parents and was in hiding during the Holocaust. He has contacted other child and adolescent survivors and has helped in documentation projects, to secure on tape eyewitness accounts of that time. He found that the child and adolescent survivors found little pride or dignity in survivorhood, unlike their adult counterparts. As adolescents and young adults, what they wanted was to be normal, to have stability in their lives, to create a new solid family unit. To illustrate the adaptability and resilience of this group, these youngsters caught up on many years of interrupted schooling, in two years or less, in a foreign language. Many of them became university educated, goal oriented, and successful.

Does this sound familiar? In our own time thousands of children and adolescents from Vietnam and Cambodia have come to this country, having survived a devastating war, deaths of family members, perilous journeys, and years in resettlement camps. Many of them worked hard at becoming part of their new culture and became more successful than their fellow American teenagers.

We do not completely understand why some adolescents become survivors and others become victims. At least one factor is that family and community values and loyalty and support can help a youngster get through some extremely bad times. That is one conclusion that can be drawn from examples as disparate at the children of Chowchilla and the children of the Holocaust. But when the family is the source of the trauma, it is much harder for the adolescent to emerge as an intact and successful survivor. The children and adolescents who are victims of incest start out with two strikes against them. Not only have they been severely victimized, but they don't have a strong family or community to fall back on. Their families became the perpetrators and the enablers of their victimization.

INCEST

Incest is not rare. It is estimated that one out of ten children and adolescents has been sexually molested by a trusted family member. In citing that statistic we are including abuse by step-parents and other members of the extended family, not just by parents and siblings. Also, we are not just talking about sexual intercourse, but including fondling, exhibitionistic behavior, and taking photographs for sexual purposes.

Our society's recognition that children are abused and sexually molested by family members has been a long time coming. We seem to have the ability to ignore the ugly side of life. If there is reason to think that something too horrible to contemplate is happening, well, we just don't contemplate it. The history of this issue over the last hundred years has been something like peeling back the layers of a rotten onion. The deeper we looked into the problem, the uglier the damage.

The discovery and rediscovery of child abuse have followed a pattern. Usually our society as a whole has been complacent. Then one person or a few people point out that something bad is happening to our children. Initially we say, "Oh no, that hardly ever happens." Or that just happens among uneducated people or poor people. Then more and more individuals in the community start noticing and we accept awareness that we really do have a problem of child abuse. Then we become incensed and pass laws. Then we worry whether some of the victims are abused more by the system than by the original perpetrator.

A Short History of Abuse and Incest

In the nineteenth century there were laws that prohibited cruelty to animals. Some of the early cases of child abuse were tried under those laws, since state legislatures had not yet passed laws that prohibited cruelty to children. Up until the 1950s it was thought that physical abuse of children was rare—partly because physical discipline of children was generally more acceptable and partly because most of us did not want to notice the fact that adults in our midst were burning children and breaking their bones. The most important breakthrough in the "discovery" and recognition of child abuse was not accomplished by a psychiatrist or social worker or pediatrician or minister, but by a radiologist in a hospital emergency room. Caffey (1946) noticed a syndrome of children with chronic subdural hematomas and also multiple fractures of their arms and legs. He published his discovery and soon it was recognized that many children brought to emergency rooms had been physically abused by caretakers. A few years later Kempe et al. (1962) published their famous article, "The Battered-Child Syndrome."

The recognition of sexual abuse of children was similar. It was known that incest occurred, but people thought that it must be very unusual and that it happens among very deviant families, usually hillbillies. Students and trainees were learning how Freud's analytic patients described how their fathers had sexually molested them, but Freud eventually decided that most of his patients must have been talking about sexual fantasies rather than real events. Our current understanding is that sexual abuse actually happens, all too often.

There was one more step. Professionals became willing to accept that children, both boys and girls, could be sexually abused. It was harder to accept that adolescents could be molested, since they supposedly would be able to fight back or protest or tell on the perpetrator. Not so, since many adolescents have found themselves in situations in which they had to submit to the aggression of a parent or sibling. It happens every which way, with mothers molesting both sons and daughters and fathers molesting both sons and daughters. The most common form of incest is father-daughter incest. It may have happened only once and in a reasonably benign form: an intoxicated father exposed himself to his teenaged daughter. It may have happened many times: a father forced his daughter to have vaginal and anal intercourse from her puberty until she left home to marry at age 17.

In the late 1970s and 1980s there was an explosion of openness about incest. Many women came out of their closets to acknowledge that their fathers or uncles or grandfathers had repeatedly molested them. Forward and Buck (1988), Goodwin (1982), and Kempe and Kempe (1984) described the victims of incest and the families of these sexually abused children and adolescents.

It is known that hospitalized psychiatric patients as well as other seriously disturbed individuals, such as violent adolescents, show a high incidence of sexual abuse history. This is true of both sexes, but girls more than boys. What this means in practice is that the clinician should maintain a high index of suspicion of the possibility of sexual abuse and should develop a comfortable technique of inquiring about these experiences as a routine part of the history of the adolescent patient.

Burgess and Holmstrom (1974) popularized the term, "rape trauma syndrome," and created a framework for understanding the sequelae of sexual victimization. They described how the psychological damage may be produced in three ways: ethically, in terms of instilling false standards regarding what constitutes usual sexual behavior between adults and children; emotionally, in terms of instilling fear, shame, and guilt; and physically, in terms of anatomic harm. Depending on the severity of the attacks and other circumstances, the clinical diagnoses may include adjustment disorder with mixed emotional features, posttraumatic stress disorder, major depression, and many other possibilities. The whole range of anxiety disorders, panic disorders, and phobias may be present.

Two Clinical Examples

One of the most important issues in the clinical outcome during treatment is whether the youngster's family, especially her mother, provide both psychological and physical support. Sally's case shows how the prognosis is more bleak when the victim does not receive the support she needs.

Sally was a 15-year-old girl who was referred for inpatient treatment after a serious suicide attempt which included slashing both her wrists. Sally had been found on the bathroom floor by her mother after she called the mother to say goodbye. After admission to the hospital, Sally revealed in individual therapy that she had been sexually abused by her stepfather from age 8 to 15. The abuse began with occasional fondling and increased in frequency until the stepfather forced Sally to have intercourse at age 11.

The incident that precipitated the suicide attempt included being impregnated by the stepfather and his pressuring her to have an abortion. At the time of hospitalization, the mother and stepfather were still living together.

Sally's treatment included having her confront the mother regarding the incest. The mother was extremely angry and denied all her daughter's allegations. This issue was processed with the mother over many weeks, and still the mother continued to deny and invalidate the client. When the client was stronger, it was agreed that both the mother and stepfather would attend a family meeting. Both parents denied and invalidated the client. They also psychologically blackmailed her by saying that if she withdrew her "outrageous" allegations, they could all "be a family again."

This clinical example indicates a difficult prognosis for the client because of lack of validation for the abuse and unwillingness of the mother and stepfather to take respon-

sibility for the abuse and betrayal of the client. It was decided that Sally would live with an aunt. She continued to
have bouts of depression and acting out.

On the other hand, the adolescent incest victim is much more
likely to benefit if the family is able to support the treatment.
That's what happened in the case of Madeline.

Madeline was a 12-year-old girl who was brought for
outpatient treatment by her mother and father. Madeline
had recently revealed an incident of incest that included
forced intercourse by a 16-year-old cousin. Madeline was
quite depressed but was willing to discuss the trauma in
individual therapy and in family meetings with her mother
and father. The parents were very supportive. In addition,
Madeline's mother was able to press charges against the boy
who was her nephew. The duration of treatment—weekly
individual and family meetings—was about six months.
Madeline was able to work through the trauma because of
family support and validation.

Treatment of Incest

Many adolescent incest victims benefit from a combination of
individual, group, and family therapy. It may be very helpful
for the therapist to guide the client in bringing information
from one treatment modality to another. This usually involves
rehearsing in one meeting what is going to happen in the next.
For instance, the therapist may use an individual therapy meeting to discuss with the client what she is going to say at the next
group meeting. At the group, the therapist may arrange for the
members to role play and for the client to practice how she will
confront her parents in the family meeting. Of course, the therapist can meet with the parents and advise them what to do when
the confrontation occurs.

Working with the families of these youngsters requires both
confrontation and diplomacy. At the initial stages, the parents
may react very negatively to the revelation that their child has
been abused, especially if the abuser is a close family member.

The parents' negative reactions may include denial and a persistent belief that the child is lying. For instance, the parents may wish to organize a "cover-up"—but the therapist may need to explain that a report to protective services may be legally and clinically required. The family may accept the fact of abuse but blame the child. This is especially true in father-daughter incest. The daughter's affectionate and flirtatious behavior toward the father may lead the mother to justify his overt sexual response. The family may accept the truth of the event and feel sympathy for the child but feel embarrassed and uncomfortable. Strong emotions of guilt, shame and fear may overwhelm the family's ability to be helpful to the victim. At times this may take the form of a narrow preoccupation with punishing the abuser, which ignores the needs of the victim. Finally, the family may be ready and emotionally able to help and yet lack sufficient understanding of the expected reactions to sexual abuse and knowledge of what they can do to help.

Forward and Buck (1988) made useful suggestions for the treatment of incest victims. Her style as a therapist is to be active, but also warm and supportive. She found that incest victims do well in group therapy because they can see that other youngsters have had similar experiences and because they can benefit from the enormous support that can be evoked. However, many of her ideas can also be employed in individual therapy. Forward does not leave the therapy agenda up to the group, since she has definite ideas about what the therapist should be accomplishing. The first step is for the therapist to help the client deal with her rage at the perpetrator and also at other family members, such as the mother who allowed or perhaps even endorsed the incest. She suggests that group members help each other by taking roles in a form of psychodrama, so that the victim can feel that she is having a dialogue with these people. Forward also encourages the clients to confront their assailants, through writing letters or in family therapy sessions. These confrontations can be extremely cathartic experiences and she structures them so that they are constructive and not simply a violent display of anger. After dealing with her rage, the client needs guidance to cope with the ensuing depression and to build the foundation for a more healthy sense of identity and self-esteem in the future. In her experience Forward found these clients to be extremely treatable—but the therapist must be assertive enough to make the diagnosis and to guide the client through her inevitable resistances.

As mentioned previously, adolescent incest victims may develop a range of psychiatric symptoms and syndromes, such as generalized anxiety, chronic depression, and posttraumatic stress disorder. It is possible with incest victims to see hysterical phenomena such as conversion symptoms, depersonalization, dissociation, and fugue states. Hysterical seizures have been described. Sometimes the dissociative states become organized into multiple personalities. Working backward in conducting an evaluation, clients with multiple personality disorder may reveal a history of incest. Bowman et al. (1985) described their work with a 14-year-old girl who developed multiple personality disorder after incestuous experiences. Bowman treated the girl with individual therapy and was able to reconstruct the origin of the personalities and could explain the steps in therapy that allowed the personalities to fuse. Bowman said that the original personality is usually a shy, introverted, bland personality who is unable to experience anger, depression, fear, or sexual excitement. The secondary personalities function to take on the roles that the original personality cannot handle. So, they can be the exact opposite of the original. The dissociations act as a defense mechanism of the ego against painful experiences or memories. Each personality may serve some purpose. One may hold the memories of the painful experiences. One may contain the anger. One may retain memories of enjoying the experience. Although not all therapists would agree with this view, it is an interesting possibility.

GETTING MUGGED

Every morning after breakfast the mother of every teenager feels like announcing what the sergeant of *Hill Street Blues* used to say: "Be careful out there!" It is hard to accept that violence is prevalent in our country and that your own child is just as vulnerable as the next one. This section describes some of the psychological sequelae to getting mugged. We are not talking about the feelings that a youngster might have after participating in a street brawl or a gang fight. In those situations the fellow has gotten involved in the fracas voluntarily and also it was an experience of group camaraderie, so the injuries wouldn't hurt so much. We are addressing here the experience of being a victim, where the adolescent was not asking for trouble, but was beaten up anyway.

The physical injuries sustained in a mugging can range from minor to life-threatening. The psychological aftermath covers the gamut. The youngster's rage at being victimized might be expressed or might be suppressed, in which case the therapist may need to help the client recognize and verbalize his anger. The youngster may describe anxiety, panic attacks, and symptoms of posttraumatic stress disorder. He may feel humiliated, ashamed, and move into a state of chronic depression. He may resent how even his friends seem to blame him for what happened. That is, peers of the victim may not want to think about their own vulnerability, so they assume that these misfortunes only happen to fellows who have messed up in some way: "Couldn't you see the guy coming?" The adolescent victim may prefer anonymity and be tired of people asking him about the traumatic event, since it reminds him of being helpless and vulnerable.

In evaluating and treating a client who has been injured in this way, it is important to sort out the psychological from the neurological complications. If the youngster had sustained a head injury—especially if associated with loss of consciousness, a period of confusion or obtundation, skull fracture, or seizure—there may be emotional symptoms which have an organic basis to them. What looks like an appropriate expression of anger may actually be the irritability, lability, and explosiveness seen in a person with personality change due to closed head injury. What looks like depression may actually be apathy and mental blunting

as a result of brain damage. Arffa (1998) reviewed the psychological manifestations of brain injury.

The following case illustrates some of psychological consequences of a head injury.

> A psychiatrist happened to read in the newspaper that a
> 10th grade student at a private school was placed in juvenile
> detention after he attacked another boy with a pipe. The
> student, Barney, had hidden behind a pillar and hit an 11th
> grader named Roger on the back and head as he went by.
> Barney was tried as an adult for aggravated assault, but was
> found not guilty. Barney's defense was that he was a wimpy
> kid who had been teased by older boys who were basketball
> players, so his swinging with the pipe was construed as self-
> defense and justifiable retaliation.

> Several months later a neurologist referred the victim of
> the attack, Roger, to the same psychiatrist for evaluation.
> Roger had sustained a depressed skull fracture, which had
> been treated without further complications. Fortunately,
> there was no apparent neurological damage. However,
> Roger had become apathetic, socially isolated, and had
> slipped academically from the honor roll to barely passing.

> In the evaluation Roger was a polite, well-mannered
> boy. He had a soft, low-key style and it was easy to see how
> his fundamental personality traits could easily turn into
> chronic passivity and depression. Roger was a strong,
> sturdy youngster who had been a successful athlete and
> was on the basketball team, but he said that he had not
> actually been one of the mean basketball players who had
> been picking on Barney. It sounded like Barney had
> picked out Roger to be his victim because Roger was the
> most mild mannered basketball player he could find.
> Roger also knew that the school administrators knew that
> Barney had made threats and had emotional problems,
> but had not taken any steps to control him.

> Roger was treated in individual therapy, an adolescent
> therapy group, and in family meetings. The group mem-
> bers asked enough questions to help Roger express his an-

ger and frustration at what had happened. He was able to describe how the criminal trial of Barney left him feeling helpless all over again. He put himself on the line by testifying, but was not vindicated by the outcome of the trial. The ventilation of these feelings also helped him make an important decision, which was whether to sue his own school for damages. He felt loyalty to the school and the principal, but he also thought that the school had put its needs above his own. The family meetings were notable in two ways. It was important to help the parents avoid compensating by becoming unnecessarily protective of Roger. Also, they were extremely uncommunicative with each other. The therapist helped them express both supportive and other feelings, so that they could be useful to each other and could also make use of the support available in the community.

Roger's case is a good example of a youngster who was injured in a mugging, although not severely. He had psychological complications, was motivated in treatment, and did well.

Denial in the Service of Recovery

The last vignette is this chapter is quite different. Harold was very seriously injured and he "treated himself" with the use of denial. Harold's denial helped him get through his day-to-day routine and it also seemed to energize him to make plans for the future. As you read this case history, think about whether you would want to use psychotherapy to remove Harold's denial and to force him to face the reality of his disability.

Harold was 16 when he was seriously injured playing football. He and a friend got involved in an informal game at a playground, where he had never been before. He was the youngest and smallest person in the game. It turned out that this was not your ordinary pick-up football game—it had a closer likeness to assault and battery. On the initial kick return Harold was running with the ball and the other players tried to take him down. Several of them pulled him down and then a whole pile of people were on his back. At first he thought he had just hurt his head, but then noticed that he could not feel anything below his neck. He told everybody to get off of him and told them to roll him over real slow. Somebody called Harold's mother and an ambulance, but then everybody scattered, except for the friend he had started out with.

Harold sustained a compression fracture of one of his cervical vertebrae, which caused an incomplete paraplegia. He was treated at a hospital that deals with serious trauma and was also at a rehabilitation center for almost a year. He was able to return home and live with his mother. Although Harold was generally confined to a wheelchair, he was able to walk for short distances. He had limited use of his left arm, with which he was able to feed himself, shave, answer the telephone, open doors, play cards, and take care of his urinary and bowel functions. Even before his injury he had not been an enthusiastic student, but Harold was able to return to high school and he graduated a year after his original class.

This boy's emotional reaction to his injury was understandable and almost predictable. He became discouraged and moody and sometimes had crying spells. He was able to express his anger at the men who had injured him; at the city for not supervising the playground better; and at the doctors for not completely fixing him up. He was frightened by noises and loud sounds, because he felt he could not protect himself if he were attacked by somebody.

Harold also employed the unconscious defense mechanism of denial. When he was at the rehabilitation center the staff noted that Harold's expectations for recovery seemed much higher than what one might realistically expect. His high expectations appeared to win out over his periods of depression. When he was seen for psychiatric evaluation after he had returned home and had graduated from high school, Harold still seemed unrealistically optimistic about the future. He was making plans to apply to a local junior college, with the idea that he would later go on to a state university and pursue a career in medicine or in law.

The psychiatrist felt that supportive counseling should be incorporated into Harold's overall physical and educational rehabilitation program. He did not need therapy to get in touch with his anger, which was apparent and was motivating Harold to make something of himself. It did not seem to make sense to treat his occasional crying spells with antidepressant medication. The question for the therapist was whether to challenge Harold's unrealistic expectations. The therapist chose not to tell Harold to forget about medical school or law school. He did encourage Harold to try to get into junior college and to think about several professions that might be possible for him, such as radio broadcasting or working in an office.

It is easy to find examples of adolescents who feel good about themselves and who succeed, despite a serious physical handicap. Sometimes a child or adolescent requires an amputation of a leg because of bone cancer. These youngsters still learn to dance, run, and ski beyond the beginner slopes. One boy whose leg was amputated was on his high school wrestling team and scored better than many of his peers.

GUIDELINES FOR TREATMENT

Here are some ideas to keep in mind when treating adolescents who have been psychologically traumatized. These are intended as suggestions which each therapist needs to edit and adapt, since it is not possible to organize this material like a cookbook.

1. *"If it ain't broke, don't fix it."* In your practice you will probably see youngsters who are brought for assessment because their parents are concerned about some traumatic event that has occurred. You may find that the incident that occurred was fleeting in duration and low in intensity. The client is able to describe what happened in an appropriate manner and with appropriate affect. The parents seem like reasonable people and are not

trying to ignore the event or to blow the incident out of proportion. You will take a thorough history and find that there is no dysfunction associated with this traumatic event. What to do? We suggest that you see this as an opportunity for crisis intervention. That means that you see the client and the parents two or three times, explore the situation, allow for ventilation of feelings, make sure that the family members are supporting each other, and educate the family about the nature of psychological trauma and signs to watch for. Then you wish them well. You may also want to set up another appointment in about three months to see how everybody is doing.

2. *If the traumatic event was serious and has resulted in psychological symptoms, recommend treatment.* It is usually helpful for the therapist to say up front, "It wasn't your fault." As a general rule it is important for the therapist to help the victim get in touch with the painful feelings associated with the trauma. That usually means fearfulness, feelings of helplessness and vulnerability, rage, and sadness. However, it is not therapeutic in itself to leave your client feeling miserable, so you need to go on to the next step.

3. *The therapist should actively find ways to develop and promote a sense of mastery in the victim.* That may take the form of confronting the aggressor, through letters or through orchestrated family meetings. It may take the form of the victim testifying at the perpetrator's trial. It may take the form of enrolling in a self-defense class and becoming the local expert in tae kwon do. It may take the form of going public and teaching other teenagers how to avoid becoming future victims.

4. *Consider group therapy or a support group.* Victims find solace in learning that they are not alone. That is, they are not alone in being victims and also they are not alone in having intense and frightening feelings afterwards. Don't expect the average victim to find the right support group on his own. The therapist may need to get on the phone, find the group, locate the coordinator, and tell the client how to get to the meeting. Sometimes the local court or mental health center has an organized victim assistance program, which might know about support groups.

5. *Make sure that the client's family and community are being supportive.* That usually means that the family should be reasonably sympathetic, should be available to discuss the trauma and the circumstances surrounding it, but should not dwell endlessly on that subject. Perhaps the family should be a little watchful and solicitous, but should not become overprotective. The therapist should inquire how the client's peers are dealing with the client's trauma. Sometimes an adolescent victim is injured even more because his former friends shun him, not knowing what to say or do in his company. For instance, a teenager whose father was murdered was afraid to return to school. His fantasy was that his friends would be so squeamish about the subject that they would avoid hanging around with him. This boy was not looking for sympathy or for any special treatment, but just wanted his old friends to include him the way they always did. If this issue seems to be a problem, the therapist could suggest that the client invite two or three friends to a therapy session. The therapist and the client should discuss ahead of time the agenda for the meeting and what they would like to accomplish with it.

6. *Don't forget that the mind lives in the brain.* If the victim you are treating sustained a head injury, the mental symptoms you notice may have a neurological rather than an emotional etiology. If this is a serious consideration, you should consult with a neurologist who is interested in the subtleties of closed head injuries. You may also wish to arrange for neuropsychological testing, which would help you and the client understand his cognitive strengths and weaknesses.

7. *Medication may be helpful for some of the symptoms,* such as intense anxiety and sleeplessness and severe depression. However, don't expect medication to solve the issues that need to be worked out in therapy.

8. *Keep an open mind.* Be creative. Depending on the clinical situation you may want to consider hypnosis (to help a client recollect important experiences), relaxation training (for chronic anxiety), in vivo desensitization (for severe phobias), and community networking (when the trauma extends through several families). Consider cognitive-behavioral therapy (March et al.,

1998), especially if the PTSD was caused by a single-incident stressor.

9. *Don't create false memories of abuse.* It is bad enough that child maltreatment is so common and that traumatic memories are as painful as they are. One thing that therapy clients do not need is to start having false memories, i.e., memories of abuse when the client had not been abused in the first place. During 1985 to 1995 in this country there was a small epidemic of false memories of childhood abuse. Most authors who have studied this phenomenon think that overzealous therapists helped to create these false memories by using overly suggestive therapy techniques (Acocella, 1999).

The message of this chapter is that adolescents who have been victimized are able to overcome a tremendous amount of adversity. Sometimes they do it on their own, through conscious strategies or through unconscious mechanisms; sometimes they persevere through the active support of their families and their communities; sometimes they benefit from the relationship and the direction offered by a skillful therapist. It would be nice to know how to plan ahead and raise children to be survivors, but so far nobody knows exactly how to do that.

CHAPTER 15

adolescents in divorced and remarried families

Since about one-half of marriages in the United States end in divorce, there are many children and adolescents whose parents are separated, divorced, and perhaps remarried. Therapists who see adolescents will become involved in this issue in a number of ways:

- by treating adolescents whose parents divorced many years earlier, during their childhood, but whose emotional wounds are still tender
- by seeing adolescents whose parents are currently divorcing and trying to deal somehow with the needs of the client, the mother, and the father
- by being roped into legal disputes regarding custody and visitation, such as being subpoenaed to testify about where the child "really wants to live"
- by seeing blended families and other complex combinations of parents, stepparents, half-siblings, and step-siblings

When the frequency of divorce increased during the 1960s and 1970s, clinicians rapidly became aware of how seriously younger children were affected by parental divorce. It was thought that the sadness and other psychological effects lasted about a year and then the child would get over it and be back to his usual self. These earlier notions have been corrected. It is now generally accepted that adolescents as well as younger children may also be profoundly hurt by parental divorce. It is also understood that the injury may affect their development and especially their interpersonal relationships for many years.

Perhaps the most significant research to document the phenomenon and effects of divorce on children and adolescents has been the work of Hetherington and her colleagues (1985, 1998) and Wallerstein and her colleagues (1980, 1985, 1989). Judith S. Wallerstein and Joan B. Kelly (1988) designed and published a major longitudinal study of the responses of normal, psychologically healthy children and their parents to divorce. The children and adolescents and their parents were studied intensively at the time of marital separation and subsequently at eighteen months post-separation and at five years post-separation.

Wallerstein and Kelly identified "three broad, overlapping stages" of divorce. The first stage is the time when the parents' marriage becomes increasingly unhappy and culminates with the decision to divorce and the departure of one of the parents from the household. During this time the children are caught up in a family process that may be violent, extremely unhappy, and disorganized. During the second stage the family members "make efforts to solve problems and experiment with new lifestyles in new settings." The family members may become involved with new partners, new careers, and move to new communities. Life may be unstable and unsettled for several years. The third stage, which may occur several years after the divorce, is marked by a "renewed sense of stability." New patterns and new relationships become established and the family feels more secure. Of course, it is possible that this fragile sense of stability may be threatened by a subsequent parental divorce or other stresses. Wallerstein does not think of these stages as following mechanically one after another. Divorcing families may follow many variations and experience recurrent advances and regressions.

Parental divorce is not always a catastrophe for the adolescent. Sometimes the youngster realizes that divorce is better than the alternative. Sometimes parents manage to go their separate ways in an unusually civilized manner, with respect for themselves and also for the needs of their children. Whether the divorce becomes a gigantic problem or just a medium problem depends on a number of factors—such as the availability of supportive friends and relatives; the adolescent's ability to remain invested in his own issues and tasks, rather than in his parents'; and whether the divorce leads to further displacement, such as a move to a different school or neighborhood. However, the factor that really causes a divorce to be traumatic is how much the parents fight with each other and how much they involve the children in the fighting. What really hurts an adolescent the most is not that his parents now live in different homes or that he lives part-time in at least two households or that he has to accommodate to one or perhaps two stepparents. What really hurts is how much his parents fought with each other and chose to fight over him or through him.

IMPLICATIONS FOR PSYCHOTHERAPY

When helping the adolescent deal with parental divorce the therapist may find it helpful to be more directive than usual. For instance, the adolescent may find himself being sucked into the parental conflict. He may find himself actively allying himself with one parent and rejecting the other. He may feel it is his job to negotiate both big and little issues between the parents. Since the divorce makes his parents miserable, he may think it is up to him to make them happy. It usually is good advice for the teenager to stay out of the fighting and to try to be reasonably neutral. That may be hard to do since the parents may be campaigning for the youngster's vote and affection.

Therapists may see youngsters whose parents divorced many years earlier and who are now referred for a completely separate reason. In such a case the adolescent may appear open and nondefensive about the details and the circumstances of his parents' divorce. He is likely to say some form of "it really doesn't bother me . . . it was a long time ago . . . it doesn't matter anyway, since there's nothing I can do about it. . . ." The therapist who pursues this matter patiently will probably find that the divorce really does matter in many ways. The youngster is likely to feel resentment that most of his childhood and adolescence has been affected by his parents' agendas. He has repeatedly had to accommodate his schedule to theirs, to move from one household and community to another, to maintain a fragile relationship with the noncustodial parent through visitation, to adapt to stepparents, to give up the closeness and simplicity of an intact nuclear family, and so on.

Another issue for the therapist to keep in mind is that it seems to be extremely common for adolescents to recapitulate their parents' behavior when they get involved in serious dating relationships. This occurs in a general way, since adolescents and young adults whose parents divorced are more likely to think that they might divorce their own mates at some future time. The phenomenon of recapitulation may also occur in a very specific manner, such as a girl choosing a boyfriend who is similar to her father, the man her mother divorced.

Joyce and her mother and stepfather moved from Los Angeles to Boston for two reasons. The explanation offered to the general public was that the stepfather was able to take advantage of an attractive job opportunity in Boston. Privately, they all agreed that the real reason was to get away from Joyce's father in L.A. The father was described as an offensive alcoholic who had been physically abusive to the mother and who continued to harass her long after their divorce. The father reportedly was a showy, flamboyant man who worked on the fringes of the motion picture industry.

Joyce had been referred for evaluation because of school refusal and academic underachievement. She readily brought up an additional concern of her own—whether she should continue the relationship with her current boyfriend in Boston. It sounded like the bass guitarist of a rock band had selected Joyce to be his girl. He dominated the relationship and took advantage of her both physically and psychologically. When they dated Joyce had to drive because his license had been suspended after driving while intoxicated. Joyce said that she enjoyed being the girlfriend of a local rock star, but she disliked the boyfriend's drinking and his behavior and his control over her.

Joyce asked the therapist what she should do about the boyfriend. The therapist sidestepped the opportunity to play parent and said that the decision was up to her, although he was perfectly happy to discuss the situation with her. He did comment a couple of times how curious it seemed that her relationship with the boyfriend was so similar to her mother's relationship with her father. Over the weeks Joyce gave the boyfriend an ultimatum to stop drinking, broke up with him, got back together again, and eventually broke up for good. She thought that she had learned something from her mother's experience. In the meantime Joyce started dating a boy from her high school who was polite, kind, good looking, and rich. He seemed too good to be true. At that point the therapist started wondering to himself how much the new boyfriend would come to resemble the stepfather.

The issue for Joyce, like so many children of divorce, was to remove herself psychologically from the drama that had enveloped her parents. It was important for her to realize that she did not have to act out the roles that had been assigned by her parents, nor did she have to recapitulate her parents' relationship. Joyce used an expression which is not unusual for an adolescent girl who lives with her mother, in that she referred to "*our* divorce from Dad." When she used that phrase, the therapist took the opportunity to explore exactly what she meant by "our divorce." The therapist pointed out the obvious—that it may have been the mother's divorce, but it wasn't Joyce's divorce at all.

COUNSELING FOR DIVORCED PARENTS

In some cases it is better to intervene by working with the parents rather than with the adolescent. For instance, the therapist may meet with the divorced parents together on a regular basis, such as once a month. The purpose of these meetings is to discuss how the two divorced parents can raise their child in a cooperative and reasonable manner. The most important aspect of this kind of counseling is simply establishing good communication between the parents. For instance, the therapist would be the moderator for discussions on topics such as: clarifying exactly what the visitation schedule is going to be over Christmas vacation this year; figuring out how the youngster can be on his high school basketball team when he is living in two households; and comparing notes on Christmas presents, so that both parents do not get the son exactly the same 10-speed bicycle. In working with divorced parents, it is necessary for the therapist to structure the meetings and keep the parents on task. That is, it does not do anybody much good if the meeting degenerates into a session for digging up old grievances and of angry backbiting (Bernet, 1995).

It is well known that most custody and visitation disputes involve trying to take custody away from the other parent or trying to limit the other parent's visitation. In working with the divorced parents of adolescents, the therapist may find each parent trying to push more visitation and more responsibility off onto the other parent. Sometimes this phenomenon of the parents' trying to unload the responsibility for the adolescent is apparent to all. It's like O. Henry's famous story, "The Ransom of Red Chief." In other cases the process is more subtle, as in the following example.

    Two parents, who were both successful professionals, consulted a psychologist who was experienced in custody and visitation evaluations. The parents were in the process of divorcing and said that they both wanted to do what was best for their two daughters, Merrie and Melodie. Merrie was 16 and Melodie was 12. They both expressed the lofty view that they did not want to take the other parent to court and have a big custody battle, but they wanted to work out what was best for the girls in a rational and cooperative manner. They both were concerned that the girls were already distraught over the divorce and were manifesting symptoms. That is, Merrie was acting out sexually and Melodie was depressed and alluding to suicidal ideation.

    The parents explained the plan that they had already worked out between themselves. Both of them had important careers and both wanted to continue to work full time. They had agreed on a schedule in which both daughters would alternate between the mother's household and the father's household on a weekly basis. They had agreed on joint custody, so that each parent would be fully responsible for the girls when they were with that parent.

The psychologist interviewed Merrie and Melodie separately and also together. They both were angry and miserable. They strongly resented the arrangement in which they had to live in two different households. The girls did not seem distressed about the divorce itself. They had strong attachments to both parents and were perfectly willing to live with either their mother or father. What they resented was having to live half the time in each household. They had figured out that the parents were putting their own desires above the needs of the girls.

The psychologist met again with the parents and determined the basic issue in the case, that neither parent was willing to take charge of the situation and to provide a fulltime home for their daughters. Each parent really wanted the other parent to take full custody of Merrie and Melodie. The psychologist explained his assessment of the girls, that their symptoms were related to feeling rejected and being constantly displaced on a week-to-week basis. The psychologist was able to propose some other options for the parents to consider. One possibility was the traditional arrangement of one parent working only part-time and being able to raise the children. The parent who continued to work full-time would, of course, provide child support. A second possibility was for the girls to alternate on a much longer cycle, such as every six months or once a year. A third possibility was for each parent to be the primary parent for one child. That is, Merrie could live with the father and visit the mother; Melodie could live with the mother and visit the father.

What is instructive in this case is the disguise. The parents had colluded in a way to look like they were only concerned about the girls' welfare, i.e., for the girls to have a continuing relationship with both mother and father. In fact, what the parents really had in mind was to avoid providing what the girls really needed, a consistent household.

Virtually every adolescent whose parents are divorced is affected emotionally, although the impact may range from the subtle to the profoundly tragic. The saddest situations involve a youngster whose entire life has been shaped and distorted by the angry warfare between his parents. For these clients, the experience of divorce was comparable to the sudden loss of both parents by death. Then the "dead" parents come back to brutally browbeat the child, by cajoling and demanding the greater share of the youngster's love and devotion. Then the child falls into the impersonal and seemingly arbitrary machinery of the legal processes. When it seems like the warfare is subsiding, some fresh battle breaks out on a new front. At times, the momentum of this process is so strong that even the most skillful or sensitive therapist is helpless. What good is a brilliant interpretation when the client's life is picked over by a courtful of determined parents, stepparents, grandparents, attorneys, and judges?

Howie was a 14-year-old boy who was referred to a social worker because of his depression. School personnel had encouraged the father to seek professional help. Howie had been living with his father ever since his parents divorced when he was 8. The father had received custody because the mother had serious psychiatric problems.

On examination, Howie was a slender, anemic-looking boy who was extremely polite and deferential. His speech was remarkable, in that he consistently expressed himself in a soft whisper. When asked to try speaking as loud as he could, he would move up to a loud whisper. He explained in a cooperative manner that his entire day-to-day life consisted of two activities: school work and talking to his mother on the telephone. Although he was not particularly smart, Howie was extremely studious. He was well behaved and conscientious in the small rural school which he attended. His afternoons, evenings, and weekends were spent diligently attending to the details of his homework. The only departure from homework occurred each evening when he spoke to his mother for about an hour on the phone. Although one could say that he was unhappy and depressed, the best way to capture Howie's personality is to say that he was extremely inhibited and constricted emotionally. Although Howie's father was supportive and well intentioned, he could do little to interrupt the mother's intrusive, pathological, and almost symbiotic relationship with her son.

The social worker initiated individual therapy and also had monthly meetings with Howie and his father together. After a while, the therapist arranged for Howie to attend an adolescent therapy group. The social worker spoke to Howie's mother occasionally by phone. As more information was collected, it seemed that Howie had been a pretty normal youngster until his parents divorced. When the mother lost custody, she reacted by becoming much more intrusive and controlling of Howie. Howie came under his mother's control and he did not see any reason why he should stand up for himself or be more assertive with his mother or with anyone else.

This story has a sad ending. Perhaps Howie's mother felt threatened by the idea that the youngster might become more independent. In any case, she went back to court and once again sought custody. She thought that the therapist's notes would be useful to her case, so she subpoenaed them. The indignant social worker resisted the subpoena, since she felt the mother's intrusiveness should not reach into the confidential progress notes of Howie's therapy. But the therapist was not to prevail, since both the mother's attorney and the father's attorney had agreed that the progress notes should be released to the parents for their perusal. The point is that this youngster was victimized by his parents' psychopathology; by the warfare of divorce; and by the legal processes that presumably should be acting in his interests.

In some situations a mere therapist is able to advise and counsel the client, but is not able to make a dent in the enormous environmental factors that are causing or perpetuating the youngster's problems. In such circumstances, it may be appropriate to recommend that the adolescent attend a boarding school or live with relatives for a while, in order to remove him from the environment. The therapist may be limited to providing a supportive relationship, hoping that time will pass and that eventually the adolescent will be able to separate both geographically and psychologically from the destructive parents.

STEPFAMILIES AND BLENDED FAMILIES

Stepfamilies or remarried families come about in three ways. Nowadays, the most common stepfamily history is that two parents got divorced and then one or both of them remarried. Each time one of the parents remarries, a stepfamily is created. It does not matter whether the child is actually living with that particular parent. Regardless of where he lives, the child of divorced and remarried parents is part of two stepfamilies: his first family is his mother, stepfather, and himself; his second stepfamily is his father, stepmother, and himself. Stepfamilies also occur when a parent has died and the surviving parent remarried. A third possibility is that an unmarried mother might later marry a man other than the child's father, so you end up with a mother, stepfather, and child. In any case, stepfamilies have certain characteristics: the family members have experienced an important loss (of the former parent), whether through divorce or death; there is a new person in the household (the stepparent), who does not necessarily fit in perfectly well; from the child's point of view, there is a "missing" biological parent who is somewhere else; and the child frequently belongs to two different households.

A blended family is a kind of stepfamily which is more complicated. For instance, two divorced individuals may marry, both of whom already have children. You end up with both of the adults being a parent (to his own child) and a stepparent (to the spouse's child). Another way to create a blended family is for the parents of a stepfamily to have another child together. In that case, one child in the family still has a stepparent, while the other child has two biological parents in the same family. To add to the confusion, some people use inconsistent terminology and mix up stepfamilies with adoptive families and foster families.

Taking a family history may require a good deal of patience, in order to get all the relationships straight. At a bare minimum, it is important in evaluating an adolescent to get straight who are the people who live in the mother's household and who lives in the father's household. It may help to draw a family tree together.

> During an evaluation interview, the therapist asked an early adolescent how many brothers and sisters he had. The youngster thought for a moment and said "eight." The therapist wanted to make a list of their names and asked the client to tell something about each sibling, from the oldest down to the youngest, who was the client himself. The boy was agreeable to this and rather painstakingly created this list. It turned out, however, that the client only had two brothers and one sister. In his mind, he had also included two sisters-in-law; one brother-in-law; a stepbrother who lived in another household; and a half-brother whom he had never seen, who lived in a distant state with his mother's second husband.

Dr. Emily Visher and Dr. John Visher (1979) have collected a good deal of information about stepfamilies, which has been based on their own personal experience, their clinical experience as a psychologist and a psychiatrist, and their study of available research. The Vishers have pointed out a number of special issues that are confronted by adolescent stepchildren. For instance, adolescence is a time of separating from the nuclear family and establishing an independent role. But if both parents have remarried, "separating from two stepfamily households can be more difficult than separating from one, and confusion over role models can lead to added tension for an adolescent." The Vishers explained that there may be conflict between what is important for the new stepfamily (such as establishing a sense of family cohesiveness) and what is important for the adolescent (such as the loosening of emotional ties with the family). The Vishers suggest that a collision course "can only be averted if the adults in the teenager's life will allow the young person considerable personal space and distance from the family." Another issue for adolescent stepchildren is the sexual relationship between the newly married couple. In intact families children tend to be more oblivious to their parents' sexual behavior, while "in remarriages the adolescents are forced to recognize sexuality as a part of the adult relationship."

The psychotherapy of adolescents within the remarried family has been described by Sager (1983). He has taken the various tasks of adolescence and compared how that task would be addressed in a nuclear family and in a remarried family. We'll take one of these tasks as an example, the task of discerning and integrating those aspects of the parents' personalities that will be helpful to the youth as an adult. In an intact family, "the environment usually lends itself to have the adolescent express various aspects of the parents' personalities." In a remarried family, the adolescent is in a loyalty bind. That is, "when the adolescent expresses a positive connection to one parent, the other parent feels betrayed. In order to survive with this parent . . . , the adolescent may need to reject . . . all aspects of the other parent." And what about the role of the stepparent as a source of identification for the adolescent? Sager said that the youth's relationship with the stepparent may be a positive influence (in that "multiple identifications can offer the adolescent a variety of extended options") or a negative influence (in that "multiple identification can lead to identity confusion, especially if parental figures operate counter to each other and thrust different values and points of view on the adolescent").

Regarding this specific task of helping the adolescent identify with aspects of his various parents and stepparents, Sager offered some good advice for therapists. Basically, the youngster needs "to integrate a realistic picture of both parents, a picture that considers each parent's strengths and weaknesses." What that means in practice is for both parents to encourage the youngster to have a good relationship with both his mother and father. That is an optimistic goal and in some cases is unreachable. Sometimes the youngster has permanently foreclosed his relationship with one of the parents, usually the noncustodial parent.

THE PSYCHOTHERAPIST AND THE COURT

The work of therapy with adolescents in divorced and remarried families can be a complex process and a nerve-wracking experience. These situations become even more problematic when it looks like the parties, i.e., the parents, are heading for a trial at court. The purpose of the trial may be to address the terms of the divorce agreement, such as the division of property or the custody of the children. Even after the divorce, the parties may return to court if there is disagreement about the way visitation is being handled or if the noncustodial parent feels that there has been a change in circumstances that would justify a change in the child's custody. Whatever the reason, a long and angry trial becomes an experience which is at a minimum very difficult and at its worst quite devastating.

The child of the disputing parents is, of course, caught in the middle. Although parents and attorneys and court officials make some attempt to protect younger children from the inevitable loyalty conflicts, adolescents are more likely to be considered fair game. That is, one or both parents may freely discuss the legal issues and strategies with an adolescent child; may expect the youngster's total commitment to that parent's position; and may ask the adolescent to spy on or steal documents from the other parent. When attorneys get involved, they usually leave younger children alone and sometimes never even meet them. However, an adolescent who is involved in a custody dispute is likely to be interviewed by one or both attorneys and asked to come up with very derogatory facts and opinions about his parents. The judge may allow or perhaps expect an adolescent to testify about his relationship with his parents in an open courtroom. Of course, none of this does much for the ideal that the children of divorced families should have a good relationship with both parents.

In general, there are two different roles that a mental health professional may have in the context of a custody dispute. One possibility is that the psychiatrist or social worker or psychologist has been asked to perform an independent custody evaluation. Such an evaluation usually consists of an assessment of the youngster and of both parents and recommendations that are intended to be in the best interests of the child. The second possible role is that the professional has already been involved as the therapist of the child or of one of the parents. In these situations a professional may choose either to be the evaluator or to be the therapist, but it rarely works to try to do both at the same time. When a new client is referred for evaluation, it is helpful to clarify from the outset whether one's role is to conduct an evaluation for the use of the court or to conduct a clinical evaluation and provide therapy.

When Asked to Conduct a Custody Evaluation

Custody disputes are more likely to involve younger children, since most children are still young when the parents' divorce occurs. Another reason why adolescents are less likely to be fought over in court is that adolescents have a much greater say as to where they want to live. That is, a judge is probably going to listen to an adolescent who has a clear and rational preference to live with one parent rather than the other. Since the parents and the attorneys know that the adolescent's own choice is going to be the determining factor, they do not bother to take the matter to court. Many state laws instruct the court to take the adolescent's opinion into consideration, although it is still up to the judge to make the final decision.

Although infrequent, there are custody disputes that involve adolescents. The general method of conducting a custody evaluation has been described by Bernet (2002), Hodges (1986), and Weiner et al. (1985). Haller (1981) has discussed some aspects of the custody evaluation as they apply specifically to adolescents. The American Academy of Child and Adolescent Psychiatry (1997c) has published practice parameters on this topic.

When an adolescent custody dispute does occur, the noncustodial parent may be alleging that the custodial parent has chronically and habitually influenced the youngster to become emotionally alienated from the noncustodial parent. In evaluating such a case, it is obviously important to keep an open mind. If information is collected in a thorough and unbiased manner, the evaluator should be able to determine how the relationship between the teenager and the parents has evolved over a period of several years. You will find that there is no set or predictable answer to these cases. The teenager's alienation from the noncustodial parent may have been instigated by the custodial parent; may have resulted from the unpleasant or unkind behavior of the complaining noncustodial parent; or may have derived from the youngster's own mental defense mechanisms, completely independent of what the two parents have done.

Tom, Dick, and Harry were three brothers who lived with their mother after their parents divorced six years previously. During that time they continued to see their father, but grew more and more distant from him. A psychiatrist was asked to evaluate the family because the father was seeking custody of the younger boys, Dick and Harry. Tom was already 19 years old and was away at college. Dick was a junior in high school and Harry was in the 8th grade. The father felt that he should have custody because he could be a good role model for his adolescent sons. Also, he contended that the mother had actively indoctrinated the boys to dislike him.

The evaluation consisted of meeting with each of the parents individually for several hours in order to obtain a detailed history. The meetings were also used to assess each parent's psychological strengths and weaknesses and each parent's attitudes toward the boys. The evaluator also met with Dick and Harry individually on two occasions, once when they were brought to the appointment by the mother and once when they were brought by the father. The boys gave a consistent and reasonable account of their feelings for both parents. They felt that they had a secure, comfortable relationship with their mother. They were willing to spend time with their father, but they found him to be overbearing, somewhat pompous, and unnecessarily controlling and dogmatic. They could not think of any reason at all to live with the father on a continuing basis. Dick and Harry had apparently arrived at their opinions on their own, without any help from their mother. Furthermore, the father's personality style and behavior with the evaluator was similar to what the boys described. To give one example of the father's desire to control, he had purchased a video camera and instructed the boys to videotape themselves and some friends at the father's household in order to demonstrate that Dick and Harry were having a good time there.

In this case, the evaluator recommended that the family maintain the status quo, that the boys would continue in the mother's custody and that they should also continue their regular visitation with the father.

Visitation disputes that involve adolescents are also uncommon. Judges realize that it does not make too much sense to tell a teenager exactly how often he or she should visit the noncustodial parent. Adolescent visitation disputes seem to happen more often when the two parents live in distant states and the issue is whether the adolescent is required to visit the noncustodial parent at all. The typical story is that the youngster, with the approval of the custodial parent, does not want to visit the noncustodial parent at all over the summer and other vacations. The noncustodial parent would go to court and ask the judge to order the custodial parent to put the teenager on the plane and send him for the visitation. In situations like this, the court may seek an evaluation from a neutral mental health professional in order to determine whether visitation is truly in the youngster's best interests, whether or not he actually wants to go.

Being the Therapist During the Custody Dispute

It is not unusual to have an adolescent who is already in therapy at the point when the parents embark on a full-fledged custody dispute. It almost always happens that the custodial parent, who was the parent who brought the youngster for therapy in the first place, and the custodial parent's attorney ask the therapist to become actively involved in the custody dispute. That usually means for the therapist to write a report that recommends that the client stay with the custodial parent and perhaps testify at a deposition or at court. All of this raises the question, What should be the role of the adolescent's therapist when one of the parents has initiated a custody dispute and the court is intending to determine the client's placement? It is our opinion that a therapist who is already involved in a therapeutic relationship should emphasize his role of helping the adolescent express his feelings, explore his fantasies, and deal with the events that are occurring in his life. In most situations it will be preferable for the therapist to emphasize the importance of his work with the youngster and decline the invitation to become actively involved in the custody dispute. That is, the therapist should confine himself to helping the adolescent deal with the process and outcome of the custody dispute and should not try to influence the outcome of the dispute by sending written reports and testifying (Bernet, 1983).

The parent and the attorney usually feel very strongly that the therapist is the ideal person to testify, since the therapist has come to understand that adolescent client so well and since the therapist can be considered an expert in these matters. The therapist should take care not to succumb to the flattery. Although it looks superficially like the adolescent's therapist is the perfect person to testify in a custody dispute, he really isn't appropriate. For one thing, the therapist is almost certainly biased in favor of the custodial parent, even though he may try very hard to feel neutral. His biases make his testimony almost worthless. Furthermore, there are risks involved in testifying. For instance, the confidential nature of the therapy will almost certainly be violated if the therapist testifies. Also, the therapist's testimony may adversely affect any future therapy with his client. The therapist's active role in influencing the outcome of the custody dispute is going to change the therapeutic alliance with the client and will also change the relationship with the client's parents.

Even when the therapist's opinion is adopted by the court, the effect on the therapy itself can be damaging, as illustrated in the following example.

> A woman had custody of her 14-year-old daughter who had anorexia nervosa. There appeared to be a symbiotic relationship between mother and daughter and both of them felt it was important for the girl to be as perfect a child as possible. The girl was in therapy with a child psychiatrist, who was also seeing the girl, the mother, and stepfather in family therapy.
>
> The father sought custody of the girl and the case went to court. The child psychiatrist agreed to testify and recommended that custody remain with the mother and stepfather. The court upheld this recommendation. The mother took the psychiatrist's testimony as unequivocal endorsement of her values and her parenting skills, so she discontinued therapy. After all, a highly credentialed child psychiatrist had stated under oath that she was a good mother.
>
> The anorexic girl later required both medical and psychiatric hospitalizations, but the mother steadfastly maintained that her family had received the official stamp of approval.

Although it is usually best for the therapist to avoid active participation in these disputes, the therapist may wish to become involved indirectly by sharing verbal information with the independent mental health professional who is performing the custody evaluation. When the therapist is invited by a parent, an attorney, or a judge to participate actively and make recommendations regarding custody, the therapist can use the opportunity to explain the possible disadvantages of his taking that role. For instance, the attorney will probably have a better case if an independent psychiatrist supports his position rather than the potentially biased therapist.

CHAPTER 16
acute psychotic episodes

Acute psychotic episodes in the adolescent often present serious diagnostic and treatment problems to the clinician. They are also very dangerous to the adolescent client since the confusion and personality disorganization of the psychosis impacts on a personality that is still immature, largely bound to an immediate time perspective, and prone to impetuous action. The diagnostic process is further complicated by the client's difficulty in communicating clearly and frequently by an inability or unwillingness to cooperate.

The key issues in management of the acute psychosis in adolescent clients are proper diagnosis, use of appropriate psychopharmacological agents, utilization of inpatient care, and long-term follow-up care including family treatment.

DIAGNOSIS OF THE PSYCHOTIC STATE

The major conditions that present as acute psychosis during adolescence include schizophrenia; the manic phase of bipolar disorder; toxic psychoses, especially those induced by hallucinogens and amphetamines; and acute and brief confusional states that do not appear directly related to the major psychoses, such as the temporary decompensation of the borderline adolescent.

The schizophrenias are the best known psychotic illnesses of adolescents. It seems clear after years of clinical observation that there is no unitary schizophrenic process but rather a range of schizophrenias. This group of illnesses is complex and includes both "positive" and "negative" symptoms. The positive symptoms include confusion, delusions, hallucinations, and some-

402

times disorders of motor function such as catatonic excitement or retardation. The negative symptoms are related more to social withdrawal, poverty of emotional life, affective blunting, and general withdrawal from social interaction. As a rule of thumb, positive symptoms often develop with rapidity and in an emotional atmosphere of anxiety and acute distress. On the other hand, negative symptoms are often insidious in onset, develop over an extended period of time, and often seem to cause little distress to the client. As a general rule, positive symptoms are more responsive to treatment, are not incompatible with a reasonable long-term outcome, and frequently develop in youngsters whose premorbid adjustment had a number of positive elements. The insidious development of negative symptoms more often signals a chronic and somewhat unresponsive course of the illness.

Schizophrenia in adolescents may be difficult to recognize and diagnose because of the particular style with which the adolescent often presents regardless of the source of his discomfort (Masterson, 1967).

A 16-year old boy was being interviewed by a medical student.

Medical student: "Why are you in the hospital?"

Patient: "It's my parents. They're mad because I smoke a little dope and like to hang around with my friends."

Medical Student: "Tell me about your friends. Who would you say is your best friend?"

Patient: "God is my best friend."

Medical student: "No, I mean regular friends like people that you have conversations with."

Patient: "I have conversations with God."

Even this flagrantly delusional adolescent tried to present himself as typical and his difficulties as entirely developmental. In long-term follow-ups of adolescent clients with apparently delinquent or behavioral problems one usually encounters a significant percentage who eventually prove to be classically schizophrenic (Gossett et al., 1983; Hartmann et al., 1984).

Schizophrenic adolescents may also be misdiagnosed because

of the reluctance to recognize and admit that the young person has such a grave and potentially chronic illness. For example, Masterson (1967) found that most adolescents diagnosed as "adolescent turmoil" later proved to be suffering from serious and profound emotional disabilities. It is important for the clinician to look honestly at the client's condition so that prescribed treatment and long-term planning can be realistic and helpful.

Perhaps the most important alternative diagnosis to consider is that of manic stage of bipolar disorder. Many manic adolescents may present as behaviorally disordered or disorganized and psychotic. In the early stages of a manic episode when the client is still relatively euphoric and well organized, it may be difficult to differentiate the manic state from adolescent rebellion, delinquent behavior, and impulsive acting out. In some adolescents, mania may present as extreme, explosive rage. According to one long-term follow-up study, the diagnoses of mania may be more likely if one can observe or obtain a history of episodes of extensive and excited behavior alternating with other periods of lethargy (Gossett et al., 1983). In the later stages of a manic episode the client may be fatigued, frustrated, and increasingly disorganized. Paranoid thinking that borders on or is even frankly delusional is a relatively common occurrence. In addition, grandiose delusions may be utilized in an effort to maintain and justify the previously enjoyed euphoria. Thinking and communication may be disrupted so that the client may appear blocked, tangential, and irrational.

Some assistance in making the differential diagnosis between manic episodes and acute schizophrenic psychoses can be gained simply by sticking very closely to *DSM-IV-TR* criteria and maintaining a high index of suspicion regarding the possibility that the illness is manic. A careful mental status with attention to the question of whether or not any delusions or hallucinations are congruent with the client's mood can be helpful. A careful family history searching for evidence of bipolar illness in close relatives may also be helpful.

The differential diagnosis between schizophrenic psychoses and toxic psychoses induced by drugs is not as easy as one might think. The history of drug ingestion may be difficult to get and may be very inaccurate. Often family members are relatively unaware of the client's drug use since this is rarely shared openly with parents. The clients themselves may distort their drug use consciously but more often may simply not remember accurately due to the disruption of their perceptions of reality. The psychotic conditions themselves may have many features in common and at times may be basically indistinguishable. The paranoid psychoses that are experienced by some heavy amphetamine users are said to be identical to paranoid schizophrenia. The psychoses caused by phencyclidine (PCP) may also mimic schizophrenic reactions although the degree of frenetic excitement, undirected hostility, and failure to respond to environmental situations may give the accurate diagnoses. Insensitivity to pain and apparent demonstrations of unusual strength may be related to the strong analgesic effect of PCP. The psychotic episode may persist for several days. LSD (lysergic acid diethylamide) psychoses are also very similar to schizophrenia although the occurrence of delusions is less frequent in the toxic LSD psychoses. Visual illusions especially emphasizing color and light, are common. LSD psychoses normally do not last for more than a few hours. A high percentage of youngsters with toxic psychosis from hallucinogen intake seem to have predisposing tendencies toward psychotic disorganization.

DSM-IV-TR requires a duration of schizophrenic symptomatology for six months to justify the diagnosis of schizophrenia. If the condition has lasted longer than one month but not as long as six months the proper diagnosis is schizophreniform psychosis. The *DSM-IV-TR* also provides for a diagnosis of brief psychotic disorder when the psychotic decompensation lasts more than one day but less than one month. This may be referred to as a reactive psychosis if the mental disturbance follows and is apparently related to some clear external stress. Some of these brief psychoses may represent temporary decompensations of clients with borderline personality. It will be instructive to follow these clients over time in an effort to elucidate more clearly their basic psychopathology.

ANCILLARY TESTING IN PSYCHOTIC CONDITIONS

The biological tests for psychiatric disorders have received a good deal of attention over the past few years. One of the most common laboratory tests performed in the country is the urine drug screen. Since the urine drug screen is associated so automatically with evaluating clients for substance abuse, it might not occur to a clinician to request a urine drug screen when seeing a psychotic client. It is advisable, however, to arrange for a urine drug screen when evaluating an acutely psychotic adolescent in an outpatient setting, in an emergency room, or in the hospital. A variety of psychotic states can be caused by or enhanced by marijuana, hallucinogens, amphetamines, and cocaine.

On rare occasions mental changes, including psychosis, can be caused by neurological conditions such as tumors. For instance, some clients with temporal lobe pathology have auditory hallucinations, but are not otherwise psychotic. When clinically indicated, the evaluator should consider an electroencephalogram (EEG); quantitative EEG (qEEG), in which a computer maps the frequency of the brain's electrical activity; magnetic resonance imaging (MRI), which gives a detailed picture of the structures of the brain; or positron-emission tomography (PET), which provides information about the metabolic functioning of brain structures.

Psychological testing can be extremely useful in confirming the diagnosis of psychoses. Careful psychological testing can also discover evidences of organic toxicity or drug effects in youngsters with possible psychoses. It is important that testing be accomplished by a skilled clinician with broad experience in testing adolescents. Adolescent norms are different from those of the adult population.

DRUG TREATMENT OF PSYCHOTIC EPISODES

Adolescents who are acutely psychotic almost always require psychotropic medication, in addition to psychosocial interventions, such as supportive counseling, education regarding the illness for the client and family members, and sometimes inpatient treatment and partial hospitalization. Some of the medications currently in use are mentioned in the chart on page 408. For more detailed information regarding the use of psychotropic medications with adolescents, the reader is referred to practice parameters published by the American Academy of Child and Adolescent Psychiatry (1997a, 1998a, 2001), Coffey and Brumback (1998), and Popper (1998).

There are many antipsychotic drugs on the market. Current consensus suggests that these medications produce beneficial effects by reducing the activity of the neurotransmitter, dopamine, in the central nervous system. They are generally applicable to psychotic symptoms occurring in a variety of contexts, including schizophrenia, mania, and organic psychosis of any etiology. Properly utilized, these medications should be effective in the vast majority of adolescent psychotic clients. Among adolescents with schizophrenia, positive symptoms such as hallucinations, paranoid delusions, and agitation are more likely to respond to medication. Negative symptoms such as apathy, withdrawal, vague thinking, and impaired judgment are less likely to respond to antipsychotic medication.

After the schizophrenic adolescent is stabilized, maintenance medication is recommended because research indicates that this greatly reduces the likelihood of relapse. This is also true for youngsters who have experienced a serious episode of depression or mania.

It is generally agreed that drug treatment is most effective when it is accompanied by supportive psychotherapy. If hospitalization is required, it should include well-structured milieu treatment and group therapy that focus on reality issues and improving social interaction.

HOSPITAL TREATMENT OF THE ACUTELY PSYCHOTIC ADOLESCENT

As a rule acute psychotic reactions in adolescents require hospital treatment. The security, structure, and careful supervision of 24-hour inpatient care are usually necessary in order to deal

PSYCHOTROPIC MEDICATION

In some clinical situations, medication is an important part of the treatment plan, in addition to psychotherapy. This outline indicates some of the indications for psychotropic medication.

Severe Depression. The earlier medications used for depression were called tricyclic antidepressants. A newer class of medication for depression is the selective serotonin reuptake inhibitors (SSRIs), which apparently reduce depression by increasing the level of serotonin in the brain. For example, Prozac, Luvox, Paxil, Zoloft, Celexa.

Bipolar Disorder. A person who is manic or hypomanic may be treated with mood stabilizers including lithium preparations (e.g., Eskalith, Lithobid) and anticonvulsants (e.g., Tegretol, Depakote).

Schizophrenia and Other Psychoses. The earlier medications for psychoses were phenothiazine tranquilizers (e.g., Thorazine, Trilafon) and similar agents (Haldol). The newer products are called atypical antipsychotics (e.g., Risperdal, Zyprexa, Seroquel, Clozaril).

Obsessive-Compulsive Disorder. Symptoms are reduced by Anafranil and by the SSRIs.

Severe Anxiety. Tranquilizer medication such as Valium, Xanax, and Buspar may be used on a short-term basis. Paxil and other SSRIs reduce the anxiety of social phobia.

Attention-Deficit/Hyperactivity Disorder. Symptoms are reduced by psychostimulants, such as Ritalin and Dexedrine.

Violence and Aggression. If the youngster is paranoid, an antipsychotic may help. If there is an affective component, lithium or Tegretol may be helpful. SSRIs reduce aggressive feelings, presumably by increasing the level of serotonin in the brain.

with the client's overwhelming anxiety. The adolescent who is undergoing a psychotic disorganization experiences extreme terror regarding the loss of the sense of self, the loss of control over his actions, and a general loss of the sense of meaning. The structure and safety of an inpatient setting are reassuring. Although it may be possible at times to manage acute psychotic reactions through rapid tranquilization, this procedure is not recommended on an outpatient basis except as an emergency alternative when hospital care is not available.

Hospital care is useful not only for initial and severe episodes of disorganization but as a brief intervention to avoid recurrences and relapses in more chronic cases. Many adolescents with relatively chronic psychotic illnesses can be managed on an outpatient basis if hospital care is quickly available at times of stress or regression.

Adolescents with psychotic reactions can respond positively to a wide range of hospital settings. As a rule they should be hospitalized in a psychiatric unit if at all possible, since the bizarreness of their behavior and their potential for agitation may be disruptive to an adult or adolescent medical unit. As a corollary, it is best for the psychotic adolescent to be treated in a center where staff are experienced in dealing with this type of client and are calm and confident in their approach. There may be some advantages to treating youngsters of this kind in a mixed adult and adolescent psychiatric population since adults are often more tolerant of the psychotic adolescent's severe regression and inability to function effectively in a group. Psychiatric units that are specialized for adolescents with a broad range of psychiatric difficulties may deal effectively with psychotic adolescents except at those times when their population is heavily weighed toward behaviorally disordered adolescents. Antisocial adolescents may be very critical of psychotic youngsters. In some cases they make scapegoats of the more disturbed youngsters and may treat them in ways that can be quite harsh.

The phenomenon of post-psychotic depression that has been described in adult clients is quite marked in the adolescent population. Although no one knows for sure whether this is primarily a psychological reaction to the experience of the psychotic episode, simply another stage in the psychotic process, or partially related to medication response, it does present additional treatment problems. Antidepressant medication seems to be relatively ineffective and the client's response to any treatment approach is slow. Based on personal clinical experience, the key elements seem to be patience, understanding the frightening impact of having lived through a psychotic episode, and a tactful acceptance of the client's reluctance to get involved in life again for fear of "rocking the boat." Gentle but firm and persistent encouragement toward greater activity is necessary over an extended period of rehabilitation.

AFTERCARE

Most adolescents who have psychotic episodes need extensive aftercare treatment. According to Gossett et al. (1983) continuation in psychotherapy following hospitalization was positively correlated with good outcome at long-term follow-up.

It is surprisingly difficult to obtain cooperation with aftercare plans in spite of the seriousness of the illness, possibly because both the family and the client would like to put this frightening episode behind them and are reluctant to be reminded of the painful period by continuing in psychiatric treatment. In addition, psychotherapy often includes concomitant psychopharmacological treatment and compliance with medication regimens is notoriously poor.

FAMILY TREATMENT

Family psychotherapy is crucial to the care of the psychotic adolescent. During the hospital stay the parents' cooperation and understanding of the treatment regimen are essential to ensure their support of the treatment program. Since the psychotic adolescent often has great difficulty in making proper choices for himself, the family's understanding and cooperation become essential. Parental cooperation is more likely to be gained by recognizing the tremendous stress involved in caring for the psychotic adolescent than if parents are viewed as basically etiological in the development of the illness. Even if distortions of the family process are important in the creation or maintenance of the psychotic adjustment, these issues are better addressed after the psychotic episode is stabilized. As discussed in chapter 7, "Family Therapy," judgmental assumptions regarding family function are usually counterproductive.

Families often require long-term treatment to support them in the continuing effort to take care of a severely disturbed adolescent. The parents of a psychotic adolescent have a very complex and confusing task thrust upon them. On the one hand, at times they may have to closely supervise and manage the behavior of a highly disturbed person losing contact with reality. On the other hand, they often need to support the developmental tasks of adolescence, encouraging their child to take a more independent and responsible role. These developmental tasks are usually particularly difficult for adolescents who have sustained psychosis. Often their confidence and security are undermined and residual chronic symptoms impair judgment, impulse control, and social skills. The parents need to learn to evaluate these complex factors in cooperation with the therapist and to seek the delicate balance between overprotection and inadequate supervision and support.

Supportive therapy, specific therapy for an individual parent, or marital therapy may be indicated on a prescriptive basis. Education is usually important. Referral to network support groups such as the Alliance for the Mentally Ill may be tremendously helpful in supplying both emotional support and practical suggestions regarding techniques for coping with this highly stressful family challenge. With tolerance, patience, and sustained educative efforts on the therapist's part, parents can sometimes gradually develop important skills that minimize the disability imposed by psychotic illnesses on maturing adolescents.

CHAPTER 17

chemical dependency in adolescents

The widespread use of psychoactive drugs exploded on the American social scene about 40 years ago. Many aspects of the pattern of drug use have shown changes and shifts. Although there have been occasional drug abuse epidemics, there is a surprising stability in the baseline frequency of drug use. About 1970 there was an epidemic of heroin use in this country. The cocaine epidemic reached its peak around 1985. There was an epidemic of marijuana use among adolescents in the late 1970s, when 10% of high school seniors were using marijuana on a daily basis; daily use was down to 2% by 1991, but subsequently went up again and down again. Between 1980 and 2000, there were periods of high use and low use of marijuana, amyl nitrite, hallucinogens, cocaine, stimulants, and sedatives among adolescents. But the use of alcohol by adolescents has remained almost constant—that is, about 80% of high school seniors had "more than a few sips" of alcohol. Alcohol is the substance most frequently abused by adolescents; marijuana is the most frequently abused illegal substance (Johnston et al., 2000).

Since substance abuse is a major national issue, much information is available to teenagers, parents, and therapists regarding drugs, statistics, and treatment programs. Information is available from the Office of National Drug Control Policy (www .whitehousedrugpolicy.gov) and the Partnership for a Drug-Free America (www.drugfreeamerica.org). The Substance Abuse and Mental Health Administration (SAMHSA) of the Department of Health and Human Services conduct the annual National Household Survey on Drug Abuse, which provides estimates of the prevalence of use of a variety of illicit drugs, alcohol, and tobacco based on interviews of people aged 12 and over.

In the 1960s the prevalence of drug usage was linked directly to social discontent. Many social critics decried what they saw as America's colorless and crushing preoccupation with cognitive skills at the expense of human passion and spontaneity (Keniston, 1965). Members of the "establishment" were viewed by the '60s youth movement as soulless robots who had sacrificed their humanity for efficiency and technological competence, accepting the bauble of material affluence as a tinseled consolation prize. This negative judgment on "technocracy" led to a questioning of the sufficiency of reasoning and rationality as bases for planning human life (Leary, 1968). For a period of time particularly on the West Coast the hippie movement was viewed as quasi-religious phenomena in which psychedelic drugs served a central ritualistic and sacramental role.

Of course, most of the people who previously were involved in the hippie lifestyle later chose to live a more ordinary life. Some of their choices are so ironic as to be comical. One could understand a metamorphosis to politician, but stockbroker? Perhaps more important than esoteric social issues is the simple fact that American culture has traditionally been very accepting of the state of intoxication. Not only has popular fiction, especially in movies and television, depicted alcohol use as highly normative behavior, it has tended to depict sobriety as dull or even worthy of suspicion. Often the inhibited hero or heroine finds meaningful emotional experiences, romance, and the joy of life only when drunk or high on marijuana.

Although the government's war on drugs has waged many battles and won some of them, the fighting isn't over. Substance abuse continues to be endemic in America and this heavy usage certainly extends to adolescents and even latency age children.

DEFINITION OF CHEMICAL DEPENDENCY

It is obvious that many adolescents use drugs, even fairly heavily, without apparent long-term negative consequences. This has led to an effort to define some drug use as social or recreational, some drug use as experimental, and only a portion of drug use as psychologically problematic. The difficulty, of course, is that there is no clear line between these categories of drug use.

The accepted definition of dependence in the past has been the occurrence of withdrawal symptoms on cessation of drug intake. This is a limiting and clinically inadequate guide, especially in the adolescent population. Adolescents are reluctant to describe unpleasant subjective feelings, prone to transmit them into action and explain them on the basis of their current surroundings, and certainly reluctant to admit that their uncomfortable feelings are related to the drug use that they maintain to be harmless. In addition, they are physically highly resilient, having been using drugs for a relatively short time compared to adult addicts, and therefore probably do not have as intense physical reactions as are seen in the older population. Therefore an adolescent may be seriously drug dependent without showing clear withdrawal symptoms.

From a practical point of view the adolescent may be considered to be chemically dependent when drugs become more important to him than human interactions or when his emotional interactions with others show clear evidence of a loss of sensitivity and empathy. This deterioration in human relationships will be even more clear when we discuss the psychology of chemical dependency. Serious chemical dependency is the likely result whenever an individual finds intoxication to be a superior substitute for human interactions in maintaining emotional stability and psychological comfort. The preference for chemicals over human contacts may be obscured to some extent by an apparent friendliness with a wide range of other people. Indeed, the adolescent's investment in being with "friends" may be so strong as to almost parody normal adolescent group membership. Unfortunately, these groups are primarily organized around the group experience of drug use. They emphasize a shared secretiveness, preoccupation with maintenance of drug supplies, a spurious sense of superiority to the "straight world," and unfortunately, frequent personal and sexual exploitation of group members.

Obviously, as the pattern of chemical dependency becomes

STAGES OF ADOLESCENT SUBSTANCE ABUSE

The use of alcohol and drugs by teenagers follows a predictable pattern. This outline has been adapted from Jaffee (1998) and is consistent with *DSM-IV-TR*.

Stage 1: Experimental, Recreational, or Social Use. For youngsters at this stage, education and counseling are appropriate, since it usually helps for them to learn about the realistic dangers of drugs and alcohol. Parents also need counseling, primarily to learn how to set appropriate limits.

Stage 2: Substance Misuse. These teenagers are actively seeking the pleasurable experiences of using alcohol and drugs, since they have learned that misuse helps them escape from feelings of frustration, depression, and inadequacy. Use is primarily on weekends. In addition to education and counseling, these youngsters need individual and group psychotherapy, family treatment, and an abstinence contract. These adolescents and their parents need specific, clear rules that provide for negative consequences for all drug and alcohol behavior.

Stage 3: Substance Abuse Disorder. These teenagers are preoccupied with using alcohol and drugs, which are used during the week. The peer group is other users. There are significant impairments in functioning. They are very secretive and deceptive. In addition to the treatment strategies mentioned above, these adolescents require an AA or NA program, cognitive and behavioral treatment, and a partial hospital program.

Stage 4: Substance Dependency Disorder. Tolerance has developed. Withdrawal symptoms may be present. Using has taken over the adolescents' lives, despite knowledge of severe consequences. Hospital or residential treatment is usually necessary.

more chronic and severe, more obvious symptoms of psychological deterioration appear including a loss of interest in previous constructive activities, academic difficulties, grossly irresponsible behavior, and even self-neglect or physical symptoms related to excessive drug use. It is important to remember that the chemically dependent adolescent's move away from people and toward drugs is initially subtle and difficult to detect. It may first appear as a slight loss of sensitivity and empathy in relationships with family and straight friends. Later it becomes more obvious as the adolescent steals from the family to obtain money to purchase drugs and treats family members as enemies if they oppose drug use in even mild terms. It is only when the illness is advanced that the adolescent may reach that desperate and chilling situation in which the youngster will use anyone in order to ensure an uninterrupted supply of a favorite drug. This progression almost always includes a pattern of growing alienation from parents and other family members that is often accompanied by intense hostility, intimidation, and cold rejection. To some extent these attitudes arise from the inner feelings of guilt that the adolescent is attempting to externalize as he provokes the parents and family members to treat him harshly, thus justifying some of his destructive behavior. However, these attitudes of hostility and disinterest also represent to some extent the psychological truth that the adolescent no longer needs the parent since the drugs and drug companions have become the most important source of comfort, solace, and pleasure. The parents are enemies with potential power to interfere with the adolescent's crucial sources of emotional supplies.

ETIOLOGY OF CHEMICAL DEPENDENCY

The etiology of drug use seems to have both biological and psychological elements. There is convincing evidence of a hereditary element in the vulnerability to addiction, especially clear in the case of severe alcoholism. The evidence for this hereditary tendency is not merely from statistical research but is confirmed by the everyday experience of clinicians who note a very high frequency of chemical dependency in the family tree of adolescents with serious drug problems. No one knows for sure how much this outcome is related to learned behavior based on the children's observation of parental drug use and how much is a purely genetic vulnerability. However, there is convincing evidence based on studies of children of alcoholics who were adopted at birth into nondrinking families which supports the likelihood that there is a pure biological element (Weinberg et al., 1998).

Other elements of family dynamics seem important in the genesis of substance abuse in adolescents. Families in which parental drug use disrupts basic family rituals seem more likely to produce a chemically dependent offspring. It has also been noted that a history of sexual and/or physical abuse in childhood occurs with great frequency in populations of youngsters with chemical dependency. Obviously, neither of these family patterns are independent of parental substance abuse since heavy drug use would impair a parent's ability to maintain family rituals and is also a factor in increasing the likelihood of child abuse.

It is obvious to most adolescent practitioners that many elements of the adolescent developmental phase may tend to encourage drug experimentation and even passing serious interest in drug usage. The adolescent's dependency needs coupled with his shame about dependence on others make the self-controlled gratifications of drugs and the capacity for self-comforting very appealing (Marohn, 1983). In addition, the adolescent's turn toward a peer culture, deliberately defined as deviant from adult norms, is also a factor in encouraging drug use. In a very literal sense, the adolescent "sins" to test the penalties and to diminish his terror before his internal inquisitor. Classic adolescent rebelliousness that is actually directed against the internal parental images in the form of the primitive superego may paradoxically increase interest in drug use. Deliberately breaking the law serves to externalize internal states of guilt, focusing the adolescent's concern on real life authority representatives such as parents and policemen whom the adolescent hopes to elude. Even if he is caught, the punishment has some limits, unlike the formless dread provoked by the primitive superego.

It is also important to remember that not all drug-using

adolescents are alike by any stretch of the imagination. Some drug-using adolescents seem primarily depressed, lonely, and inhibited. Drugs for them seem to be a vehicle for acceptance, lessening of inhibition, and amelioration of painful social anxiety. Another large group of substance-abusing adolescents seem more sociopathic, grandiose, and arrogant. They use drugs to maintain their sense of excitement, euphoria, and power over themselves and others. A final group of adolescents seem merely dedicated to self-destruction. They use drugs in such a massive, random, and nondiscriminating manner as to regularly threaten their very existence without showing any concern for their own survival, much less their well-being. It seems obvious that we are dealing with a complex interaction of genetic vulnerability, life experience, social expectation, and individual biological responses to specific doses and frequencies of the various chemical agents readily available to adolescents these days. Each case must be carefully evaluated in order to understand the specific youngster's vulnerability to chemical dependency so that gradually we may better understand the basic patterns in this serious illness.

Serious substance abuse is often comorbid with other serious psychiatric conditions, so this possibility should be considered in conducting a clinical assessment. (American Academy of Child and Adolescent Psychiatry, 1997b). Many of the youngsters who are heavy drug users fall within the group of youngsters described earlier as those with "malignant" defenses related to severe impairment of their sense of competence. After their chemical dependency and addictive behavior are treated directly, their evaluation and treatment often resembles that described in chapter 4.

THE PROGRESSION OF CHEMICAL DEPENDENCY

Chemical agents will never provide satisfactory answers for the problems that young people experience because of two inherent characteristics of psychoactive drugs. First of all, all drugs have a number of effects on the body. Those that are desired are seen as the drug's pharmacological action while those that are undesired are classified as side effects. Some of these side effects are merely unpleasant while others may actually damage the body.

The second problem with drug use is that the body gradually develops tolerance to the desired effects of any drug. Ever larger doses are required to produce the same effect if the drug is taken with any frequency. Consequently the higher dosage produces more and more of the unwanted effects, many of which are unaffected by tolerance, including those that are harmful. Even the most dedicated drug users have to eventually recognize, if only briefly and sporadically, that the drugs they are taking are producing negative effects. For example, any adolescent who uses large amounts of marijuana and alcohol will eventually begin to recognize that memory and capacity for concentration are impaired. The adolescent who uses cocaine regularly will eventually experience some withdrawal depression, damage of the nasal mucosa, or simply severe personal and practical problems occasioned by the escalating costs of the habit.

The negative side effects are not merely biological. Regular drug use also impairs the development of ego skills by lowering signal anxiety, obscuring the consequences of behavior, and by producing an illusory sense of well-being without any need for achievement. Interestingly enough, it is not simply "serious" skills that are adversely affected. Adolescents who use drugs regularly and in large amounts blunt their ability to have fun and to find pleasure in everyday activities. The drug dependent adolescent often has few interests or hobbies and indeed is unaccustomed to engaging in any leisure activity except in the intoxicated state. The common final pathway for all of these negative psychological effects is a state of chronic boredom that is only imperfectly relieved by periodic intoxication.

Human relationships, particularly with adults, are severely impaired by heavy drug use. Partly because of guilt over their behavior and partly because of the actual opposition of caring adults, these adolescents come to view most concerned adults as enemies since they might potentially interfere with access to the desired chemical. The adolescents' relationships with others become increasingly dishonest, manipulative, and hostile so that the need for the drug is actually increased since there is diminished opportunity for meeting needs through interpersonal relationships.

The factors just outlined explain why drug dependency is almost always a progressive illness characterized by an increasingly blind and desperate dependency on drugs with a narrowing and ever more intense preoccupation with drug issues. In a curious kind of way, these adolescents have recreated the infantile dependency that they so feared and so desperately were trying to avoid. Rather than becoming omnipotent and self-sufficient, they become increasingly helplessly dependent on the availability of the needed drug and also on people who will supply the agents to them. At this point in the illness there is an astonishing degree of denial. Although the most casual objective observer would see the person's life as massively impacted by blind dependency on the drug, the client maintains that this is totally untrue. Often the client will stop using the drugs for a period of time to demonstrate that he can "take them or leave them," but, of course, he always returns to the same pattern of heavy drug use in a relatively brief period. This classical pattern of denial probably represents an emergency measure designed to defend the person against the recognition of the true state of affairs. An honest viewing of the actual situation would be simply too devastating. These adolescents would have to recognize that rather than being omnipotent they have become helplessly dependent on someone else. Of course, they would also have to recognize that they would have to give up drugs to change this state of affairs. That is an unacceptable idea because at this point they regard the drugs as their only practical source of support, pleasure, and self-esteem.

CHARACTERISTICS OF ABUSED SUBSTANCES

The popularity of specific drugs may vary over time. In addition to the process by which a particular individual selects his own drug of choice, broader sociological and economic factors may affect a drug's availability and popularity. These factors include issues such as the supply of a drug in a particular community; the influence of adolescent role models; and the "marketing" of new drug products, such as designer drugs and crack cocaine.

Caffeine and Nicotine

These substances are mentioned because they are the most extensively used drugs in our country. It is also notable how unpredictable adults are regarding a common issue such as adolescent smoking. Lawmakers and school boards come down on this issue along a very long continuum from very permissive to very restrictive. Some high schools have designated smoking lounges for students; many schools don't encourage smoking, but just look the other way; some schools go to the trouble to actively discourage smoking by teenagers; and in some communities it is illegal for minors to have tobacco in their possession on school property and teenagers are routinely arrested and charged.

Alcohol

Alcoholism is a progressive disease that can start at any age. It clusters in families and most likely has a biological, inherited predisposition. Although it takes 5 to 15 years for an adult to become an alcoholic, an adolescent can become an alcoholic in 6 to 18 months of heavy drinking. Adolescent alcoholics obviously have greatly impaired social and academic functioning. The physical effects of chronic heavy drinking (such as dementia, delirium tremens, cirrhosis, impotence, and so on) will catch up with them in later life.

Cannabis

Marijuana is the most widely used illegal drug. Among adolescents, its use is associated with tobacco use. That is, adolescents who smoke cigarettes are five times more likely to also use marijuana. In addition to the desired effect of euphoria, marijuana has side effects of impairing short-term memory, concentration, and fine motor skills. It is very dangerous to smoke pot and drive. The "amotivational syndrome" has been hashed over many times, so to speak. There are two schools of thought: one, that chronic marijuana use leads to apathy and loss of ambition; the second, that apathetic individuals with low ambition are the people who are likely to become chronic marijuana users.

Cocaine

Many people feel that cocaine use is the most important issue facing our government today. Even people who consider themselves jaded to the media have been impressed by drug busts netting several tons of cocaine at one location; the epidemic of drug-related murders in many cities; and other evidence of an illegal billion dollar industry. Our adolescent clients have been swept into this calamity in several ways—as users, as family members of addicted individuals, and as drug dealers.

Cocaine is a white powder extracted from the leaves of a common tropical plant, Erythroxylon coca. In addition to being a local anesthetic, it is a very strong stimulant that gives a very strong illusion of limitless power and energy. That's why they say, "cocaine lies." Up until recently, cocaine was almost always used by snorting the white powder through the nose or by dissolving it and injecting it with a needle.

Crack cocaine is made by mixing ordinary cocaine with a solution of baking soda in water. A chemical reaction occurs in which cocaine is changed from a salt into a freebase crystalline alkaloid. The result is that crack can be smoked and it is absorbed through the lungs as a vapor, which means that it has an immediate powerful effect. Both regular cocaine and crack cocaine are highly addictive. Not only does it make the user feel extremely good, the rebound effect as the drug wears off makes the user feel extremely bad. The only way to keep feeling good is to keep using. In addition to making the user feel bad, "cocaine kills" by causing heart attacks and heart failure.

Opiates

Opiates or narcotics are a class of drugs that are used legitimately for pain-reduction and cough-suppression. Naturally occurring opiates such as morphine and heroin come from the Asian poppy plant. Other narcotics, such as Demerol, have been synthesized and are used medically as analgesics. Although opiate addiction is more likely to occur in adults than in adolescents, there have been flurries of heroin abuse, overdose, and deaths among adolescents in some communities.

Hallucinogens

The classic hallucinogen was lysergic acid diethylamide (LSD). It causes visual hallucinations and other perceptual distortions, which some people find frightening and other people find pleasurable. Phencyclidine (PCP) is also considered a hallucinogen, although it usually causes agitation and paranoia rather than pretty hallucinations. Clinicians were very concerned about these drugs in the 1960s and 1970s, but they are used less frequently now by adolescents. Hallucinogens used to be considered quite trendy among teenagers, but now they are mentioned by youngsters who are socially out of the mainstream. It is good to be aware, however, that LSD and PCP can be manufactured with simple equipment and chemicals that are fairly easy to obtain, so sometimes they are manufactured and sold locally.

Inhalants

Inhalants are breathable chemicals that produce mind-altering vapors. Most of the inhalants that are abused are actually manufactured for some other purpose, such as gasoline, glue, paint thinners, nail polish remover, cleaning fluid, hair spray, and White-Out. Some inhalants, such as amyl nitrate and butyl nitrate, are packaged in small breakable capsules or bottles that are intended to be broken and the contents inhaled. Inhalants are much more popular among children and adolescents than among adults. While small amounts cause a sense of lightheadedness and stimulation, high doses cause unconsciousness and sudden death.

Sedatives

Sedatives, hypnotics, or "downers" include tranquilizers and sleeping pills, that is, barbiturates (such as Seconal), benzodiazepines (such as Valium), methaqualone (Quaalude), chloral hydrate (Noctec). Sedatives are dangerous because they cause both physical and psychological dependence. Larger doses cause unconsciousness, respiratory depression, and death. It is particularly dangerous to combine sedatives with alcohol. Rohypnol is a sedative that is not marketed in the United States, although it is available in other countries. It has achieved notoriety for its use in date rape, since it is added to a woman's alcoholic beverage to reduce her inhibition to engage in sexual activities.

Amphetamines

Dexedrine and other forms of "speed" can also be abused. Symptoms include anxiety, agitation, and paranoia. Dexedrine and Ritalin are sometimes prescribed for adolescents with attention-deficit/hyperactivity disorder. It is unlikely that an adolescent would become dependent on these medications if they are taken in low to moderate doses for the purpose of relieving an attention deficit. It would be dangerous, however, for an adolescent to take high doses for the purpose of getting a buzz. "Ectasy" is a methamphetamine derivative that has been called a designer drug.

Anabolic Steroids

Anabolic steroids refers to testosterone and various synthetic analogues, which have legitimate medical applications. They are also widely used by men who want to increase muscle mass and strength. High school athletes sometimes obtain steroids for this purpose, either with or without the knowledge of their coaches. Males who use steroids may develop testicular atrophy, sterility, and short stature (because of premature closure of bony epiphyses).

THE DIAGNOSIS OF CHEMICAL DEPENDENCY IN ADOLESCENTS

The primary factors interfering with the diagnosis of chemical dependency in adolescents are the client's denial, the tendency of the family to deny the illness, and the chemically dependent adolescent's suspiciousness and animosity toward adults. The result of all these factors is that adolescents typically minimize their drug use or even lie about the role that it plays in their life. At the same time the adolescents usually give indirect evidence of the problem to therapists and other caring adults since they are basically concerned about themselves and retain some hope that someone will be able to help them. They may broach the subject of drugs indirectly through discussion of friends who use drugs or through theoretical discussions about the hypocrisy and overreaction of the adult world to adolescent drug use or in some of the other ingenious ways that adolescents introduce topics into discussion. At other times their approach is more direct—they come to therapy sessions drunk or high on marijuana. Of course, sometimes the diagnosis is made when a urine screen for drugs produces positive results.

The denial of parents is almost as striking as that of their teenagers. This pattern of denial is based on a complex family adaptation to the chemical dependency pattern—a pattern of behaviors known in the chemical dependency treatment field as "enabling." Enabling behavior on the part of the family refers to those methods of approaching the chemically dependent adolescent which permit or even encourage continued drug use. They include not only denying the existence of the problem in the face of rather obvious evidence of serious drug involvement but also rescuing the youngster from consequences of the drug dependent behavior and in other ways subtly accepting the youngster's self-identification as an addict. The dynamics behind this pattern are complex and may include some elements of family system pathology that require deviant behavior in the child in order to maintain family homeostasis. In other cases the pattern of enabling appears to be a self-protective response to the stress created by the presence in a family of an addicted individual since chemically dependent people often behave with callous disregard for the rights of others and coldness toward other family members. Enabling, in these cases, is designed to simply pretend that this heartbreaking behavior isn't happening. As one mother put it, "I was a happy little blind lady." In any case, one cannot totally count on families to recognize and identify adolescents who need treatment for chemical dependency problems.

Diagnosis is fairly obvious in the full pattern of advanced chemical dependency which includes a change in associates, deterioration of adaptive functioning in school and at home, and wide variations in mood, communicativeness, and level of consciousness. When these are accompanied by recurrent obvious episodes of intoxication the diagnosis of chemical dependency alone or in combination with other psychiatric problems needs to be made even if the adolescent and the family minimize or attempt to deny the importance of these occurrences.

Diagnosis can be more difficult in other cases where the youngster manages to avoid some of the more clear-cut external manifestations of the problem behavior and instead functions as a "closet addict." In these instances one's suspicion should be roused by more subtle signs such as a loss of interest in previous constructive activities such as academics or extracurricular activities and organizations. These changes are usually rationalized as a simple change in interest patterns, but if they are not replaced by other constructive activities, this explanation should be viewed with some skepticism. Intense degrees of felt and expressed anger toward parents in the face of relatively benign behavior on the part of the parents should also be a warning sign of the possible presence of drug involvement. As mentioned earlier it is sometimes possible to pick up subtle evidence of heavy drug use from the nature of the adolescent's response to the psychotherapeutic process itself.

If suspicion is aroused, the issue can be addressed as any other resistance or problem in the therapeutic process. That is, the question can be raised as to whether appropriate progress can be made in treatment in the face of regular drug use on the part of the client. Since the client, due to denial, is likely to be unaware of the negative impact of the drug usage, it may be necessary to apply considerable pressure utilizing the leverage of the treatment contract and one's expert status as a psychotherapist. It is wise to avoid a parental or superego approach to the issue and it is unwise to issue ultimatums unless the parents are in total agreement and everyone is prepared to back up the ultimatums with firm insistence on hospitalization or residential treatment if the youngster continues to use drugs. Instead, it may be useful to suggest to the client that a period of one month of abstinence would be a useful way to determine whether the concerns about drug use are justified. Obviously if the client is unable to stay away from drugs for even one month this might demonstrate to him the intensity of his attachment. On the other hand, when youngsters do completely give up drugs for a month there are often changes in their ability to concentrate, plan for their future, modulate affect, and be aware of their own feelings, which are obvious to them. This trial period gives a good basis for continuing careful attention to this issue as the psychotherapy goes on.

ISSUES IN THE TREATMENT OF ADOLESCENTS WHO ABUSE SUBSTANCES

The outpatient treatment of these youngsters is complicated by their difficulty in forming a strong attachment to the therapist. As described above they are, in a sense, more attached to their drugs of choice than human beings when chemical dependency reaches advanced stages. This almost phobic resistance to dependent attachments will certainly extend to the therapist. In the emotional life of the severely chemically dependent adolescent a therapist is merely a means to an end and manipulation and exploitation of the therapist is the common event.

An intelligent 17-year-old boy hospitalized after a near fatal accidental drug overdose had been in psychotherapy for over a year on an outpatient basis. Early in his hospital treatment he bragged of convincing his outpatient therapist to prevail on his parents to allow him access to the area of the city where he obtained his drugs. He felt no remorse for this and held an attitude of amused contempt toward the therapist whom he felt he had outsmarted.

The therapist who treats a youngster with a serious drug problem needs to recall that these youngsters have found human dependency extremely uncomfortable and unrewarding. They avoid their anxiety about dependent relationships by constantly trying to prove that they are smarter than adults and that they have no need for their help. As a rule, abstinence must be a requirement for successful treatment of these youngsters. If abstinence can be obtained, underlying feelings of depression, yearnings for support, and feelings of anxiety may come to the fore for psychotherapeutic management. However, it is usually not possible for the therapist to compete with the instant and complete solutions to these problems which the drugs provided, at least in the early and middle phases of usage. One must expect to be compared unfavorably with the drug life. This is particularly true as the youngsters regain some of the benefits of abstinence. As their physical and emotional vigor returns, they tend to forget the negative effects of drug use and may idealize the pleasant and gratifying aspects of intoxication. Clients in treatment for severe chemical dependency will periodically be tempted to use drugs. These temptations come from both yearnings for remembered gratifications and urges to self-medicate in the face of some of the emotional discomfort created by life or indeed by the psychotherapeutic process itself.

In outpatient therapy it usually is necessary to provide some external support to assist in maintaining abstinence in the face of these temptations. Regular random monitoring of drug urines and membership in support groups such as Alcoholics

Anonymous (AA) and Narcotics Anonymous (NA) that encourage continuing abstinence and remind members of the dangers of drug use are useful and perhaps necessary adjuncts to outpatient psychotherapy. Family support and resolution of enabling behaviors in the family system are also crucial.

INPATIENT TREATMENT

Obviously, there are many seriously drug-involved youngsters who cannot maintain abstinence on an outpatient basis even with the support of family and treatment procedures such as those described above. For these youngsters, treatment must be started in a controlled, drug free environment where a period of abstinence can be ensured while they gain at least beginning control over their compulsive drug use.

There are several ways to organize an inpatient treatment program for adolescents who abuse drugs and alcohol. Two approaches that are quite different from each other are the medical psychiatric treatment approach and the recovering-community treatment model. The medical psychiatric treatment approach started as an attempt to treat adolescents who abuse substances on units that are actually intended for youngsters with psychiatric conditions. The recovering-community treatment approach for adolescents is derived from the adult-oriented "Twelve Step" Alcoholics Anonymous program. These two models have different philosophies and therapeutic practices. For instance, the traditional psychiatric approach would involve dealing with the anxiety that is created as the youngster gradually gives up his denial of his condition; in the recovering-community model, the client may be confronted vigorously about his denial. A traditional medical psychiatric program is more likely to include individual therapy and medication; the recovering-community model emphasizes the power of group therapy and a highly structured educational component. The staff in a traditional psychiatric program are more likely to allow a greater degree of freedom of expression, while recovering-community staff may insist on a very strict dress code and rules about hairstyle. In both models family therapy is considered very important.

It is likely that the best treatment approach for adolescent substance abusers is neither of these models, in their original pure form. King and Meeks (1988) described two inpatient programs where they attempted "to merge the expertise of the recovering community with the psychological and developmental insights of adolescent psychiatry. . . ." The treatment included components of a traditional psychiatric inpatient treatment program (daily formal group psychotherapy, prescribed individual therapy, special education, and a variety of activity therapies) and also components of the recovering-community treatment approach (the Twelve Step program and didactic and process-oriented meetings with substance abuse counselors). The family involvement was intensive.

In both outpatient and inpatient treatment the trained drug counselors, particularly those who have previously been addicted themselves, are an invaluable aid to the treatment process. They provide both an empathic understanding of the joys and horrors of chemical dependency and a seismographic awareness of the manipulations and self-delusions that characterize the illness. They do not usually need to see gross evidence of a return to drug use in addicted adolescents because they recognize the very subtle evidences of the mind set that usually precedes or accompanies a relapse. Their comfort in confronting the adolescent drug addict is usually higher than therapists who have not been drug addicted, both because they have the sense of having "been there" but also because they usually have a conviction of the correctness of their assessment that "straight" therapists find very difficult to maintain in the face of blatant denial.

FAMILY THERAPY AND INDIVIDUAL THERAPY

The role of family therapy has already been mentioned. Obviously, intensive family therapy focusing on enabling patterns is very important if the adolescent is to be strongly encouraged to find the strength to persist in new lifestyle patterns. If the family continues to encourage and permit chemical dependency, the adolescent's own temptations to return to drug use will find ready support and likely expression. Adequate therapy for parents of this kind includes major educational efforts to be sure that they understand the nature of chemical dependency, peer support (especially from other families who have successfully dealt with the problem), and appropriate therapy for family system psychopathology that might lead to a need for a scapegoated child.

If these special parameters of therapy are carefully attended to, the chemically dependent youngsters will gradually turn away from compulsive drug use. As a rule, as they give up drug use and abandon the fantasy that drug use in the future will solve their problems, the basic underlying psychopathology will tend to become more obvious and more available to traditional psychotherapy. This change is accompanied by the development of a genuine transference relationship and a strong human attachment to the therapist. At this point in treatment the client's motivation to maintain this relationship and explore it becomes a very important element in avoiding drug use. Since the therapist is now more important than the chemical substance, the balance has shifted and traditional psychotherapy becomes possible.

However, it should be remembered that a youngster who has been chemically dependent may continue to find the prospect of chemical solutions attractive in the face of unusual stresses, especially those that relate directly to therapy. The time of termination, for example, may be fraught with risk for these youngsters as they deal with the major loss of giving up the therapist. Vacation times and periods of disillusionment with the therapist also raise the specter of relapse as a treatment complication. This reality should be recognized by the therapist and also conveyed to the parents so that these episodes of return to drug use can be seen for what they are rather than being misdiagnosed as a simple continuation of the drug pattern in which the therapist has just been conned for a longer period than usual.

CHAPTER 18

medical and neurological issues

Therapists who work with adolescents frequently have the opportunity to use medical consultation as well as their own understanding of biology in evaluating and treating their clients. It is easy to find many interfaces between the emotional, physical, and medical lives of these youngsters. These issues don't end after you take the medical history and wrap up the evaluation, since many of the adolescent's concerns in therapy may be expressed in physical or medical terms. Treating adolescents is work that requires assessing and integrating and taking seriously much medical and neurological data.

How many ways can there be for medical topics to come up with adolescents?

On a developmental level, every adolescent is intrigued with and concerned about the physical changes that occur during and after puberty. Many times the teenagers who end up in therapy have not been able to ask the right questions and get the right answers through the usual channels that most adolescents use to get information about sexuality and physical development—such as peers and parents and family doctors. These inhibited and conflicted youngsters may be able to get basic information from a therapist, as long as the therapist is not inhibited and conflicted himself.

Actually, adolescents are curious about many parts of their bodies in addition to the parts related to sex. A youngster who has a serious learning disability may find it both educational and reassuring to have somebody explain how her brain works. It may be that a teacher or psychologist tried to do that when the disability was documented back at age 7, but it may not be until age 14 that the client has the mental and conceptual ability to follow a simple explanation. An adolescent may find herself very interested in learning about her genetics, as in inheritance. As her own sense of identity unfolds, she may become very interested in sorting out what parts of her personality may have been inherited and what parts were learned and what parts she created on her own. Although the main job for the adolescent therapist is not to teach a biology class, he may frequently find his own professional education a valuable resource in communicating with these youngsters.

A therapist can learn a lot about a youngster by the way the patient deals with both acute and chronic illness. An acute medical condition may be an opportunity to get some mileage out of one's courage and daring. That is probably the dynamic that has perpetuated the nickname of "the kissing fever" for several generations of mononucleosis-prone adolescents. A teenager who has broken a leg playing football or on a ski trip usually looks pretty happy when his or her buddies visit in the hospital, especially when they bring pizza. On the other hand, a chronic and debilitating condition may be the basis for much resentment, anger, depression, and social withdrawal.

Many neurological and medical conditions have prominent emotional and behavioral symptoms. Maybe it is true that "anybody who sees a psychiatrist should have her head examined." The adolescent therapist should at least be wondering whether his patient's psychological symptoms have some kind of neurological basis. Neurological conditions that should be kept in mind range from the common (complex partial seizures or temporal lobe epilepsy) to the unusual (Tourette's disorder) to the rare (frontal lobe cyst) to the downright scarce (Klein-Levin syndrome). These diagnoses are mentioned just to make a point and the list is not meant to be comprehensive. Some of these conditions will be discussed later in the chapter.

To mention another way that medical topics come up in therapy with young people, the therapist needs to know the physiological effects of alcohol and abused drugs and other substances that adolescents put in their bodies. If your patient is a self-proclaimed expert on cannabis, it is good to know enough about the topic to judge whether the patient really knows what she is talking about. When the patient is taking psychiatric or other medication, the therapist has an important role in educating the patient about both therapeutic effects and side effects. For instance, it may be important to ask a young man who is taking antidepressant or antipsychotic medication whether there has been a change in his ability to have an erection or ejaculate. He might be very concerned about it and it probably would not occur to him that this change in his potency is related to the medication that is supposed to make him feel better.

The adolescent therapist will find many ways in which psychological and physical phenomena interact. Perhaps the most important are conversion disorder (in which unconscious conflicts cause the loss of or alteration of physical functioning, but without permanent physical changes in any organ) and psychosomatic conditions, such as asthma and peptic ulcer disease (in which psychological factors are related to the initiation or exacerbation of demonstrable organic pathology). Anorexia nervosa is also a good example of an illness in which both the physical and the mental aspects must be given equal attention, so we will use it later in this chapter to illustrate our message.

PSYCHOSOMATIC ILLNESS

DSM-IV-TR does not use the term psychosomatic disorders, but uses the terminology "somatoform disorders." The somatoform disorders include: somatization disorder (characterized by multiple physical complaints not fully explained by a general medical condition); conversion disorder (symptom affects voluntary motor or sensory function); pain disorder (psychological factors have important role in initiating or perpetuating pain); hypochondriasis (preoccupation with having a serious disease), and body dysmorphic disorder (preoccupation with imagined defect in appearance).

The classic psychosomatic disorders described by Franz Alexander (1950) included hypertension, asthma, ulcerative colitis, peptic ulcer, neurodermatitis, rheumatoid arthritis, and hyperthyroidism. Although we no longer think that each type of illness is caused by specific unconscious conflicts, we continue to make use of the Alexandrian notion that psychosomatic conditions arise from the interaction of multiple variables. That is, a psychosomatic disorder may arise when the person has a biological predisposition to the particular disorder, a susceptible or vulnerable personality style, and experiences a significant psychosocial stress. The psychosomatic conditions that are most likely to occur in adolescents are respiratory disorders, such as hyperventilation syndrome and asthma; gastrointestinal disorders, such as irritable bowel syndrome, peptic ulcer, regional ileitis, and ulcerative colitis; obesity; and chronic pain, especially abdominal pain.

There is not a consensus among psychotherapists regarding the treatment of psychosomatic disorders. Thompson (1988) advocated an integration of medical and psychological treatments. For the treatment of peptic ulcer, for instance, he would endorse the use of medication to block the production of gastric acid and also the use of psychotherapy to address psychological conflicts and maladaptive defenses, if those conflicts are obviously present in that particular client. Other authors (Wilson and Mintz, 1989) emphasize psychoanalytic treatment of the underlying personality disorder. They claim that the premature removal of psychosomatic symptoms could lead to another substituted psychosomatic symptom, addictive disorder, or other psychological symptoms.

The adolescent with a psychosomatic disorder may resist seeing a therapist or a counselor because she thinks that somebody is trying to tell her that her illness is all in her head. She has been experiencing very real epigastric pain and has even seen a very real x-ray of a peptic ulcer after her upper GI series, so nobody is going to get off easy by saying that she has some kind of emotional problem. During the course of the initial evaluation these youngsters usually appreciate a straightforward explanation of how psychosomatic symptoms occur. It may be as simple as something like this: "Your ulcer is caused partly by physical factors and partly by psychological factors. You may have been born with some kind of predisposition for this kind of illness. You probably have a particular gram-negative bacterium, Helicobacter pylori, in the wall of your digestive tract. Your smoking two packs of cigarettes a day may be aggravating the ulcer. We also know that you have put yourself under a great deal of stress recently, since you have the idea that you need to get straight A's in order to become valedictorian of your graduating class. And the fact that your parents got divorced last year hasn't helped. We need to take all of these factors into consideration in order to help your duodenum heal up and stay healed. We need to work together—your pediatrician will be prescribing some medication; I am going to help you figure out how to avoid putting yourself under so much pressure; and you can help yourself by not smoking so much."

The following case illustrates how the recognition of the underlying conflict can help in the resolution of a psychosomatic illness.

Sandra was a 17-year-old high school senior who was referred by the social worker attached to the medical clinic of a large private hospital. The girl had several episodes of low abdominal pain which interfered with her attendance at school and at times was severe enough to cause her to collapse to the ground. A comprehensive medical and gynecological evaluation had been completely normal. The gynecologist considered scheduling the patient for endoscopy, because he thought that the pain could be caused by endometriosis. He decided to postpone that procedure and recommended instead that the patient have psychiatric evaluation and treatment.

During the early part of treatment it became apparent to the therapist and to the youngster that she was a dedicated, extremely responsible, and overly conscientious person who identified greatly with her father. Sandra was the best student in her school in her particular area of interest, which involved math and science; the father was an engineer who was tops in his field, to the point where he occasionally had testified before Congressional committees. It was hard for her to reconcile her wish to be dutiful and another wish to have a good time, like other high school students. Furthermore, the more she identified with her father, the more arrogant she became at school and the more she distanced herself from peers. She set extremely high standards for female peers and for boy friends, which few kids were willing to put up with.

The low abdominal, vaguely gynecological pain appeared to have several psychological determinants. It probably started with the patient's awareness of ordinary menstrual cramps. Sandra was a very intense and driven youngster who seemed to exaggerate the pain in the same way that she exaggerated other emotions and attitudes. The intense pain and the episodes of collapsing seemed to occur at times when some important event was about to occur, which could either turn out to be a great success for Sandra or else what she perceived as an utter failure. Finally, the pain seemed to protect her from becoming physically involved with her boy friend.

Sandra's treatment was a combination of individual, group, and family meetings. The therapist's observations helped Sandra understand that these pains could have a number of interesting explanations and that it would be worthwhile for her to figure out which ones might apply to herself. She learned that it is really nice to have fun some of the time and that a person does not have to be successful in absolutely everything. Finally, she needed permission to identify with some aspects of her father's personality, without being obligated to become a reproduction of him. It also seemed to help for Sandra to graduate from high school and to move on in her life. When she was seen after a semester of college, she was much happier and was not having abdominal pains.

ANOREXIA NERVOSA

The eating disorders that occur in adolescence include anorexia nervosa, bulimia nervosa, and obesity. Both anorexia and bulimia have occurred more often in recent years. The increasing incidence may be related to cultural factors, such as the general popularity of fitness and thinness. Perhaps more of our children become preoccupied with food because our society enjoys an abundance and an unusual variety of food. Anorexia occurs more often in the middle and upper classes, which are the people who patronize gourmet supermarkets and are barraged with advertising and commentary on nutrition, good food, bad food, and dieting. A child growing up in this culture is going to get the idea that there is something very important about food and what you do with it.

Anorexia and bulimia have been portrayed many times in television shows, movies, and in printed media. As a result, adolescents are much more aware of these conditions. It used to be that an adolescent female would have to discover completely on her own that self-starvation can provide enough primary gain and secondary gain to make it worthwhile. Now all she has to do is read a few magazines or watch popular television shows to learn that anorexia and bulimia are options to be considered.

DSM-IV-TR requires four criteria for the diagnosis of anorexia nervosa:

- Refusal to maintain body weight at or above a minimally normal weight for age and height. That is taken to mean keeping one's weight at least 15% below what would be expected.
- Intense fear of gaining weight or becoming fat, even though underweight.
- Disturbance in the way in which one's body weight or shape is experienced. For instance, the person may feel that one area of the body is "too fat" even when obviously underweight.
- In females, absence of at least three consecutive menstrual cycles when otherwise expected to occur. This may be either primary or secondary amenorrhea.

There are other symptoms that commonly occur in youngsters with anorexia. Usually the illness starts with a period of purposeful dieting, which may be undertaken in order to be more attractive, more fit, or a more competitive ballet dancer or wrestler. During the course of dieting the patient may become preoccupied with issues related to food, such as calories and the size of portions and she may achieve a detailed but flawed knowledge of nutrition. She may start exercising in order to lose even more weight, which can take the form of getting up early in the morning to complete a regimen of calisthenics or jogging.

The most striking psychological symptom is the way the client distorts her image of herself. Although her cachexia is obvious to family members and her entire physical education class, the patient will insist that she is still a little too chubby in certain places. High school students are aware of this aspect of anorexia nervosa and they sometimes make the diagnosis. In one case, a physical education class sat on the floor and refused to play any more volleyball until the teacher and the school nurse agreed to refer an anorexic student for a professional evaluation.

Clients with anorexia nervosa have characteristic personality traits. These youngsters frequently have been obedient, compliant, and overly conscientious. They have often been hard working in school with good academic records. They were popular with parents and teachers and other adults, but did not succeed at the important adolescent task of forming peer friendships. In general the anorexic adolescent seems to prefer the role of an asexual, dependent, younger child with intense ties to parents, rather than forging ahead into adolescence. At times the condition of anorexia nervosa occurs in conjunction with other neurotic, psychotic, or personality disorders.

Anorexia and bulimia have been studied extensively from both a physiological and a psychiatric point of view. The etiologies of both conditions probably start with a genetic predisposition. In twin studies of anorexia and bulimia, the concordance rate for monozygotic twins was much greater than the concordance for dizygotic twins. It has been suggested for anorexia nervosa that there is an abnormality in the hypothalamus and dysregulation of neurotransmitters, such as serotonin, norepinephrine, and dopamine. Recent reviews have been published by Steiner and Lock (1998) and Halmi (2000).

It is possible, of course, to conceptualize this illness in psychological and psychodynamic terms. Bruch (1973) organized the psychological aspects of anorexia and concluded that three criteria should be fulfilled to establish the diagnosis. First, there must be a convincing disturbance of body image, to the point of being delusional. Second, there is a distortion in the accuracy of bodily sensations. For instance, these youngsters do not interpret accurately feelings of hunger, fatigue, discomfort, and sexuality. Third, these patients are concerned with being in control, so they find elaborate ways to accomplish that goal.

For the practicing clinician it usually does not matter whether the physiological or the psychological pathology occurred first, since the therapist still needs to address both aspects of the illness. It is most useful to collaborate with the youngster's pediatrician. If outpatient treatment is indicated, the pediatrician or her nurse can meet weekly with the patient to monitor her weight and to give advice about how to select a healthy diet. The therapist can provide the individual and family therapy and can consider using psychotropic medication. In some cases it may be preferable for separate therapists to handle the individual and the family meetings. If the pediatrician and the therapist(s) communicate periodically, the patient will experience a truly coordinated and holistic approach to this complex illness.

In evaluating a patient with anorexia nervosa the therapist must consider the treatment options that are available and make recommendations to the youngster and her family. Hospitalization should be considered for youngsters who are more seriously disturbed, as indicated by an unusually great loss of weight; by severely abnormal electrolytes; by the patient's lack of insight and denial of the seriousness of her fasting; by her lack of willingness to gain weight; and by the lack of family support.

If it appears that outpatient treatment should be tried, the therapist then needs to choose between seeing the patient himself and referring the patient to an outpatient treatment program intended specifically for anorexics. A youngster who has persistent distortions of body image and who does not appreciate the seriousness of her condition may do better in an eating disorders treatment program, since the other group members and the educational component of the program will tune her into the gravity of her illness. However, youngsters who have a "mild" case of anorexia nervosa can be treated in a general outpatient practice. For instance, these patients do well in a heterogeneous adolescent therapy group, in which the patients are dealing with common adolescent issues. It seems to help these patients see that they are struggling with some of the same feelings and conflicts as other teenagers.

One way to approach the outpatient treatment of a patient with anorexia nervosa is to combine the modalities of individual psychotherapy, group therapy, and family therapy. For instance, the patient could have two appointments a week. On one day each week she could come to an adolescent group. The second appointment could alternate between an individual therapy session and a family meeting. It is usually helpful to address the issue of weight on a regular basis, but then spend most of the therapy on other issues.

It may also be helpful to develop a contract that includes the patient, the parents, the pediatrician, and the therapist. For instance, suppose the girl's usual weight should be 120 pounds, but she has been fluctuating between 90 and 95. The parents and the doctors could decide that the absolutely minimal acceptable weight will be 105 pounds. It is arranged for the patient to be officially weighed at the pediatrician's office once a week, perhaps on the way to the individual therapy appointment. If her weight is 105 or above, it is agreed that for the following week she herself will be in control of what she eats and her activity level. If her weight is less than 105, for the following week the parents will take over control, by selecting the menu, dishing up her plate, monitoring her consumption, and regulating her level of exercise.

That may seem like a simple behavioral contract, but it should be done in a way to communicate important messages. For one thing, the patient and her parents are not supposed to argue about her eating and her weight all week long. If the family is cooperative, the patient's weight is discussed only once a week. Second, the therapist may need to explain that it is a worthy ambition to find ways to get your parents off your case and out of your hair. This contract expresses in a concrete manner that the anorexic patient can be more grown up and more self-sufficient by simply reaching a weight of 105, in which case her parents will leave her alone for a week.

The reader will immediately point out that the typical patient with anorexia nervosa may simply want to be an immature, dependent child rather than an adolescent striving for independence. That's the whole point! The patient will be insisting that she is willing and ready to take responsibility for herself, but then she'll let her weight slip below 105, which will cause the parental infantry to assemble. The discrepancy between her words and her actions will give you something to talk about in therapy.

EPILEPSY AND RELATED SYNDROMES

In patients with epilepsy it can be a challenge to sort out the psychological phenomena from the neurological phenomena. In some cases it may not be possible at all. There are several ways that psychological and neurological symptoms can be related and can be confused with each other:

- Adolescents with epilepsy can have the same feelings as other patients with a chronic illness, such as secondary depression, apathy, and resentment.
- For some reason, suicide attempts and actual suicide occur more often in epileptics than in the general population.
- Whatever caused the epilepsy could be causing other neuropsychiatric symptoms, such as attention-deficit/hyperactivity disorder.
- Some forms of seizure activity, such as complex partial seizures or temporal lobe epilepsy, may be manifested by prominent mental and behavioral symptoms.
- Even when the seizure itself is not occurring, during the interictal period epileptics may have characteristic personality traits and mental symptoms that could be mistaken for psychiatric conditions.
- Some patients may have pseudoseizures, either purpose-

fully or through unconscious mechanisms, which may look a whole lot like real seizures.

- The chronic use of some anticonvulsant medications, especially barbiturates, may create symptoms such as mental dulling.

Temporal Lobe Epilepsy

Of all the epileptic disorders, temporal lobe epilepsy has interested and intrigued psychiatrists the most. Temporal lobe seizures have also been called psychomotor seizures or limbic seizures. Neurologists frequently use the terminology proposed by the International League Against Epilepsy—in that nomenclature temporal lobe seizures are called complex partial seizures if loss of consciousness is involved and simple partial seizures if consciousness is maintained.

A typical temporal lobe seizure begins with an aura; the subsequent ictal episode is usually marked by unconsciousness and a variety of automatisms; and the postictal period follows. If the patient is unconscious during the seizure, he will be amnesic for what he may do during that time. The patient usually manifests automatisms, which are repetitive, stereotyped movements, such as lip-smacking or scratching or fingering a button or a utensil. Both the aura and the not-remembered part of the seizure tend to be brief, highly stereotyped, and unique for a given patient. The first observable event tends to be the interruption of ongoing activity. But if the seizure discharge is only slight, the patient may continue doing what he was doing and yet have no memory. He may look "conscious" to the casual observer because he is still sitting or standing or walking about. One patient continued to ride a bicycle during a temporal lobe seizure.

Dramatic mental symptoms can occur during the aura and the postictal period associated with temporal lobe seizures. The patient may spontaneously experience strong emotions, including a sense of doom or intense anxiety or, for that matter, intense happiness. As the seizure activity spreads through the association areas of the temporal cortex, the patient may experience visual or auditory hallucinations. General mental confusion, tiredness, and a feeling of depression usually mark the postictal period.

The Interictal State

It is easy to understand the occurrence of mental symptoms as the electrical discharge starts at the epileptic focus and moves through other parts of the brain. What is more interesting and more pertinent to psychiatry is that patients with temporal lobe epilepsy have characteristic mental experiences and personality traits during the interictal state, when they are not having a seizure at all. David Bear and other authors (Bear and Fedio, 1977; Bear et al., 1984) have described an epileptic personality that occurs in patients with temporal lobe seizures, which is characterized by hyperreligiosity, hyposexuality, circumstantiality, and hypergraphia. The idea is that these personality traits are caused by the seizure focus. That is, during the interictal state the seizure focus is not strong enough to precipitate a full seizure, but it is strong enough to influence and mold nearby parts of the brain. Fyodor Dostoyevsky was a famous epileptic who illustrates Bear's syndrome. Dostoyevsky certainly was preoccupied with religious and philosophical issues; what the neurologist would call hypergraphia, other folks call great literature.

While the personality and behavior changes may be subtle in nature, the mood changes may be more striking and more serious. Overall the patients tend to be hyperemotional and intense. Hyperactivity and catastrophic rages have been described in children and adolescents with temporal lobe epilepsy. Episodic outbursts of anger or rage, which contrast with an otherwise good-natured and affectionate disposition, may occur. Parents may comment on the "Jekyll and Hyde" nature of the youngster's behavior. The anger is often mixed with a depressive mood, and such dysphoric episodes and even prolonged depressions may be the most disturbing symptoms. Treatment with carbamazepine (Tegretol) can be helpful.

Other psychiatric syndromes occur in patients with epilepsy, especially temporal lobe epilepsy (Ferguson and Rayport, 1984; Mendez, 2000). Epileptic patients have presented with a schizophrenia-like syndrome and a bipolar-like syndrome. It is important for the adolescent therapist to realize that these syndromes are part of the epilepsy and not a separate illness. It is hard enough for the teenager and his family to cope with the burden of a chronic illness such as epilepsy. It would be an unnecessary hardship to lay on them the conclusion that the youngster has two serious illness, that is, epilepsy and also schizophrenia. An epileptic patient who also has paranoid, delusional, or hallucinatory symptoms may be treated with anticonvulsant medication and perhaps with a trial of an antidepressant or antipsychotic medication.

Julie had experienced generalized tonic-clonic seizures and complex partial seizures since early childhood. Although she was taking anticonvulsant medication, she continued to have a seizure two or three times a year. Julie came for psychiatric evaluation because of depression, poor peer relationships, and academic underachievement. Julie became actively involved in an outpatient adolescent psychotherapy group and she benefited from it. Her psychiatrist also saw her individually every other week and had family meetings about once a month.

After about a year of therapy Julie was functioning better in school and was more assertive with peers. One day during an individual therapy meeting she greatly surprised her psychiatrist by explaining in a matter-of-fact manner that the captain of the basketball team was in love with her, but that he was having a hard time expressing his true feelings to her. Julie said that she could use her thoughts to control the boy. For instance, if she were in the cafeteria line in back of him, she could mentally induce him to take a brownie instead of apple pie. She also felt that she had a special relationship with the boy's mother, who could communicate with the patient because she once had been a guidance counselor.

At the next family meeting the psychiatrist asked Julie if

she wanted to tell her parents about her feelings about her friend, the basketball player. She readily did so. Her parents asked a few questions and elicited, in a rather sensitive manner, a complicated delusional system. This schizophrenia-like mental disorder had apparently started during the course of psychiatric treatment, since the patient described it as a new development and it was news to both the therapist and to the parents. The psychiatrist prescribed an antipsychotic medication and the delusional thoughts abated.

Julie continued to improve in her functioning in school and also in her peer relations. As she felt more confidence in herself, Julie decided to exercise her sense of independence by discontinuing both the anticonvulsant and antipsychotic medications she had been taking. She did that without telling anybody, including her therapist. After a few weeks it became obvious that something was wrong, because she was having seizures and she also was ruminating again that the basketball player had a romantic interest in her. After the situation was investigated and the medications were reinstated, both the seizures and the delusions were controlled.

Temporal Lobe Syndrome, but No Seizures

It seems clear that adolescents who have temporal lobe epilepsy sometimes have personality traits and psychiatric symptoms which are caused by the seizure focus and its electrical activity. But is it possible for a patient to have temporal lobe personality traits without actually having epilepsy? In other words, is it possible to have temporal lobe dysfunction which is severe enough to have a chronic neurochemical effect on that part of the brain, but which is not severe enough to cause actual seizures? That idea is worth keeping in mind, especially when the adolescent's condition has been refractory to traditional treatments.

Kenny, age 14, was referred for inpatient psychiatric evaluation because of extraordinarily severe temper tantrums. Kenny would become frustrated over some minor disappointment, go into a violent rage that might last an hour, and be quite remorseful when it was over. He had cooperated in outpatient exploratory psychotherapy, which had no beneficial effect on the severe tantrums.

This youngster had a family history of temporal lobe epilepsy in a paternal uncle. He also had a history of neonatal hypoxia. Since Kenny had been impulsive and distractible as a child, the pediatrician thought that he had attention-deficit/hyperactivity disorder. He prescribed methylphenidate, which had been helpful. All in all, there were reasons to think about a neurological basis for Kenny's outrageous behavior.

Kenny's parents pointed out that it was not simply that he would become extremely angry. Kenny experienced many emotions and expressed many feelings in an extreme manner. When he was feeling good, he became frenzied with excitement. When he was disappointed, he became very sad very quickly. In clinical terminology, Kenny was overly intense and was not able to modulate affect along a number of parameters.

The neurological evaluation and the routine EEG were normal. In addition, however, it was arranged for Kenny to have a quantitative or computerized EEG, which mapped the electrical activity of the brain. The quantitative EEG is able to pick up very subtle changes and also compare the patient's pattern to a normal population. Kenny's study was markedly abnormal, in that it showed disorganized and impaired conduction in both temporal regions, as well as in other parts of the brain.

Although it is hard to be conclusive in these matters, the clinical history and the quantitative EEG data seemed consistent with the diagnosis of organic personality disorder. Kenny was treated with an anticonvulsant, carbamazepine, with some success. Although the medication did not make him a whole new person, it did mean that the rages were less often and less severe. It also helped Kenny become more amenable to psychotherapy.

Pseudoseizures

Pseudoseizures or psychogenic seizures can come about in several ways. The easiest and probably the most common way is for a youngster who actually has epilepsy to discover that it is possible to have additional "seizures" through either conscious or unconscious processes. Sometimes clients are familiar with the epilepsy of a family member or a friend, so they borrow the symptom from the other individual. Finally, it may be that a frightened or anxious youngster starts by simply having a fainting spell. Thereupon, the concerned parents and concerned doctors investigate the fainting spell and may go so far as to conduct EEGs and other studies of the youngster's brain. That may plant the idea for future spells, which look more like seizures.

It sometimes is possible to distinguish between epileptic seizures (with a neurological basis), pseudoseizures that have an unconscious origin; and malingered seizures on clinical grounds (Mendez, 2000). Goodyer (1985) described five adolescents with pseudoepileptic seizures. In comparing epilepsy with pseudoseizures, epilepsy is more likely to have stereotyped aura; to have cyanotic skin changes; to include self-injury, such as severe tongue biting; to cause incontinence; to be nocturnal; and to be followed by postictal confusion. In observing an episode, the body movements in epilepsy are stereotyped, with tonic and clonic phases. The movements in pseudoseizures are variable, random, asynchronous, and frequently involve truncal and pelvic thrusting.

If in doubt, the best solution may be to refer the youngster to a specialized inpatient epilepsy center which is able to diagnose the condition with certitude. The way it is done is to monitor the patient continually for several days. That is, the patient's EEG is recorded and the patient is videotaped continually. When an episode does occur, it is possible to correlate exactly the patient's behavior with any EEG changes.

Tourette's disorder has the distinction of being almost the only psychiatric condition in *DSM-IV-TR* to retain its eponym. That seems a suitable recognition for the man who was able to separate out this group of tiqueurs from all the other patients who visited the clinic at Salpétrière with involuntary movements. The role of Georges Gilles de la Tourette and the history of his syndrome was described by Walkup et al. (1998).

The tic disorders are usually thought of as constituting a continuum from benign to serious conditions. If a child or adolescent has had a motor or vocal tic for less than four weeks, it does not merit a specific diagnosis in *DSM-IV-TR*. If the tics have continued nearly every day for at least four weeks, but less than a year, the diagnosis is transient tic disorder. If the youngster has experienced either vocal or motor tics, but not both, for more than a year, the diagnosis is chronic vocal tic disorder or chronic motor tic disorder. If the youngster has had both vocal and motor tics for more than a year, the diagnosis is Tourette's disorder.

This illness usually starts during childhood. Each patient may exhibit a variety of motor tics (such as eye blinking, grimacing, clenching the fists, shrugging shoulders, etc.) and vocal tics (coughing, making a barking sound, clearing throat, etc.). These tics come and go and one form of tic is replaced by another. The most striking symptoms, which occur infrequently and are not necessary for the diagnosis of Tourette's disorder, are echolalia (repeating the word or phrase of another person) and coprolalia (using obscene words and phrases) and copropraxia (using obscene gestures). By the time the youngster reaches adolescence he and his parents can usually list a number of tics which he has experienced.

The adolescent therapist will occasionally see a patient who has had multiple tics for years and was never diagnosed as having Tourette's disorder. This happens less often than previously, because the Tourette Syndrome Association has greatly increased the awareness of this illness among the general public and among medical professionals. Several years ago Tourette's disorder was highlighted on a popular television program—a fictional medical examiner portrayed by Jack Klugman investigated the case of a person with this illness. Many people diagnosed themselves after seeing that show.

This is a neurological condition, so why is it in psychiatric textbooks at all? There have been at least three ways to account for the relationship between the neurological and the psychological aspects of Tourette's disorder. In the past, psychoanalytic writers conceptualized Tourette's disorder as a psychosomatic condition, i.e., that the cause was basically psychological and unconscious. The second point of view was exactly the opposite, that Tourette's disorder is an organic condition which, in itself, did not have a psychological etiology or psychological manifestations. The adherents of that view would say that psychological symptoms that did sometimes occur in individuals with Tourette's disorder were simply the person's response to the illness. A third way to look at this condition is to say that Tourette's disorder is caused by dysfunction in neurochemical systems of the brain, which cause both neurological and psychological symptoms. The advocates of the third view would say that the tics and the behavioral symptoms (restlessness, impulsivity) and mental symptoms (obsessions, compulsions, impaired concentration) are all caused by some basic organic pathology.

How can an adolescent therapist be helpful to a teenager with Tourette's disorder? You can certainly help by making the diagnosis and explaining the condition to the patient and to the parents. You can imagine how weird an adolescent must feel to find that his body insists on being out of control, sometimes in the most embarrassing manner. In one case, a youngster at a Catholic boarding school found himself spouting off with, "Holy shit, Harry," in a loud, clear voice at morning prayers. An accurate diagnosis and scientific explanation would help the patient feel that he is neither crazy nor deviant.

The next step would be to discuss with the patient and the parents the pros and cons of medication to suppress the tics and also, perhaps, the obsessiveness, which can also be disabling. In general, medication should not be used if the symptoms are mild and do not greatly interfere with school or with the youngster's peer relations. When medication is used, sometimes the youngster does very well on a rather low dosage.

The therapist can also be helpful by explaining this unusual condition to school personnel, since some of these patients have special educational needs. It may be that the teacher or the guidance counselor is baffled by the student because they don't know what Tourette's disorder is. Many children and adolescents with Tourette's disorder have learning disabilities, which may not fit into the typical categories used at the local schools. Sometimes the therapist may need to meet with school personnel to facilitate the youngster's placement in an appropriate program, which usually means a resource room for students with learning disabilities. If the patient has unusually severe behavioral or psychological symptoms associated with the Tourette's disorder, he may require placement in a school program for emotionally disturbed students.

The therapist can be supportive by referring the family to the Tourette Syndrome Association. The best way to access the organization is to search the Internet for "Tourette Syndrome Association"—that turns up the national office and also the web sites of many local or state associations. Local chapters are in many cities and are quite helpful to families who are learning about this illness. The best part of the TSA newsletter is called "Tourette Victories," which are vignettes of members who have accomplished some goal, such as "graduating school, getting married, earning a scouting award, being elected Congressman."

Psychotherapy does not cure Tourette's disorder, but it may help the adolescent cope with his disability. If the youngster feels good about himself and is pursuing the tasks of adolescence, there is no point to proposing psychotherapy. But if the patient is chronically depressed and avoids social situations and can't make plans for the future, he would benefit from either individual counseling or a heterogeneous coed adolescent therapy group.

LOOKING FOR ZEBRAS

Now that Tourette's disorder is better known, it is recognized more and more often and many child and adolescent therapists treat several patients with that condition. There are other illnesses which occur much less frequently and it is not really possible to know the details of every obscure medical syndrome. However, it is possible to keep an open mind and to wonder actively whether there is something going on that is more than meets the eye. It is a little like being a detective and looking for clues, even though no crime has been reported.

Oftentimes youngsters with physical illness first come to the attention of a psychotherapist, whom they reached through a school counselor or simply through the yellow pages. A girl was referred for "depression," manifested by tiredness and drooping eyes, and later was found to have myasthenia gravis. Another patient was underachieving and chronically depressed, and it turned out he had hypothyroidism. An older adolescent was hospitalized on a psychiatric unit because of a schizophrenia-like illness. The routine screening test for syphilis turned out to be positive, after the tests on several thousand other patients had been negative. On rare occasions tumors and other mass lesions in the brain are found in psychiatrically hospitalized adolescents.

An interesting condition that ranks high in the annals of psychiatric trivia is the Kleine-Levin syndrome. This is a rare medical condition that presents with dramatic psychiatric symptoms. In the case described by Gillberg (1987), various specialists had labeled the patient as having drug addiction, schizophrenia, hysteria, and depression before the correct diagnosis was made. Orlosky (1982) reviewed the literature and tabulated the psychiatric symptoms which occurred in the thirty-three cases which he studied.

The Kleine-Levin syndrome usually occurs in male adolescents. It is characterized by recurrent episodes of sleepiness, compulsive eating, and psychiatric disturbances. The sleep disturbance is usually described as periods of profound sleepiness which may continue for several days, interrupted only by eating and trips to the bathroom. Unusual eating behavior was described. Although these patients do not crave food or seek it, they eat food compulsively when it is presented to them.

Patients with this illness manifested a variety of psychiatric symptoms, which Orlosky divided into three areas. The most common disturbances of behavior were sexual disinhibition, apathy, withdrawal, and agitation. He found disturbances of mood, such as irritability, depression, and euphoria. Most interesting were the disturbances of thought, which included confusion, amnesia, delusions, and hallucinations.

Here is something to think about. It was suggested by Young (1975) that the Kleine-Levin syndrome and anorexia nervosa are mirror images. The Kleine-Levin syndrome occurs in male adolescents and is characterized by decreased physical activity, increased eating, and hypersexuality. Anorexia nervosa occurs in female adolescents and is characterized by increased physical activity, decreased eating, and hyposexuality. Perhaps both illnesses are caused by hypothalamic dysfunction, but through opposing neuroendocrine systems.

TAKE A PEDIATRICIAN TO LUNCH

It is not realistic to suggest that every adolescent who comes for counseling should have a physical examination. In fact, a pediatrician is likely to take a superficial history and run through a perfunctory physical examination when he is asked to see a patient for no particular reason. It makes more sense for the psychotherapist to refer the youngster to a pediatrician or some other specialist when a specific question needs to be addressed. It also makes sense to have an ongoing dialogue with pediatricians, so that patients do not slip between the cracks.

Howie, a 14-year-old boy, was referred for psychiatric evaluation by his pediatrician because of fainting spells. These incidents occurred at times of emotional excitement and were thought to be psychogenic. For instance, this shy youngster attended a school function and asked a girl to dance for the first time in his life. When the dance was over he "fainted" and was briefly unconscious. At the conclusion of the evaluation the psychiatrist said that there seemed to be a psychological basis for these spells and recommended outpatient therapy, but suggested that he and the pediatrician keep in touch to make sure that no physical problem was being overlooked.

The boy did not show up for his next appointment. The psychiatrist called the patient's mother, who apologized for not calling to cancel the appointment, but on the preceding day the youngster had been hospitalized for open-heart surgery. It turned out that the boy had a myoma in the wall of the heart. It was removed and that cured the fainting spells. The pediatrician had continued to follow the patient and heard a murmur that had not previously been present.

The lesson, of course, is to keep an open mind about how psychological symptoms come about and to maintain open communication with other members of the treatment team.

BON VOYAGE

Psychotherapy with adolescents can be a satisfying, frustrating, exciting, tedious, stimulating, monotonous, rewarding, discouraging activity. The duration of psychotherapy is sometimes very brief, with meaningful resolution occurring after three or four meetings; it may be quite long, extending for many months or several years. Some cases seem very simple and require familiar, straightforward interventions; other situations are complicated, requiring much weaving and turning, moving forward and backward and forward again.

Even the cases that are relatively simple involve a complexity that is usually absent when therapists work with younger children or adult clients. That is, psychotherapy with adolescents involves addressing multiple relationships, since almost every teenager must deal with parents; other adults, such as teachers, probation officers, and extended family; siblings; peers; and, of course, the therapist. Within these relationships the adolescent struggles with multiple conflicts: desires for dependence vs. autonomy; compliance vs. arguing; selfishness vs. self-sacrifice; altruism vs. hedonism. And sometimes these clients are insightful and clever; sometimes defensive and obtuse; and sometimes simply confused.

For therapists navigating these rough seas, the beacon is the therapeutic relationship with the adolescent client. This relationship may vary from fragile to robust to nonexistent, depending on the case and the vicissitudes within each individual case. As expressed in this book, the therapeutic relationship with adolescents relies on certain values and principles: that the therapist seeks to team up with the part of the client that wants to be healthy and autonomous, not dependent and enmeshed; that the therapist and youngster together seek to understand the reasons for his behavior, be they conscious or unconscious; and that they learn to respect each other and each other's opinions, even if they disagree. Even while emphasizing the importance of establishing and nurturing the therapeutic relationship with the teenager, the therapist must also keep in mind the needs of the client's parents, the safety of others in the community, and the laws of society.

We hope that this book provides a chart through these waters. We don't expect it to be the only word or the last word. Therapists need to find their own ways to conceptualize their cases, address important issues, and communicate with their clients. We simply hope that *The Fragile Alliance* helps you find your own route and that you enjoy the trip.

references

The number(s) in brackets refer to the chapter(s) in which the citation occurs.

Ackerman N. W. (1958), *The Psychodynamics of Family Life*. New York: Basic Books. Nathan W. Ackerman was a pioneer in the study of the psychology of family life. He described the treatment of families with "integrative family therapy." [7]

Ackerman N. W. (1982), *The Strength of Family Therapy: Selected Papers of Nathan W. Ackerman*, Bloch D., Simon R., eds. New York: Brunner/Mazel. This is a good survey of Ackerman's work. [7]

Acocella J. (1999), *Creating Hysteria: Women and Multiple Personality Disorder*. San Francisco: Jossey-Bass. Joan Acocella related the modern history of multiple personality disorder (MPD), which is now known as dissociative identity disorder. She posed the question—Why did the diagnosis of MPD explode during 1985–95 and then suddenly fall to the level of an unusual, rare disorder? [14]

Adams P. R., Adams G. R. (1984), Mount Saint Helens ashfall: evidence for a disaster stress reaction. *American Psychologist* 39: 252–260. This is a good example of the systematic study of a population that experienced together a traumatic event. [14]

Adatto C. P. (1966), On the metamorphosis from adolescence into adulthood. *Journal of the American Psychoanalytic Association* 14: 485–509. Adatto discussed adult patients whom he had treated earlier as adolescents. He focused on their memories of their earlier treatment. [9]

Aichorn A. (1925), *Wayward Youth*. Chicago: Northwestern University Press, 1983. August Aichorn was a student of Sigmund Freud. He applied psychoanalytic principles to the treatment and management of unruly teenagers in Vienna in the 1920s and created one of the first residential programs for delinquent boys. [1, 4]

Alexander F. (1950), *Psychosomatic Medicine: Its Principles and Applications*. New York: W. W. Norton. A classic investigation of psychosomatic disorders, such as peptic ulcer and rheumatoid arthritis. Although dated, it is still an interesting study. [18]

American Academy of Child and Adolescent Psychiatry (1997a), Practice parameters for assessment and treatment of children and adolescents with bipolar disorder. *Journal of the American Academy of Child and Adolescent Psychiatry* 36 (10 Supplement): 157S-176S. The AACAP and other professional organizations publish practice parameters or practice guidelines on a variety of topics. Some of them are referenced in this bibliography. [16]

American Academy of Child and Adolescent Psychiatry (1997b), Practice parameters for assessment and treatment of children and adolescents with substance use disorders. *Journal of the American Academy of Child and Adolescent Psychiatry* 36 (10 Supplement): 140S-156S. [17]

American Academy of Child and Adolescent Psychiatry (1997c), Practice parameters for child custody evaluation. *Journal of the American Academy of Child and Adolescent Psychiatry* 36 (10 Supplement): 57S-68S. [15]

American Academy of Child and Adolescent Psychiatry (1998a), Practice parameters for the assessment and treatment of children and adolescents with depressive disorders. *Journal of the American Academy of Child and Adolescent Psychiatry* 37(10 Supplement): 63S-83S. [11, 16]

American Academy of Child and Adolescent Psychiatry (1998b), Practice parameters for the assessment and treatment of children and adolescents with language and learning disorders. *Journal of Child and Adolescent Psychiatry* 37 (Supplement): 46S-62S. [10]

American Academy of Child and Adolescent Psychiatry (1998c), Practice parameters for the assessment and treatment of children and adolescents with posttraumatic stress disorder. *Journal of the American Academy of Child and Adolescent Psychiatry* 37 (10 Supplement): 4S-26S. [14]

American Academy of Child and Adolescent Psychiatry (1999), Practice parameters for the assessment and treatment of children and adolescents who are sexually abusive of others. *Journal of the American Academy of Child and Adolescent Psychiatry* 38 (12 Supplement): 55S-76S. [13]

American Academy of Child and Adolescent Psychiatry (2001), Practice parameter for the assessment and treatment of children and adolescents with schizophrenia. *Journal of the American Academy of Child and Adolescent Psychiatry* 40 (7 Supplement): 4S-23S.

American Psychiatric Association (2000), *Diagnostic and Statistical Manual of Mental Disorders*, Fourth Edition, Text Revision. Washington, D.C.: American Psychiatric Association. This book lists and defines all the mental disorders that are currently recognized. It also has other useful information, such as how to work through a differential diagnosis. The title is frequently abbreviated to *DSM-IV-TR*. [throughout]

Anthony E. J. (1988), The creative therapeutic encounter at adolescence. *Adolescent Psychiatry* 15: 194–216. James Anthony, one of the most gifted and creative child and adolescent psychiatrists, relates his experiences with several gifted, creative adolescent patients. [5]

Arffa S. (1998), Traumatic brain injury. In: *Textbook of Pediatric Neuropsychiatry*, Coffey C. E., Brumback R. A., eds., pp. 1093–1140. Washington, D.C.:

American Psychiatric Press. This is the first major textbook to merge the study of the psychiatric aspects of neurological conditions and the neurological aspects of psychiatric conditions of children and adolescents. [14]

Aug R. G., Bright T. P. (1970), A study of wed and unwed motherhood in adolescents and young adults. *Journal of the American Academy of Child Psychiatry* 9: 577–594. This study is old, but it is still a good description of some of the psychosocial forces that drive teenage pregnancy. [13]

Azima F. J. C., Richmond L. H., eds. (1989), *Adolescent Group Psychotherapy.* Madison, CT: International Universities Press. Fern Azima, Ph.D., and Lewis Richmond, M.D., have been active in the American Group Psychotherapy Association. This book is part of the monograph series of the AGPA. [6]

Bear D., Fedio P. (1977), Quantitative analysis of interictal behavior in temporal lobe epilepsy. *Archives of Neurology* 34: 454–467. The authors used a questionnaire to study the personality traits of individuals with temporal lobe epilepsy, who were found to be humorless, dependent, circumstantial, and possessing strong philosophical interests. [18]

Bear D., Freeman R., Greenberg M. (1984), Behavioral alterations in patients with temporal lobe epilepsy. In: *Psychiatric Aspects of Epilepsy,* Blumer D., ed., pp. 197–227. Washington, D.C.: American Psychiatric Press. David Bear, M.D., and his colleagues have studied the interesting behavioral syndromes that occur in individuals with seizures, particularly temporal lobe epilepsy. [18]

Belfer M. L., Krener P. K., Miller F. B. (1988), AIDS in children and adolescents. *Journal of the American Academy of Child and Adolescent Psychiatry* 27: 147–151. The authors emphasize that AIDS has impacted the neuropsychological, psychological, and social functioning of children and adolescents. [13]

Berkovitz I. H., ed. (1972), *Adolescents Grow in Groups: Experiences in Adolescent Group Psychotherapy.* New York: Brunner/Mazel. Irving Berkovitz, a child and adolescent psychiatrist, edited one of the first books that specifically addressed talking group therapy for adolescents. [6]

Berkovitz I. H. (1995), The adolescent and the schools: a therapeutic guide. *Adolescent Psychiatry* 20: 343–363. An expert in school consultation, Irving Berkovitz relates how mental health professionals and school personnel can work together to help disturbed children. [6]

Bernet W. (1982), The technique of verbal games in group therapy with early adolescents. *Journal of the American Academy of Child Psychiatry* 21: 496–501. This article describes techniques that can be used in group therapy with early adolescents, who are notoriously difficult to engage in constructive psychotherapy activities. [6]

Bernet W. (1983), The therapist's role in child custody disputes. *Journal of the American Academy of Child Psychiatry* 22: 180–183. The message of this paper is that it is usually not a good idea for the therapist of a child or adolescent to conduct a custody evaluation and testify in court, since it confuses the two roles. [15]

Bernet W. (1993), Humor in evaluating and treating children and adolescents. *The Journal of Psychotherapy Practice and Research* 2: 307–317. This article provides many examples of how humor can be used in understanding and communicating with young clients. [5]

Bernet W. (1995), *Children of Divorce: A Practical Guide for Parents, Attorneys, and Therapists*. New York: Vantage Press. This book is about two issues that affect children of divorce: *conflict* and what to do about it; *stability* and how to provide it as much as possible. [15]

Bernet W. (2002), Child custody evaluations. *Child and Adolescent Psychiatric Clinics of North America* 11: 781–804. This article summarizes the procedures that a mental health professional can use in conducting a child custody evaluation or a parenting-time evaluation. [15]

Berstein E., Duquette J. S. (1995), Inpatient group psychotherapy program: a model. *Journal of Child and Adolescent Group Therapy* 5: 35–45. Edith Berstein and Jacquelynn Duquette describe how the adolescent inpatients pass through the following stages of group therapy: joining; introduction; getting to know; trust; working; and termination. [6]

Blos P. (1962), *On Adolescence: A Psychoanalytic Interpretation*. New York: Free Press of Glencoe. This important, scholarly book provided a comprehensive framework for understanding the phases of adolescence. [1, 3, 13]

Blos P. (1967), The second individuation process of adolescence. *Psychoanalytic Study of the Child* 22: 162–186. Blos suggests that adolescence is a second opportunity to work through issues of attachment and independence. [1, 8, 9]

Blos P. (1983), The contribution of psychoanalysis to the psychotherapy of adolescents. *Adolescent Psychiatry* 11: 104–124. Blos relates a case from his own experience in which he treated an adolescent girl with psychotherapy (weekly for five months), not psychoanalysis. [5]

Blumenthal S., Bergner L. (1973), Suicide and newspapers: a replicated study. *American Journal of Psychiatry* 130: 468–471. This was one of the earliest attempts to show that new suicides occur after publication of a news story about a suicide. [11]

Bowen M. (1978), *Family Therapy in Clinical Practice*. New York: J. Aronson. Murray Bowen first started using the term "Family Systems Theory" in 1966. He thought that a person can differentiate himself from his family of origin only after a careful assessment of the historical context of the family, which is organized in an elaborate genogram. [7]

Bowman E. S., Blix S., Coons P. M. (1985), Multiple personality in adolescence: relationship to incestual experiences. *Journal of the American Academy of Child Psychiatry* 24: 109–114. Although this is a single case report, the authors discuss the broader question of the relationship between physical and/or sexual abuse and the occurrence of multiple personality disorder, which is now called dissociative identity disorder. [14]

Bruch H. (1973), *Eating Disorders: Obesity, Anorexia and the Person Within.* New York: Basic Books. This is Hilda Bruch's classic study of the psychology and psychodynamics of anorexia nervosa. [18]

Burgess A. W., Holmstrom L. L. (1974), Rape trauma syndrome. *American Journal Psychiatry* 131: 981–986. In this important article, Ann Burgess (a nurse) and Lynda Holmstrom (a sociologist) documented the existence of a "rape trauma syndrome" and delineated its symptomatology as well as that of two variations, the "compounded reaction" and the "silent reaction." [14]

Caffey J. (1946), Multiple fractures in long bones of infants suffering from chronic subdural hematoma. *American Journal of Roentgenology* 56: 163–173. This article by John Caffey, M.D., a pediatrician and radiologist, marked the rediscovery of severe child abuse among children brought to hospital emergency rooms. [14]

Campbell R. J. (1996), *Psychiatric Dictionary,* 7th edition. New York: Oxford University Press. This dictionary, which was first published in 1940, has definitions of words such as "psychotoxicomania" and "suigenderism." [5]

Centers for Disease Control (1988), HIV-related beliefs, knowledge, and behaviors among high school students. *JAMA* 260: 3567–3570. For additional information, see the web page of the CDC National Prevention Information Network: www.cdcnpin.org. [13]

Chused J. (1990), Neutrality in the analysis of action-prone adolescents. *Journal of the American Psychoanalytic Association* 38: 679–704. A talented psychoanalyst, Judith Chused, M.D., described how action during analysis may serve both neurotic conflicts and developmental tasks. A neutral stance allows the therapist to avoid countertransference problems. [5]

Coffey C. E., Brumback R. A., eds. (1998), *Textbook of Pediatric Neuropsychiatry.* Washington, D.C.: American Psychiatry Press. Edward Coffey (a psychiatrist and neurologist) and Roger Brumback (a neurologist and neuropathologist) have assembled topics that pertain to both pediatric neurology and child and adolescent psychiatry. [16]

Coles R., photographs by Lee J., Moses J. (1997), *The Youngest Parents: Teenage Pregnancy as it Shapes Lives.* New York: W. W. Norton. Robert Coles has learned a lot about teenagers by simply sitting down and talking with them. [13]

Coolidge J. C., Willer M. L., Tessman E., Waldfogel S. (1960), School phobia in adolescence: a manifestation of severe character disturbance. *American Journal of Orthopsychiatry* 30: 599–607. This classic study related a pattern of adolescent behavior (refusal to go to school) to a pattern of psychological disturbance (overly anxious and dependent on their mothers). [10]

Coolidge J. C., Brodie R. D. (1974), Observations of mothers of 49 school phobic children: evaluated in a 10-year follow-up study. *Journal of the American Academy of Child Psychiatry* 13: 275–285. In a follow-up study, John Coolidge found that almost all of the school phobic children had returned to school and remained in school, but their subjects, who were then adolescents, remained phobic and constricted. [10]

Corder B. F. (1994), *Structured Adolescent Psychotherapy Groups*. Sarasota, Florida: Professional Resources Press. Billie Corder translates her extensive clinical experience into specific techniques and activities that may be used in a variety of clinical settings. [6]

Deutsch H. (1967), *Selected Problems of Adolescence (with Special Emphasis on Group Formation)*. New York: International Universities Press. Helene Deutsch, one of the first mental health professionals to study the life cycle of woman, also wrote *The Psychology of Women*. She lived from 1884 to 1982. [1]

Dewald P. A. (1965), Reactions to the forced termination of therapy. *Psychiatric Quarterly* 39: 102–126. Dewald had to move and carefully described the varying relations to termination over his complete case load. [9]

Elkind D. (1997), *All Grown Up and No Place to Go: Teenagers in Crisis*, revised edition. Reading, MA: Addison-Wesley. David Elkind, a prolific author and psychologist, also wrote *The Hurried Child: Growing Up Too Fast Too Soon* and about twenty other books. [1, 8]

Erikson E. H. (1958), *Young Man Luther*. New York: W. W. Norton. This is a good example of psychohistorical research, which is the psychological investigation of historical events and individuals. [1]

Erikson E. H. (1963), *Childhood and Society*. New York: W. W. Norton. This book contains Erik Erikson's epigenetic chart of the eight stages of man, which seems timeless. It also contains his psychoanalytic interpretation of the Sioux and Oglala Indians, which is flawed and dated. [1, 8]

Erikson E. H. (1968), *Identity: Youth and Crisis*. New York: W. W. Norton. This book is one of Erickson's classic works on identity formation. [1, 2]

Esman A. H. (1995), Adolescence and Society. *Adolescent Psychiatry* 20: 89–108. This article, which was abstracted from the author's book, *Adolescence and Culture*, is an interesting discussion of the changing concept of adolescence. [1]

Feinstein S. C. (1982), Manic-depressive disorder in children and adolescents. *Adolescent Psychiatry* 10: 256–272. Sherman Feinstein described various ways—especially disordered conduct—in which bipolar disorder may present in adolescents. [2]

Ferguson S. M., Rayport M. (1984). Psychosis in epilepsy. In: *Psychiatric Aspects of Epilepsy*, Blumer D., ed., pp. 229–270. Washington, D.C.: American Psychiatric Press. Several forms of psychosis occur more often in persons with epilepsy than in non-epileptics. [18]

Fodor I. G. (1992), *Adolescent Assertiveness and Social Skills Training: A Clinical Handbook.* New York: Springer. This book is devoted to the treatment of specific problems for adolescents, that is, assertiveness, anger, and social skills. [6]

Forward S., Buck C. (1988), *Betrayal of Innocence: Incest and Its Devastation.* New York: Penguin Books. Susan Forward, a social worker, was one of the first clinicians to talk openly about incest on radio and television. [14]

Foster H. W. (1999), Keynote address: Taming the tempest of teen pregnancy. *American Journal of Obstetrics and Gynecology* 181: S28-S31. Henry W. Foster, Jr., M.D. developed a program, "I Have a Future," to reduce teen pregnancy. Intended for both female and male adolescents, it emphasizes the values of self-esteem, physical and mental well-being, completion of school, sexual responsibility, and self-control. [13]

Frank A. (1953), *The Diary of a Young Girl.* New York: Pocket Books. The classic book by an adolescent victim of the Holocaust. [14]

Freud A. (1958), Adolescence. *Psychoanalytic Study of the Child* 13: 255–278. Although Anna Freud viewed adolescence as an inherently destabilizing development, her description of the tasks of adolescence is still of value. [1]

Freud A. (1966), *The Ego and the Mechanisms of Defense,* revised edition. New York: International Universities Press. Anna Freud wrote several books that relate to child and adolescent development. She introduced the concept of lines of psychological development. [1]

Freud S. (1958), The dynamics of transference. In: *The Standard Edition of the Complete Psychological Works of Sigmund Freud, Volume 12,* pp. 97–108. London: Hogarth Press. As he developed the technique of psychoanalysis, Sigmund Freud defined the concepts of transference and countertransference. [3]

Friedman L. (1969), The therapeutic alliance. *International Journal of Psychoanalysis* 50: 139–153. This is an excellent review article regarding the concept of the therapeutic alliance. [3]

Fromm-Reichmann F. (1950), *Principles of Intensive Psychotherapy.* Chicago: University of Chicago Press. Frieda Fromm-Reichmann pioneered the use of intensive psychotherapy with psychotic patients. She worked for many years at Chestnut Lodge, a hospital in Maryland, and was the psychiatrist featured in the book and movie, *I Never Promised You a Rose Garden.* [5]

Galatzer-Levy R. M. (1985), The analysis of an adolescent boy. *Adolescent Psychiatry* 12: 336–360. It is uncommon to recommend and conduct psychoanalysis for adolescent clients. Robert Galatzer-Levy, however, described the successful psychoanalysis (four times a week for three and a half years) of a depressed 14-year-old boy. [5]

In re Gault (1967), 387 U.S. 1. This was the landmark case in which the U.S. Supreme Court defined the legal rights of adolescents in court. [12]

Gemelli R. (1996), *Normal Child and Adolescent Development*. Washington, D.C.: American Psychiatric Press. Ralph Gemelli, M.D., considers contemporary research on development and presents a comprehensive biopsychosocial model for mental development. [1, 8]

Gesell A., Ilg F. L., Ames L. B. (1974), *Infant and Child in the Culture of Today: The Guidance of Development in Home and Nursery School*, revised edition. New York: Harper & Row. Arnold Gesell, M.D., was the director of the Clinic of Child Development at Yale University for many years. He and has collaborators—such as Frances L. Ilg, M.D. and Louise Bates Ames, Ph.D.—wrote many books that became standard references, including *The First Five Years of Life* and *The Child from Five to Ten*. [8]

Gillberg, C. (1987), Kleine-Levin syndrome: unrecognized diagnosis in adolescent psychiatry. *Journal of the American Academy of Child and Adolescent Psychiatry*. 26: 793–794. Professor Gilberg says, "This uncommon diagnosis in child and adolescent psychiatry should always be considered in unusual cases with puzzling periodic symptomatology." [18]

Godenne G. D. (1995), Forming a therapeutic alliance with teenagers. *Adolescent Psychiatry* 20: 289–298. Baroness Godenne offers practical tips on how to develop a therapeutic alliance, based on her extensive personal experience. [5]

Godenne G. D. (1997), Hearing the S.O.S.: assessing the lethality of a youth in distress. *Adolescent Psychiatry* 21: 211–233. A sensitive account of how to assess suicidality in depressed adolescents, by the former director of Counseling and Psychiatric Services, Johns Hopkins University. [11]

Goodwin J. (1982), *Sexual Abuse: Incest Victims and Their Families*. Boston: J. Wright. This book by Jean Goodwin was one of the early books about incest. [14]

Goodyer I. M. (1985). Epileptic and pseudoepileptic seizures in childhood and adolescence. *Journal of the American Academy of Child Psychiatry*. 24: 3–9. This article describes how pseudoseizures were diagnosed using telemetry EEG. [18]

Gossett J. T., Lewis J. M., Barnhart F. D. (1983). *To Find a Way: The Outcome of Hospital Treatment of Disturbed Adolescents*. New York: Brunner/Mazel. The findings of an extended clinical research study regarding factors involved in successful and unsuccessful hospital treatment. [16]

Gould M. S., Shaffer D. (1986), The impact of suicide in television movies: evidence for imitation. *New England Journal of Medicine* 315: 690–694. This study found an increase in adolescent suicides after the broadcast of three television movies about suicide. But see Phillips and Paight (1987). [11]

Greenson R. R. (1967), *The Technique and Practice of Psychoanalysis, Volume I*. New York: International Universities Press. A master analyst describes how to do psychoanalysis with careful attention to "the working alliance." [3]

Greenspan S. I., Pollock G. H, eds. (1991), *The Course of Life, Volume IV, Adolescence*. Madison, CT: International Universities Press. Stanley Greenspan and George Pollock have edited a series of books on developmental stages, with chapters written by distinguished clinicians. [8]

Haley J. (1971), *Changing Families: A Family Therapy Reader*. New York: Grune & Stratton. Jay Haley developed strategic family therapy. In this approach, the therapist solves presenting problems by giving the family instructions—that may be paradoxical—designed to interrupt maladaptive patterns. [7]

Haley J. (1980), *Leaving Home: The Therapy of Disturbed Young People*. New York: McGraw-Hill. Jay Haley thought that the diagnosis (whether schizophrenic, depressed, or delinquent) is less important than the behavior (e.g., failure to grow up and leave home). This book advises therapists how to help older adolescents achieve psychological independence. [7]

Hall G. S. (1904), *Adolescence: Its Psychology and Its Relations to Physiology, Anthropology, Sociology, Sex, Crime, Religion, and Education*. New York: D. Appleton. G. Stanley Hall, Ph.D., who was the first president of the American Psychological Association, wrote the original systematic, scientific study of adolescence. When he was the president of Clark University, Worcester, Massachusetts, Dr. Hall invited Sigmund Freud to the campus to give a series of lectures. [1, 8]

Hallahan D. P., Kauffman J. M., Lloyd J. W. (1999), *Introduction to Learning Disabilities,* 2nd edition. Boston: Allyn and Bacon. This is a college text book by Daniel Hallahan, James Kauffman, and John Lloyd. It covers basic information such as definitions, causes, characteristics, educational approaches, and theories. [10]

Haller L. H. (1981), Before the judge: the child-custody evaluation. *Adolescent Psychiatry* 9: 142–164. Lee Haller, a child and adolescent psychiatrist, discusses issues in custody evaluations that pertain particularly to adolescents. [15]

Halmi K. A. (2000), Eating disorders. In: *Comprehensive Textbook of Psychiatry,* 7th edition, Sadock B. J., Sadock V. A., eds., pp. 1663–1676. Philadelphia: Lippincott Williams & Wilkins. Katherine Halmi, a professor of psychiatry, has written extensively on eating disorders. [18]

Harris J. R. (1998), *The Nurture Assumption: Why Children Turn Out The Way They Do*. New York: Free Press. The "group socialization theory" of Judith Rich Harris emphasizes that both children and adolescents identify very strongly with peers, even if it means giving up their identification with parents. Since children and adolescents are tremendously influenced by the culture that they grow up in, this theory minimizes the lasting influence of parents. [1, 6]

Hartmann E., Milofsky E., Vaillant G., Oldfield M., Falke R., Ducey C. (1984), Vulnerability to schizophrenia: prediction of adult schizophrenia using childhood information. *Archives of General Psychiatry.* 41: 1050–1056. The authors had detailed information on 1,000 boys, that had been collected 40 years previously. Of the 1,000 original subjects, 24 subsequently had a diagnosis of adult schizophrenia. They then compared those records with matched controls to identify indicators of vulnerability to schizophrenia. [16]

Hauser S. T., Powers S. I., Noam G. G. (1991), *Adolescents and Their Families: Paths of Ego Development.* New York: Free Press. Stuart Hauser and his colleagues say that adolescents and their families interact in several ways to create quite different paths through the process of adolescence. [8]

Hechtman L., Weiss G., Perlman T., Tuck D. (1981), Hyperactives as young adults: various clinical outcomes. *Adolescent Psychiatry* 9: 295–306. The second stage of a long-term follow-up study of hyperactive children. [10]

Hetherington E. M., Cox M., Cox R. (1985), Long-term effects of divorce and remarriage on the adjustment of children. *Journal of the American Academy of Child Psychiatry* 24: 518–530. Mavis Hetherington, Ph.D., was a pioneer in studying the effects of parental divorce on children. In this paper, for instance, she reported that while divorce had more adverse effects for boys, remarriage was more disruptive for girls. [15]

Hetherington E. M., Bridges M., Insabella G. M. (1998), What matters? What does not? Five perspectives on the association between marital transitions and children's adjustment. *American Psychologist* 53: 167–184. The authors devised a "transactional model" that accounted for the interacting factors that impact children of divorce: individual vulnerability and risk; family composition; stress; parental distress; and disrupted family process. [15]

Hiatt H. (1965), The problem of termination of psychotherapy. *American Journal of Psychotherapy* 19: 607–615. A classic description of the issues of termination in adult patients. [9]

Hine T. (1999), *The Rise and Fall of the American Teenager.* New York: Avon Books. An interesting and entertaining account of the history of adolescence and of the concept of teenagerhood. [1]

Hodges W. F. (1986), *Interventions for Children of Divorce: Custody, Access, and Psychotherapy.* New York: Wiley. William Hodges, a psychology professor, blended theory, research, and clinical experience in this book. [15]

Holinger P. C. (1989), Epidemiologic issues in youth suicide. In: *Suicide Among Youth: Perspectives on Risk and Prevention,* Pfeffer C. R., ed. Washington, D.C.: American Psychiatric Press. Paul C. Holinger, M.D., M.P.H., has studied the longitudinal epidemiological data of suicide during the twentieth century. In general he found that suicide rates for 15- to 24-year-olds showed statistically significant increases and decreases with increases and decreases, respectively, in their proportion of the population. In contrast, adult groups showed the reverse, i.e., decreases and increases in suicide rates with increases and decreases, respectively, of their proportion of the population. [11]

Hollander H. E., Turner F. D. (1985), Characteristics of incarcerated delinquents: relationship between development disorders, environmental and family factors, and patterns of offense and recidivism. *Journal of the American Academy of Child Psychiatry* 24: 221–226. Harriet Hollander and Floyd Turner, both psychologists, studied incarcerated male juvenile offenders and found that many of them had low intelligence, personality disorders, and/or a developmental disorder. [12]

Hoy E., Weiss G., Minde K., Cohen N. (1978), The hyperactive child at adolescence: cognitive, emotional, and social functioning. *Journal of Abnormal Child Psychology* 6: 311–324. The first stage of a long-term follow-up study of hyperactive children. [10]

Inhelder B., Piaget J. (1958), *The Growth of Logical Thinking from Childhood to Adolescence*. New York: Basic Books. Piaget's classic study on the stages in development of cognition and thought. [8]

Jaffe S. L. (1998), *Adolescent Chemical Dependency Recovery*. Washington, D.C.: American Psychiatric Press. This manual is a guide for teenagers to work the first five steps of a twelve-step program as part of a chemical dependency treatment program. [6, 17]

Johnson A. M. (1949), Sanctions for superego lacunae of adolescents. In: *Searchlights on Delinquency: New Psychoanalytic Studies*, Eissler K. R., ed., pp. 225–245. New York: International Universities Press. This paper, an oldie but goodie, was written by Adelaide Johnson. Her thesis was that "parents may find vicarious gratification of their own poorly integrated forbidden impulses in the acting out of the child, through their conscious or more often unconscious permissiveness or inconsistency toward the child in these spheres of behavior." [4]

Johnson A. M., Szurek S. A. (1952), The genesis of anti-social acting out in children and adults. *Psychoanalytic Quarterly* 21: 323–343. This classic paper described the "superego lacunae" of antisocial parents. [4]

Johnston L. D., O'Malley P. M., Bachman, J. G. (2000), The Monitoring of the Future National Results on Adolescent Drug Use: Overview of Key Findings, 199. (NIH Publication No. 00-4690). Bethesda, MD: National Institute on Drug Abuse. [17]

Josephson A. M., Moncher F. J. (1998), Family treatment. In: *Handbook of Child and Adolescent Psychiatry, Volume 6*, Noshpitz J. D., ed., pp. 294–312 New York: Wiley. This is a good recent outline and summary of the conceptual frameworks and clinical processes in family therapy. [7]

Kagan J., Gall S. B., eds. (1997), *The Gale Encyclopedia of Childhood & Adolescence*. Detroit, MI: Gale Research. Jerome Kagan, the executive editor, is a professor at Harvard. [8]

Kalogerakis M. G. (1998), Adolescent violence—twentieth century madness: a critical review of theories of causation. *Adolescent Psychiatry* 22: 251–275. This is a good review of one of the hot topics of this decade. [12]

Katz P. (1995), The psychotherapeutic treatment of suicidal adolescents. *Adolescent Psychiatry* 20: 325–341. Philip Katz, M.D., a Canadian psychiatrist, has many practical ideas about psychotherapy with adolescents. [11]

Katz P. (1998), Establishing the therapeutic alliance. *Adolescent Psychiatry* 23: 89–105. Phillip Katz gives several interesting examples of ways to establish a relationship with young clients, including what to say in the very first sentence. [5]

Katz S. (1998), The role of family interactions in adolescent depression: a review of research findings. *Adolescent Psychiatry* 23: 41–58. Steven Katz, Ph.D., says that families may contribute to or maintain depression in adolescents. [11]

Kavale K. A., Forness S. R. (1995), *The Nature of Learning Disabilities: Critical Elements of Diagnosis and Classification.* Mahwah, N. J.: Erlbaum. Kenneth Kavale and Steven Forness are psychologists. This book in intended for graduate students in school psychology and others interested in the scientific study of learning disabilities. [10]

Keith C. R. (1968), The therapeutic alliance in child psychotherapy. *Journal of the American Academy of Child Psychiatry* 7: 31–43. This article is old but good, an overview of the "unholy alliances" that occur in psychotherapy with children and adolescents. [3]

Kelly J. B. (1988), Longer-term adjustment in children of divorce: converging findings and implications for practice. *Journal of Family Psychology* 2: 119–140. Joan Kelly was also the co-author of *Surviving the Break-up*, the longitudinal study of the reaction of normal children and adolescents to parental divorce. [15]

Kempe R. S., Kempe C. H. (1984), *The Common Secret: Sexual Abuse of Children and Adolescents.* New York: W. H. Freeman. Henry Kempe, his wife, and his colleagues published many articles and books on child abuse. [14]

Kempe C. H., Silverman F. N., Steele B. F., Droegemueller W., Silver H. K. (1962), The battered-child syndrome. *JAMA* 181 (1): 17–24. This was an extremely influential article. After its publication and subsequent publicity the federal government and all states pass laws requiring that child abuse be reported. [14]

Keniston K. (1965), *The Uncommitted: Alienated Youth in American Society.* New York: Harcourt, Brace & World. Kenneth Keniston was a social critic who described the adolescents during the Vietnam era of the 1960s. [17]

Kernberg O. F. (1984), *Severe Personality Disorders: Psychotherapeutic Strategies.* New Haven, CT: Yale University Press. Otto Kernberg emphasized object relations in understanding and treating individuals with narcissistic and borderline personality disorders. [4]

King J. W., Meeks J. E. (1988), Hospital programs for psychiatrically disturbed, drug-abusing adolescents. *Adolescent Psychiatry* 15: 522–534. Joe King and John Meeks shared their experiences in developing and running inpatient programs for chemically dependent teenagers. [17]

King P. (1988), *Sex, Drugs & Rock 'n Roll: Healing Today's Troubled Youth.* Bellevue, Washington: Professional Counselor Books. Paul King, a high school teacher who became a psychiatrist, studied the relationship between adolescent substance abuse and the violent and satanic themes in music. [1]

Klerman G. L. (1989), Suicide, depression, and related problems among the baby boom cohort. In: *Suicide Among Youth: Perspectives on Risk and Prevention,* Pfeffer C. R., ed., pp. 63–81. Washington, D.C.: American Psychiatric Press. Gerald L. Klerman, M.D., studied the nature and treatment of depression and developed a form a treatment called interpersonal therapy. [11]

Kohlberg L. A. (1981), *The Philosophy of Moral Development, Moral Stages, and the Ideal of Justice: Essays on Moral Development, Volume 1.* San Francisco: Harper & Row. Lawrence Kohlberg defined stages of moral development, including: preconventional morality (decisions based on self-interest); conventional morality (conforms to standards of society); and postconventional morality (values derived from philosophical, religious, or personal principles). [1]

Kohut H. (1971), *The Analysis of the Self: A Systematic Approach to the Psychoanalytic Treatment of Narcissistic Personality Disorders.* New York: International Universities Press. Heintz Kohut developed the concepts of self psychology and defined mirroring, idealizing, and alter-ego transferences. [4]

Kolb L. C. (1987), A neuropsychological hypothesis explaining posttraumatic stress disorders. *American Journal of Psychiatry* 144: 989–995. Lawrence Kolb and others defined posttraumatic stress disorder after studying the veterans of World War II, the Korean War, and the Vietnam War. [14]

Krell R. (1985), Therapeutic value of documenting child survivors. *Journal of the American Academy of Child Psychiatry* 24: 397–400. Robert Krell, a child survivor of the Holocaust, later became a psychiatrist in Canada. [14]

Kymissis P., Halperin D. H., eds. (1996), *Group Therapy with Children and Adolescents.* Washington, D.C.: American Psychiatric Press. The editors have collected articles that address specific aspects of group therapy, such as work with inpatients, substance abusers, youngsters with eating disorders, and suicidal adolescents. [6]

Lantz J. E., Thorward S. R. (1985), Inpatient family therapy approaches. *Psychiatric Hospital* 16: 85–89. This article discusses the importance of education and support for families in crisis. [7]

Leary T. (1968), *The Politics of Ecstasy.* New York: G. P. Putnam's Sons. Timothy Leary was the fellow who got into LSD and said, "Tune in. Turn on. Drop out." [17]

Levine M. D. (1987), *Developmental Variation and Learning Disorders.* Cambridge, MA: Educators Publishing Service. Melvin Levine, a pediatrician, tried to integrate what was known about children with learning problems from different perspectives, including neurology, speech and language pathology, psychiatry, and developmental pediatrics. [10]

Levine M. D. (1998), *Educational Care: A System for Understanding and Helping Children with Learning Problems at Home and in School.* Cambridge, MA: Educators Publishing Service. This book has practical and effective suggestions for parents of children with learning disabilities. [10]

Lewis D. O., Balla D. A. (1976), *Delinquency and Psychopathology.* New York: Grune and Stratton. Dorothy Otnow Lewis and her colleagues studied the relationship between delinquency and psychiatric disorders and neurological abnormalities. They found that a careful examination and a thorough history turned up significant psychological and neurological pathology, such as paranoia, hallucinations, and seizures. [12]

Lewis D. O., Lovely R., Yeager C., Della Femina D. (1989), Toward a theory of the genesis of violence: a follow-up study of delinquents. *Journal of American Academy of Child and Adolescent Psychiatry* 28: 431–436. Dorothy Lewis, M.D., a child and adolescent psychiatrist, intensively studied incarcerated adolescents and followed them up years later, when they were adults. She was looking for the causes of adult violent crime. She found that the adolescents who were most likely to go on to commit violent crimes as adults had both intrinsic vulnerabilities (multiple cognitive, psychiatric, and neurological handicaps) and a history of child abuse and/or family violence. [12]

MacLennan B. W., Dies K. R. (1992), *Group Counseling and Psychotherapy with Adolescents,* 2nd edition. Beryce MacLennan and Kathryn Dies have contributed important work in the description, teaching, and research of group psychotherapy. [6]

Mahler M. S., Pine F., Bergman A. (1975), *The Psychological Birth of the Human Infant: Symbiosis and Individuation.* New York: Basic Books. In this classic work, Margaret Mahler described the steps of separation-individuation: differentiation; practicing, rapprochement, and consolidation. [4]

Malekoff A. (1997), *Group Work with Adolescents: Principles and Practice.* New York: Guilford Press. Andrew Malekoff is a social worker who gives specific advice on how to create and maintain an adolescent therapy group, which he illustrates with numerous clinical vignettes. [6]

March J. S., Amaya-Jackson L., Murray M. C., Schulte A. (1998), Cognitive-behavioral psychotherapy for children and adolescents with posttraumatic stress disorder after a single-incident stressor. *Journal of the American Academy of Child and Adolescent Psychiatry* 37: 585–593. John March, M.D., and his colleagues have designed cognitive-behavioral treatment manuals for use with children and adolescents who have obsessive-compulsive disorder, posttraumatic stress disorder, and other emotional problems. [2, 14]

Marohn R. C. (1983), Adolescent substance abuse: a problem of self-soothing. *Clinical Update in Adolescent Psychiatry.* New Canaan, CT: Nassau Publications. Richard Marohn was a prolific writer who had many insights into adolescent psychology. [17]

Massie H. N. (1988), Intensive psychodynamically oriented treatment of two cases of adolescent psychosis. *Adolescent Psychiatry* 15: 487–504. Henry Massie presented case histories of two psychotic youngsters, who were treated with intensive psychotherapy, collateral work with the parents, family meetings, hospitalization, and psychotropic medication. [5]

Masterson J. F. (1967), *The Psychiatric Dilemma of Adolescence.* Boston: Little, Brown. This book is an early classic on adolescent psychotherapy. [8, 16]

Masterson J. F. (1981), *The Narcissistic and Borderline Disorders: An Integrated Developmental Approach.* New York: Brunner/Mazel. James Masterson spent a career studying and treating adolescents with serious personality disorders. His view is that the narcissistic personality disorder is fixated before the development of the rapprochement crisis, while the borderline personality disorder is an inability to resolve the rapprochement crisis. [4]

Mauk G. W., Sharpnack J. D. (1998), A light unto the darkness: the psychoeducational imperative of school-based suicide postvention. *Adolescent Psychiatry* 23: 179–205. This is an excellent article for how to organize school-based postvention services following a student suicide. The authors emphasize planning ahead and identification of at-risk survivors. [11]

McAnarney E. R., Hendee W. R. (1989), Adolescent pregnancy and its consequences. *JAMA* 262: 74–77. This article has statistics and other information on teen pregnancy. [13]

Meeks J. E. (1973), Structuring the early phase of group psychotherapy with adolescents. *International Journal of Child Psychotherapy* 2: 391–405. This early article explained some of the technical aspects of group therapy with adolescents. [6]

Meeks J. E. (1974), Adolescent development and group cohesion. *Adolescent Psychiatry* 3: 289–297. In this early paper Meeks observed that the therapist for an adolescent group should have "an honest commitment to interpretive psychotherapy, a sensitivity to unspoken emotional currents, and a basic understanding of adolescent behavior." [6]

Meeks J. E. (1997), Psychotherapy of the adolescent. In: *Handbook of Child and Adolescent Psychiatry, Volume 3,* Noshpitz J. D., ed., pp. 381–394. New York: Wiley. This chapter is the "Cliffs Notes edition" of the book you are now reading. [3]

Meeks J. E., Dupont P. J. (2003), *The Learning Alliance: A Handbook for School-Oriented Psychotherapy.* Rockville, MD: DMS Press. This recent book emphasizes the multidisciplinary approach of school-based mental health programs. [10]

Mendez M. F. (2000), Neuropsychiatric aspects of epilepsy. In: *Comprehensive*

Textbook of Psychiatry, 7th edition, Sadock B. J., Sadock V. A., eds., pp. 261–273. Philadelphia: Lippincott Williams & Wilkins. There are many interesting relationships between neurological conditions and psychological symptoms and phenomena. [18]

Menninger K. (1958), *Theory of Psychoanalytic Technique*. New York: Basic Books. Karl Menninger was a famous and important psychiatrist. He and his brother (Will Menninger) and their father (C. F. Menninger) founded a distinguished hospital and training program in Topeka, Kansas. [9]

Miller D. (1998), Psychiatric contributions to improve the effectiveness of juvenile justice. *Adolescent Psychiatry* 22: 113–140. Derek Miller advocated for the adequate evaluation of youngsters referred by the juvenile courts in order to clarify the biological, psychological, and social etiology of delinquent behavior. [12]

Minuchin S. (1989), *Families and Family Therapy*. Cambridge, MA: Harvard University Press. Salvador Minuchin developed structural family therapy, which addresses the organization of the family, the persistent patterns and rules within the family, alliances, coalitions, and the continuum of enmeshment and disengagement. [7]

Minuchin S., Nichols M. P. (1993), *Family Healing*. New York: Free Press. Some readers considered this to be Salvador Minuchin's best book, since he was an experienced family therapist who grew wiser as he grew older. [7]

Mogul S. L. (1969), Clinical assessment of adolescent development. *Seminars in Psychiatry* 1: 24–31. This older article makes a point that all therapists of adolescents should understand, that a particular type of behavior could have totally different explanations in different teenagers. [10]

Moskovitz S. (1983), *Love Despite Hate: Child Survivors of the Holocaust and their Adult Lives*. New York: Schocken Books. Sarah Moskovitz studied children who survived the Holocaust and followed them up as adults. She found three factors that seemed to contribute to the resilience of these victims: adaptability, appeal to adults, and assertiveness. [14]

Moskovitz S. (1985), Longitudinal follow-up of child survivors of the Holocaust. *Journal of the American Academy of Child Psychiatry* 24: 401–407. [14]

Murphy W. D. (1989), Assessment and modifications of cognitive distortions in sex offenders. In: *Handbook of Sexual Assault: Issues, Theories, and Treatment of the Offender*, Marshall W. L., Laws D. R., Barbaree H. E., eds. New York: Plenum Press. William Murphy, Ph.D., shares his extensive experience in evaluating and treating adolescent sex offenders. [13]

Myers P. I., Hammill D. D. (1990), *Learning Disabilities: Basic Concepts, Assessment Practices, and Instructional Strategies*, 4th edition. Austin, Texas: PRO-ED. This book by Patricia Myers and Donald Hammill is intended for professionals who work with children and adolescents with learning problems. [10]

Newman C. J. (1976), Disaster at Buffalo Creek. Children of disaster: clinical observations at Buffalo Creek. *American Journal of Psychiatry* 133: 306–312. This study preceded the official introduction of the term, posttraumatic stress disorder, in 1980. [14]

Noshpitz J. D., ed. (1997, 1998), *Handbook of Child and Adolescent Psychiatry*. New York: Wiley. This is an encyclopedic work in seven volumes, which is a good reference for many aspects of adolescent development and psychopathology. [1]

O'Connor J. J., Hoorwitz A. N. (1984), The bogeyman cometh: a strategic approach for difficult adolescents. *Family Process* 23: 237–249. The "bogeyman experience" is the use of unpredictable or threatening events to treat difficult adolescents for whom usual solutions have been ineffectual. [4, 5]

Offer D. (1969), *The Psychological World of the Teenager: A Study of Normal Adolescent Boys*. New York: Basic Books. Dr. Daniel Offer, his wife, and his colleagues studied the phenomenon of normality among adolescents and other age groups. [1]

Offer D. (1987), The mystery of adolescence. *Adolescent Psychiatry* 14: 7–27. This is a good summary of Offer's research on normal adolescents. [1]

Offer D., Offer J. B. (1975), *From Teenage to Young Manhood: A Psychological Study*. New York: Basic Books. [1]

Oldfield D. (1986), The adolescent crisis: a hero's journey. *The Early Adolescent Magazine* 1(2): 20–27. David Oldfield designed a creative, modern-day version of the adolescent rite of passage. [6]

Orlosky M. J. (1982), The Kleine-Levin syndrome: a review. *Psychosomatics* 23: 609–621. An interesting review of a rare condition that causes psychological symptoms in children and adolescents. [18]

Orton S. T. (1937), *Reading, Writing and Speech Problems in Children: A Presentation of Certain Types of Disorders in the Development of the Language Faculty*. New York: W. W. Norton. Samuel T. Orton was a pioneer in the identification and classification of learning disabilities. He coined the term strephosymbolia, which referred to the perception of letters reversed as in a mirror. He thought that it was caused by incomplete or inconsistent dominance of the right hemisphere of the brain by the left hemisphere. [10]

Osofsky J. D., ed. (1997), *Children in a Violent Society*. New York: Guilford Press. The individual chapters in this book were written by experts on the effects of exposure to violence, the epidemiology of firearms, violence in the media, etc. [12]

Ostrov E., Offer D., Howard K. I., Kaufman B., Meyer H. (1985), Adolescent sexual behavior. *Medical Aspects of Human Sexuality* 19 (May): 28–36. The authors reported their survey of teenagers in two Chicago-area high schools. [13]

Perry B. (1994), Neurobiological sequelae of childhood trauma: PTSD in children. In: *Catecholamine Function in Posttraumatic Stress Disorder: Emerging*

Concepts, Murburg M.M., ed., pp. 233–255. Washington, D.C.: American Psychiatric Press. Bruce Perry, M.D., has championed research in the area of neurobiological consequences of chronic child abuse. [14]

Pfeffer C. R. (1998). Suicidal behavior. In: *Handbook of Child and Adolescent Psychiatry, Volume 5*, Noshpitz J. D., ed., pp. 111–113. New York: Wiley. This short chapter by Cynthia Pfeffer, M.D., an authority on suicide, provides a schematic decision tree for the assessment and management of suicidal children and adolescents. [11]

Pfefferbaum B. (1997), Posttraumatic stress disorder in children: a review of the past 10 years. *Journal of the American Academy of Child and Adolescent Psychiatry* 36: 1503–1511. Dr. Pfefferbaum, a physician and an attorney, reviewed recent research regarding the etiology and the treatment of PTSD in children and adolescents. [14]

Phillips D. P., Carstensen L. L. (1986), Clustering of teenage suicides after television news stories about suicide. *New England Journal of Medicine* 315: 685–689. The authors found adolescent suicides increased during the week following network news stories about suicide. This effect was particularly noticeable in adolescent girls. [11]

Phillips D. P., Carstensen L. L., Paight D. J. (1989), Effects of mass media news stories on suicide, with new evidence on the role of story content. In: *Suicide Among Youth: Perspectives on Risk and Prevention*, Pfeffer, C. R., ed., pp. 101–116. Washington, D.C.: American Psychiatric Press. David Phillips, Ph.D., and his colleagues have studied many aspects of the relationship between the portrayal of suicide in the media and the later occurrence of adolescent suicide. [11]

Phillips D. P., Paight D. J. (1987), The impact of televised movies about suicide: a replicative study. *New England Journal of Medicine* 317: 809–811. This study did not find an increase in adolescent suicides after the broadcast of three television movies about suicide. [11]

Piaget, J. (1972), Intellectual evolution from adolescence to adulthood. *Human Development* 15: 1–12. Jean Piaget was an early and prolific researcher of child development. This article pertains to his ideas on adolescence. [1]

Pittel E. M. (1998), How to take a weapons history: interviewing children at risk for violence at school. *Journal of the American Academy of Child and Adolescent Psychiatry* 37: 1100–1102. Elliot Pittel, a child and adolescent psychiatrist in Boston, found four groups of students who carry weapons to school: deniers ("I didn't know the gun was in my backpack."); innocents ("I found the gun in my desk."); fearfuls ("I need the gun for safety."); and defenders ("I need the gun when I get into fights."). [12]

Ponton L. E. (1997), *The Romance of Risk: Why Teenagers Do the Things They Do*. New York: Basic Books. Dr. Lynn Ponton, a child and adolescent psychiatrist, presented 15 case histories of adolescents who were unable to avoid dangerous risk-taking. [8]

Popper C. W. (1998), Clinical aspects of child and adolescent psychopharma-cotherapy. In: *Handbook of Child and Adolescent Psychiatry, Volume 6,* Noshpitz J. D., ed., pp. 200–269. New York: Wiley. This chapter and several others in the *Handbook* provide a comprehensive view of the use of psychotropic medication in adolescents. [16]

Rachman A. W., Raubolt R. R. (1984), The pioneers of adolescent group psychotherapy. *International Journal of Group Psychotherapy* 34: 387–413. This is an interesting history of this topic. [6]

Ralph N., Lochman J., Thomas T. (1984), Psychosocial characteristics of preg-nant and nulliparous adolescents. *Adolescence* 19: 283–294. The authors compared the family history and psychosocial information of pregnant and nulliparous African-American teenagers. The pregnant group had lower maternal educational level, later sex education, more brothers, better family adjustment, but poorer vocational adjustment. [13]

Reinecke M. A., Ryan N. E., DuBois D. L. (1998), Cognitive-behavioral ther-apy of depression and depressive symptoms during adolescence: a review and meta-analysis. *Journal of the American Academy of Child and Adolescent Psychiatry* 37: 26–34. These authors concluded that CBT seems effective for treating depressive symptoms in adolescents during both short-term and long-term follow-ups. [2]

Richter S. K. (1997), Overview of normal adolescent development. In: *Hand-book of Child and Adolescent Psychiatry, Volume 3,* Noshpitz J. D., ed., pp. 15–25. New York: Wiley. The *Handbook* is an encyclopedia of child and adoles-cent psychiatry. [8]

Rosenberg M. L., Eddy D. M., Wolpert R. C., Broumas E. P. (1989), Develop-ing strategies to prevent youth suicide. In: *Suicide Among Youth: Perspec-tives on Risk and Prevention,* Pfeffer C. R., ed., 203–225. Washington, D.C.: American Psychiatric Press. Mark Rosenberg, M.D., tried to find out whether there would be a consensus among experts as to how to prevent adolescent suicide. For example, he found that most experts thought it would be helpful to restrict the access of adolescents to fire-arms, but few experts thought it would be helpful to restrict the access of adolescents to medications or to high places. [11]

Rotenberg L. (1985), A child survivor/psychiatrist's personal adaptation. *Jour-nal of the American Academy of Child Psychiatry* 24: 385–389. A child survi-vor of the Holocaust, the author reflects on the survival skills that helped him persevere. [14]

Sacks H. S., Sacks H. L. (1980), Status offenders: emerging issues and new approaches. In: *Child Psychiatry and the Law,* Schetky D. H., Benedek E. P., eds., pp. 156–193. New York: Brunner/Mazel. The authors review the controversy as to whether the concept of status offenses serves the needs of either adolescents or the rest of us. [12]

Sager C. J. (1983), *Treating the Remarried Family.* New York: Brunner/Mazel. Clifford Sager is a psychiatrist who gives much practical advice. [15]

Salameh W. A., Fry W. F., eds. (2001), *Humor and Wellness in Clinical Intervention.* Westport, CT: Praeger. Waleed A. Salameh (a psychologist) and William F. Fry, Jr. (a psychiatrist) have researched psychological and physiological aspects of humor and have written extensively on the importance of humor in psychotherapy. [5]

Sarri R. C. (1985), Treatment alternatives in juvenile justice programs: a selected review. In: *Emerging Issues in Child Psychiatry and the Law,* Schetky D. H., Benedek E. P., eds., pp. 191–213. New York: Brunner/Mazel. Rosemary C. Sarri, a social worker at the University of Michigan, reviewed creative residential treatment facilities for delinquent youth, including specific programs in Colorado, Illinois, Kansas, Massachusetts, Minnesota, and New Jersey. [12]

Satir V. (1983), *Conjoint Family Therapy: A Guide to Theory and Technique,* third edition. Palo Alto, CA: Science and Behavior Books. If Nathan Ackerman was the father of family therapy, perhaps Virginia Satir was its mother. [7]

Scharff D. E., Scharff J. S. (1991), *Object Relations Family Therapy.* Northvale, N. J.: J. Aronson. David Scharff and Jill Savege Scharff have developed an object relations view of sex, the family, and family therapy. They use psychoanalytic methods to help family members achieve insight and psychological change. [7]

Schiffer M. (1984), *Children's Group Therapy: Methods and Case Histories.* New York: Free Press. Mortimer Schiffer wrote several books about group therapy with children and adolescents, usually in collaboration with S. R. Slavson. [6]

Schwartz R. S. (1984), Confidentiality and secret-keeping on an inpatient unit. *Psychiatry* 47: 279–284. Tensions may occur regarding confidentiality when therapists, especially those on inpatient programs, shift back and forth between work with an individual and work with a group. [5]

Shaffer D., Garland A., Gould M., Fisher P., Trautman P. (1988), Preventing teenage suicide: a critical review. *Journal of the American Academy of Child and Adolescent Psychiatry* 27: 675–687. David Shaffer, M.D., is an authority on suicide. He and his research associates developed a model for suicide causation, that included consideration of the individual's predisposition, the social milieu, and the trigger factors. [11]

Shaffer D., Vieland V., Garland A., Rojas M., Underwood M., Busner C. (1990), Adolescent suicide attempters: response to suicide-prevention programs. *JAMA* 264: 3151–3155. David Shaffer, M.D., and his colleagues questioned whether suicide prevention programs increase or decrease suicidal tendencies among the participants. [11]

Shapiro E. R., Freedman J. (1987), Family dynamics of adolescent suicide. *Adolescent Psychiatry* 14: 191–207. The authors believe that adolescent suicide may represent not only a consequence of the youngster's personal psychodynamics, but also a response to unconscious dynamic issues within their families. [11]

Shaw J. A., ed. (1999), *Sexual Aggression*. Washington, D.C.: American Psychiatric Press. Dr. Jon Shaw is experienced in evaluating and treating children and adolescents who have been sexually abusive of others. [13]

Shore J. H., Tatum E. L., Vollmer W. M. (1986), Psychiatric reactions to disaster: the Mount St. Helen's experience. *American Journal of Psychiatry* 143: 590–595. The authors are a psychiatrist, a psychologist, and a social worker. They used the Diagnostic Interview Schedule, a structured interview designed for administration by trained paraprofessionals, that had recently been developed. [14]

Siegel L. I. (1987), Confrontation and support in group therapy in the residential treatment of severely disturbed adolescents. *Adolescence* 22: 681–690. This article describes a style of group therapy that may be useful in a residential treatment program. [6]

Sigafoos A. D., Feinstein C. B., Damond M., Reiss D. (1988), The measurement of behavioral autonomy in adolescence: the autonomous functioning checklist. *Adolescent Psychiatry* 15: 432–462. Ann Sigafoos, Carl Feinstein, and the other authors took the concept of autonomy, which is a central feature of adolescent development, defined it in behavioral terms and developed a checklist that parents fill out. It is possible to compare a specific teenager with a normative sample. [9]

Silver L. B. (1989), Psychological and family problems associated with learning disabilities: assessment and intervention. *Journal of the American Academy of Child and Adolescent Psychiatry* 28: 319–325. Larry Silver emphasizes that children with learning disabilities must be understood holistically. Most of these youngsters have secondary emotional, social, and family problems. [10]

Silver L. B. (1998), *The Misunderstood Child: Understanding and Coping with Your Child's Learning Disabilities,* 3rd edition. New York: Times Books. This book by Larry B. Silver, a child and adolescent psychiatrist, is intended for parents. It discusses the psychological problems that often accompany learning disabilities; the pros and cons of medication; recent revisions to federal and state laws regarding discrimination; and controversial therapies. [10]

Slavson S. R., Schiffer M. (1975), *Group Psychotherapies for Children: A Textbook.* New York: International Universities Press. S. R. Slavson has been called the father of group psychotherapy. He formed groups for adolescents known as "Self-Culture Clubs" in Brooklyn, New York, which was in 1911! He later wrote almost 200 articles, chapters, and books on play therapy, activity group therapy, and activity-interview group therapy. [6]

Steiner H., Lock J. (1998), Anorexia nervosa and bulimia nervosa in children and adolescents: a review of the past 10 years. *Journal of the American Academy of Child and Adolescent Psychiatry* 37: 352–359. A good recent review of the epidemiology, etiology, assessment, and treatment of eating disorders in adolescents. [18]

Stierlin H. (1973), A family perspective on adolescent runaways. *Archives of General Psychiatry* 29: 56–62. Helm Stierlin was a creative and insightful author on how adolescents are influenced by family issues. [12]

Stierlin, H. (1977), *Psychoanalysis and Family Therapy*. New York: J. Aronson. In a series of essays, Helm Stierlin tried to develop a theory and a language that could unify psychoanalysis and family therapy. [7]

Stoiber K. C., Kratochwill T. R., eds. (1998), *Handbook of Group Intervention for Children and Families*. Boston: Allyn and Bacon. The two editors organized chapters by more than 40 authors into an encyclopedic handbook on group work with youth and their families. [6]

Sugar M. (1987), Diagnostic aspects of underachievement in adolescents. *Adolescent Psychiatry* 14: 427–440. This article by Max Sugar presents the differential diagnosis of academic underachievement and some interesting clinical vignettes. [10]

Terr L. C. (1979), Children of Chowchilla: a study of psychic trauma. *Psychoanalytic Study of the Child* 34: 547–623. Lenore Terr, a child psychiatrist in San Francisco, has studied the psychological effects of trauma on children in many different contexts. [14]

Terr L. C. (1981), Psychic trauma in children: observations following the Chowchilla school-bus kidnapping. *American Journal of Psychiatry* 138: 14–19. [14]

Terr L. C. (1983), Chowchilla revisited: the effects of psychic trauma four years after a school-bus kidnapping. *American Journal of Psychiatry* 140: 1543–1550. [14]

Terr L. C. (1987), Treatment of psychic trauma in children. In: *Basic Handbook of Child Psychiatry, Volume 5*, Noshpitz, J. D., ed., pp. 414–425. New York: Basic Books. [14]

Thompson T. L. (1988), Psychosomatic disorders. In: *American Psychiatric Press Textbook of Psychiatry*, Talbott J. A., Hales R. E., Yudofsky S. C., eds., pp. 493–532. Washington, D.C.: American Psychiatric Press. The author advocated a holistic approach to treatment. [18]

Visher E. B., Visher J. S. (1979), *Stepfamilies: A Guide to Working with Stepparents and Stepchildren*. New York: Carol Publishing Group. This book was written by a husband-and-wife team consisting of a psychiatrist and a psychologist. The Vishers emphasize the importance of the stepfamily and its differences from the nuclear family. [15]

Vitiello B., Stoff D. M. (1997), Subtypes of aggression and their relevance to child psychiatry. *Journal of the American Academy of Child and Adolescent Psychiatry* 36: 307–315. This is a good review of several articles that categorize the types of aggression in children and adolescents. Identifying the type of aggressive behavior has implications when developing a treatment approach. [12]

Walkup J. T., Amos T. M., Riddle M. A. (1998), Tics and Tourette syndrome.

In: *Textbook of Pediatric Neuropsychiatry*, Coffey C. E., Brumback R. A., eds., pp. 939–959. Washington, D.C.: American Psychiatric Press. This is a good recent review of both the psychological and neurological aspects of Tourette's disorder. [18]

Wallach G. P., Butler K. G., eds. (1994), *Language Learning Disabilities in School-Age Children and Adolescents: Some Principles and Applications*. New York: Merrill. This book was edited by Geraldine Wallach and Katherine Butler. It focuses on specific strategies for facilitating language learning and literacy learning. [10]

Wallerstein J. S., Kelly J. B. (1980), *Surviving the Breakup: How Children and Parents Cope with Divorce*. New York: Basic Books. Judith Wallerstein, Ph.D., was the principal investigator of a longitudinal study of families who were undergoing divorce. This was known as the California Children of Divorce Study. [15]

Wallerstein J. S. (1985), Children of divorce: preliminary report of a ten-year follow-up of older children and adolescents. *Journal of the American Academy of Child Psychiatry* 24: 545–553. This article related the follow-up to the California Children of Divorce Study. [15]

Wallerstein J. S., Blakeslee S. (1989), *Second Chances: Men, Women, and Children a Decade after Divorce*. New York: Ticknor and Fields. This book also related the follow-up to the California Children of Divorce Study. [15]

Weinberg N. Z., Rahdert E., Colliver J. D., Glantz M. D. (1998), Adolescent substance abuse: a review of the past 10 years. *Journal of the American Academy of Child and Adolescent Psychiatry* 37: 252–261. Naimah Weinberg and colleagues at the National Institute on Drug Abuse have reviewed and synthesized the recent scientific literature on adolescent substance abuse. [17]

Weiner B. A., Simons V. A., Cavanaugh J. L. (1985), The child custody dispute. In: *Emerging Issues in Child Psychiatry and the Law*, Schetky D. H., Benedek E. P., eds., pp. 59–75. New York: Brunner/Mazel. This is a good outline for how to do a custody evaluation. [15]

Weiss G., Hechtman L., Milroy T., Perlman T. (1985), Psychiatric status of hyperactives as adults: a controlled prospective 15-year follow-up of 63 hyperactive children. *Journal of the American Academy of Child Psychiatry* 24: 211–220. The third stage of a long-term follow-up study of hyperactive children. [10]

Weiss G., Hechtman L. T. (1993), *Hyperactive Children Grown Up, Second Edition*. New York: Guilford Press. Gabrielle Weiss and Lily Hechtman, child and adolescent psychiatrists from McGill University, followed hyperactive children and matched controls for at least 15 years to see what became of them as adolescents and adults. [10]

Weist M. D., Warner B. S. (1997), Intervening against violence in the schools. *Adolescent Psychiatry* 21: 349–359. The authors provide several specific suggestions for preventing violence and for dealing with students' reactions after violence has occurred. [12]

Wender P. H. (1987), *The Hyperactive Child, Adolescent and Adult: Attention Deficit Disorder through the Lifespan.* New York: Oxford University Press. Dr. Paul Wender was one of the first clinicians to describe how hyperactive children become hyperactive adolescents and sometimes hyperactive adults. [10]

Wiesel E. (1972), *One Generation After.* New York: Avon Books. Elie Wiesel was a teenager during the Holocaust and lived to tell the world about his experiences. [14]

Williams F. S. (1986), The psychoanalyst as both parent and interpreter for adolescent patients. *Adolescent Psychiatry* 13: 164–177. Frank Williams related a case history in which parenting, education, and guidance were required before serious psychotherapy could occur with an adolescent patient. [5]

Wilson C. P., Mintz I. L., eds. (1989), *Psychosomatic Symptoms: Psychodynamic Treatment of the Underlying Personality Disorder.* Northvale, N.J.: J. Aronson. A psychoanalytic outlook on psychosomatic disorders. [18]

Yochelson S., Samenow S. E. (1976), *The Criminal Personality.* New York: J. Aronson. Samuel Yochelson and his colleague, Stanton Samenow, studied criminals who had been committed to the forensic program of St. Elizabeths Hospital, Washington, D.C., and developed an approach for the treatment of antisocial personality disorder. [4]

Young J. K. (1975). A possible neuroendocrine basis of two clinical syndromes: anorexia nervosa and the Kleine-Levin syndrome. *Physiological Psychology* 3: 322–330. An interesting proposal that pertains to the relationship between mind and brain. [18]

Yudofsky S. C., Silver J., Yudofsky B. (1989), Organic personality disorder, explosive type. In: *Treatments of Psychiatric Disorders, Volume 2,* American Psychiatric Association Task Force, pp. 839–852. Washington, D.C.: American Psychiatric Association. The authors explain that the choice of psychotropic medication depends on the etiology of the aggressive behavior. [12]

Zinner J. (1978), Combined individual and family therapy of borderline adolescents: rationale and management of the early phase. *Adolescent Psychiatry* 6: 420–447. John Zinner described how to combine and organize individual psychotherapy, conjoint family therapy, and sometimes couple therapy for the parents in treating borderline adolescents. [5]

index

Authors are not listed in this Index. Authors who are mentioned in the text are in the References, where there is a notation of the chapter(s) pertaining to each author's work.

481